Prompting Tailwind CSS for Frontend Development

Build Responsive Tailwind CSS Interfaces, shadcn/ui Components, Modern Dashboards, and Production Frontends Faster with AI Prompt Engineering

Charles Reis Ribeiro

www.orangeava.com

First Published: July 2026

Published By: Orange Education Pvt Ltd, AVA®

Address: 9, Daryaganj, Delhi, 110002, India

275 New North Road Islington Suite 1314 London,
N1 7AA, United Kingdom

ISBN (PBK): 978-81-69646-35-2
ISBN (E-BOOK): 978-81-69646-36-9

Scan the QR code to explore our entire catalogue

www.orangeava.com

Get a Free eBook

We hope you're enjoying your recent book purchase! Your feedback is incredibly valuable to us and helps other readers discover books that truly make a difference.

If you found this book useful or enjoyable, we'd greatly appreciate it if you could leave a short review with a 5-star rating on Amazon. Your review supports our work and allows us to reach more learners worldwide.

As a thank-you, we're happy to offer you a **free digital copy of this book** plus a **30% discount code** for your next purchase on our official websites:

www.orangeava.com

www.orangeava.in (For the Indian Subcontinent).

☑ **How it works:**

Leave your review on Amazon, take a screenshot of the confirmation or use the following link to submit the claim and email it to **info@orangeava.com.** Once received the required detail, we will send your rewards within 24 hours, **along with one month free subcription to the book on AVA SkillShelf!**

Claim Form

https://rebrand.ly/4d2477

Thank you for your support—it truly means a lot to us.

Downloading the code bundles and colored images

Please follow the links or scan the QR codes to download the **_Code Bundles and Images_** of the book:

https://github.com/ava-orange-education/Prompting-Tailwind-CSS-for-Frontend-Development

The code bundles and images of the book are also hosted on ***https://rebrand.ly/mqkwxx5***

In case there's an update to the code, it will be updated on the existing GitHub repository.

Errata

We take immense pride in our work at **Orange Education Pvt Ltd**, and follow the best practices to ensure the accuracy of our content to provide an indulging reading experience to our subscribers. Our readers are our mirrors, and we use their inputs to reflect and improve upon human errors, if any, that may have occurred during the publishing processes involved. To let us maintain the quality and help us reach out to any readers who might be having difficulties due to any unforeseen errors, please write to us at:

errata@orangeava.com

Your support, suggestions, and feedback are highly appreciated.

Dedicated to

The Global Developer Community from
Brazil to South Korea,
Striving to Build a More Efficient and Creative Web.

About the Author

Charles Reis Ribeiro is a software developer and technical author with over eight years of experience building modern web applications across global markets, including Brazil and South Korea. Specializing in frontend engineering, he has worked extensively with Angular, TypeScript, and scalable UI architectures, contributing to enterprise systems that serve thousands of users. His work emphasizes performance, maintainability, and clean design.

In recent years, Charles has focused on the intersection of frontend development and Artificial Intelligence (AI). He explores AI-augmented workflows, where tools like GitHub Copilot and Large Language Models (LLMs) act as collaborative partners in the development process. His perspective encourages developers to move beyond traditional coding, and adopt a more strategic role such as designing systems, guiding AI outputs, and optimizing for efficiency.

A strong advocate of utility-first design, Charles highlights the synergy between Tailwind CSS and AI-driven development. He demonstrates how structured prompting and design systems can produce consistent, scalable, and high-performance interfaces. His approach promotes thinking in systems and abstractions, using AI to accelerate repetitive tasks while maintaining architectural control.

Beyond frontend development, Charles is deeply interested in Edge AI and Small Language Models (SLMs), particularly for industrial IoT applications. He explores how lightweight models can operate in resource-constrained environments, enabling intelligence closer to the data source.

As a business-minded technologist, Charles is committed to helping developers navigate the "post-execution" era of software engineering—where success depends not just on writing codes, but on designing workflows, making informed decisions, and collaborating effectively with intelligent systems.

About the Technical Reviewers

Kartik Bhat is a software developer and writer from Dharwad, Karnataka, India. He holds a Bachelor's degree in Computer Science and Engineering from the Visvesvaraya Technological University, Belagavi. With over six years of experience in web development, he has worked on a variety of projects involving modern technologies such as Laravel, JavaScript, and Tailwind CSS.

Kartik enjoys working across both front-end and back-end development, and is particularly interested in building practical and efficient web applications. Outside his professional work, Kartik spends time exploring new tools and trends in web development, and occasionally writes in Kannada.

Mahdieh Karimi is a Product Designer with over four years of experience designing user-centered digital products across startups, product teams, and creative agencies. Her work focuses on transforming complex problems into intuitive, scalable experiences through product thinking, design systems, and user-centered methodologies. Throughout her career, she has collaborated closely with product managers and engineering teams to bridge user needs, business goals, and technical constraints, delivering thoughtful solutions from concept to execution.

Passionate about simplicity, systems thinking, and meaningful product experiences, Mahdieh approaches design as a balance of strategy, empathy, and execution. She is particularly interested in designing products that are not only functional and scalable, but also clear, human, and impactful. Through her work and writing, she enjoys sharing practical insights at the intersection of product design, technology, and problem solving.

Acknowledgments

There are many people I wish to thank for their continued support throughout the writing of this book. First and foremost, I am grateful to my family for their patience and encouragement during the long hours of research and writing.

I would like to extend my sincere gratitude to the technical reviewers and the editorial team at Orange Education Pvt Ltd for their meticulous scrutiny and valuable feedback. Their insights were instrumental in refining the complex projects within these pages.

I also want to acknowledge the mentors and colleagues I have worked with across international borders. The diverse technical perspectives I gained while working in Brazil and South Korea deeply influenced the "AI-augmented" philosophy of this book. Finally, I would like to thank the open-source contributors of Tailwind CSS and the innovators in the Generative AI space, whose tools have fundamentally changed how we build for the web.

Preface

The landscape of frontend development is undergoing its most significant shift since the advent of responsive design. We are moving away from an era of manual syntactic execution and entering the age of AI orchestration. This book serves as a roadmap through this transition, acknowledging that traditional CSS development often involves repetitive boilerplate and time-consuming debugging. Tailwind CSS revolutionized this by providing a utility-first framework that Large Language Models (LLMs) now treat as a clean "API for styling".

Bridging Natural Language and High-Performance Architecture

This book is exclusively designed to help you master the synergy between natural language prompts and technical implementation. It focuses on developing the architectural oversight and strategic mindset required to build scalable, production-ready interfaces in a fraction of time. We begin by establishing a strong foundation in Tailwind CSS v4 and the core mechanics of Generative AI, moving beyond simple code snippets to master specialized AI-powered generators. As the text progresses, you will engage with practical, real-world applications such as building a web scraper, a dynamic data dashboard, and interactive UI components. All source codes, project assets, and final configurations discussed in these chapters are available in the official GitHub repository at **https://github.com/charlesribeiro/prompt-to-tailwind**.

Each chapter provides a blend of theory and hands-on experimentation, featuring "AI vs. Human" code comparisons and prompt engineering tips designed to solidify your understanding. You will implement "Shift Left" security measures, accessibility audits, and Responsible AI (RAI) principles to ensure that your generated code remains architecturally sound and predictable. Thus, whether you are a junior developer looking to accelerate your career or a seasoned architect optimizing your team's workflow, this guide empowers you to navigate the evolving landscape of modern web development. By the end of this journey, you will possess a sophisticated mental model for collaborating with AI assistants and a future-proof set of skills for the post-execution era of software engineering.

DID YOU KNOW

Did you know that Orange Education Pvt Ltd offers eBook versions of every book published, with PDF and ePub files available? You can upgrade to the eBook version at **www.orangeava.com** and as a print book customer, you are entitled to a discount on the eBook copy. Get in touch with us at: **info@orangeava.com** for more details.

At **www.orangeava.com**, you can also read a collection of free technical articles, sign up for a range of free newsletters, and receive exclusive discounts and offers on Print Books and eBooks.

PIRACY

If you come across any illegal copies of our works in any form on the internet, we would be grateful if you would provide us with the location address or website name. Please contact us at **info@orangeava.com** with a link to the material.

ARE YOU INTERESTED IN AUTHORING WITH US?

If there is a topic that you have expertise in, and you are interested in either writing or contributing to a book, please write to us at **business@orangeava.com**. We are on a journey to help developers and tech professionals to gain insights on the present technological advancements and innovations happening across the globe and build a community that believes Knowledge is best acquired by sharing and learning with others. Please reach out to us to learn what our audience demands and how you can be part of this educational reform. We also welcome ideas from tech experts and help them build learning and development content for their domains.

REVIEWS

Please leave a review. Once you have read and used this book, why not leave a review on the site that you purchased it from? Potential readers can then see and use your unbiased opinion to make purchase decisions. We at Orange Education would love to know what you think about our products, and our authors can learn from your feedback. Thank you!

For more information about Orange Education, please visit **www.orangeava.com**.

Table of Contents

CHAPTER 1
Introduction to Generative AI in Programming

Introduction

Welcome to **Prompt to Tailwind CSS**. In an era where digital experiences are constantly evolving, the way we design and build for the web is undergoing its most significant transformation yet. Artificial Intelligence, particularly Generative AI is no longer a futuristic concept; it is a powerful copilot in the developer's toolkit, fundamentally reshaping our workflows.

This chapter serves as your essential foundation, providing a comprehensive overview of Generative AI and its increasing relevance in programming. We will embark on a journey through AI's fascinating history, tracing its evolution from early rule-based systems to the sophisticated Large Language Models (LLMs) that now power tools such as GitHub Copilot and ChatGPT. Understanding this journey is crucial, as it illuminates *how* we arrived at the current AI boom and *why* these technologies are so impactful for modern web development.

Beyond the historical context, we will delve into the core concepts of Generative AI explore the prominent tools that are changing the game, and critically examine their transformative role across the entire software development lifecycle. We will also establish the fundamental principles of effective human-computer interaction with LLMs, setting the stage for the prompt engineering mastery you will develop throughout this book. By the end of this chapter, you will have a clear understanding of what Generative AI is, how it works, and why its synergy with utility-first frameworks such as Tailwind CSS is revolutionizing the creation of stunning, responsive user interfaces.

Structure

In this chapter, we will cover the following topics:

- The Emergence and Strategic Significance of Generative AI

- Tailwind CSS: A Conceptual Overview
    - The Role of Tailwind CSS in Accelerating Frontend Development
    - The Synergy between AI and Tailwind CSS
- A Brief History of AI:
    - The Dawn of AI: Rule-Based Systems (1950s–1980s)
    - A Glimpse into the Future: The Perceptron
    - Symbolic AI (Good Old-Fashioned AI, or GOFAI)
    - The Data Revolution: The Shift to Statistical Learning (1990s–2010s)
    - The Deep Learning Revolution: Unleashing Neural Networks (2010s)
    - The Era of LLMs and AI-Assisted Coding (2019–Today)
    - The Transformer Architecture: The Engine behind Modern AI
    - The Black Box Challenge and the Rise of Explainability
- Introduction to Prominent Generative AI Tools and Their Role in the Software Development Lifecycle:
    - The Concept of Prompt in AI
    - Prominent Generative AI Tools
- Understanding the Role of AI throughout the Software Development Lifecycle:
    - Planning and Requirements Gathering
    - Design and Prototyping
    - Development
    - Testing
    - Deployment
    - Monitoring and Maintenance
- Basic Principles of Human-Computer Interaction with LLMs:
    - Prompt as Interface
    - Iterative Dialog
    - Mental Model Alignment
    - Error Tolerance and Uncertainty
    - Natural Language as Meta-Language
- Concept Walkthrough: AI Generating a Basic UI Component

The Emergence and Strategic Significance of Generative AI

At the time of writing this book, we find ourselves in a transformative era: one where Artificial Intelligence (AI) is not just influencing the future of technology but reshaping the fabric of society itself. From education to healthcare, from logistics to entertainment, AI is being woven into nearly every aspect of our lives. Among these changes, one development stands out: the rise of Generative AI.

It is no exaggeration to say we may be living through a major inflection point, a moment some have compared to the invention of the internet or even the advent of electricity. The current wave of AI advancements, driven by breakthroughs in machine learning and natural language processing, is often referred to as a new chapter in the ongoing Industrial Revolution. This shift is not merely technological but epistemological, as it changes how we produce, consume, and even think about knowledge.

Every day, we are exposed to a growing list of AI-related buzzwords: ChatGPT, GPT-4, Copilot, LLMs, diffusion models, transformers, and more. While these terms are ubiquitous in headlines and tech circles, they often lack accessible explanations for the broader public. What do they actually mean? And more importantly, how do they affect the way we build software, especially web interfaces?

Before we dive into practical workflows using tools such as Tailwind CSS and AI prompting, it is essential to establish a strong conceptual foundation. When people talk about "AI" post-2020, they are most often referring to a specific subset of artificial intelligence known as *Generative* AI. This class of AI does not merely recognize patterns or classify data; it creates. It writes code, composes emails, designs layouts, and even drafts marketing campaigns.

Understanding the power and limitations of Generative AI requires us to zoom out slightly and examine the broader context. What exactly is AI, and how did we get here? What distinguishes the current wave from previous ones? And why is it especially relevant to modern frontend development?

In the rest of this chapter, we will answer these questions by:

- Tracing the history of AI, from symbolic systems to statistical models and beyond.
- Exploring the rise of Large Language Models (LLMs) and why they represent a paradigm shift.
- Reviewing practical use cases of AI in programming, including code generation, debugging, and refactoring.
- Introducing the core tools we will use in this book: GitHub Copilot, GPT-based assistants, and prompt engineering techniques for web development.

Grasping these fundamentals will allow you to go beyond the hype and start using AI as a true creative partner: one that can help you write better Tailwind CSS, faster, and with greater clarity and maintainability.

Tailwind CSS: A Conceptual Overview

Tailwind CSS is a **utility-first CSS framework** designed for the rapid creation of stunning, responsive user interfaces. Unlike traditional CSS frameworks that provide pre-designed components (such as buttons or cards), Tailwind provides low-level **utility classes**. These classes, such as `bg-blue-600` for a background color or `rounded-lg` for rounded corners, allow developers to apply styles directly within their HTML markup.

The Role of Tailwind CSS in Accelerating Frontend Development

Tailwind CSS significantly speeds up the development process by reshaping how styles are applied and managed:

- **Bypassing Manual Layouts:** It allows developers to move from prototype to production code faster by removing the need to hand-code basic layouts from scratch.
- **Simplified Responsiveness:** Managing responsive states across different devices is handled through built-in breakpoints, such as using `flex-col` for mobile and `flex-row` for larger screens.
- **Built-in Design Systems:** It includes utilities for complex combinations, such as dark mode variants, hover states (for example, `hover:bg-blue-700`), and shadows (for example, `shadow-md`), ensuring visual consistency without leaving the HTML file.
- **Improved Maintainability:** By using a standardized set of utility classes, developers can achieve greater clarity and maintainability in their codebases.

The Synergy between AI and Tailwind CSS

The true power of modern web development lies in the synergy between Generative AI and utility-first frameworks. Because Tailwind CSS is structured around predictable, descriptive utility classes, it is an ideal match for the pattern-recognition capabilities of LLMs.

Generative AI tools can understand high-level design concepts and translate them directly into structured HTML with precise Tailwind classes. This enables developers to use natural language prompts to generate entire components, explore complex utility combinations, and even automate refactoring or bug fixes within their Tailwind configuration files. Throughout this book, you will learn to harness this partnership to build sophisticated layouts with unprecedented speed and precision.

Brief AI History – From Rules to Revolution

To truly appreciate the power of today's AI in web development, especially its synergy with tools such as Tailwind CSS, it is helpful to understand the journey of Artificial Intelligence (AI). AI is not a sudden phenomenon; it is a field with a rich history, marked by periods of great optimism, quiet research, and groundbreaking breakthroughs. This section provides a concise overview of the eras that shaped what we now call Generative AI (Gen AI).

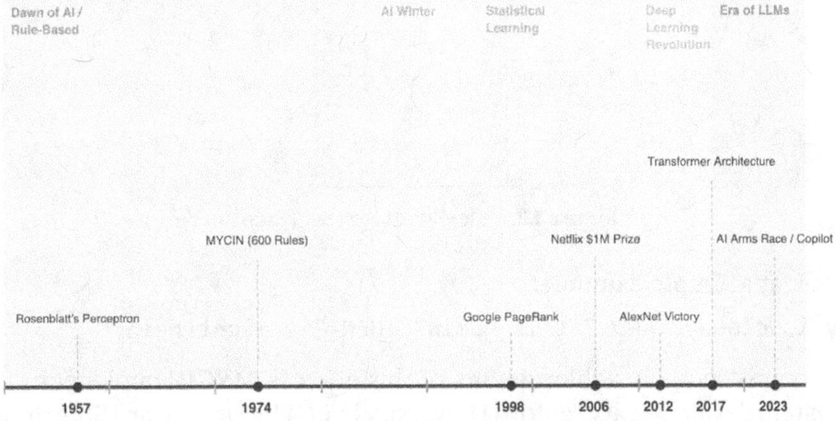

Figure 1.1: *Timeline of the AI Development*

The Dawn of AI: Rule-Based Systems (1950s–1980s)

Imagine a world where computers needed every single instruction spelled out, like a detailed recipe for a meal. This was the philosophy behind early Artificial Intelligence, characterized by **Rule-Based Programming**. During this era, AI systems operated on explicit, predefined rules, meticulously crafted by human programmers. This can be conceptualized as programming a computer with a comprehensive set of conditional instructions.

A typical rule-based system comprises three fundamental components:

- **Knowledge Base:** This was the system's brain, containing a vast collection of facts (data) and rules, predominantly expressed as "**`if-then`**" statements. For example, a rule might be: "IF the patient has a fever AND the patient has a cough THEN the patient might have a cold."

- **Inference Engine:** This component was the system's detective. Its job was to apply the rules from the Knowledge Base to the available facts to deduce new information. It determined which rules were relevant, the order in which to apply them, and when to stop the deduction process. Just like a detective uses a notebook full of logical steps to solve a case, the inference engine used its rules and facts to reach conclusions.
- **Working Memory:** This served as the system's scratchpad, that is, a temporary storage area for all the facts it knew and any new facts it inferred during its processing.

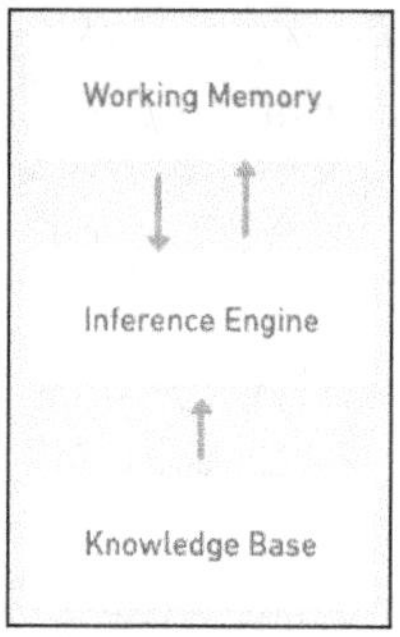

***Figure 1.2**: Rule-Based System Diagram*

Let us look at a simple example:

```
IF "sky is cloudy" AND "it is humid" THEN "it might rain."
```

One of the most notable achievements of this era was **MYCIN**, a pioneering medical expert system developed at Stanford University in 1974 by Dr. Edward Shortliffe. MYCIN was designed to identify bacteria causing severe blood infections and recommend appropriate antibiotics. It leveraged a knowledge base of approximately 600 rules and would engage doctors in a series of "Yes/No" questions. The outcome was a prioritized list of potential bacteria, coupled with a confidence level for each diagnosis.

While MYCIN[1] and other rule-based systems showcased impressive capabilities for their time, they had significant limitations:

- **Brittleness:** These systems were highly rigid. Small deviations or unexpected inputs could often cause the entire system to break down or produce incorrect results. Imagine adding a new, slightly different "if" condition; the entire system might need a rewrite.

[1] *Although* MYCIN *demonstrated strong diagnostic performance for bacterial infections and antibiotic recommendations, it was never deployed in real clinical practice. This was not due to limitations in accuracy but rather to a combination of ethical, legal, and technical concerns. Physicians and institutions hesitated to rely on a system whose diagnostic errors could raise liability concerns. More critically, the lack of integration technologies at the time meant* MYCIN *functioned as an isolated, text-based interface requiring manual data entry, which was impractical for routine clinical workflows.*

- **Poor Handling of Ambiguity:** They struggled immensely with uncertainty, exceptions, or incomplete data. Real-world scenarios are rarely black and white, and rule-based systems often could not cope with the nuances.
- **Maintenance Nightmare:** As knowledge bases grew, maintaining and updating the vast number of interconnected rules became an extremely complex and time-consuming task.

Despite these challenges, rule-based systems laid crucial groundwork, demonstrating that computers could indeed exhibit forms of "intelligence" and tackle complex problems. They paved the way for future AI advancements by formalizing knowledge representation and logical inference.

A Glimpse into the Future: The Perceptron

Even while rule-based systems dominated early AI, another revolutionary concept was quietly taking shape, one that would lay the very groundwork for the sophisticated Artificial Intelligence we interact with today: the **Perceptron**.

Conceived in the 1940s, the perceptron is considered the most fundamental building block in what would eventually evolve into **neural networks**. Actually, a perceptron can be considered a single-layer neural network. Its core idea was to mimic the behavior of the human brain, specifically how individual neurons process information. Imagine a simplified, digital neuron that takes multiple inputs, performs a calculation, and then produces an output.

This groundbreaking concept moved from theory to tangible experimentation in **1957**, when American psychologist Frank Rosenblatt successfully tested a physical perceptron on an IBM 704 computer. He later solidified his research in a pivotal paper titled, "*The Perceptron: A Probabilistic Model for Information Storage and Organization in the Brain.*" This theoretical work was soon followed by a dedicated hardware implementation, the **Mark I Perceptron**, which further demonstrated its capabilities.

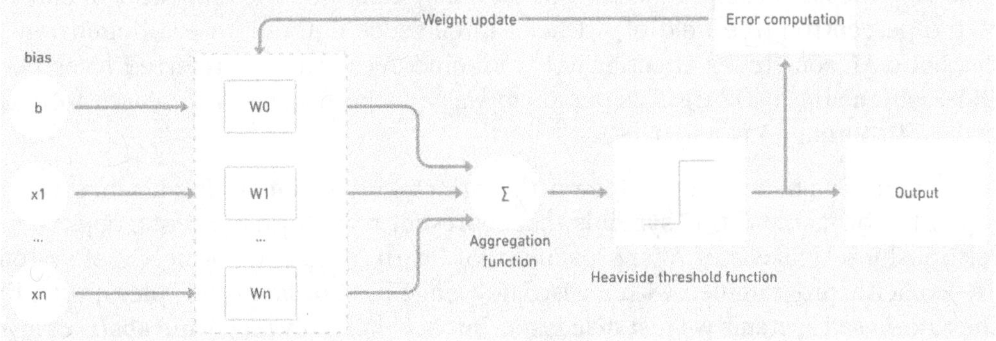

Figure 1.3: *Diagram of a thresholded perceptron model, illustrating how weighted inputs are summed and passed through a Heaviside threshold function to classify linearly separable data*

The perceptron's promise was immense: it offered a pathway for machines to learn from data, rather than being explicitly programmed with every rule. This was a radical departure from the brittle, rule-based systems of the era. However, despite its early excitement, the initial perceptron had significant limitations, particularly in its ability to solve more complex problems (such as those requiring non-linear decision boundaries).

Consequently, the profound implications of the perceptron and the neural network concepts it foreshadowed would not be fully realized for another **70 years**. The true "boom" for these ideas would await advancements in computational power, vast amounts of data, and more sophisticated algorithms, eventually leading to the powerful **Large Language Models (LLMs)** that are at the heart of our discussion in this book. For now, understand that this humble concept planted a vital seed for the future of AI.

***Figure 1.4**: Rosenblatt and the Perceptron*
(Source: Wikimedia Commons https://commons.wikimedia.org/wiki/File:330-PSA-80-60_(USN_710739)_(20897323365).jpg)

Symbolic AI (Good Old-Fashioned AI or GOFAI)

Following the early explorations of rule-based systems and the foundational concept of the perceptron, the field of Artificial Intelligence entered an era dominated by **Symbolic AI**, sometimes affectionately, or sometimes critically referred to as **Good Old-Fashioned AI (GOFAI)**. This paradigm was a major force in AI research from the mid-1950s through the mid-1990s.

At its core, Symbolic AI operates on the principle that human intelligence can be replicated by manipulating **symbols** that represent real-world concepts, objects, and relationships. Unlike later AI approaches that "learn" from data, Symbolic AI systems are explicitly programmed with a vast knowledge base of facts and rules, much **like the rule-based systems we just discussed, but at a more advanced and abstract level**. Imagine defining "dog" as an animal that "barks," "has four legs," and "is a mammal." These are symbols and logical assertions that the AI system can then process.

Key Characteristics of Symbolic AI:

- **Human-Readable Information:** The "symbols" in Symbolic AI are designed to be easily understood by humans. This makes the internal workings of the system highly transparent.
- **Explicit Knowledge Representation:** All knowledge is encoded directly by human experts. This means there is **no training required** in the way modern machine learning models need it; the inputs are considered static and reliable, leading to predictable outputs. There are no "guesses" involved in its core operations.
- **Logical Reasoning:** Symbolic AI systems excel at applying formal logic (such as **propositional logic** or first-order logic) to deduce new information or make decisions based on their encoded knowledge. This is a fundamental type of logic in which statements (propositions) are either true or false, and they can be combined using logical operators such as:
  - **AND (∧):** Both propositions must be true for the combined statement to be true.

    Example: "The sky is cloudy, AND it is humid." (Only true if both conditions are met.)
  - **OR (∨):** At least one of the propositions must be true for the combined statement to be true.

    Example: "I will eat pizza, OR I will eat pasta." (True if you eat one, or both.)
  - **NOT (¬):** Reverses the truth value of a proposition.

    Example: "NOT (it is raining)." (True if it is not raining.)
  - **IF-THEN (→):** Also known as implication. If the first proposition (the "if" part) is true, then the second proposition (the "then" part) must also be true.

    Example: "IF the alarm sounds THEN evacuate the building."

Many experts during this era held strong beliefs that Symbolic AI would eventually lead to **Artificial General Intelligence (AGI)**, a hypothetical AI with human-level cognitive abilities. The idea was that if we could just encode enough knowledge and enough rules, the system would become truly intelligent.

The Challenges and the "AI Winter":

Despite the initial optimism, Symbolic AI faced considerable hurdles that ultimately contributed to what is known as the **"AI Winter"**. This period, roughly from the late 1980s to the early 1990s, saw a significant decline in funding and interest in AI research. Some of the primary causes were:

- **The "Knowledge Acquisition Bottleneck":** Building the vast knowledge bases required for complex real-world problems proved highly labor-intensive and expensive. Imagine trying to explicitly define every piece of common-sense knowledge a human possesses.
- **Brittleness and Scalability:** While transparent, these systems struggled with exceptions, ambiguity, and the sheer volume of knowledge needed to handle the messy, unpredictable nature of the real world. Small changes often require significant reengineering.
- **Weak Capacity for Learning from Experience:** Unlike approaches that would emerge later, Symbolic AI was not inherently designed to learn and adapt from new data or experiences. Its knowledge was static, defined by its human creators.

The Enduring Legacy: Expert Systems and Transparency:

Even with its limitations, Symbolic AI left a significant legacy. A considerable amount of the AI we use today, particularly in niche applications, is still based on Symbolic AI principles. These are often referred to as **Expert Systems**.

There are excellent reasons for their continued use:

- **Transparency and Explainability:** This is arguably the greatest strength of Symbolic AI. Because the logic is explicitly coded in human-readable symbols and rules, a programmer can easily trace *why* a system arrived at a particular conclusion. The system can even explain its reasoning steps ("Because rule X was true, and fact Y was present, I concluded Z"). This is vital in fields where trust and accountability are paramount, such as finance, legal, or medical diagnostics.
- **Reliability for Well-Defined Problems:** For domains where knowledge can be clearly codified and ambiguity is low, Symbolic AI provides robust and predictable solutions without the need for vast datasets or complex training.

While the dream of AGI through pure Symbolic AI did not materialize, its principles continue to underpin critical systems. It also laid foundational ideas about knowledge representation and logical reasoning that informed subsequent AI paradigms, including the powerful statistical methods that drive today's Generative AI and Large Language Models.

The Data Revolution: The Shift to Statistical Learning (1990s–2010s)

As the limitations of Symbolic AI (GOFAI) became increasingly apparent—especially its struggles with the messy, ambiguous, and ever-changing nature of the real world—AI research underwent a pivotal transformation. The grand promises of AGI through explicit rule-encoding faltered, leading researchers to turn towards a radically different approach: **Statistical Learning**.

This new paradigm fundamentally changed how machines "think" and "learn." Instead of relying on human-defined rules, Statistical Learning models derive insights and make predictions by identifying patterns and relationships within vast amounts of data. Imagine no longer needing to tell a computer every single rule about what a "cat" looks like, but instead showing it thousands of images of cats and letting it figure out the common features itself. This was the crucial shift that paved the way for later, more advanced AI paradigms, including the Large Language Models we will explore extensively.

How Is Statistical Learning Different from GOFAI (Symbolic AI)?

To fully grasp the significance of this shift, let us compare the core philosophies of these two dominant AI approaches:

Feature	GOFAI (Symbolic AI)	Statistical Learning
Knowledge Source	Manually encoded rules by experts.	Learned automatically from data.
Representation	Symbols and logic (for example, if-then rules, and first-order logic).	Numeric features, vectors, and probabilities.
Reasoning	Deductive and rule-based inference.	Inductive and probabilistic inference.
Strengths	Transparent, interpretable, and logical.	Scalable, handles uncertainty, and noise.
Weaknesses	Brittle, hard to scale, and a knowledge bottleneck.	Less interpretable and dependent on data quality.

Table 1.1: GOFAI *(Symbolic AI) and Statistical Learning Comparison*

Let us unpack these differences:

- **Knowledge Source:** While GOFAI demanded that human experts painstakingly define every rule and fact, Statistical Learning models are fed raw data, millions of examples. The "knowledge" is not programmed in; it is *discovered* by the algorithm as it processes the data. This overcomes the infamous "knowledge acquisition bottleneck" that plagued Symbolic AI.
- **Representation:** Instead of abstract symbols such as "is-a" or "has-part," Statistical Learning represents information numerically, often as features and vectors, and then uses probabilities to express relationships and make predictions.
- **Reasoning:** GOFAI used *deductive* reasoning (applying general rules to specific cases, for example, "All birds fly; Tweety is a bird; therefore, Tweety flies").

Statistical Learning, conversely, primarily uses *inductive* reasoning (drawing general conclusions from specific observations, for example, "Most images with fur, pointy ears, and whiskers are cats, so this new image with those features is likely a cat"). This probabilistic approach allows it to handle ambiguity and uncertainty far better.

The Impact and Early Successes:

This new paradigm, where computers were fed examples instead of modeled data, was revolutionary. It allowed AI to tackle complex, real-world problems that were simply too dynamic or nuanced for rigid rule-based systems.

Statistical Learning models quickly began powering many applications that became common in our daily lives:

- **Spam Filters:** One of the earliest and most widespread successes, statistical models learned to distinguish between legitimate emails and unwanted spam by analyzing patterns in text, sender information, and other features.

- **Recommendation Systems:** Think of the suggestions you get on e-commerce sites or streaming platforms. These are often driven by statistical algorithms that learn your preferences from your past interactions and compare them to those of others.

- **Basic Image and Speech Recognition:** Early versions of these technologies relied heavily on statistical methods to identify patterns in pixels or audio waveforms.

- **Search Engine Ranking:** Algorithms learned to determine the relevance of web pages by analyzing keywords, links, and user behavior.

While Statistical Learning offered immense scalability and robustness in handling noisy, incomplete data, it was not without its own challenges. These models were often less transparent and interpretable than their symbolic counterparts; it was harder to understand *why* a particular prediction was made, beyond the statistical correlation. They also heavily depended on the quality and quantity of the data they were trained on.

Despite these new challenges, the shift to Statistical Learning marked a critical turning point. It proved that AI could learn directly from the world's vast data, laying essential groundwork for the subsequent advancements that would lead to the intricate neural networks and Generative AI models shaping our present.

The Deep Learning Revolution: Unleashing Neural Networks (2010s)

While Statistical Learning significantly broadened AI's capabilities, a monumental turning point occurred in the early 2010s, ushering in the era of **Deep Learning**. This paradigm took the foundational concept of the Perceptron, which we briefly touched upon earlier, and scaled it to unprecedented levels, unlocking astonishing performance in complex tasks.

The pivotal moment for Deep Learning arrived in **2012**. That year, a deep learning model named **AlexNet** achieved a groundbreaking victory in the ImageNet Large Scale Visual Recognition Challenge (ILSVRC2012)[2]. AlexNet won by a significant margin, dramatically outperforming all previous approaches to image recognition. This victory was very important, demonstrating the immense potential of deep neural networks.

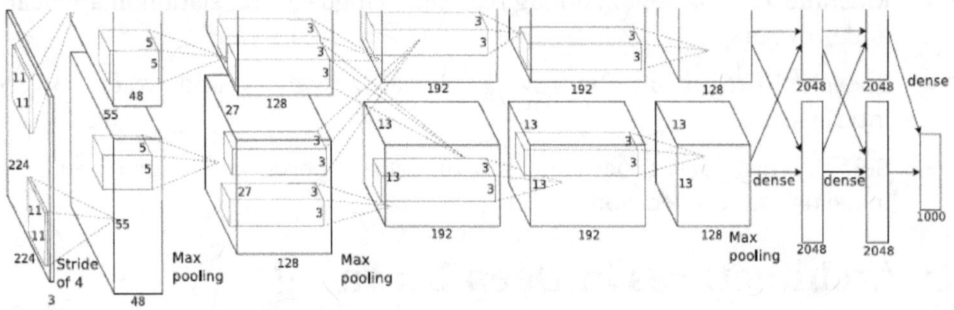

Figure 1.5: *Architecture of AlexNet, the pioneering convolutional neural network* (CNN) *for image classification, illustrating its division of computational tasks across two* GPUs.
Source: Krizhevsky, Alex; Sutskever, Ilya; Hinton, Geoffrey E. (2017)

Introduction to Deep Learning

At its heart, Deep Learning uses **Multi-Layer Perceptrons (MLPs)**, which are essentially neural networks with multiple "hidden" layers between the input and output layers. These layers progressively learn more abstract and complex feature representations from the data. The "deep" in deep learning refers to the presence of these many layers.

This resurgence of neural networks was made possible by three converging factors:

1. **Vast Data Availability:** The digital age produced an explosion of data, providing the fuel these data-hungry models needed to learn intricate patterns.
2. **Computational Power:** The evolution of **GPU (Graphics Processing Unit) hardware**, originally designed for gaming graphics, proved to be perfectly suited for the parallel computations required to train large neural networks. This drastically cut down training times from months to days or even hours.[3]

[2] *https://www.image-net.org/challenges/LSVRC/*

[3] *GPUs are highly optimized for parallel processing, with thousands of smaller cores designed to perform many operations simultaneously. This architecture aligns perfectly with the needs of training neural networks, where large matrix and tensor computations can be executed in parallel. Unlike CPUs, which are optimized for sequential serial processing and general-purpose tasks, GPUs can perform the repetitive arithmetic-heavy operations in backpropagation and gradient descent far more efficiently, drastically reducing training time for deep learning models.*

3. **Algorithmic Innovations:** New techniques for training deep networks, such as better activation functions and regularization methods, helped overcome the previous hurdles.

Thanks to these advancements, Deep Learning quickly found applications in a multitude of fields, revolutionizing areas such as:

- **Image Recognition:** Powering facial recognition, object detection in self-driving cars, and medical image analysis.
- **Machine Translation:** Enabling real-time language translation in applications and browsers.
- **Speech Recognition:** Improving virtual assistants and voice-controlled interfaces.
- **Self-Driving Cars:** Processing sensor data to perceive the environment and make navigation decisions.

Key Architectures in Deep Learning

Beyond simple MLPs, two architectural innovations were particularly impactful during this period:

- **Convolutional Neural Networks (CNNs):** CNNs, in a sense, are an evolution of the MLP approach specifically designed for processing grid-like data, such as images. Their key innovation lies in using "convolutional layers" where each neuron is connected only to a small, localized region of the input. Crucially, these connections use the same set of weights across different positions in the input (known as **weight sharing**). This design makes CNNs highly effective at identifying features (such as edges, textures, or shapes) regardless of where they appear in an image, and significantly reduces the number of parameters needed for training.
- **Recurrent Neural Networks (RNNs):** RNNs were designed to handle sequential data, such as text, speech, or time series. Unlike traditional neural networks, where inputs are independent, RNNs have connections that form directed cycles, allowing information to persist from one step to the next. This "memory" made them powerful for tasks such as natural language processing and speech generation.

The Rise of Deep Learning Libraries

The burgeoning interest and success of Deep Learning (DL) led to the rapid development of open-source libraries and frameworks, democratizing access to these powerful tools. Here is a timeline of some major releases that shaped the ecosystem:

Year	Library / Framework	Milestone / Description
2012	AlexNet (published)	Won the ImageNet competition; popularized deep CNNs and GPU-based training.
2013	Theano (v0.6)	Gained popularity in academia for symbolic differentiation and GPU support.
2014	Caffe (by Berkeley)	Optimized for image classification tasks, it became widely used in early Computer Vision (CV) applications.
2014	Torch7	Lua-based deep learning framework used at Facebook; precursor to PyTorch.
2015	TensorFlow (v1.0 beta)	Released by Google, flexible graph-based computation quickly became an industry standard.
2015	Keras (initial release)	Simplified neural network API built on Theano (later supported TensorFlow and CNTK).
2016	MXNet	Chosen by Amazon for AWS; supported dynamic and static computation graphs.
2017	PyTorch (v0.1)	Released by Facebook, a dynamic computation graph; quickly adopted by researchers.
2017	TensorFlow (v1.0 stable)	Officially reached stable 1.0 release, marking production-readiness.
2018	FastAI (v1)	Built on top of PyTorch, popularized transfer learning and user-friendly abstractions.

***Table 1.2**: Deep Learning Library/Framework Timeline*

Challenges and the Path Forward

Despite their successes, early Deep Learning architectures also faced limitations, particularly RNNs when dealing with very long sequences of data:

- **Vanishing Gradients[4]:** As sequences grew longer, RNNs struggled to "remember" information from distant past steps. Gradients (signals used for learning) would become tiny, making it difficult for the network to update its weights effectively for earlier parts of the sequence.
- **Training Instability:** Training RNNs on long sequences could be slow and computationally unstable, hindering their ability to learn long-range dependencies.

[4] *In neural networks, a gradient measures how much a model's output changes in response to small changes in its parameters (weights). During training, gradients are computed using backpropagation and guide the optimization process, typically through a gradient descent, by indicating the direction and magnitude of weight updates that will reduce the model's error. When gradients become extremely small (vanishing) or extremely large (exploding), training can stall or destabilize, especially in deep or recurrent architectures. This is a key challenge in learning long-term dependencies in sequences.*

These challenges eventually led to further innovations, setting the stage for the next monumental leap in AI: the development of **Transformer architectures** and the emergence of **Large Language Models**, which are central to the prompt engineering techniques we will master in this book.

The Era of LLMs and AI-Assisted Coding (2019–Today)

The evolution of Deep Learning, particularly the advancements in neural network architectures, culminated in a new era defined by **Large Language Models (LLMs)** and their profound impact on every aspect of computing, including the very way we write the code.

***Figure 1.6**: Théâtre D'opéra Spatial, an award-winning AI-assisted artwork created by Jason Michael Allen using Midjourney*

A key enabler of this era was the **Transformer Architecture**, which gained dominance across various domains. Models such as BERT and Vision Transformers (ViT) demonstrated superior capabilities, often replacing traditional CNNs and RNNs in many tasks. This paved the way for the development of truly large-scale, general-purpose models, capable of understanding and generating human-like text with unprecedented fluency.

The Transformer Architecture: The Engine behind Modern AI

While the Deep Learning revolution introduced powerful concepts such as CNNs and RNNs, a single innovation fundamentally changed the landscape of Large Language Models (LLMs) and AI-assisted coding: The Transformer Architecture.

This architecture, introduced in the 2017 paper "Attention Is All You Need[5]," is the core innovation that makes modern LLMs, including GPT (Generative Pre-trained Transformer), possible. It addressed significant limitations of earlier sequential models, such as RNNs, which struggled with the "vanishing gradient" problem and were inefficient due to their reliance on processing data sequentially.

Transformer Architecture: Parallel Processing and Attention

The Transformer architecture revolutionized sequence modeling by abandoning the sequential processing of traditional RNNs in favor of parallel processing. This allows models to handle entire sequences of data (such as a whole sentence or block of code) simultaneously, dramatically speeding up training and enabling the creation of much larger models.

The secret behind the Transformer's success is a mechanism called attention.

Imagine reading a complex paragraph of code. As a human, you do not read it one word at a time in a vacuum; you constantly refer back to previous variables, function definitions, and comments to understand the current line. The attention mechanism works similarly.

It allows the model to weigh the importance of different parts of the input sequence when processing a specific element. When generating a word or a line of code, the Transformer can "attend" to relevant words or context hundreds of steps earlier in the sequence. This ability to capture long-range dependencies (how distant words or tokens relate to each other) is crucial for understanding the nuances of language and the structure of code.

The "T" in GPT

The significance of the Transformer architecture for Generative AI cannot be overstated. The "T" in GPT (Generative Pre-trained Transformer) directly refers to this architecture.

By leveraging the Transformer, models such as GPT are capable of handling vast amounts of data and generating coherent, contextually relevant output. For developers working with tools such as GitHub Copilot or Cursor, the Transformer architecture is what enables the AI to understand complex coding contexts and generate accurate, context-aware suggestions and components, **including sophisticated Tailwind CSS** layouts. It is the engine that powers the era of AI-assisted coding.

---

[5] *Vaswani, A., Shazeer, N., Parmar, N., Uszkoreit, J., Jones, L., Gomez, A. N., Kaiser, Ł., & Polosukhin, I. (2017). Attention is all you need. Advances in neural information processing systems, 30.*

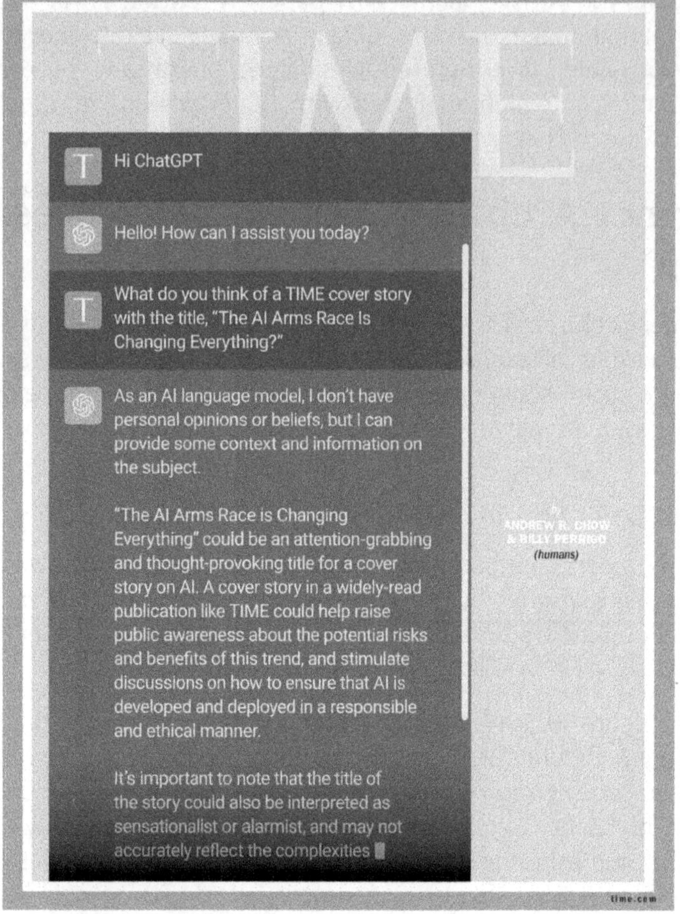

***Figure 1.7**: February 2023 Time magazine cover illustrating the global "AI arms race" via a ChatGPT conversation. (Source: Wikimedia Commons https://commons.wikimedia.org/wiki/File:The_AI_Arms_Race_Is_Changing_Everything.webp)*

The arrival of foundational LLMs such as **GPT-2 (2019)**, **GPT-3 (2020)**, and later **GPT-4**, fundamentally revolutionized how we interact with AI. These models are not trained for a single, specific purpose; instead, they are "**foundational**" in the sense that they are:

- **Massively Pre-Trained on Varied Data:** This includes immense volumes of text, code, images, and other digital content. This broad exposure allows them to develop a generalized understanding of language and patterns.
- **Scalable to Many Applications:** Their general training enables them to be adapted for a wide range of tasks, from complex coding challenges and machine translation to detailed summarization and even the scaffolding of user interfaces.

- **Promptable:** Critically, these models can be controlled and guided through simple, natural language instructions, known as **prompts**. This intuitive interaction method is at the core of prompt engineering.
- **Adaptable:** Beyond their initial training, foundational models can be further refined through fine-tuning or, more commonly, guided through sophisticated prompting for specific use cases.

The power of these models lies in their ability to perform diverse tasks, including code generation, translation, summarization, and UI scaffolding, all driven by these natural language prompts. This is where the potential of "**Prompt to Tailwind CSS**" truly begins.

The Black Box Challenge and the Rise of Explainability

However, as deep learning models, particularly those emerging between 2012 and 2018, began to consistently outperform traditional algorithms, developers and researchers encountered a growing, perplexing problem: *why* did these models work so well?

Neural networks, especially the deeper ones, were often described as "**black boxes**"—systems that could make astonishingly accurate predictions, yet offered little to no transparency into *how* those decisions were made. This lack of interpretability raised serious concerns, particularly in sensitive fields where understanding the rationale behind a decision is critical:

- **Healthcare:** "Why was this tumor classified as malignant?"
- **Finance:** "Why was this loan application rejected?"
- **Criminal Justice:** "Why was this recidivism risk rated so high?"

The challenge was clear: If AI was to be broadly trusted and adopted into critical systems, its decisions absolutely needed to be explainable to humans. This gave rise to the field of **Explainable AI (XAI)**, dedicated to making AI systems more understandable and transparent.

Explainability in AI-Assisted Frontend Development:

This "black box" challenge directly parallels a crucial need in the world of AI-assisted frontend development. Just as data scientists and domain experts wanted to understand *why* a model made a prediction, frontend developers and designers now demand to understand *why* AI generates a given piece of code.

With the advent of powerful tools such as **ChatGPT**, **GitHub Copilot**, and specialized AI CSS generators, the developer is no longer hand-coding every line of markup or styling. Instead, they are increasingly guiding AI to do the heavy lifting. But this shift does not remove the need for understanding; it rather redefines it. Developers still critically need to grasp:

- "Why is this layout structured this way?"
- "Why are these specific utility classes applied in Tailwind CSS?"
- "Is this generated markup accessible and semantically correct?"
- "Is the generated code optimized for performance and maintainability?"

In essence, it is no longer enough for AI to simply generate the "right" UI from a visual perspective. The generated code must also be legible, maintainable, performant, and accessible. This parallels the broader explainability movement in AI: understanding *how* AI arrives at its solutions is just as important as the solution itself, especially when that solution becomes part of a critical and evolving codebase. This book aims to equip you with the prompt engineering skills to not only generate effective Tailwind CSS but also to guide AI towards producing transparent, understandable, and maintainable frontend solutions.

Introduction to Prominent Generative AI Tools and Their Role in the Software Development Lifecycle

Generative Artificial Intelligence (AI) has opened up exciting new possibilities for human-computer interaction, particularly through the advancement of Large Language Models (LLMs). The ability to communicate with these powerful models using natural language is revolutionary, but doing so effectively requires a specialized skill set: **prompt engineering**.

Prompt engineering focuses on crafting effective prompts to unlock the capabilities of LLMs. By carefully designing these inputs, users can provide the context, instructions, and examples necessary to guide the AI toward a specific, desired output. In essence, a prompt acts as a roadmap for the AI, enabling it to understand intent and follow human instructions.

The Concept of Prompt in AI

In the context of AI, a prompt is the input provided to the model to elicit a specific response. This input can vary widely, ranging from simple keywords or questions to complex instructions, code snippets, or even creative writing samples. The quality and relevance of the AI's output are directly influenced by the effectiveness of the prompt provided.

Prominent Generative AI Tools

Several prominent Generative AI tools are reshaping programming and software development:

- **GitHub Copilot and GPT:** Tools such as Copilot and GPT can be prompted to generate code, such as Tailwind CSS.
- **ChatGPT and Google's Gemini (formerly Google Bard):** These are prime examples of Large Language Models (LLMs) capable of conversing in natural language and generating text. ChatGPT, for instance, can generate text based on prompts to compose emails, summarize research papers, or generate marketing slogans.
- **Other Generative AI for Content:** Generative AI models extend beyond text, capable of producing music, videos, or images. Examples include Google's "DeepMind" for piano music, the "Auxuman" algorithm, the "Endel" app, "DeepL" for translation, and "DALL-E 3" and "Midjourney" for AI-generated artwork. These tools demonstrate the broader capabilities of generative AI to create content that, if human-made, would satisfy copyright conditions.

These tools leverage the ability of AI models to learn patterns from vast datasets and apply that learning to generate new, relevant outputs.

Understanding the Role of AI throughout the Software Development Lifecycle

Generative AI is no longer a mere novelty in development—it has become a versatile partner across the entire Software Development Lifecycle (SDLC). From initial ideation and planning to deployment and ongoing maintenance, AI's presence is reshaping how teams work, how systems evolve, and how code is written and understood.

Here is how AI plays a transformative role at each stage:

Planning and Requirements Gathering

The SDLC begins with defining objectives. AI can significantly accelerate this phase by analyzing existing documentation or stakeholder input to summarize product requirements, generate detailed user stories, and even create precise acceptance criteria. Tools such as ChatGPT and other custom LLMs can transform vague business goals into concrete, testable objectives.

- **Example Prompt:**
  - "Generate user stories and acceptance criteria for a responsive e-commerce checkout flow, including desktop and mobile variations, payment processing, and confirmation pages."
- **Example Output (AI-Generated User Story):**
  - "As a user, I want to see a confirmation of my order immediately after payment so that I know my purchase was successful."

Design and Prototyping

AI tools assist UX/UI designers and developers in rapidly generating wireframes, design mockups, and component hierarchies based on prompts. This accelerates the transition from concept to tangible prototype.

- **AI + Tailwind Synergy:** Generative AI tools can translate design concepts (for example, from Figma or a description) directly into structured HTML with Tailwind CSS classes. This allows developers to move from prototype to production code faster, bypassing the need to hand-code basic layouts.
- **Example Prompt:**
    - "Convert this Figma design screenshot into a responsive hero section using Tailwind CSS. Use `flex-col` on mobile and `flex-row` on larger screens. Ensure it includes a `shadow-lg` on hover."

Development

This is the stage where AI's impact is most visible and transformative:

- **Code Completion and Scaffolding:** Tools such as GitHub Copilot complete code snippets contextually, drastically reducing typing and cognitive load.
- **Refactoring and Translation:** GPT-based tools can refactor existing code, document functions automatically, and even translate logic between programming languages.
- **Tailwind-Specific Assistance:** Developers can prompt AI to write entire Tailwind components, manage responsive states using breakpoints, implement dark mode variants, and explore complex utility combinations.

Testing

AI accelerates the testing phase by generating boilerplate test code and identifying potential issues.

- **Unit and Integration Tests:** AI can write unit and integration tests based on a function's behavior, saving significant time.
- **Simulated QA:** AI can simulate Quality Assurance (QA) personas to test for edge cases, performance bottlenecks, or accessibility compliance, potentially identifying flaws a human tester might miss.
- **Example Prompt:**
    - "Write Jest unit tests for the following Angular service function that calculates shipping costs, including tests for free shipping, international orders, and large orders."

Deployment

AI assists with streamlining the deployment process by generating configuration files and deployment scripts.

- **CI/CD Pipeline Setup:** AI can help set up Continuous Integration/Continuous Deployment (CI/CD) pipelines and detect configuration mismatches.
- **Example Prompt:**
  - "Write a GitHub Actions workflow that automatically builds and deploys a Tailwind-based Angular site to Vercel upon a successful merge to the main branch."

Monitoring and Maintenance

In the ongoing maintenance phase, AI provides the following proactive insights:

- **Log Analysis and Anomaly Detection:** AI can summarize logs, detect anomalies in system behavior, and predict potential failures.

Suggested Fixes: AI can suggest fixes for common issues, such as outdated dependencies, security vulnerabilities, or deprecated class usage in a Tailwind configuration file.

Basic Principles of Human-Computer Interaction with LLMs

Interacting with a large language model is not just about issuing a command—it is a collaboration with a creative and highly capable partner. Understanding this relationship is key to crafting effective prompts and harnessing LLMs productively in coding tasks.

Prompt as Interface

When using an LLM, your prompt *is* the user interface. Unlike traditional graphical user interfaces (GUIs), where visual cues (affordances) guide interaction, prompting is akin to "invisible UX": your intent must be explicit and clearly communicated.

- **Bad Prompt:**
  - `fix css bug` (Too vague, provides no context or code.)
- **Better Prompt:**
  - `This Tailwind UI component shifts unexpectedly on mobile. Here is the HTML structure and the applied Tailwind classes.`

`Suggest a fix for the responsiveness issue, and explain why the original code failed to render correctly.` (Provides context, specifies the issue, and requests both a solution and an explanation.)

Iterative Dialog

Unlike a traditional compiler that provides a static error message, LLMs support a back-and-forth clarification process. Prompt engineering is inherently dialogic: you refine your input based on the model's output, and the model refines its output based on your new input.

- Start with a simple request and progressively add specificity.
- Always ask for explanations, not just solutions, to better understand the AI's reasoning.

Mental Model Alignment

Just as designers build a mental model of their users, developers must learn the LLM's model of the world. Understanding that an LLM predicts based on patterns rather than "knowing" your codebase means we must facilitate this prediction process by:

- Including essential context in prompts (for example, the specific Tailwind configuration, relevant library versions).
- Avoiding ambiguity in instructions.
- Specifying intended use cases and desired output formats (for example, "Respond only with the HTML code block," "Ensure this follows accessibility best practices", "Make sure this code is modular and reusable across the rest of the application").

Error Tolerance and Uncertainty

LLMs may "hallucinate," outputting confident but incorrect code. The human-AI loop requires:

- **Critical Verification:** Always review and test AI-generated code.
- **Intuition and Experience:** Combining AI output with your own development intuition.
- **Seeking Explanations:** Asking the AI to explain its logic to validate the code's correctness.

Natural Language as Meta-Language

AI enables non-programmers to express complex programming intentions using natural language. This significantly lowers the barrier for collaboration, allowing designers, product managers, and junior developers to contribute more directly to the codebase.

- **Prompt Example:**
    - "Create a responsive image gallery using Tailwind CSS. Ensure it uses a masonry layout, includes hover effects to slightly enlarge the image, and optimizes images for fast loading."

Concept Walkthrough: AI Generating a Basic UI Component

In this walkthrough, we will explore a simple, illustrative example of how Generative AI can assist in generating basic code for a user interface component. This example demonstrates the fundamental concept of using a natural language prompt to produce functional code, specifically leveraging the utility-first nature of Tailwind CSS.

Our Objective: We want to generate the HTML markup and Tailwind CSS classes for a simple, styled button.

The Prompt

We begin by providing the AI with a clear, specific instruction detailing the desired component, the styling, and the framework to be used:

"Generate a primary button element using Tailwind CSS. It should have a blue background color, white text, rounded corners, and padding. The button should change color slightly when hovered over."

The AI Output

The AI processes this natural language request and generates the following code snippet:

HTML

```html
<button class="bg-blue-600 hover:bg-blue-700 text-white font-bold py-2
px-4 rounded-lg shadow-md transition duration-300 ease-in-out">
  Get Started
</button>
```

Figure 1.8: *An LLM-generated button in Tailwind Play, showing the translation of utility classes to traditional CSS.*

Analysis: From Prompt to Code

This simple example illustrates the powerful capability of Generative AI to understand intent and apply context.

1. **Understanding the Request:** The AI understood the request for a "primary button element" and used the appropriate HTML tag (**`<button>`**).
2. **Applying Tailwind Utilities:** Based on the instructions ("blue background color," "white text," and "rounded corners"), the AI correctly translated these concepts into corresponding Tailwind utility classes (**`bg-blue-600`**, **`text-white`**, **`rounded-lg`**).
3. **Handling Interactions:** The prompt requested a hover effect ("change color slightly when hovered over"). The AI accurately implemented this using Tailwind's `hover:` variant (**`hover:bg-blue-700`**). It also added **`shadow-md`** and **`transition duration-300 ease-in-out`** classes to enhance the visual appeal and provide a smooth interaction.

This process demonstrates how AI can rapidly scaffold functional and visually correct components, translating high-level design descriptions into executable code. As we explore further, we will learn how to refine our prompts to generate increasingly complex and precise outputs.

Conclusion

As we reach the end of this foundational chapter, we have journeyed through the fascinating history of Artificial Intelligence, from the early rule-based systems to the revolutionary Transformer architecture that powers today's Large Language Models. We have seen how AI has evolved, overcoming previous limitations to deliver unprecedented capabilities in understanding and generating content, particularly a code.

This chapter has established the essential context for our exploration of prompt engineering and Tailwind CSS. We have understood that Generative AI is not merely a tool for automation but a versatile partner transforming every stage of the Software Development Lifecycle, from planning and design to development, testing, and maintenance. Crucially, we have recognized that effective interaction with these powerful LLMs hinges on mastering the principles of human-computer collaboration, treating the prompt as our primary interface and engaging in iterative dialogue.

The era of AI-assisted coding is here, and with it comes a powerful shift in the developer's role. It is no longer just about writing every line of code. It is about expertly guiding AI to generate intelligent, efficient, and maintainable solutions. By grasping these foundational concepts, you are now well-prepared to embrace this new paradigm.

In the upcoming chapters, we will move from theory to practice, diving deeper into specific prompt engineering techniques and applying them hands-on to build stunning, responsive user interfaces with Tailwind CSS. The knowledge you have gained here will be your compass as we navigate the exciting future of web development, empowering you to harness AI to its fullest potential.

Exercises and Reflections

This section provides opportunities to pause and reflect on the concepts discussed in this chapter and apply them to your own understanding of web development workflows. These exercises are designed to encourage critical thinking, spark curiosity, and help you recognize the profound transformation AI is bringing to the coding landscape.

Remember, the goal is self-learning, encouraging you to question and reflect on your own experiences.

Identifying AI Opportunities in Your Current Workflow

Think about a typical day in your development environment. Consider the tasks you perform regularly, such as writing boilerplate code, debugging errors, or searching for documentation.

- Identify three specific tasks that currently take up significant time but could potentially be accelerated or automated using Generative AI tools such as GitHub Copilot, Gemini, or ChatGPT.

- For each task, describe *how* AI might change your process.
- What immediate benefits (for example, faster development, reduced cognitive load) do you anticipate from integrating AI into these tasks?

The Shift from "Writing Code" to "Prompting Intent."

The rise of LLMs introduces a fundamental shift: developers are increasingly becoming prompt engineers.

- Reflect on the difference between writing a function from scratch and providing a detailed prompt for an AI to generate that same function.
- How does the required skill set change in this scenario? Consider the importance of clarity, context-setting, and understanding the AI's limitations.
- Discuss the challenges of relying on AI-generated code for complex projects, particularly regarding code quality and maintaining consistency.

The Evolving Role of the Developer

As AI takes on more low-level coding tasks, the role of the human developer is transforming.

- If AI handles routine code generation and debugging, what skills will become most valuable for frontend developers? (for example, architectural design, critical thinking, validation, prompt refinement, complex problem-solving, and human skills).
- Discuss the importance of human supervision and verification when using AI-generated output. How do you ensure accountability for code that you did not write yourself?
- Consider the ethical implications of using AI in your development workflow (for example, potential biases in AI-generated code and security vulnerabilities).

By engaging with these reflections, you begin to integrate AI concepts into your professional mindset, preparing for the AI-assisted workflows that are central to this book.

Multiple Choice Questions

1. Rule-Based systems operate on which primary principle?
    a. Learning patterns from vast datasets
    b. Explicitly coded "if-then" rules defined by programmers
    c. Inductive, probabilistic inference
    d. Utilizing multi-layer perceptrons

2. Which component of a rule-based system applies rules from the knowledge base to available facts to deduce new information?
   a. Working Memory
   b. Knowledge Base
   c. Inference Engine
   d. Working Knowledge
3. The concept of the Perceptron is considered the most fundamental building block in what type of AI?
   a. Rule-Based Systems
   b. Neural Networks
   c. Symbolic AI
   d. Expert Systems
4. Symbolic AI (GOFAI) systems are primarily based on:
   a. Numeric features and probabilities
   b. Inductive reasoning and probabilistic inference
   c. Symbols representing physical world concepts and logic
   d. The Transformer Architecture
5. Which of the following was a primary challenge that contributed to the "AI Winter" for Symbolic AI?
   a. The inability to apply logical reasoning.
   b. The "Knowledge Acquisition Bottleneck."
   c. The lack of available GPUs for training.
   d. Poor handling of transparent systems.
6. How did the paradigm of Statistical Learning differ from Symbolic AI (GOFAI) regarding the knowledge source?
   a. Statistical Learning required manually encoded rules by experts.
   b. Statistical Learning relied on static and reliable inputs without guesses.
   c. Statistical Learning automatically learned knowledge from data, rather than requiring manually encoded rules.
   d. Statistical Learning primarily used deductive, rule-based inference.
7. What event in 2012 marked a pivotal turning point for Deep Learning?
   a. The release of TensorFlow by Google.
   b. The development of the Transformer architecture.

   c. AlexNet's victory in the ImageNet Large Scale Visual Recognition Challenge.
   d. The introduction of the first publicly available ChatGPT model.

8. Which Deep Learning architecture is specifically designed for processing grid-like data (such as images) and utilizes "weight sharing"?
   a. Recurrent Neural Networks (RNNs)
   b. Multi-Layer Perceptrons (MLPs)
   c. Convolutional Neural Networks (CNNs)
   d. Generative Pre-trained Transformers (GPTs)

9. What is a core characteristic of "foundational" Large Language Models (LLMs)?
   a. They require extensive fine-tuning before they can be used for any task.
   b. They are trained for a single, specific purpose rather than general usage.
   c. They are massively pre-trained on varied data and are scalable to many applications.
   d. They exclusively use inductive reasoning and avoid deductive logic.

10. According to the Basic Principles of Human-Computer Interaction with LLMs, why is it crucial for developers to verify AI-generated code?
    a. LLMs frequently "hallucinate," outputting confident but incorrect code.
    b. AI is incapable of understanding natural language prompts.
    c. AI cannot generate complex UI components, such as those in Tailwind CSS.
    d. LLMs are only useful for summarizing documentation, not generating code.

Answers

1. b
2. c
3. b
4. c
5. b
6. c
7. c
8. c
9. c
10. a

CHAPTER 2
Setting up the Environment

Introduction

Welcome to *Chapter* 2. In the world of software development, your editor is often part of a larger suite of tools called an Integrated Development Environment (IDE)[1], is more than just a place to write code. It is your cockpit! It is the command center from which you navigate complex projects, orchestrate tools, and, in the modern era, collaborate with an AI co-pilot. A well-configured environment is the foundation for a seamless and productive workflow, ensuring your tools do not get in the way, but instead act as a natural extension of your intent.

By the end of this chapter, you will have a fully configured, professional-grade development environment, ready to generate exceptional frontend solutions with Tailwind CSS and AI. We will guide you through setting up your editor of choice, understanding that different developers have different needs. We will cover two distinct paths:

- Visual Studio Code (VS Code): The versatile and powerful industry standard.
- Cursor: The AI-first editor for a deeply integrated experience.

You would not just follow the installation steps; you will understand the "why" behind each choice, empowering you to select the path that best suits your style. Once your cockpit is set up, you will be ready to move from theory to practice and start building.

To get started, you will need a GitHub account, which is essential for using tools such as Copilot. If you do not have one, do not worry as we will provide a quick guide to create one. A basic familiarity with using a code editor and the command-line terminal will also be beneficial as we build your new AI-powered workspace.

[1] An **Integrated Development Environment (IDE)** *is a software application that bundles common developer tools into a single Graphical User Interface (GUI). It typically consists of a source code editor, build automation tools, and a debugger.*

Structure

In this chapter, we will cover the following topics:

- Before Choosing Your AI-Powered Editor
- Initializing Your Tailwind CSS Project
    - Path A: The Industry Standard (Visual Studio Code)
    - Path B: The AI-First Experience (Cursor)
- Managing API Keys Safely (For External Tools)
    - Best Practices for Storing API Keys
- Understanding Your Tools and Writing Your First Prompts
    - Meet Your AI Assistants: Different Tools for Different Jobs
    - A Quick Note on Context
    - Your First Prompts: A Systems Check

Before Choosing Your AI-Powered Editor

Your editor is the single most important tool in your daily workflow. The right choice can make your interaction with AI assistants feel seamless and intuitive, while the wrong one can introduce friction. There is no single "best" editor for everyone; the choice depends on your personal preferences, your comfort with customization, and what you want from your AI-human collaboration.

In this section, we will explore two excellent but distinct paths to setting up your AI-powered development environment. Read through each and choose the one that best aligns with your working style. The core concepts and prompting techniques we cover later in this book will apply to all of them.

Before we dive into the specific editors, there is one foundational piece of technology we need: **`Node.js`**. Modern web development, especially using build tools and managing packages for projects with Tailwind CSS, relies on **`Node.js`** and its Node Package Manager (**`npm`**). The recommended way to install **`Node.js`** is with a version manager, which prevents permission issues and lets you easily switch between different versions.

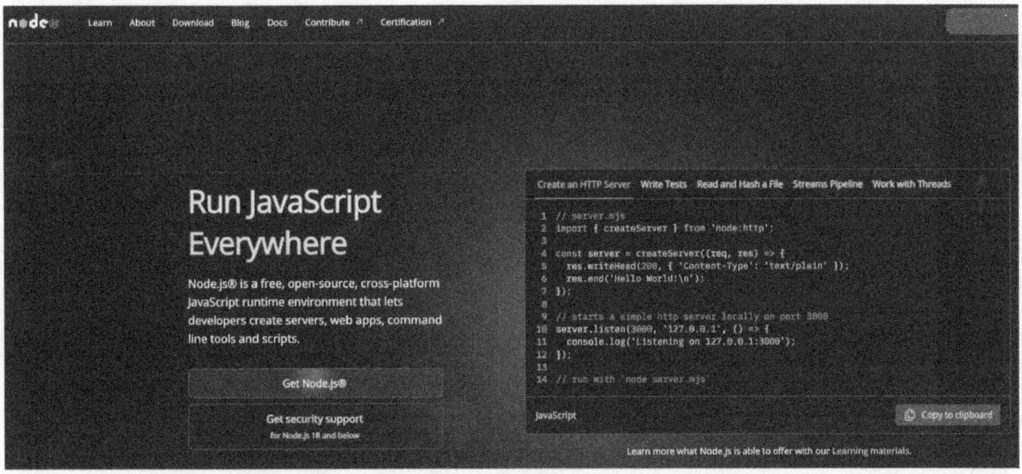

Figure 2.1: *Screenshot of Node.js Official Homepage*

From the main homepage, navigating to the downloads section presents you with the latest stable releases. Here, you can select the specific installer tailored to your exact operating system and architecture—whether that is macOS, Windows, or Linux.

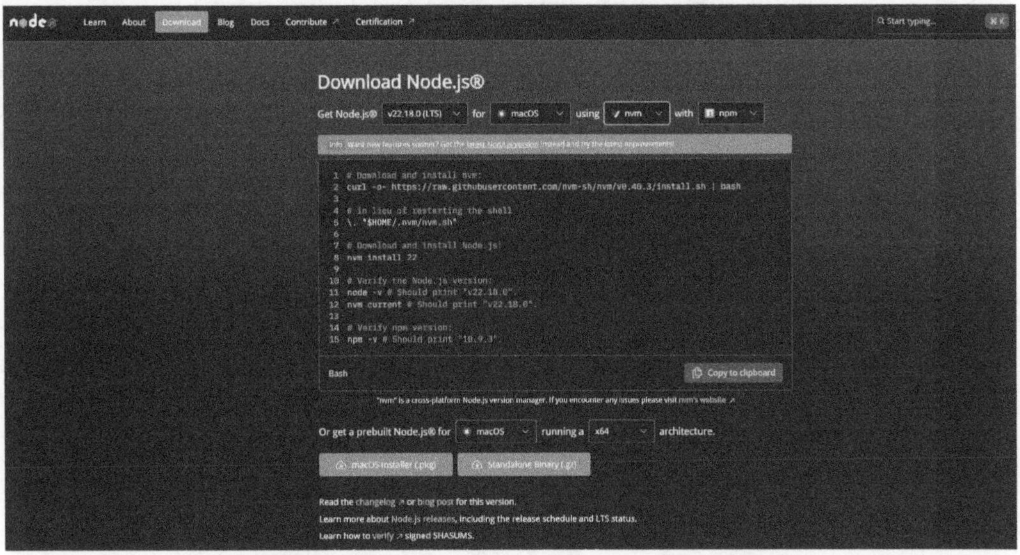

Figure 2.2a: *Screenshots of Node.js Download Page*

Once you have selected and downloaded the appropriate installer for your system, locate the downloaded file and launch it. This will open the setup wizard to guide you step-by-step through the local installation.

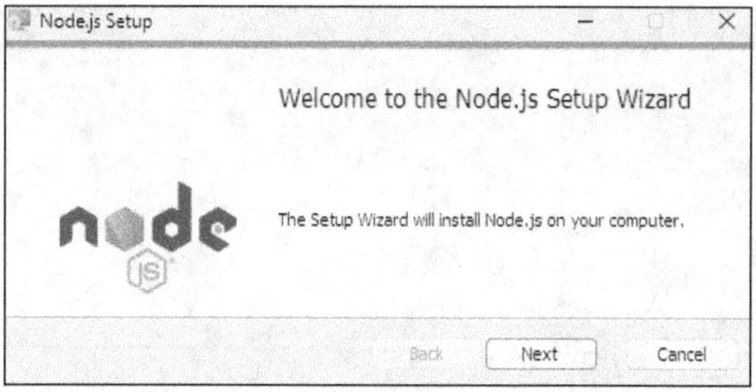

Figure 2.2b: *You Will be Welcomed by This Installer When Double Clicking the Installer (for Windows). The Install Process Will be Quite Similar for MacOS*

After advancing past the initial welcome and license agreement screens, the installer will present options for additional tooling.

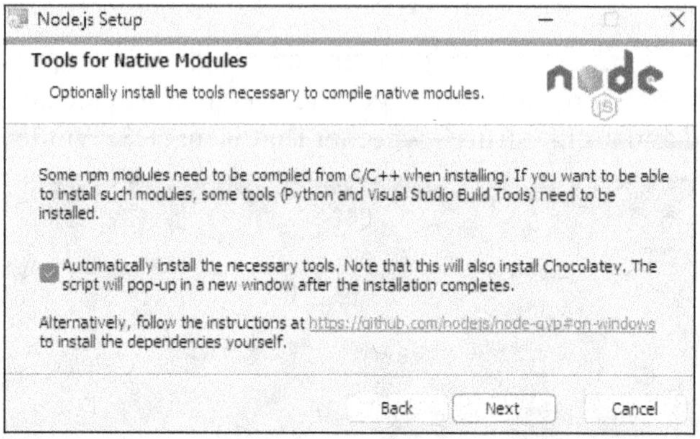

Figure 2.2c: *It is a Nice Idea to Install the Suggested Tools If You are Using Windows. It Will Also Install Chocolatey, a Package Manager That Works Like Brew*[2] *(for MacOS/Linux)*

With your tool preferences selected, click `Next` to reach the final confirmation screen before the system begins making changes to your hard drive.

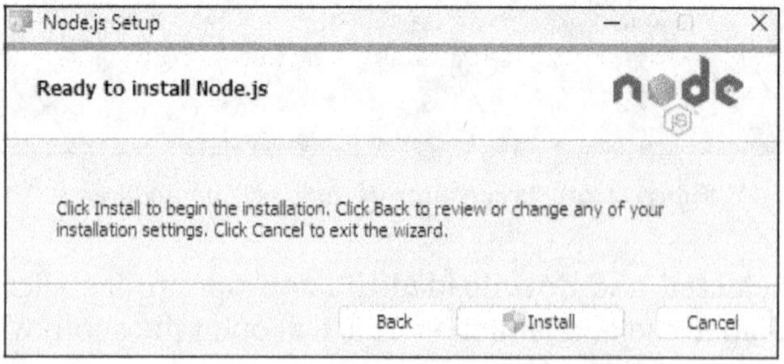

Figure 2.2d: *You Will be Now Ready to Install. Click* `Install`*, and Give Administrative Permissions If Needed*

[2] *https://brew.sh/*

The setup wizard will take a few moments to extract and configure the necessary files. Upon completion, you will be greeted with a final screen confirming the successful installation.

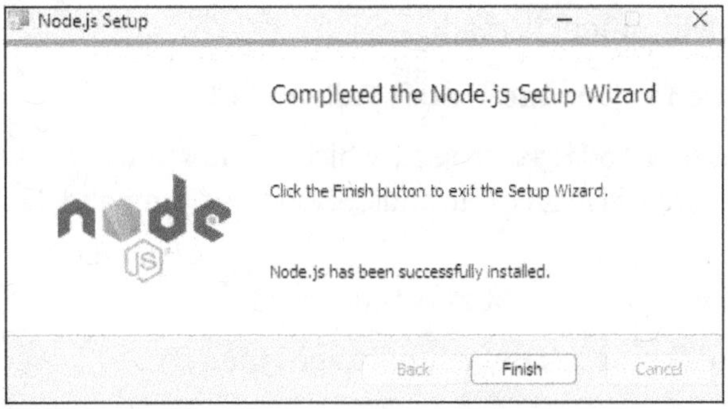

Figure 2.2e: *Congratulations, You have Installed Node.js Successfully*

We recommend using **`nvm`** (Node Version Manager), which you can obtain here https://github.com/nvm-sh/nvm or **`nvm-windows`**, obtainable here https://github.com/coreybutler/nvm-windows[3]. You can install it using the script from its official repository and then install the latest Long-Term Support (LTS) version with **`nvm install --lts`**.

Initializing Your Tailwind CSS Project

After successfully installing **`Node.js`**, the next step is to create a project folder and install the Tailwind CSS framework (version 4). You can do this with or without an IDE. These steps should be performed in your terminal.[4]

Step 1: Create and Enter Your Project Directory

First, create a dedicated folder for your project and navigate into it. We will name ours **`tailwind-playground`**.

```
mkdir tailwind-playground
cd tailwind-playground
```

Step 2: Verify Your `Node.js` Installation

Before proceeding, confirm that **`Node.js`** and **`npm`** (Node Package Manager) are installed correctly. Run the following commands:

---

[3] *It is important to note that **`nvm`** and **`nvm-windows`** are two separate projects, despite their similar names and purpose. The original **`nvm`** is a command-line tool written for macOS and Linux-based systems (such as Ubuntu) and will not work on native Windows. **`nvm-windows`** is a completely different program, built specifically for the Windows environment, that provides the same core functionality. While their commands are very similar for convenience, they are not the same tool. macOS/Linux users should install the original **`nvm`**, while Windows users must install **`nvm-windows`**.*

[4] *If you prefer to skip the manual folder creation and start with the pre-configured environment used throughout this book, you can clone the official starter repository at: https://github.com/charlesribeiro/prompt-to-tailwind.*

```
node -v
npm -v
```

These commands should output the version numbers for **Node.js** and **npm**, respectively, confirming your environment is ready.

Step 3: Initialize the Project and Install Tailwind CSS

Next, we will initialize a **Node.js** project, which creates a **package.json** file to manage dependencies. Then, we will install Tailwind CSS and its Command-Line Interface (CLI) tool.

```
npm init -y
npm install -D tailwindcss @tailwindcss/cli
```

- **npm init -y** creates a default **package.json** file.

Step 4: Create Your Source CSS

It is now time to create your CSS file that will contain the file customizations we will perform in the future.

```
mkdir src
touch src/input.css
```

Inside `src/input.css`, use a Tailwind v4 import:

```
@import "tailwindcss";

/* Any theme overrides now go here, not in a JS file */
@theme {
  --font-display: "Inter", sans-serif;
}
```

Step 5: Run the Tailwind CLI Build Process

Finally, run the Tailwind CLI tool to scan your template files and build your final **output.css** file.

```
npx tailwindcss -i ./src/input.css -o ./src/output.css --watch
```

Let us break down this command:

- **npx tailwindcss** executes the Tailwind CLI tool.
- **-i ./src/input.css** sets your source file as the **input**.
- **-o ./src/output.css** sets the file where the generated CSS will be saved as the **output**.
- **--watch** tells the CLI to continue running in the background and automatically rebuild your output.css file whenever you make changes to your HTML or input.css files. This creates a live-development environment.

Your terminal will now be running the Tailwind watch process. You can now start using Tailwind classes in your HTML.

Path A: The Industry Standard (Visual Studio Code)

For most web developers today, Visual Studio Code (VS Code) is the default choice. It is a free, open-source, and incredibly powerful editor backed by Microsoft that has become the industry standard due to its versatility, performance, and massive extension marketplace. For developers looking for a stable, well-supported, and flexible environment, VS Code is the perfect starting point.

Its greatest strength for our purposes is its best-in-class support for AI integration through extensions. Because of its popularity, companies such as GitHub prioritize it for their flagship AI tools.

This guide will walk you through setting up VS Code from scratch to create an optimal environment for AI-assisted Tailwind CSS development.

Step 1: Install Visual Studio Code

First, you need to install the editor itself.

a. Navigate to the official Visual Studio Code website at code.visualstudio.com.

b. The site will automatically detect your operating system (Windows, macOS, or Linux). Click the prominent download button to get the installer.

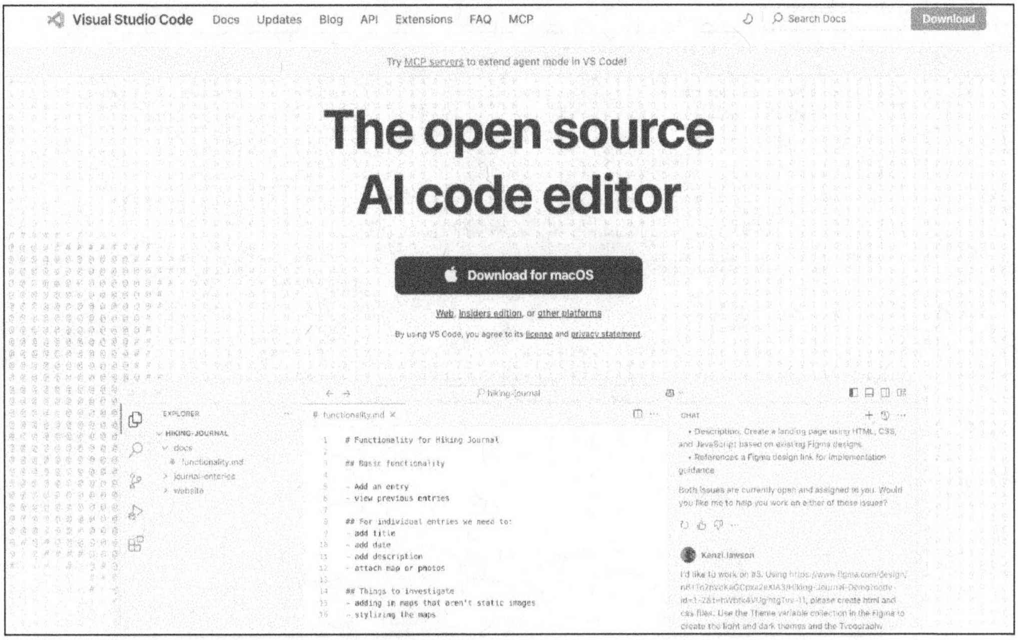

Figure 2.3: *Screenshot of the Official Visual Studio Code Download Page, Showing the Main Download Button for the User's Detected OS (in This Case MacOS) and Links for Other Operating Systems*

c. Run the installer and follow the on-screen instructions to complete the installation.

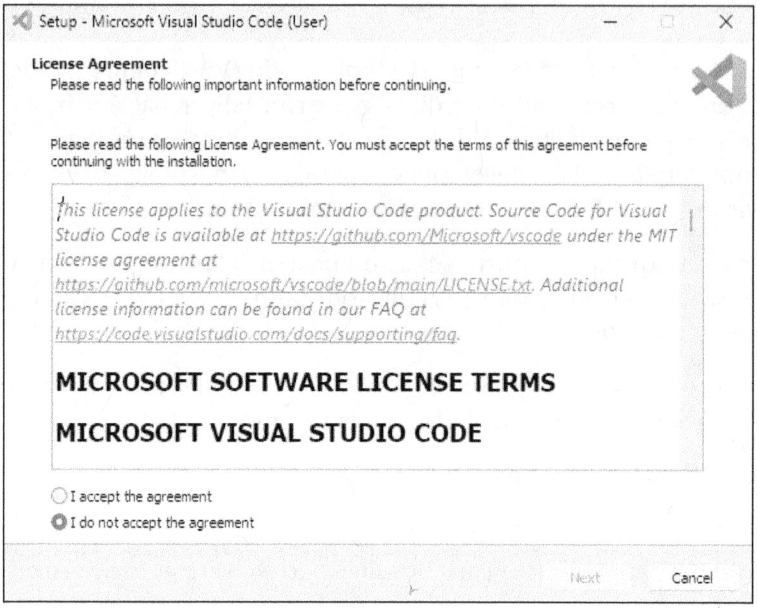

Figure 2.4: *After Clicking the Executable on Windows, Read the License Agreement, Select "I Accept the Agreement" and Click the next Button*

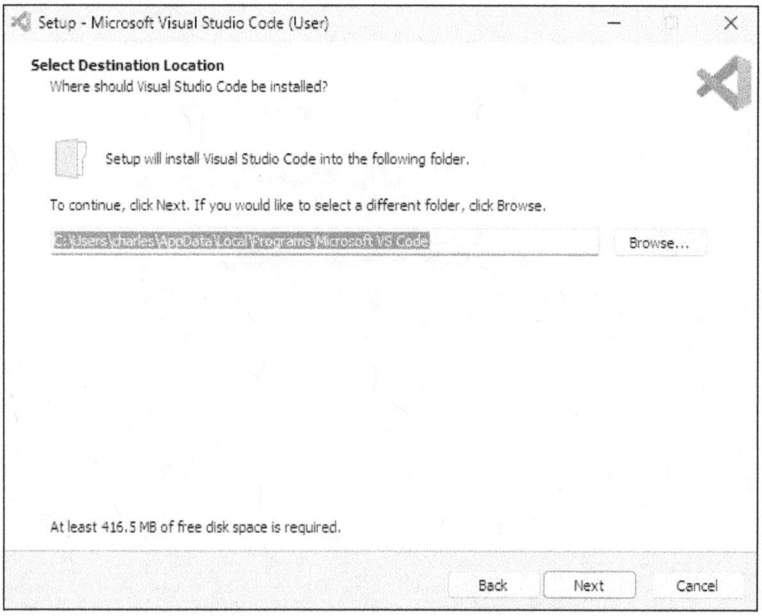

Figure 2.5: *Select the Destination Folder*

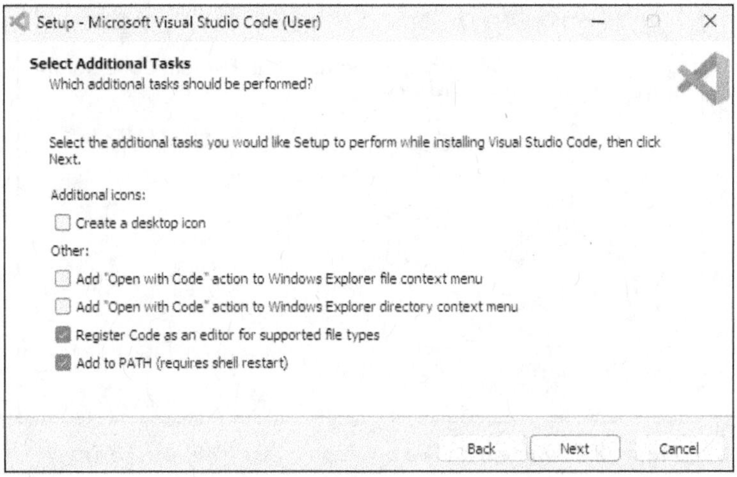

Figure 2.6: Select Any Additional Tasks

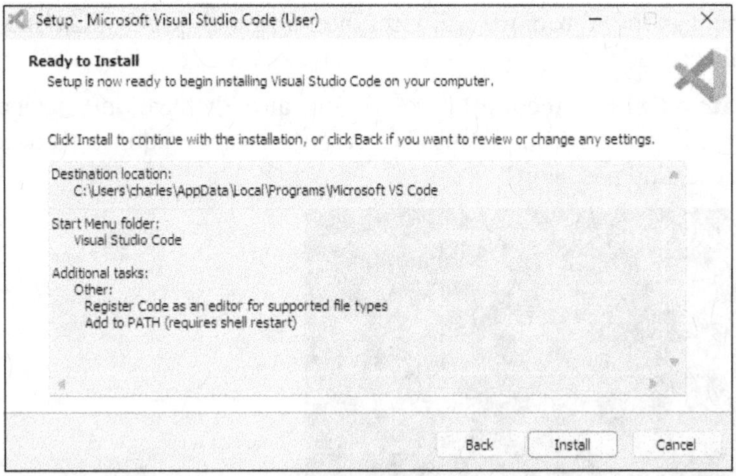

Figure 2.7: Check the Install Path and Click `Install`

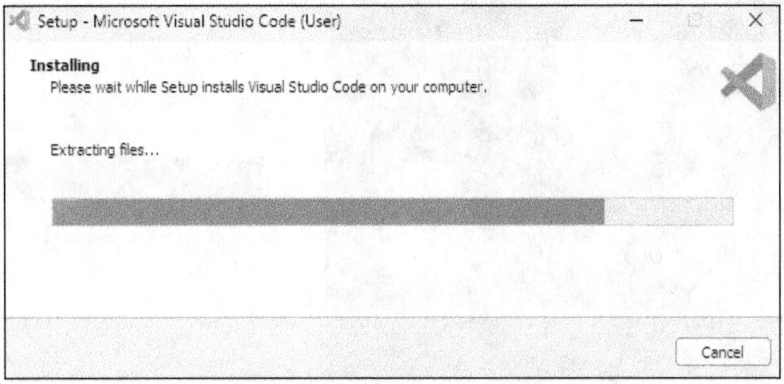

Figure 2.8: Wait for the Install Process to Complete

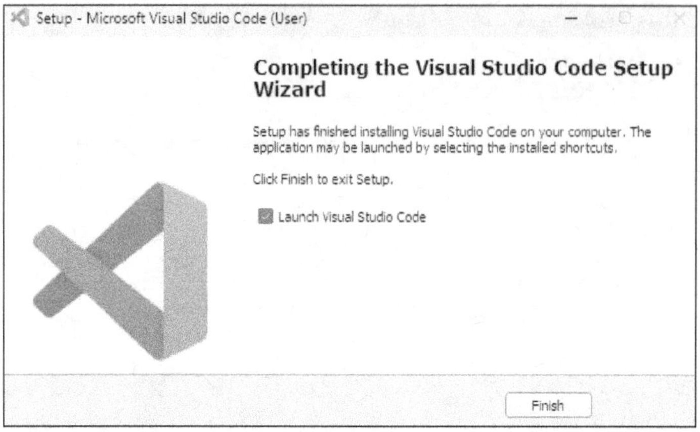

Figure 2.9: *You Should See a Window Like This. Click* `Finish`

Step 2: Set Up Your GitHub Account and Copilot Subscription

GitHub Copilot is the AI tool we will integrate, and it requires a GitHub account and an active subscription.

a. **Create a GitHub Account:** If you do not already have one, navigate to github.com and sign up. The process is straightforward, requiring a username, email address, and password.

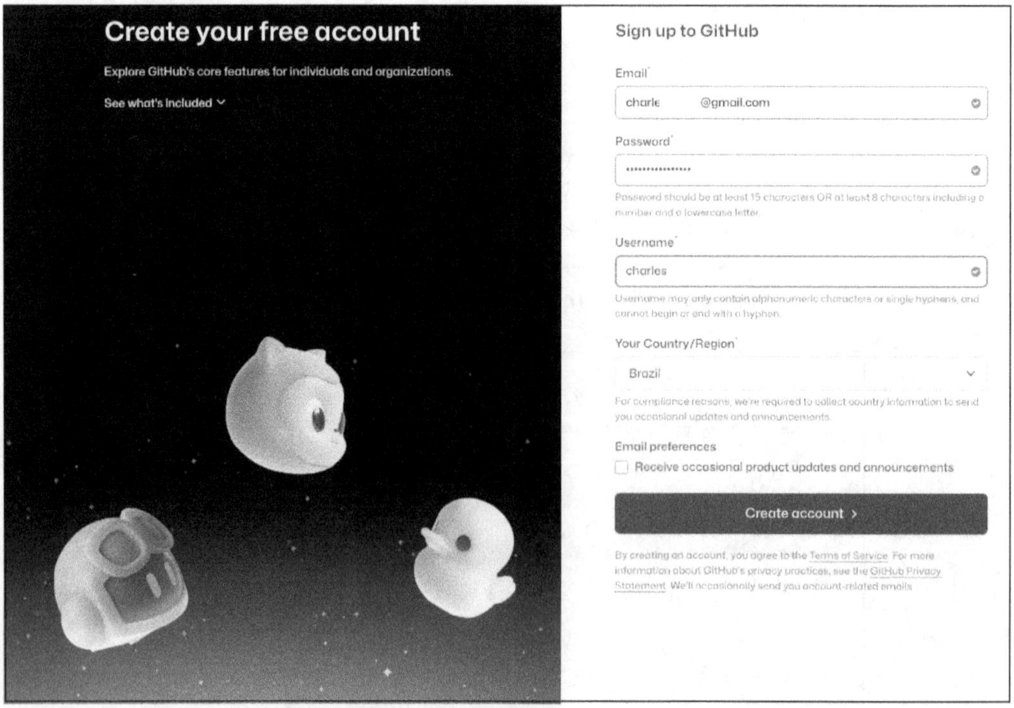

Figure 2.10: *GitHub Account Creation Screen*

Later, you will need to validate your email address.

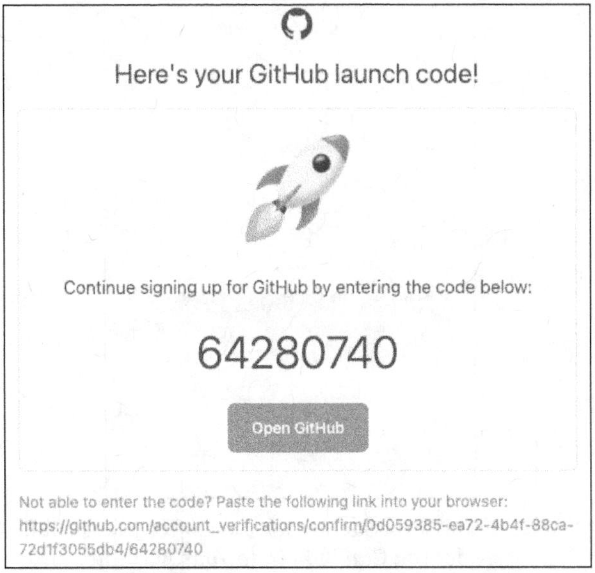

Figure 2.11a: *You Will be Prompted to Enter the Code That was Sent to Your Email You Just Used to Register on GitHub*

Check your email inbox for the verification message from GitHub. It will contain the numeric launch code required to prove your identity and proceed with the registration.

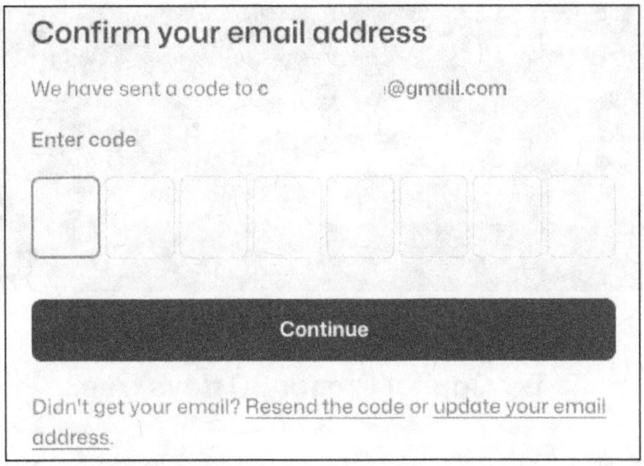

Figure 2.11b: *Enter the Code GitHub Sent You*

Carefully type or paste this code into the input fields provided on the GitHub website. Once the system validates your code, your account setup is complete, and you are ready to log in.

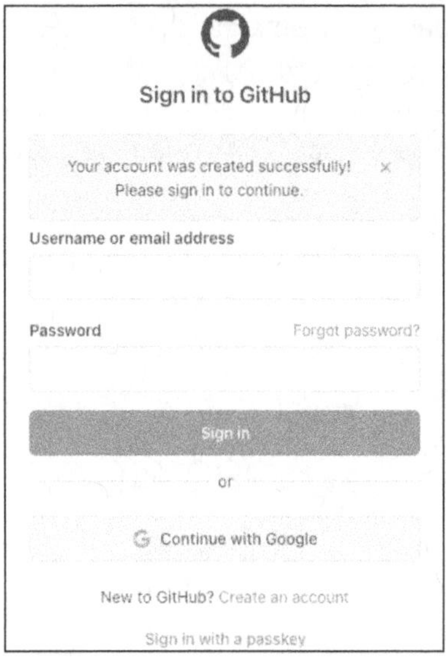

Figure 2.12: *You Should See a Success Message after the Account Activation! Now, You Can Sign in to Your Account*

b. **Subscribe to GitHub Copilot**: Copilot is a subscription-based service. Navigate to the GitHub Copilot page (https://github.com/features/copilot) to sign up. There is typically a free trial available, and if you are a student, you may be able to get it for free through the GitHub Student Developer pack.

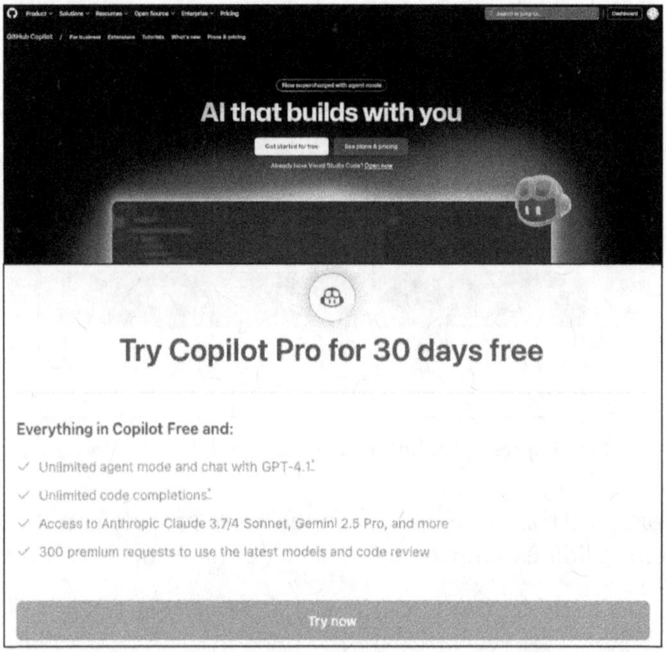

Figure 2.13: *Copilot Home Page and Copilot Pro Free Trial Offer*

Step 3: Install and Configure Your AI Engine

Now, we will install the core AI tools into VS Code.

Open VS Code. On the left-hand side, you will see a vertical toolbar called the "Activity Bar." Click the **`Extensions`** icon (it looks like four squares, with one flying off).

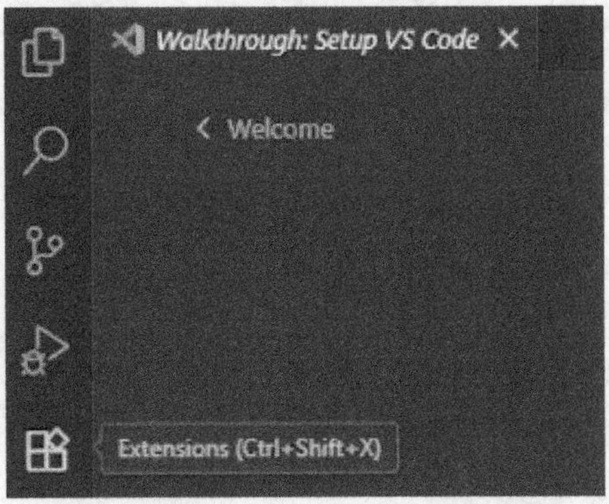

Figure 2.14: *Extensions Menu on VSCode*

In the search bar that appears, type **`GitHub Copilot`**

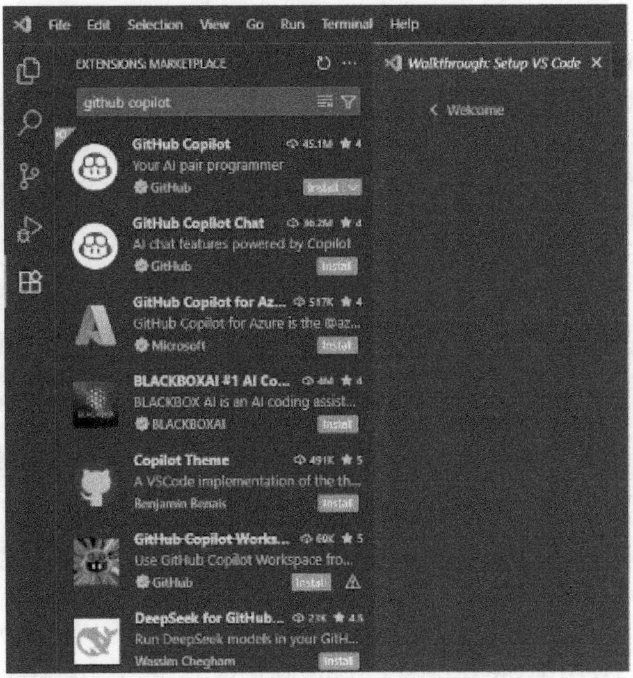

Figure 2.15: *Github Copilot Extension by Github on VSCode*

Find the extension named "**`GitHub Copilot`**" published by "**`GitHub`**" and click the **`Install`** button.

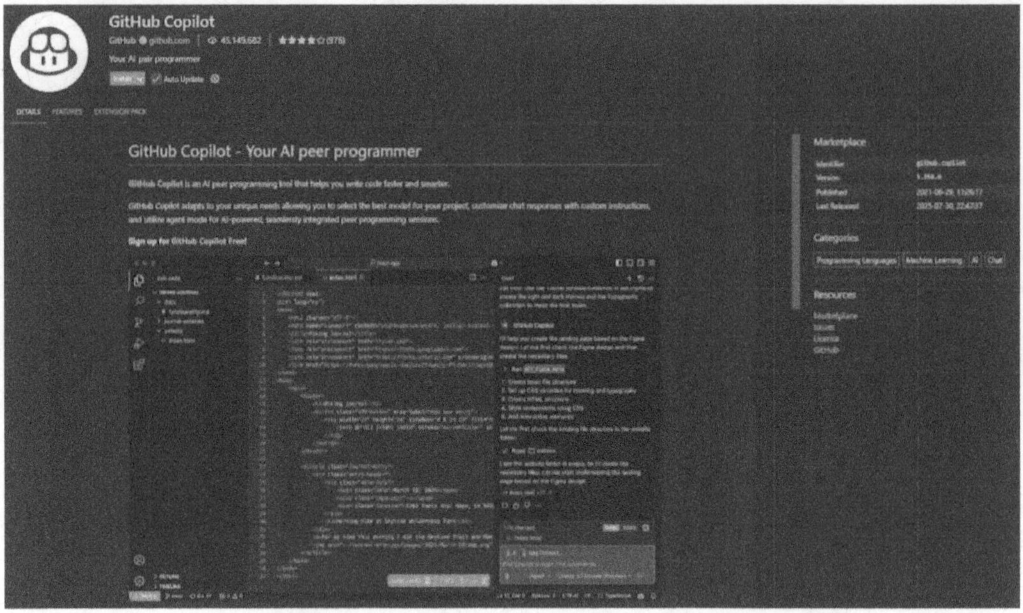

Figure 2.16: *Github Copilot Extension by Github on VSCode*

Once installed, a pop-up will appear at the bottom right, prompting you to sign in to GitHub. Click **`Sign in to GitHub`**.

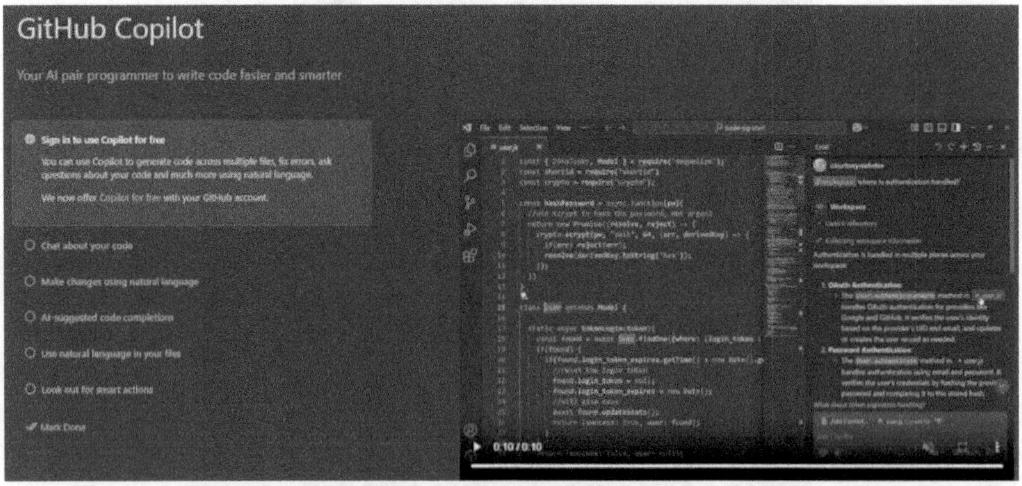

Figure 2.17: *Github Copilot Setup Screen, Where You Will be Prompted to Sign in*

You will be redirected to your browser to authorize VS Code to use your GitHub account. Click **`Authorize Visual-Studio-Code`** to grant permission. After authorization, you can close the browser tab and return to VS Code.

Figure 2.18: *Sign in Screen for Copilot*

Step 4: Install Essential Companion Extensions

To create the best possible workflow, we need three more extensions that work hand-in-hand with our AI assistant.

a. **Tailwind CSS IntelliSense:** This extension is a critical companion to your AI workflow. While Copilot generates Tailwind class names, this extension will validate them, provide autocompletion, and show you the underlying CSS for each class, giving you immediate feedback on the AI's output.

   - In the Extensions view, search for `Tailwind CSS IntelliSense.`
   - Install the official extension published by "`Tailwind Labs`."

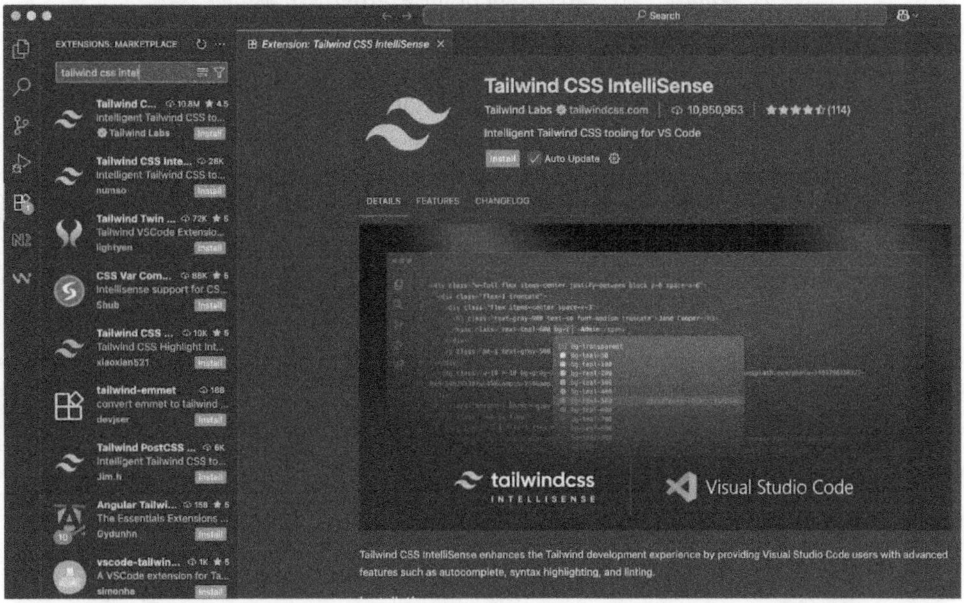

Figure 2.19: *Screenshot of the VS Code Extensions View Showing the Official "Tailwind CSS IntelliSense" Extension by Tailwind Labs, Ready to Install*

b. **Prettier - Code Formatter:** Keeping your code consistently formatted is crucial. A clean codebase provides clearer context for AI tools, leading to better and more accurate suggestions. In the Extensions view, search for **`Prettier - Code Formatter`**. Install the official extension. To make it fully automatic, you can set it as your default formatter and enable "**`Format on Save`**" in your VS Code settings.

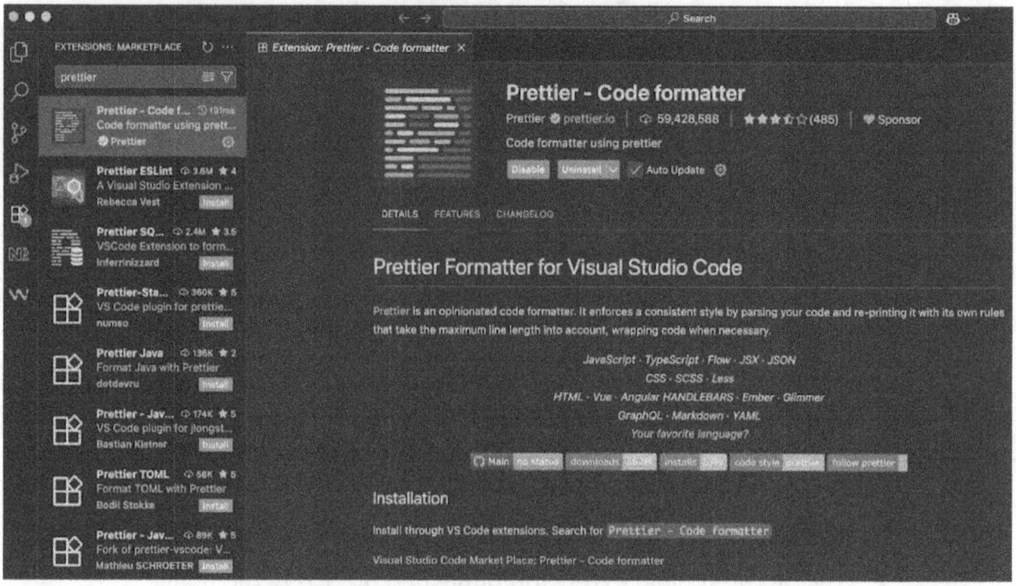

Figure 2.20: *Screenshot of the Prettier Extension*

c. **Live Server:** When generating UI with AI, you need to see your results instantly. Live Server creates a rapid feedback loop by automatically reloading your browser whenever you make changes. In the Extensions view, search for **`Live Server`** and install the popular extension by Ritwick Dey. Once installed, you can right-click your HTML file and select **`Open with Live Server`**, or click the **`Go Live`** button in the status bar to see your AI-generated designs update in real-time.

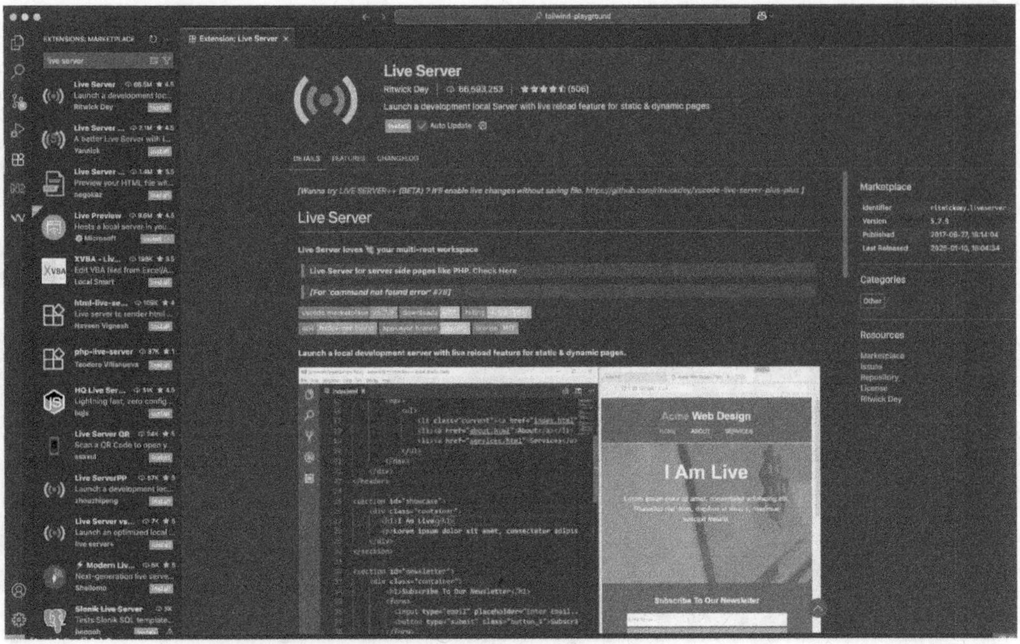

Figure 2.21: *Screenshot Showing the Extension Live Server on the Extensions Marketplace. Click* **`install`**

Figure 2.22: *You Should See a Go Live Button on VSCode's Bottom Bar after the Install Process*

Step 5: Verification: Your First AI-Generated Component

With everything installed and configured, let us verify that it is all working together.

a. Create a new folder on your computer, open it in VS Code (**`File`** > **`Open Folder...`**).

b. Create a new file named `index.html`.

c. Inside the file, type the following comment “ ” and press *Enter*.

d. **Wait a moment.** GitHub Copilot should now display a "ghost text" suggestion for the complete HTML button element.

e. Press the `Tab` key to accept the suggestion. Your editor should now contain the AI-generated code.

f. Finally, hover your mouse over one of the Tailwind CSS classes in the generated code (for example, **`bg-blue-500`**). A pop-up from Tailwind CSS IntelliSense should appear, showing you the exact CSS that class applies.

This confirms your setup is complete: Copilot is generating code, and IntelliSense is validating it. You are now ready to start building with your AI co-pilot.

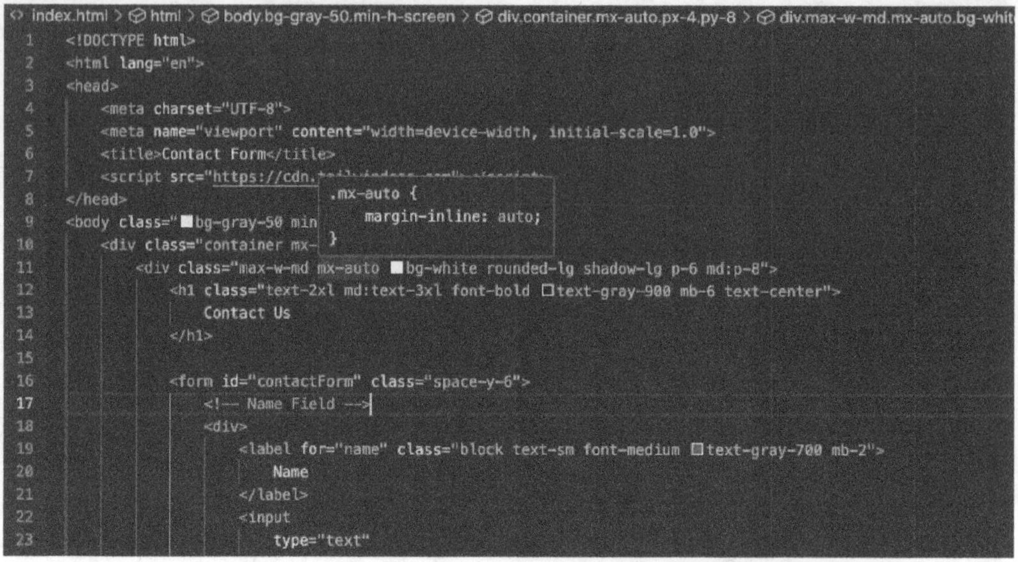

Figure 2.23: *Example of a Working Setup of VSCode*

Path B: The AI-First Experience (Cursor)

If you want an editor that was not simply adapted for AI but was built for it from the ground up, Cursor is your ideal choice. Cursor is a fork of VS Code, meaning it will feel instantly familiar if you have used VS Code before, but it has been re-engineered to place AI at the very core of the editing experience.

Unlike VS Code, where AI is added via extensions, Cursor integrates AI as a native feature. This leads to a more cohesive and powerful workflow for developers who want to fully embrace AI-assisted programming. This guide will walk you through setting up Cursor and understanding its unique, AI-native features.

Step 1: Install Cursor

First, you will need to download and install the editor.

a. Navigate to the official Cursor website at cursor.sh.

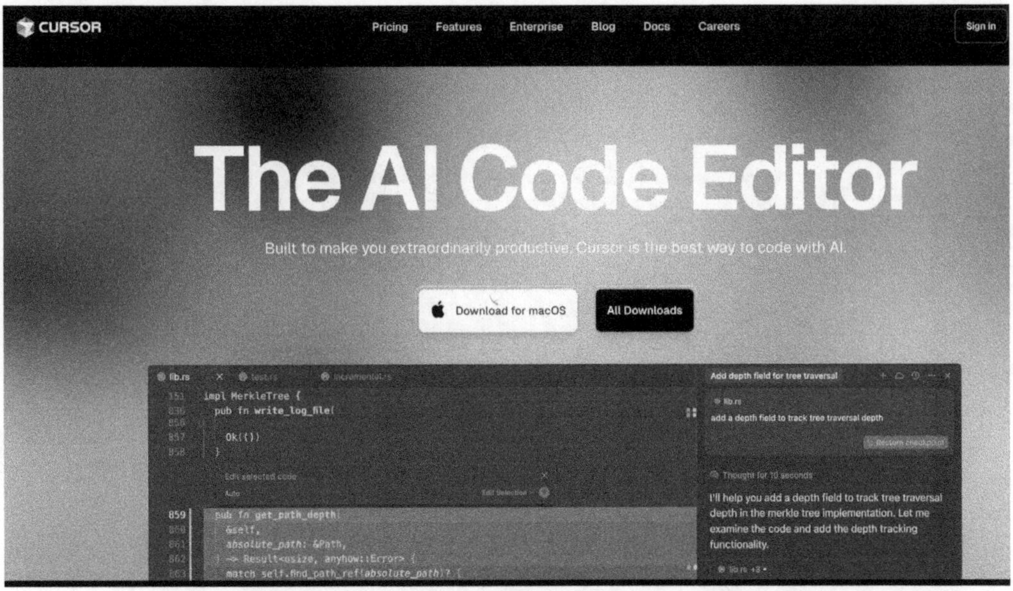

Figure 2.24: *Screenshot of the Official Cursor Download Page, Showing the Main Download Buttons for Different Operating Systems*

b. The website will present download options for your operating system (Windows, macOS, Linux). Download the appropriate installer.

c. Run the installer and follow the on-screen instructions.

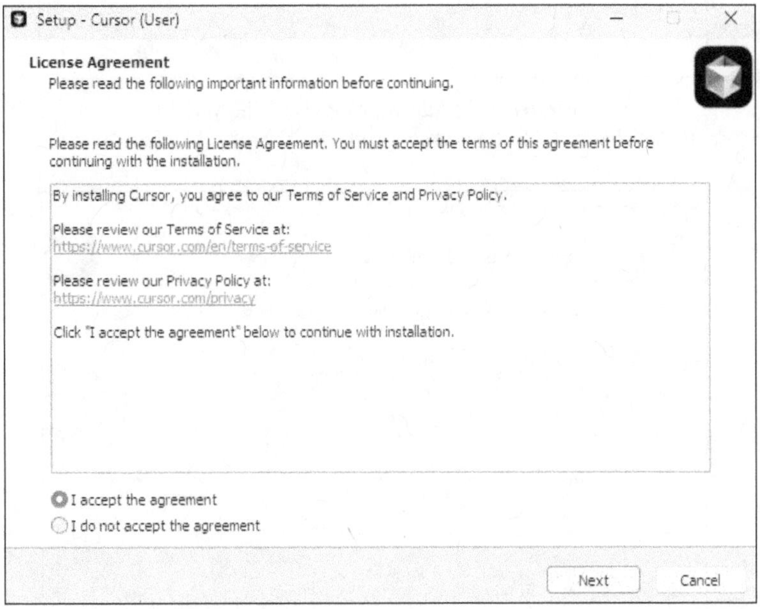

Figure 2.25: *Select Accept the Agreement and Next (the Install Process Will be Really Similar to the Regular VSCode)*

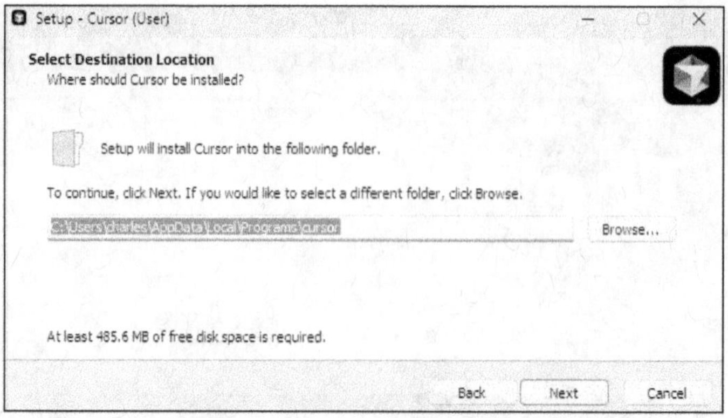

Figure 2.26: *Select the Install Folder*

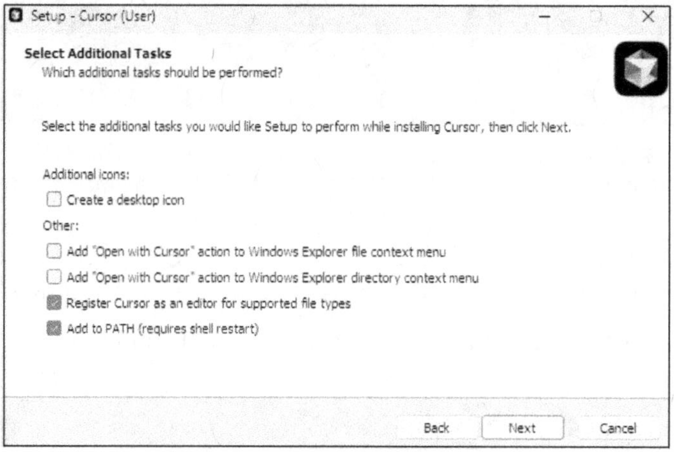

Figure 2.27: *Adding to PATH Will Make It Possible to Call the Cursor from the Terminal. Select "Next"*

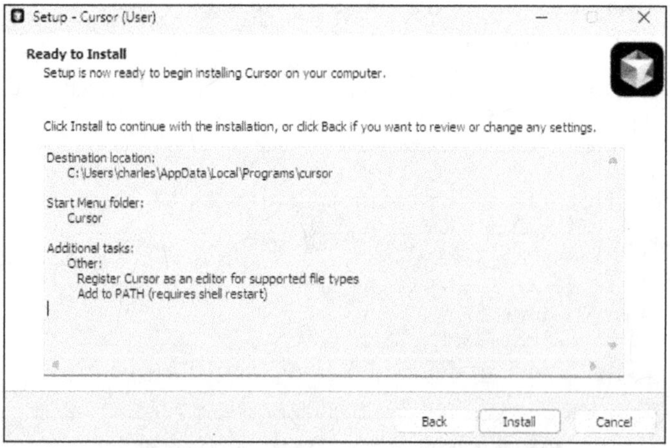

Figure 2.28: *Double Check the Install Options*

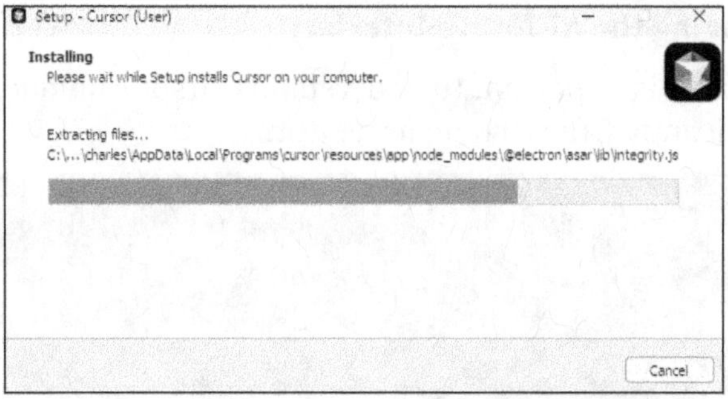

Figure 2.29: *Wait for the Installation to Finish*

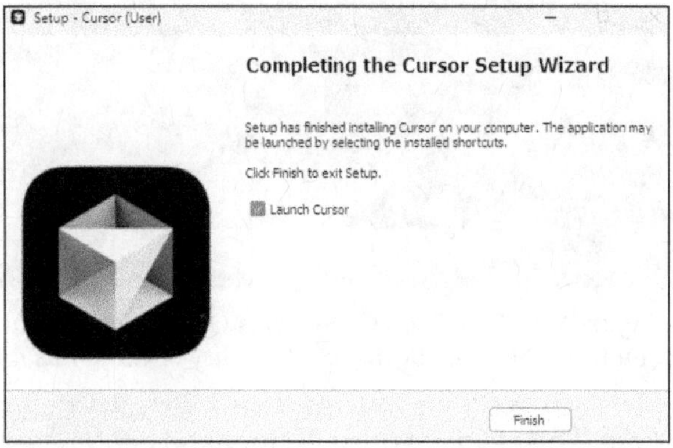

Figure 2.30: *You are Ready to Launch the Cursor*

Step 2: Account Setup and AI Configuration

Cursor's power is unlocked by connecting it to an AI model. This is done by logging into your account. Upon launching Cursor for the first time, you will be greeted with a welcome screen that prompts you to `Log In` or `Sign Up`. Create a Cursor account to get started.

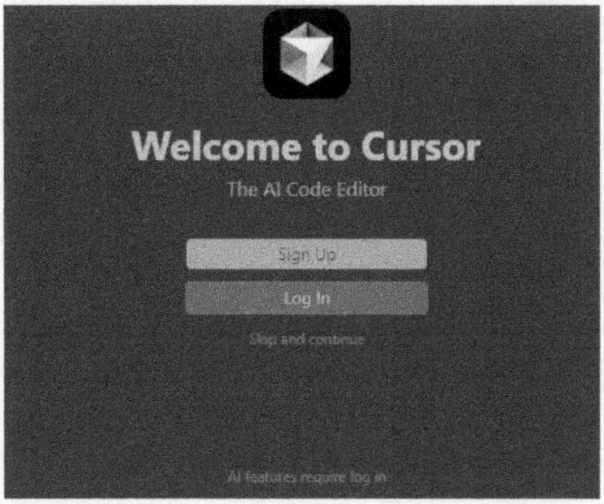

Figure 2.31: *You Will be Prompted to Login or Sign up to Use the AI Functionality*

Step 3: Understanding the AI-Native Interface

Before writing code, it is important to understand Cursor's unique interface elements, which differ significantly from a standard editor.

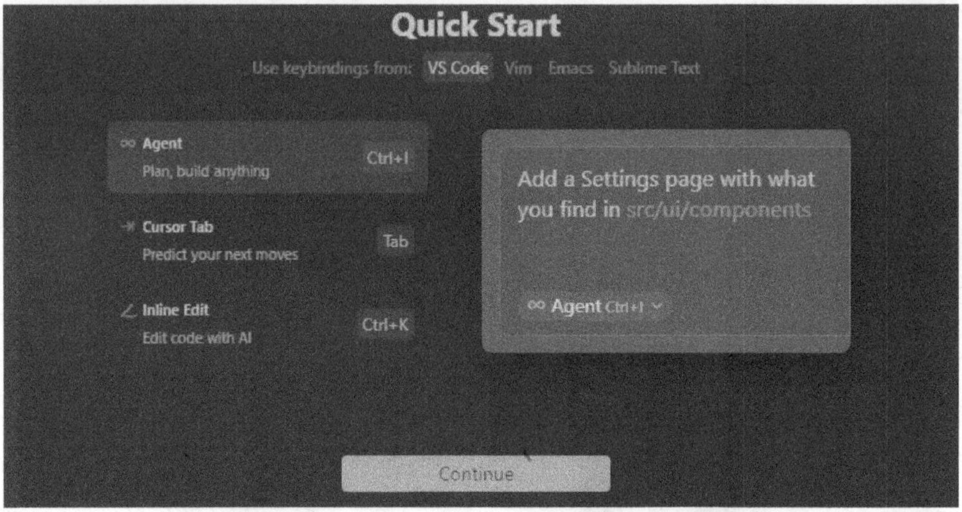

***Figure 2.32:** You Can Will See This Quick Start Modal, Where You Can Check the Basic Functionality of Cursor as an AI Tool*

- **The Chat Panel:** This is your primary command center, typically docked on the right or left. Instead of writing comments in your code to trigger AI, you will write the detailed prompts here.
- **Context with `@`:** In the chat, you can use the `@` symbol to specify the context for your prompt. For example, **`@code`** tells the AI to read your entire project, while **`@file`** tells it to focus only on that specific file.
- **Inline Editing (*Cmd/Ctrl* + K):** This is for making targeted changes. You can highlight a block of code, press *Cmd* + K (on macOS) or *Ctrl* + K (on Windows), and give the AI a direct command such as "Refactor this into a reusable function" or "Translate these comments to Spanish." The AI will then perform the edit directly in your file.

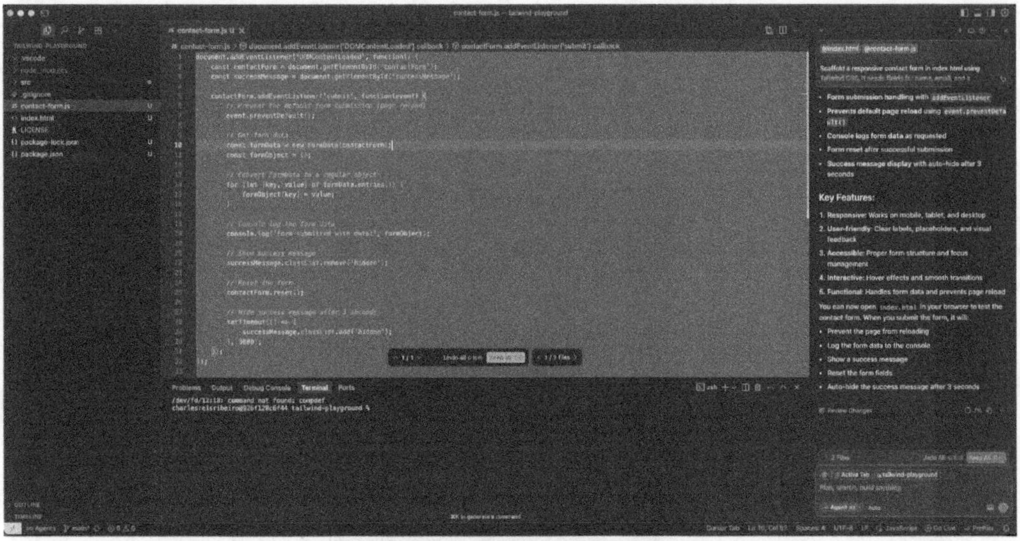

Figure 2.33a: *Screenshot of Cursor. Note the Right Sidebar, Where You Can Interact with an LLM Model That Knows about Your Codebase!*

To give you a better idea of how this interaction works, let us zoom in on that right sidebar. This dedicated chat panel acts as your primary command center, where you can type detailed instructions and use tools such as the @ symbol to feed specific files directly into the AI's context.

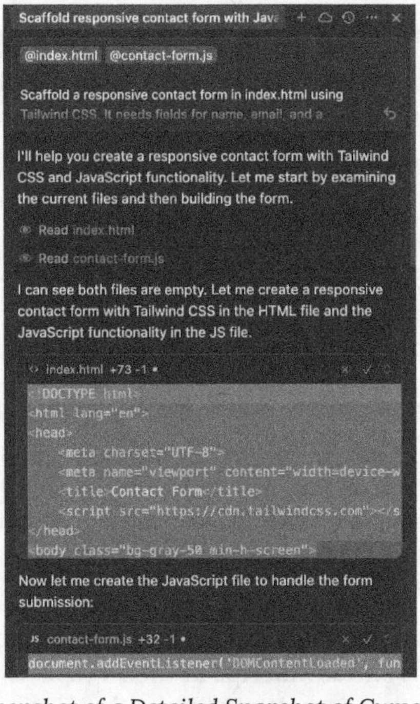

Figure 2.33b: *Screenshot of a Detailed Snapshot of Cursors' Chat Interface*

Step 4: Installing the Tailwind CSS Companion

Since, Cursor is a fork of VS Code, it has access to the same extension marketplace. To get the best Tailwind CSS experience, we will install the same IntelliSense extension.

a. Click the Extensions icon in the Activity Bar.

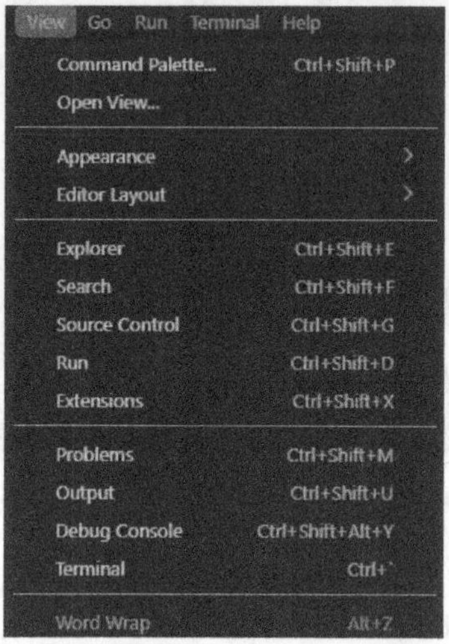

Figure 2.34: *Look for the "Extensions" Icons on the Left Sidebar. If You Cannot Find It from There, You May Open the Extensions from the View Menu, Then Selection Extensions (Also Accessible from the Ctrl+Shift+X)*

b. Search for **`Tailwind CSS IntelliSense`**.

c. Install the official extension published by "Tailwind Labs." This will give you the same validation and autocompletion features as in VS Code.

d. Do the same for **`Prettier`** and **`Live Server`** extensions.

Step 5: Verification: A Truly AI-Native Workflow

Let us see Cursor's power in action by performing a task that would be difficult in a traditional editor.

a. Open the **`tailwind-playground`** folder you created earlier in Cursor.

b. Create two new empty files: **`index.html`** and **`contact-form.js`**.

c. In the Chat panel, type the following prompt: `@index.html @contact-form.js Scaffold a responsive contact form in index.html using Tailwind CSS. It needs fields for name, email, and a message. Then, in contact-form.js, write the JavaScript to handle form submission, console.log the data, and prevent the default page reload.`

d. Press Enter. Cursor will analyze your request, read both files, and write the appropriate HTML and JavaScript in their respective files. This demonstrates its ability to work across multiple files with a single prompt.

e. Hover over one of the generated Tailwind CSS classes in **`index.html`** to confirm that the IntelliSense extension is working correctly.

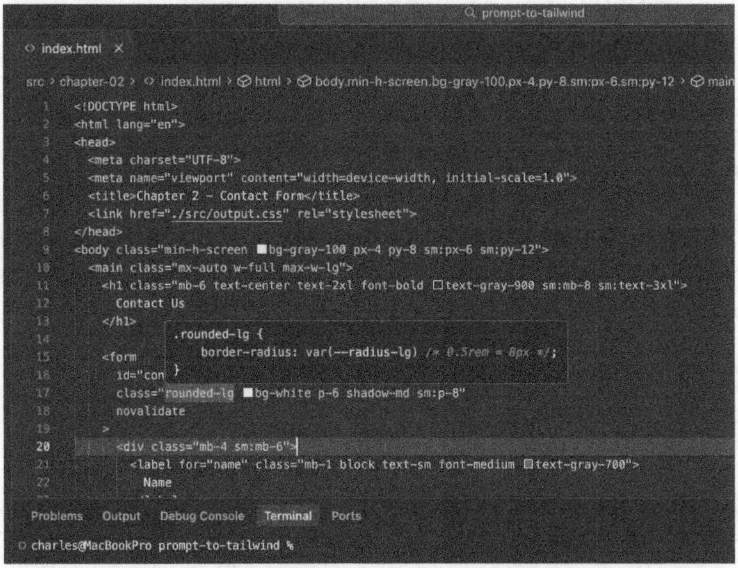

Figure 2.35: *Screenshots of the Cursor Chat Panel Showing the Multi-File Prompt. The Editor View has a Tab for index.html*

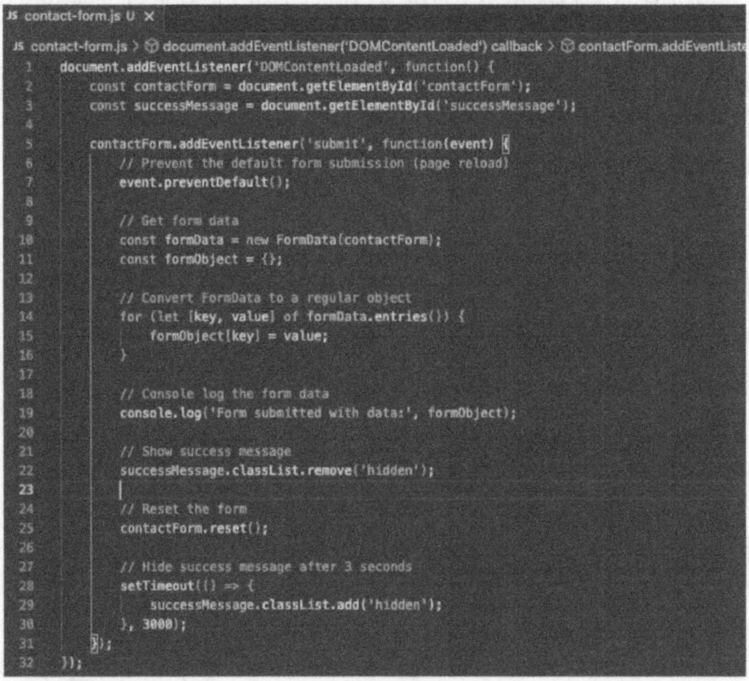

Figure 2.36: *Screenshot of the Cursor Chat Panel Showing the Multi-File Prompt. The Editor View has a Tab for contact-form.js*

This workflow showcases the fundamental difference in Cursor: you are orchestrating changes across your codebase from a central, conversational interface. You are now set up with a powerful, AI-first development environment.

Managing API Keys Safely (For External Tools)

While integrated tools such as GitHub Copilot is seamless; you may want to connect your editor to other powerful AI services directly. You might want to experiment with the very latest models from OpenAI, or use a specialized service such as Anthropic's Claude, or simply have more granular control over your AI provider.

To do this, your editor needs to prove it has permission to use the service. This is done with an **API Key**. Managing these keys safely is one of the most important security practices for a modern developer.

Introduction to API Keys

Think of an API Key as a secret password or a unique digital keycard for your application. It is a long, unique string of characters that you get from an AI service provider (such as OpenAI).

When your editor sends a request to the AI service, it includes this key. The key serves two main purposes:

Authentication: It proves that the request is coming from you and that you are an authorized user of the service.

Tracking and Billing: It allows the service to measure your usage, enforce rate limits, and handle billing.

Because this key is directly tied to your account and billing information, you must protect it as carefully as you would protect your bank account password.

The Golden Rule: NEVER Hard-Code Your Keys

This is the most critical lesson in this section. **NEVER** save an API key directly in your code. This is known as "hard-coding."

A Bad Example (What NOT to do):

```
// DANGER: Do NOT do this!
const OPENAI_API_KEY = "sk-xxxxxxxxxxxxxxxxxxxxxxxxxxxxxxxxxxxxxxxx";
// ... rest of your application code
```

If you commit a file containing a hard-coded key to a public repository on GitHub, malicious bots that constantly scan the platform can find your key in *seconds*. They can then use your key to make their own requests, potentially running up a huge bill on your account before you even realize what has happened.

Best Practices for Storing API Keys

So, if you cannot put the key in your code. Where do you put it? You use a method that keeps the key separate from your codebase.

Method 1: Environment Variables (`.env` files) - The Universal Approach

This is the most common and versatile method, and it works across all editors and operating systems.

Create a `.env` file: In the root directory of your project, create a new file named `.env`.

Add your key: Inside this file, add your API key in a `KEY=VALUE` format. By convention, the key's name is in all caps.

```
OPENAI_API_KEY="sk-xxxxxxxxxxxxxxxxxxxxxxxxxxxxxxxxxxxxxxxx"
```

IGNORE This File: This is the most important step. Open your `.gitignore` file (create one if it does not exist) and add `.env` on a new line. This tells Git to **never** track this file or include it in any commits.

Your editor or application code can then be configured to securely load this variable from the `.env` file without the key itself ever being part of your version control history.

Method 2: Using Your Editor's Secure Storage

Modern editors provide secure ways to store secrets, which are often used automatically by extensions.

For VS Code / Cursor:

These editors have a built-in Secret Storage API. When you install an extension that needs a key (for example, an OpenAI or a Claude extension), it will typically provide a settings input field.

When you paste your key into this field, the extension uses the editor's API to store it securely in a location on your machine *outside* of your project folder. This is often the most user-friendly method, as the extension handles the security for you.

Understanding Your Tools and Writing Your First Prompts

Your AI-powered editor is now installed and configured. The next crucial step is learning how to communicate effectively with your new assistants. A common mistake is to treat all AI tools as if they were the same. The key to an efficient workflow is understanding the unique strengths of each, knowing when to rely on a quick inline suggestion versus when to engage in a detailed conversation to scaffold an entire feature.

This section will guide you through the different roles your AI assistants play and provide you with your first set of prompts to verify your setup and start exploring their capabilities.

Meet Your AI Assistants: Different Tools for Different Jobs

Think of your AI toolset as a team of specialists. You would not ask a junior assistant to design a skyscraper, nor would you ask a chief architect to fetch you coffee. Assigning the right task to the right tool is essential.

- **GitHub Copilot (The "Over-the-Shoulder" Pair Programmer):** This is the AI that provides inline, "ghost text" suggestions. It is constantly watching what you type and anticipating your next move. Its strength lies in its immediate context awareness of the file you are editing.
- **AI Chat (The "Architect" or "Consultant"):** This is your conversational partner (for example, Copilot Chat, Cursor's chat). It is best for higher-level, more complex tasks. You can provide it with detailed instructions, paste large blocks of code for analysis, or ask it to brainstorm solutions.

Here is a simple guide for when to use which:

Task at Hand	Best Tool	Why?
Finishing the line of code you are typing.	Inline Suggestions (Copilot)	It excels at short-term, predictive completion.
Generating a full function or class boilerplate.	Inline Suggestions (Copilot)	Writing a function signature or a comment often gives it enough context to scaffold the rest.
Scaffolding a new component from scratch.	AI Chat	You can provide a multi-line, detailed prompt describing the component, its state, and its styling.
Explaining a block of code you do not understand.	AI Chat	You can paste the code directly into the chat and ask, "What does this do?" or "Explain this to me like I am a beginner."
Refactoring or improving existing code	AI Chat	This is perfect for providing a function and asking, "Can you make this more efficient?" or "Refactor this to use modern JavaScript syntax."
Brainstorming different approaches.	AI Chat	You can describe a problem, such as "What are the best ways to create a responsive grid layout with Tailwind CSS?" and get multiple options.

Table 2.1: *Contrasting the Usage of GitHub Copilot and AI Chat*

A Quick Note on Context

The single most important factor for getting good results from AI is **context**. An AI with no context is like a programmer with no requirements.

- **Inline Suggestions** get their context automatically from the content of the file you are currently editing, and sometimes from other files you have open in your editor. The more relevant information you have on screen, the better the suggestions will be.
- **AI Chat** relies on the context *you provide* in your prompt. If you ask a vague question such as "Fix my code," it cannot help you. You must paste the relevant code, describe the error message, and explain what you are trying to achieve. In editors such as Cursor, you can use `@` symbols to give the chat direct access to your project files, which is a powerful way to provide context.

Your First Prompts: A Systems Check

Let us write our first prompts. The goal here is not to build anything complex, but to verify that your tools are working and to get a feel for the interaction. We will use the AI Chat for this.

The Verification Prompt

This prompt checks that the AI can generate a complete, working file. It is a great way to get a "Hello, World!" from your setup.

"Create a basic HTML5 boilerplate file. Inside the `<head>`, include the script tag for the Tailwind CSS Play CDN. In the `<body>`, add an `<h1>` tag with the text 'AI Setup Complete!' and style it with Tailwind to have large, bold, blue text that is centered on the page."

The Configuration Prompt

AI is excellent at handling boilerplate configuration files. This prompt tests its ability to generate code for your project's tooling.

"Show me a basic `tailwind.config.js` file. In it, extend the theme to add a new brand color called 'brand-purple' with the hex value #5D3A9B."

The Learning Prompt

Finally, remember that your AI assistant is also an incredibly powerful learning tool. Use it to ask questions you might otherwise search for online.

"Explain the difference between `justify-content` and `align-items` in CSS Flexbox. Please provide examples using Tailwind CSS classes."

By running these three prompts, you will have confirmed that your setup is working, seen how AI can help with project configuration, and experienced its power as an on-demand tutor.

Conclusion

Congratulations! You have successfully navigated one of the most crucial parts of your journey into AI-assisted development. You have moved beyond theory and have now built a tangible, powerful, and professional development environment. Whether you chose the industry-standard versatility of Visual Studio Code or the deeply integrated, AI-first experience of Cursor, your cockpit is ready, and you are in the pilot's seat.

In this chapter, you installed and configured not merely an editor, but a new way of working. You integrated a powerful AI co-pilot into your workflow, whether through the seamlessness of GitHub Copilot or a connection to a local LLM. You have also learned the vital principles of this modern toolkit: Understanding when to use quick inline suggestions versus a detailed AI chat, the critical importance of managing API keys safely, and how to write your first prompts to verify your setup and begin the human-AI conversation.

With your environment now fully operational, you are ready to put it to the test. The setup phase is complete, and the real creative work can begin. In the next chapter, we will take these newly configured tools and start building, using our AI assistant to tackle the fundamentals of crafting responsive UI elements with HTML and Tailwind CSS. The foundation is laid. Let us start creating.

Exercises and Reflections

The goal of this section is to solidify what you have learned through hands-on practice and critical thinking. Do not only complete the tasks; reflect on the process and how these new tools are shaping your workflow. This self-learning is key to mastering AI-assisted development.

Hands-on: Your First AI-Generated Component

Now that your environment is fully configured, let us put it to a practical test. Your task is to generate a complete UI component from scratch using your AI assistant.

Task: Using your editor's AI Chat (Copilot Chat or Cursor Chat), write a single, detailed prompt to generate the HTML for a "User Profile Card."

Requirements for the Prompt:

The card should have a white background, rounded corners, and a subtle box shadow.

It must contain a placeholder for an avatar image (you can use a service such as `picsum.photos`).

It should include a user's name (for example, "Alex Doe"), a job title (for example, "Frontend Developer"), and a short bio.

Use Tailwind CSS for all styling. The name should be bold and larger than the other text.

After generating the code, hover over the utility classes to verify that Tailwind CSS IntelliSense is working correctly.

Hands-on: API Key Safety Drill

This exercise will reinforce the single most important security lesson from this chapter: Never commit your secret keys.

Ask: Create a new, temporary folder on your machine.

Steps:

1. Initialize a Git repository inside the folder (`git init`).
2. Create a file named `.env` and add a fake API key to it, such as `MY_SECRET_KEY="12345-this-is-a-test"`.
3. Create a `.gitignore` file and add .env as a new line inside it.
4. Create another file, `index.html`.
5. Add all files to be tracked by Git (`git add .`).
6. Run the command git status.

Verification: Look at the output of git status. It should list `index.html` and `.gitignore` as new files, but the `.env` file should be absent. This confirms you have successfully told Git to ignore your secrets.

Reflection: The Two Modes of AI

The difference between inline suggestions and conversational chat is fundamental. Explore this difference for yourself.

Task: Think about the "User Profile Card" from the first exercise.

First, try to generate it again, but this time **only** by writing comments in your HTML file to trigger inline suggestions from GitHub Copilot.

Now, compare that experience to using the AI Chat panel.

Questions to Ponder:

Which method felt faster for the initial creation?

Which method gave you more precise control over the final output?

Describe a scenario where the inline suggestion approach would be superior, and a scenario where the AI Chat is the obvious choice.

Reflection: Your Evolving Workflow

The introduction of powerful AI assistants transforms how development gets done.

Task: Think about a web development project you completed before reading this chapter.

Questions to Ponder: Identify two specific, time-consuming tasks from that project (for example, writing boilerplate HTML for multiple pages, creating a complex responsive layout, and debugging a tricky CSS issue).

How would you approach those same tasks differently now, using the tools you configured in this chapter? Be specific about the prompts you might use or the features you would leverage.

Multiple Choice Questions

1. What is the primary purpose of an Integrated Development Environment (IDE)?
    a. To run web servers locally.
    b. To bundle common developer tools such as a code editor, debugger, and build tools into a single interface.
    c. To manage API keys and project secrets.
    d. To write and send emails to a development team.
2. When setting up a project, what is the most critical step to ensure your `.env` file is secure?
    a. Encrypting the `.env` file
    b. Naming it `secrets.txt` instead
    c. Adding `.env` to your `.gitignore` file
    d. Storing it in a separate folder outside the project
3. Which task is best suited for an AI Chat assistant (like Copilot Chat) rather than inline suggestions?
    a. Completing the second half of a variable name you started typing
    b. Generating a standard for a loop

    c. Automatically closing an HTML tag
    d. Refactoring a large, complex function and asking for an explanation of the changes

4. Why is the "Tailwind CSS IntelliSense" extension considered a critical companion for an AI workflow?
    a. It automatically generates all your Tailwind CSS code for you.
    b. It validates the utility classes generated by the AI and shows you the underlying CSS on hover.
    c. It allows you to chat with the creators of Tailwind CSS directly.
    d. It replaces the need for a `tailwind.config.js` file.
5. What is the recommended way to install `Node.js` to avoid permission issues and manage multiple versions easily?
    a. Downloading the installer directly from the `Node.js` website
    b. Using a version manager such as `nvm` (Node Version Manager)
    c. Installing it as a VS Code extension
    d. Compiling it from source code
6. What is the primary danger of "hard-coding" an API key into your source code?
    a. It can slow down your application's performance.
    b. It makes the key difficult for other team members to find.
    c. If committed to a public repository, the key can be stolen and used maliciously.
    d. It prevents the AI from understanding your code's context.

Answers

1. b
2. c
3. d
4. b
5. b
6. c

CHAPTER 3
Coding Fundamentals with AI – Building Basic UI Elements with Tailwind CSS

Introduction

In this chapter, we focus on using AI to assist with fundamental coding tasks while mastering Tailwind CSS basics. We will cover core Tailwind concepts, including the utility-first approach, layout techniques, responsive design, pseudo-classes for interactive states, and theming (dark mode), and show how AI tools such as GitHub Copilot or ChatGPT can accelerate these tasks. The goal is to learn how to validate and understand AI-generated code as we build a simple responsive UI component (a card with an image, title, and button). Throughout, we provide prompt engineering tips, brief comparisons between AI-generated and human-written code, and exercises to solidify your understanding. By the end of this chapter, you will have solid knowledge about how to use Tailwind CSS with the most common generative AI tools.

Structure

In this chapter, we will discuss the following topics:

- Tailwind Core Concepts
  - Base Styles: Preflight
  - Utility Classes for Styling
  - Flexbox Utilities for Layout
  - Grid Layout Utilities for Layout
  - Pseudo-Class Variants for Hover, Focus, and More
  - Responsive Design and Mobile-First Breakpoints
  - Dark Mode Support (Class-Based Strategy)

   - Z-Index and Layering (Stacking Contexts)
   - Typography Utilities and Font Styles
   - Color Palette and Usage in Tailwind
   - Working with SVGs and Icons
   - Theme Configuration and Extending Tailwind
   - Removing Unused CSS (Purging with JIT)
   - Tailwind's CSS Directives and Functions (@apply, theme(), and so on)
- AI Integration as a Support Layer in Coding
   - AI-Powered Code Suggestions (Copilot, and so on.)
   - AI Code Generation with ChatGPT
   - Prompting AI for Tailwind Snippets (Examples)
   - AI for Fixing Styling Bugs
   - AI for Refactoring and Optimization
- Concept Walkthrough: Building a Responsive Card Component (with AI Assistance)
   - Step 1: Initial Structure – Base HTML and Styling
   - Step 2: Enhancing with Responsive Behavior
   - Step 3: Adding Dark Mode Support
   - Step 4: Polish – Hover and Focus States, Accessibility

Tailwind Core Concepts

Before diving into AI-assisted coding, it is essential to understand Tailwind CSS fundamentals. Tailwind is a **utility-first CSS framework**, meaning it provides many small, single-purpose classes (utilities) that map directly to specific CSS properties. Instead of writing custom CSS rules for each new component, you compose these utility classes directly in your HTML. This approach keeps styling close to the markup and speeds up development by reducing context-switching between HTML and CSS files.

Let us explore the key Tailwind concepts you will use throughout this chapter.

Quick Note: Refresher on HTML and CSS

- **HTML (HyperText Markup Language):** The standard markup language for structuring web content. HTML provides the elements that define a page's structure (such as headings, paragraphs, buttons, images, or forms).

- **CSS (Cascading Style Sheets):** The styling language that controls how HTML elements look (colors, layout, typography, spacing, and so on). CSS works by applying rules that target elements and define their presentation.

Tailwind sits on top of CSS. Instead of writing your own style rules in a stylesheet, you apply predefined utility classes directly to HTML elements. This keeps structure (HTML) and presentation (CSS) in the same place, streamlining the development process.

Quick Note: Using Tailwind Play

For many examples in this chapter, we will use **Tailwind Play**, the official online playground provided by Tailwind CSS. It is a browser-based tool that allows you to:

- Experiment with Tailwind classes in real time.
- See instant results of changes without configuring a project locally.
- Share live examples or snippets with others easily.

You can access Tailwind Play at https://play.tailwindcss.com. It is a convenient way to test utilities quickly before integrating them into a full project.

Base Styles: Preflight

Every web browser applies its own default styling to HTML elements, which can often lead to frustrating visual inconsistencies. To prevent this and provide developers with a truly blank canvas, Tailwind establishes a standardized baseline before any utility classes are applied.

- Tailwind includes an opinionated (that is, assertive and dogmatic) set of base styles called Preflight, which is automatically applied when you import Tailwind into your project. Preflight is essentially Tailwind's modern CSS reset built on top of Normalize.css[1]. Its purpose is to smooth over cross-browser inconsistencies and ground elements on a clean slate. Most Preflight styles are subtle and go unnoticed, but some are more noticeable:
- **Default Margins are Removed:** All the default browser margins on elements (such as the top margin on paragraphs or headings) are reset to zero. This prevents accidental reliance on browser styles that are not part of your design system.

[1] *Normalize.css is a small CSS library created by Nicolas Gallagher and Jonathan Neal that provides cross-browser consistency by correcting common styling inconsistencies in HTML elements. Unlike older CSS resets that removed nearly all default styles,* ***`Normalize.css`*** *preserves useful defaults while fixing bugs and ensuring elements render more uniformly across browsers. Tailwind's Preflight builds upon Normalize.css by adding additional resets and adjustments specifically designed for utility-first development.*

- **Border Styles are Reset:** Tailwind sets all elements to **`border: 0 solid`** (with box-sizing: border-box), so that adding a utility such as border will always produce a 1px solid border by default. This means simply adding **`class="border"`** gives you a visible border without further specification.

- **Headings and Lists are Unstyled:** All heading **`<h1>...<h6>`** elements do not carry browser-default font sizes or boldness; they inherit the base font styles. Similarly, lists **`<ul> / <ol>`** have no default list-style or padding. This may surprise newcomers (your **`<h1>`** looks the same as normal text until you style it), but it ensures you explicitly apply consistent styling via utilities rather than relying on inconsistent defaults. (Tailwind's creators argue this forces conscious design decisions and prevents deviating from your chosen type scale unintentionally.)

In practice, Preflight gives you a blank canvas where everything is consistent – for example, headings will not have huge default sizes, and paragraphs will not have unexpected margins. You then build up your design with Tailwind's utility classes. If needed, you can override or add base styles by injecting your own CSS into Tailwind's base layer (using the **`@layer`** base directive), but generally, Preflight's defaults are a solid foundation.

Utility Classes for Styling

Tailwind's basic building blocks are its **utility classes**. Each class corresponds to a single CSS declaration (such as a color, spacing, font size, and so on). For example, **`text-center`** sets **`text-align: center, bg-blue-500`** applies a specific blue background color, and `p-4` adds padding of 1rem (16px) on all sides. You combine these classes on an element to achieve the desired design. This can result in quite long **`class`** attribute values, but each piece is purposeful and descriptive.

For instance:

```
<button class="bg-blue-500 text-white font-semibold px-4 py-2 rounded">
  Click Me
</button>
```

This snippet gives the button a blue background, white text, semi-bold font, horizontal padding of **`1rem (px-4)`** and vertical padding of **`0.5rem (py-2)`**, and slightly rounded corners. There is no custom CSS, such as **`.btn-primary`**; we describe the styling directly on the element. Utility-first styling might feel unusual at first, but it makes the markup a clear blueprint of the UI. You might see markup such as:

```
<div class="bg-gray-800 text-white p-5 rounded-lg shadow-lg"> ... </div>
```

This describes "a dark gray box with white text, some padding, rounded corners, and a shadow" entirely through classes. In summary, **utility classes let you build designs in HTML** by mixing and matching predefined styles. They are intuitive for humans and predictable for AI assistants, which have been trained on common Tailwind class patterns.

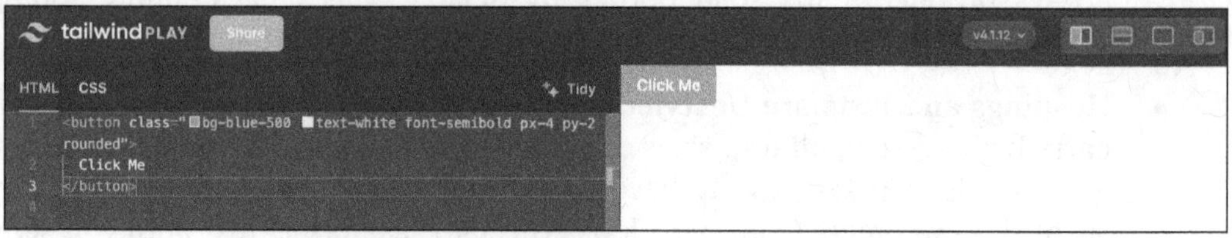

Figure 3.1: *Example of an HTML Button Element Styled with Multiple Tailwind Utility Classes*

Flexbox Utilities for Layout

Modern web layouts often rely on **Flexbox** for arranging elements, and Tailwind provides comprehensive utilities for Flexbox. To start using flexbox, add the class **`flex`** to a container element, which applies **`display: flex`**. By default, this makes child elements lay out in a row (horizontal axis). Tailwind includes utilities to control flex **direction**: use **`flex-row`** (the default) or **`flex-col`** to arrange children horizontally or vertically, respectively (and **`flex-row-reverse`** or **`flex-col-reverse`** for reversed order). For example:

```
<div class="flex flex-col md:flex-row">
  <div class="p-4">Column 1</div>
  <div class="p-4">Column 2</div>
</div>
```

In the above code, we create a flex container that stacks its items in a column on small screens (**`flex-col`**), but switches to a row on medium screens (**`md:flex-row`**). The child **`<div>`** elements are now flexible items that can be aligned and spaced using additional flexbox utilities.

Tailwind offers classes for **flex wrapping** as well. By default, a flex container will try to fit all items on one line. You can use **`flex-wrap`** to allow items to wrap onto multiple lines, or **`flex-nowrap`** to prevent wrapping. If you want items to only wrap in reverse order, there is **`flex-wrap-reverse`**. These utilities correspond to the CSS **`flex-wrap`** property.

Alignment in flexbox is controlled with Tailwind's **`justify-**`** and **`items-**`** classes, which map to **justify-content** (alignment along the main axis) and **align-items** (alignment along the cross axis), respectively. For example, **`justify-between`** distributes items with space between them, **`justify-center`** centers them horizontally, and **`items-center`** centers them vertically within the container's cross-axis. If we extend the previous example:

```
<div class="flex flex-col md:flex-row items-center justify-between">
```

```
  <div class="p-4">Left Item</div>
  <div class="p-4">Right Item</div>
</div>
```

Here, in the flex container, **`items-center`** ensures both items are vertically centered (useful when in a row), and **`justify-between`** ensures there is space between the left and right item, pushing them to the container edges. Tailwind also provides **`gap-x-*`** and **`gap-y-*`** (or the shorthand **`gap-*`**) utilities to easily put consistent space between flex items without needing extra margins. For instance, adding **`gap-4`** to a flex container inserts a 1rem gap between all children.

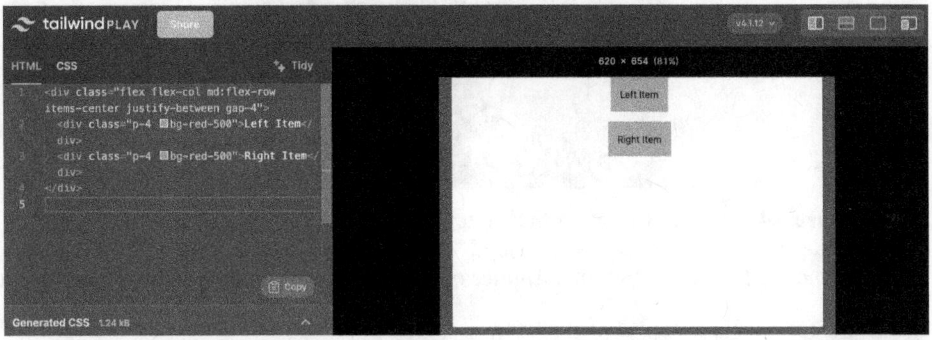

Figure 3.2: *Screenshot of a Mobile Screen of a Flex Container with Two Items Aligned with Justify-between and Items-Center. Notice the md Breakpoint is not A ctivated Due to the Screen Size (Notice That the Mobile Icon on the Top Right is Activated)*

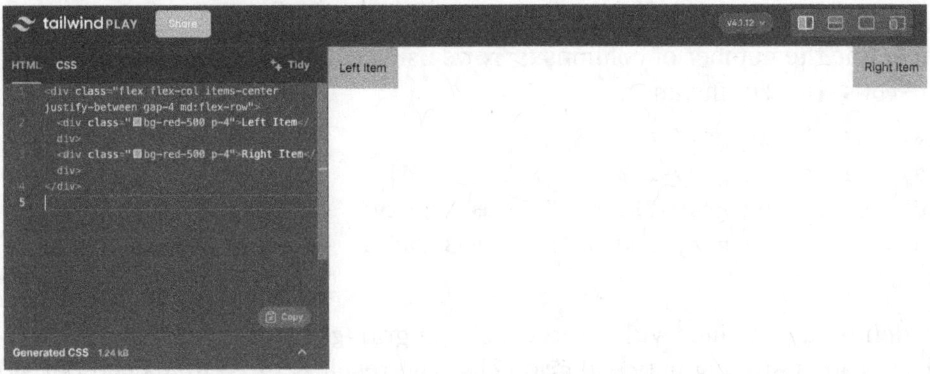

Figure 3.3: *Notice That This Time the Breakpoint has been Activated (the Screen's Width is Larger Than 48rem), and That the Flex-row Style has been Applied*

Flexbox utilities make it straightforward to create responsive, mobile-first layouts. Since Tailwind's flex classes are just CSS under the hood, AI assistants can infer their usage if you prompt them. For example, asking ChatGPT to "center content with flexbox using Tailwind" would likely yield a combination of **`flex`**, **`items-center`**, and **`justify-center`** classes. As always, you should verify AI suggestions, but Tailwind's flex utilities are highly intuitive.

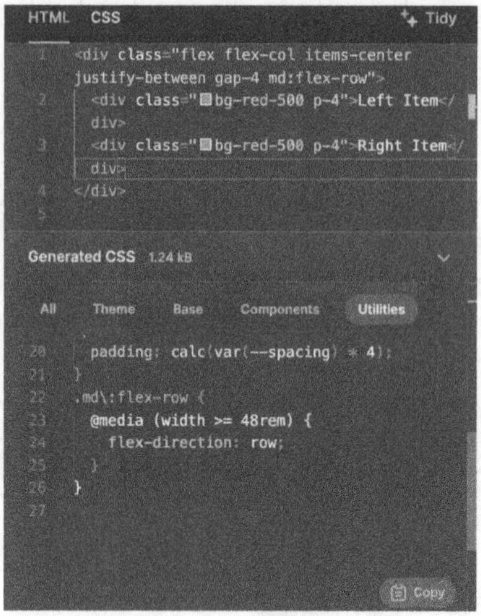

Figure 3.4: *You Can Check on the Generated CSS Section from Tailwind Play, under Utilities, That under the Hood, Tailwind has Created a Flex-row CSS Class for the md Breakpoint, Which Applies over Screens of Width is Larger Than 48rem*[2]

Grid Layout Utilities for Layout

In addition to flexbox, Tailwind supports CSS **Grid** layout with utility classes. Grid is useful for two-dimensional layouts. For example, arranging items in rows and columns. To use a grid, add the class **`grid`** to a container, which applies **`display: grid`**. You can then define the number of columns or rows using classes such as **`grid-cols-{n} or grid-rows-{n}`**. For instance:

```
<div class="grid grid-cols-3 gap-4">
  <div class="bg-gray-200 p-2">Item 1</div>
  <div class="bg-gray-200 p-2">Item 2</div>
  <div class="bg-gray-200 p-2">Item 3</div>
</div>
```

This defines a container with a three-column grid (**`grid-cols-3`**), and uses **`gap-4`** to add consistent spacing between grid cells. The result is three items laid out side by side with a 1rem gap. On smaller screens, you might want fewer columns; you can use responsive prefixes (covered below), such as **`sm:grid-cols-2`** or **`md:grid-cols-3,`** to change the number of columns at different breakpoints.

---

[2] *The rem unit stands for "root em" and is a relative unit in CSS. One rem equals the font size defined on the root element (**`<html>`**). By default, most browsers set this to 16 pixels, so 1rem = 16px, 2rem = 32px, and so on. Using rem for spacing, sizing, and breakpoints ensures consistent scaling across devices, since it adapts if the root font size is changed (for accessibility or user preferences). Tailwind's spacing scale, padding, and breakpoints often map to rem values, making designs more predictable on mobile and desktop screens.*

Tailwind's grid utilities also allow controlling the **row arrangement** and **flow**. By default, grid items fill each row before wrapping to the next (flowing in row direction). You can change this with **`grid-flow-row`** (the default), **`grid-flow-col`** (to fill columns first), or **`grid-flow-row-dense`** and **`grid-flow-col-dense`** to use the dense packing algorithm (which backfills gaps). Additionally, you can set specific column or row spans on child elements using classes such as **`col-span-2`** or **`row-span-3`** to make an item span multiple grid tracks.

For example, consider a photo gallery where one item is larger:

```
<div class="grid grid-cols-4 gap-2">
  <img class="col-span-2 row-span-2" src="feature.jpg" alt="Featured">
  <img src="pic1.jpg" alt="1">
  <img src="pic2.jpg" alt="2">
  <img src="pic3.jpg" alt="3">
  <!-- ... -->
</div>
```

Here, the first image spans 2 columns and 2 rows, occupying a larger area in the grid, while the others fill one cell each. The **`gap-2`** provides a small gap between all images.

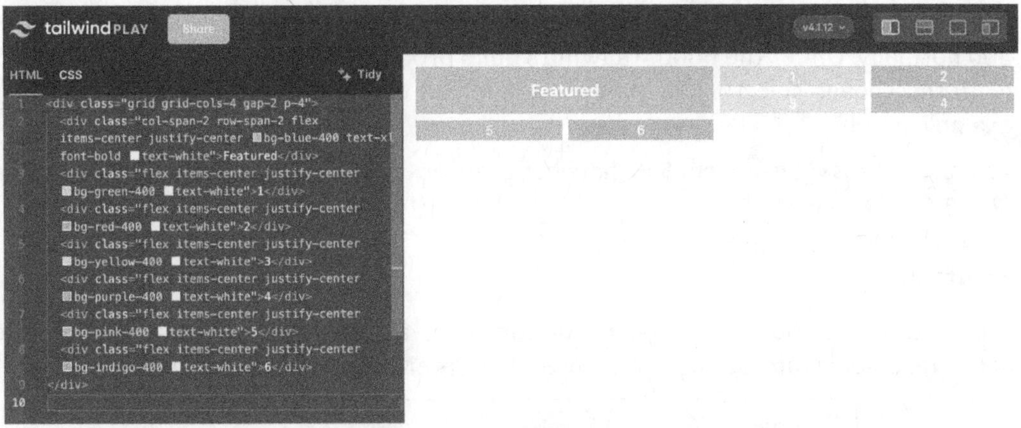

Figure 3.5: *Example of a Grid Layout with Items of Different Sizes and a Gap-2*

Using grid in Tailwind is powerful for complex layouts. AI assistants are generally aware of Tailwind's grid classes if prompted clearly. For instance, if you ask for "a three-column gallery layout with Tailwind grid," the AI might produce a structure with **`grid grid-cols-3 gap-*`** and possibly use **`object-cover`** on images. Always double-check the output: Ensure the number of columns and gaps match your intent. If the AI suggests a deprecated or incorrect grid approach, cross-check with the Tailwind documentation. (In our card example later, we primarily use flexbox, but one could achieve a similar layout with grid – and indeed, if one AI solution uses flex, a follow-up might try CSS grid with Tailwind's grid utilities to give you alternative options.)

Pseudo-Class Variants for Hover, Focus, and More

Interactive states such as hovering, focusing, or clicking are handled in Tailwind by **variant prefixes** for pseudo-classes. Every utility class in Tailwind can be applied conditionally by prepending a state to the class name. Common variants include **`hover:`**, **`focus:`**, **`active:`**, **`disabled:`**, and **`visited:`**. For example, **`hover:bg-blue-700`** will apply a different background color when the user hovers over an element, and **`focus:outline-none`** removes the outline when an element is focused. Tailwind's consistency in variant naming makes it easy to pick up: If you know the CSS pseudo-class, you can guess the Tailwind variant. The syntax is simply **`state:utility`**.

Using these variants is straightforward. If we extend our button example with a hover state:

```
<button class="bg-blue-500 hover:bg-blue-700 text-white font-semibold
px-4 py-2 rounded">
  Hover Me
</button>
```

Now, the button's background will darken to blue-700 on hover, while remaining blue-500 normally. Under the hood, Tailwind's build process generates the appropriate CSS (with the `:hover` selector) for that class. You can chain multiple variants as well, for example:

```
<button class="bg-green-500 hover:bg-green-600 active:bg-green-700 text-
white ...">
  Click Me
</button>
```

This button uses `hover:bg-green-600` for hover and `active:bg-green-700` for the active (pressed) state, giving a slightly darker green on press than on hover.

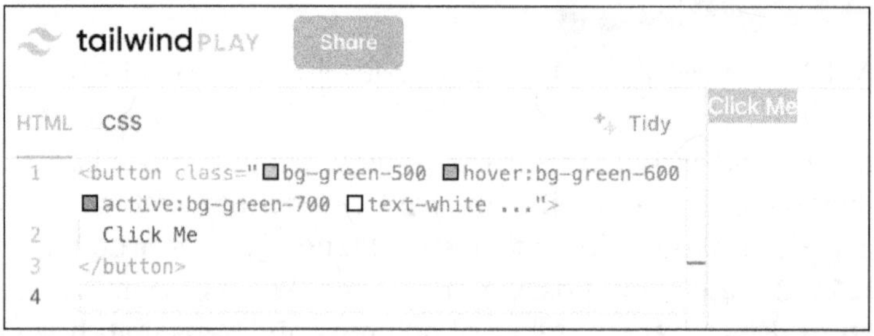

Figure 3.6: *Example of a Button Using Its Base Background Class*

As the user moves their mouse over the element, the **`hover:bg-green-600`** utility class takes effect, instantly providing visual feedback by darkening the button's background.

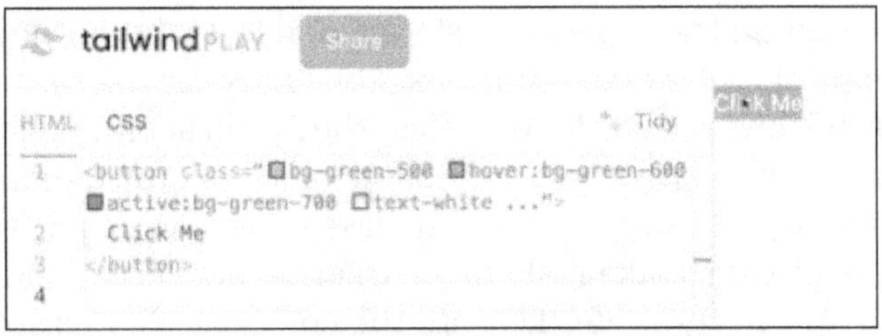

***Figure 3.7**: The Button Now is Hovered by the Cursor, and has Its Background Color Changed*

Furthermore, at the exact moment the user clicks or presses the button, the active: **`bg-green-700`** state is triggered. This darkens the color even further to simulate a physical pressing action.

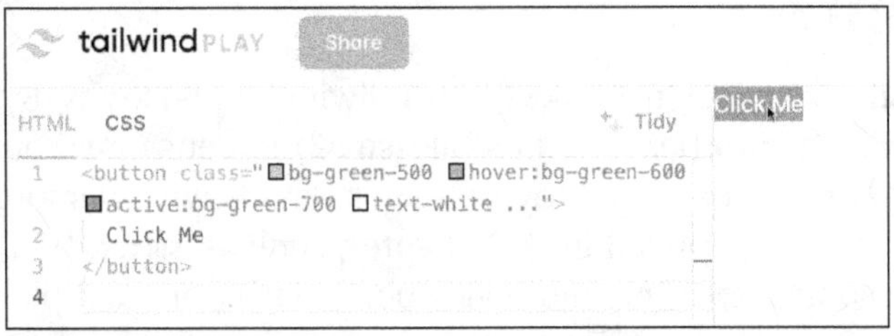

***Figure 3.8**: The Button Now is Now by the Cursor, and has Its Background Color Changed to an Even Darker Shade of Green*

Tailwind supports many pseudo-class variants beyond the basics. A few useful ones are:

- **Focus and Focus-Within: `focus:*`** Applies when an element is focused (for example, an input clicked or a button tabbed to), and **`focus-within:*`** applies when any child element has focus. These help with accessibility (highlighting form groups when a field is active, for instance).
    - **Active: `active:*`** Applies during the moment an element is being pressed/clicked.
    - **Disabled: `disabled:*`** Applies when an element (such as a button) is disabled (**`disabled`** attribute present).
    - **Visited: `visited:*`** For styling visited links.
    - **Group Hover/Focus:** These allow parent-child interactivity. By adding **`class="group"`** to a parent container, you can use **`group-hover:*`** or **`group-focus:*`** on child elements to style them when the parent is hovered or focused. For example, if you want a button label to appear only when a card is hovered, you might give the card **`class="group"`** and the label **`class="opacity-0 group-hover:opacity-100"`** so it fades in on hover of the whole card.

Tailwind's variant system thus covers most common UI states without writing custom CSS. As you prompt AI to generate code, you can explicitly ask for these states. If you say "include a hover state" or "add focus styles," the AI will likely include the appropriate **`hover:`** or **`focus:`** classes. If not, you can follow up to ask for them. One benefit of AI is that it can remember dozens of Tailwind class names and their variant forms. You might describe the effect ("make it slightly darker on hover" or "dim the button when disabled") and the AI can translate that into the correct utility classes. Still, verify the output: Ensure the classes exist and are spelled correctly, because older AI training data might include outdated class names. In general, however, Tailwind's pseudo-class variants are simple and predictable to use.

Responsive Design and Mobile-First Breakpoints

Responsive, mobile-first design is baked into Tailwind's philosophy. By default, the styles you apply with Tailwind utilities target mobile (small) screens first. You can then override or add styles for larger breakpoints by prefixing classes with responsive abbreviations that we briefly saw being applied in this chapter, such as **`sm:`**, **`md:`**, **`lg:`**, **`xl:`**, and **`2xl:`**. Each prefix corresponds to a minimum viewport width (for example, **`sm`** is 640px, **`md`** is 768px, **`lg`** is 1024px, and so on, unless customized in your Tailwind config).

The idea is simple: You write your base styles (which apply to all screens, especially small devices) as unprefixed classes, then add prefixed classes to adjust the design on larger screens. This ensures a **mobile-first** approach – the default looks good on mobile, and you enhance it as the screen size increases.

For example, consider the following code:

```
<div class="p-4 sm:p-6 lg:p-8">
  <p class="text-base sm:text-lg lg:text-xl lg:text-red-800">Responsive
text</p>
</div>
```

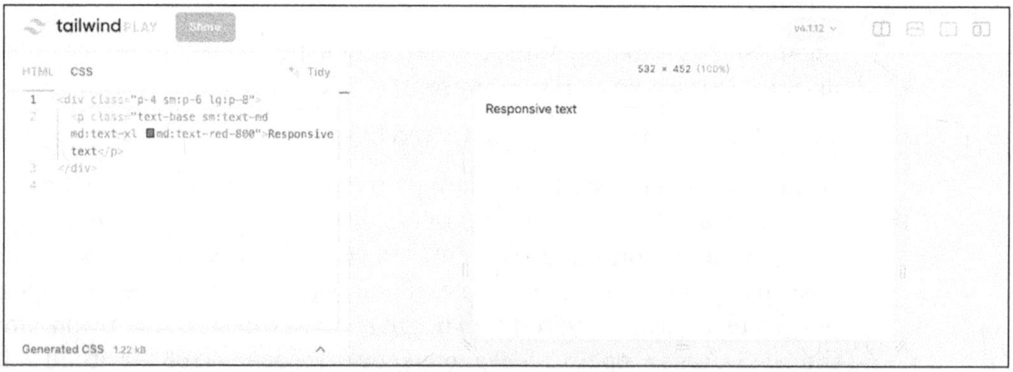

Figure 3.9: *The Text Size for a Small Mobile Screen is Text-md*

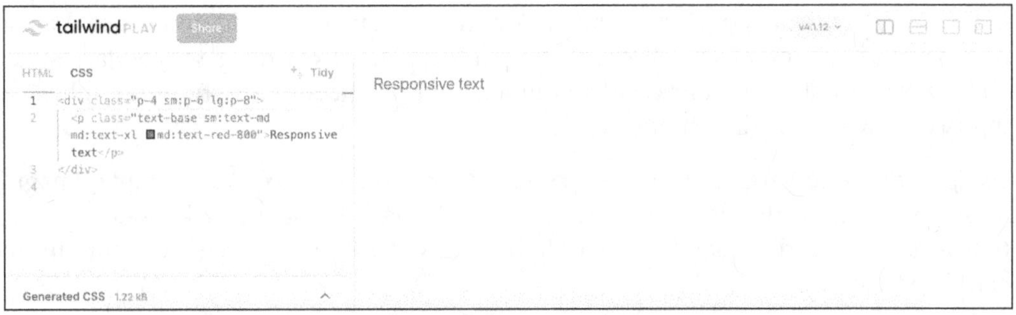

Figure 3.10: *And the Text for Anything Larger Than a md-Sized Screen is Red-800 and of the Text-xl Size*

In this snippet, the container **<div>** has **`p-4`** (1rem padding) applied on mobile and all screens by default, but on small screens and up (`sm:`), it uses **`p-6`** (1.5rem), and on large screens and up (**`lg:`**), it uses **`p-8`** (2rem). Similarly, the paragraph text is **`text-base`** normally, but becomes larger (**`text-lg`**) on small screens, and even larger (**`text-xl`**) on large screens. Tailwind interprets **`sm:p-6`** as "apply **`p-6`** when the screen is at least the small breakpoint width (640px) or larger." The original unprefixed padding (**`p-4`**) still applies on smaller screens by default, because **mobile-first means styles cascade up.**

The official Tailwind documentation summarizes this pattern as: *"just throw a screen size prefix in front of any utility class to apply it at that breakpoint"*. **This approach ensures your UI is usable on small devices first, and then progressively enhanced for larger viewports.** It aligns with modern CSS best practices (using min-width media queries for responsive design).

Even AI code assistants understand this convention. If you ask ChatGPT or Gemini to "make an image full-width on mobile but a fixed width on desktop using Tailwind," it might produce an answer with classes such as **`class="w-full md:w-1/2"`** – meaning 100% width by default (mobile), and 50% width at the `md` breakpoint and above. This shows that the model has knowledge of Tailwind's responsive class syntax and mobile-first approach. When using AI, remember to specify breakpoints in your prompt if you have a responsive behavior in mind (for example, "two-column on large screens, one-column on mobile") to get the appropriate **`sm:`**, **`md:`**, **`lg:`** classes in the output.

Dark Mode Support (Class-Based Strategy)

Many websites support a dark mode theme, and Tailwind provides built-in support for styling in dark mode. By default, Tailwind's **`dark:`** Variant allows you to define styles that apply when the user or system prefers a dark color scheme. There are two main strategies: The **media-based** strategy (using the OS preference) and the **class-based** strategy (explicitly toggling dark mode via a class). We will focus on the class-based approach, as it offers more control in a UI.

In the class-based strategy, you manually control dark mode by adding a **`class="dark"`** on a parent element (often the **`<html>`** tag or a top-level **`<div>`**) to toggle dark styles. Tailwind's variant prefix **`dark:`** Works much such as, **`hover:`** or **`sm:`** – it applies the utility only when the dark mode is active.

Using dark mode variants is as easy as using any other prefix. For example, imagine a card component that is white with dark text in light mode; in dark mode, we want to invert it to a dark background with light text. With Tailwind, we could mark up the card like this:

```
<div class="bg-white dark:bg-gray-800 text-gray-900 dark:text-gray-100
p-6 ...">
  <h2 class="text-xl font-bold mb-2 text-gray-900 dark:text-gray-
100">Title</h2>
  <p class="text-gray-700 dark:text-gray-300 mb-4">Card content...</p>
  <button class="bg-blue-500 dark:bg-blue-600 text-white px-4 py-2
rounded">Action</button>
</div>
```

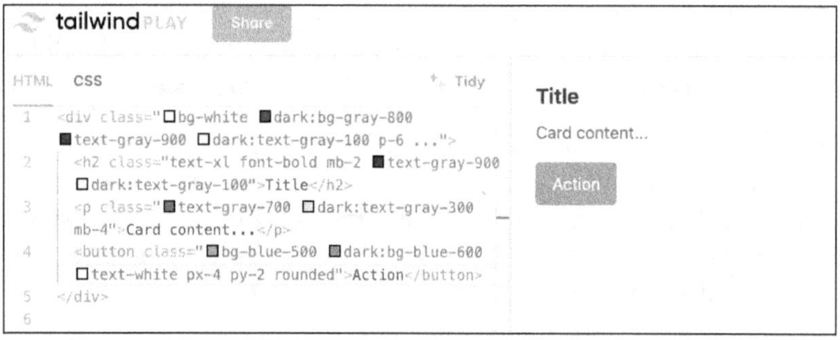

Figure 3.11: *Example of Our Component When the Light Mode is on*

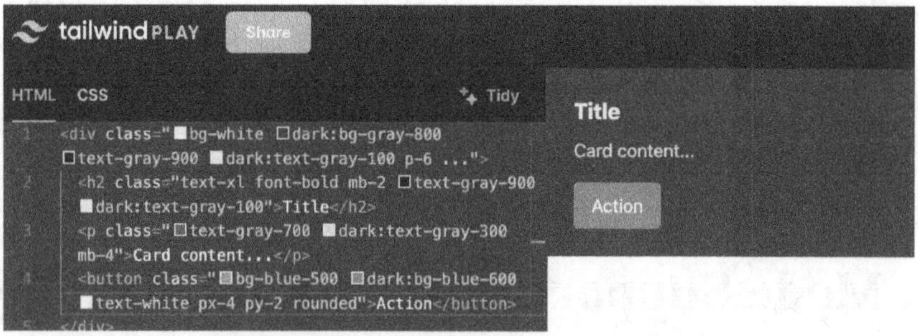

Figure 3.12: *The Component Will Change*
Its Theme Once the Dark Mode is Defined by the Browser/OS

In this snippet, each color-related class has a **`dark:*`** counterpart for the dark theme. The container's background goes from white to gray-800 in dark mode; the text color on the title goes from gray-900 to gray-100; the paragraph text from gray-700 to gray-300; and even the button background changes from blue-500 to a slightly darker blue-600 when dark mode is on. If we also wanted the button to have a different hover color in dark mode, we could add **`dark:hover:bg-blue-700`** (meaning: On dark mode *and* hover).

Under the hood, if your Tailwind configuration is set up with **`darkMode: 'class'`**, adding the **`dark`** class to the root will activate all these **`dark:`** Styles. This approach lets you easily create a themed design without writing separate CSS files – you just pepper **`dark:`** Variants alongside normal classes in your HTML. The result is a component that automatically restyles for dark mode without any additional CSS logic, once the **`dark`** class is present on a parent.

Tailwind's documentation provides examples of this pattern of adding **`dark:`** Utilities alongside normal ones. Simply remember to enable class-based dark mode in your **tailwind.config.js** by setting **`darkMode: 'class'`**. Then, toggling dark mode in your application (for instance, via a button that adds/removes the **`dark`** class on the **`<html>`** element) will switch the theme.

Tip: *AI assistants are aware of Tailwind's dark mode variants. If you prompt "give me a dark mode toggle component in Tailwind," the AI might produce an HTML snippet with both light and dark classes included on elements, as we saw above. Always ensure the classes the AI provides match your design intent. If something does not appear to work (say, your dark classes have no effect), check that the **dark** class is indeed being applied to a parent element and that your config enables class-based dark mode.*

Z-Index and Layering (Stacking Contexts)

Web UIs often have overlapping elements – think of modals, dropdown menus, or tooltips that layer on top of other content. The **z-index** property controls the stack order of elements along the z-axis (vertical stacking order), and Tailwind provides utility classes for managing z-index values. By default, Tailwind includes a set of predefined numeric z-index classes (for example, **`z-0, z-10, z-20, ... z-50`**) as well as **`z-auto`** (which uses the CSS **`auto`** value). Higher numbers stack above lower numbers, as seen in *Figure* 3.13, where the z-index 3 stacks over the lower ones.

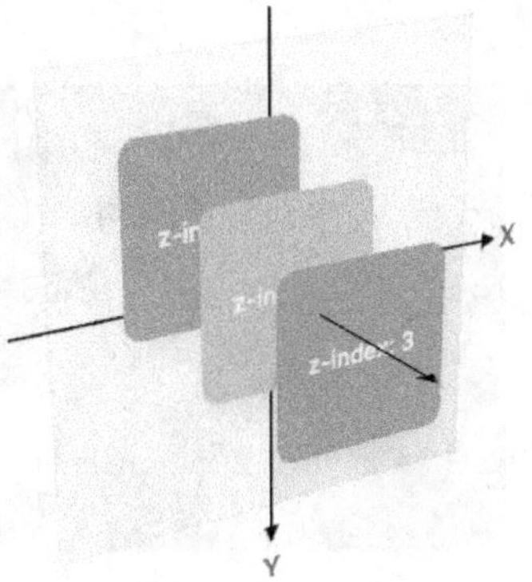

Figure 3.13: *A 3D representation of the browser's coordinate system, illustrating how the z-axis (z-index) controls the stacking order of elements*

For example, an element with **`z-10`** will appear above an element with **`z-0`** (assuming they overlap in the same stacking context). If you need an element to overlay everything, you might use a higher value, such as **`z-50`** (common for modals or overlays). Tailwind's default scale covers common needs, but you can configure additional values in your theme if necessary. You can also use arbitrary values: for instance, **`z-[99]`** would set **`z-index: 99`** if you needed a specific number.

However, **z-index only works as expected if the element is in a positioning context that allows stacking**. Typically, an element needs a position other than static (for example, relative, absolute, fixed, or sticky) to establish a stacking context or to be positioned above others. Tailwind has utilities such as **`relative`**, **`absolute`**, **`fixed`**, and **`sticky`** to set an element's position. For instance, a dropdown menu might be absolutely positioned within a relative parent, with a **`z-20`** to ensure it appears above the parent; meanwhile, a modal dialog might be fixed positioned to cover the viewport with a **`z-50`** so it overlays all content.

It is also important to understand **stacking contexts**: Certain conditions (such as a positioned element or an element with certain CSS properties, such as **`opacity`** less than 1) create a new stacking context for their descendants. This means an element with a lower z-index can appear above another element with a higher z-index if they belong to different stacking contexts. In practice, if you run into a case where **`z-index`** is not behaving, you may need to adjust the HTML structure or the positioning strategy.

As an example, consider a modal overlay and dialog:

```
<div class="relative">
  <!-- Page content here -->
  <div class="fixed inset-0 bg-black bg-opacity-50 z-40"></div>
  <div class="fixed inset-0 flex items-center justify-center z-50">
    <div class="bg-white p-6 rounded shadow-lg">Modal content</div>
  </div>
</div>
```

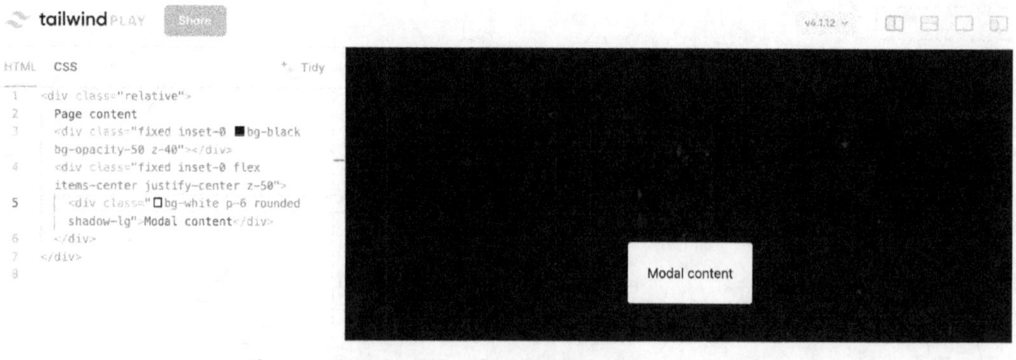

Figure 3.14: *Example of a Modal Using the z-Index*

In this code, we have a full-screen semi-transparent overlay (**bg-opacity-50** makes the black background 50% opaque) with **z-40**, and the modal content container above it with **z-50**. Both are **fixed** and cover the viewport (**inset-0** is a shorthand for top/right/bottom/left 0). The result is the modal content stacking above the overlay, which stacks above the page content. The outer **<div class="relative">** here is not strictly necessary for stacking, but if the overlay and modal were intended to be within a certain section, using **relative** on the parent and **absolute** on children could scope the stacking context.

Tailwind makes these layering and positioning tasks easier by providing the classes, but you still need to design the structure. AI can assist by recalling the proper classes (**z-50, fixed**, **inset-0**, etc.) if you ask for an overlay or a popup. If you prompt something such as "create a modal with Tailwind CSS," the AI should include an overlay with a certain z-index and a content box with a higher z-index. Nonetheless, always test and adjust stacking context issues manually: AI might not perfectly account for the context every time. A good practice is to keep high-level elements, such as modals, at the end of your HTML and use high z-index values on them to avoid conflicts. You can also modify the default z-index scale in your Tailwind configuration if your design system requires specific stacking order values, but the defaults (0 through 50) suffice for most cases.

Typography Utilities and Font Styles

Styling text is a big part of UI design. Tailwind includes a range of typography-related utilities to control font family, size, weight, line-height, letter spacing, and so on. For example, classes such as font-sans, font-serif, and font-mono will set common sans-serif, serif, or monospace font stacks for an element. You also have numeric font weights (**font-light**, **font-bold**, and so on), italic (**italic**), and alignment classes (**text-left**, **text-right**, and so on).

For font sizing, Tailwind provides a typographic scale out of the box (typically a set of sizes from **text-xs** up to **text-9xl** or so). Each size maps to a specific font-size and line-height combination optimized for readability. For example, **text-base** is ~1rem (16px), **text-lg** maybe 1.125rem, **text-xl** 1.25rem, etc. There are also relative sizing utilities such as **text-sm** and **text-2xl**, and so on. The key is that Tailwind's sizes are named by purpose (**sm, base**, **lg**, **xl**) rather than exact pixel values, making it easy to adjust in design without remembering numbers.

One important thing Tailwind does (via Preflight) is remove all default browser styling on headings and other text elements. That means **<h1>** is not automatically huge or bold; it starts like normal text until you apply classes. This might initially confuse developers ("why is my **<h1>** so small?"), but it ensures you have full control. You will not accidentally use an **<h2>** somewhere and get an unintended style – you explicitly choose the text size and weight with classes such as **text-2xl** font-bold for a heading, for example. This approach avoids inconsistent heading sizes that are not in your design system.

For multi-paragraph content (such as blog posts or articles), manually adding classes to every element can be tedious. Tailwind offers an official plugin called Typography (the **"`@tailwindcss/typography`"** plugin) that generates a special set of prose classes. By adding **`class="prose"`** to a container (such as an **`<article>`**)[3], you automatically get beautifully formatted text styles for all the content inside (headings, lists, paragraphs, blockquotes, and so on.) This plugin is essentially a pre-designed set of typography defaults (it is how this very Tailwind documentation styles its blog posts.) We will not dive deeply into plugins yet, but keep in mind that Tailwind can handle complex text formatting needs either via its core utilities or extensions such as this plugin.

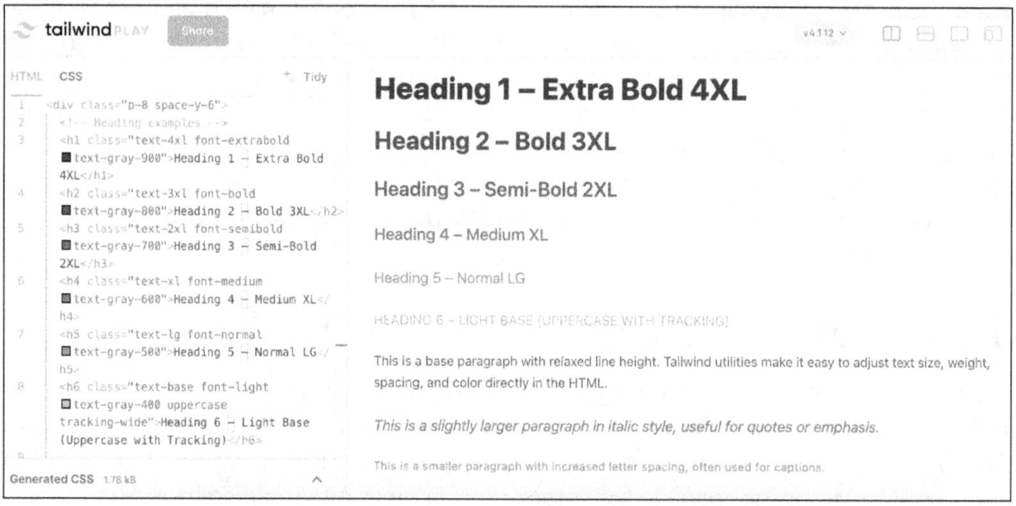

Figure 3.15: *Example of Text Styled with Tailwind Typography Utilities, Including Headings and Paragraphs*

Tip: *Always define your font families and include the fonts you need (for example, via a Google Fonts import or self-hosted fonts). Tailwind's default theme includes generic stacks (font-sans is a stack of system UI sans-serif fonts), but you can customize these in the theme configuration if you have specific brand fonts. Use the* `@import` *at the very top of your CSS for external fonts, then configure Tailwind's theme or use utilities such as* `font-[CustomFont]` *to apply them.*

[3] *The* **`<article>`** *element is an HTML5 semantic tag used to represent a self-contained, independent piece of content that could be distributed or reused on its own. Examples include a blog post, a news story, a forum entry, or a product description. Using* **`<article>`** *helps both accessibility tools and search engines understand the structure and meaning of the page, as it indicates that the enclosed content is a standalone unit of information.*

Color Palette and Usage in Tailwind

One of Tailwind's most lauded features is its **extensive default color palette**. Tailwind CSS includes a vast set of colors out-of-the-box – all carefully chosen and calibrated.

The palette is organized by color name (such as red, green, blue, and so on) and a **numeric scale** from 50 up to 900 (and in newer versions, 950 for some extra-dark shades). In general, 50 *is the lightest tint and* 900 *the darkest shade* for a given color. For example, "blue-50" is an extremely light baby-blue, while "blue-900" is a very dark navy. This numeric scale makes it easy to pick lighter or darker variants systematically – a higher number is a deeper/richer color.

Tailwind's color classes follow a consistent naming: **`{property}-{colorName}-{shade}`**. For instance, **`text-blue-500`** sets the text color to medium blue, **`bg-green-100`** gives a very light green background, and **`border-pink-700`** would be a border in a dark pink hue. The **entire palette** is available across all color-related utilities (text, background, border, outlines, and so on). This means if "indigo" or "emerald" or "rose" are in the palette, you can use them for any element's text or background just by changing the prefix.

For example, here are a few class usages:

- **`text-gray-700`** – medium gray text (good for body text on light backgrounds).
- **`bg-yellow-200`** – a pale yellow background (maybe for a highlight or warning box).
- **`border-teal-500`** – a teal border line.
- **`outline-red-500`** – if using focus outlines, makes the outline red.
- **`shadow-blue-500`** – if you have a colored box shadow, this sets its color (Tailwind's ring and shadow utilities support coloring too).

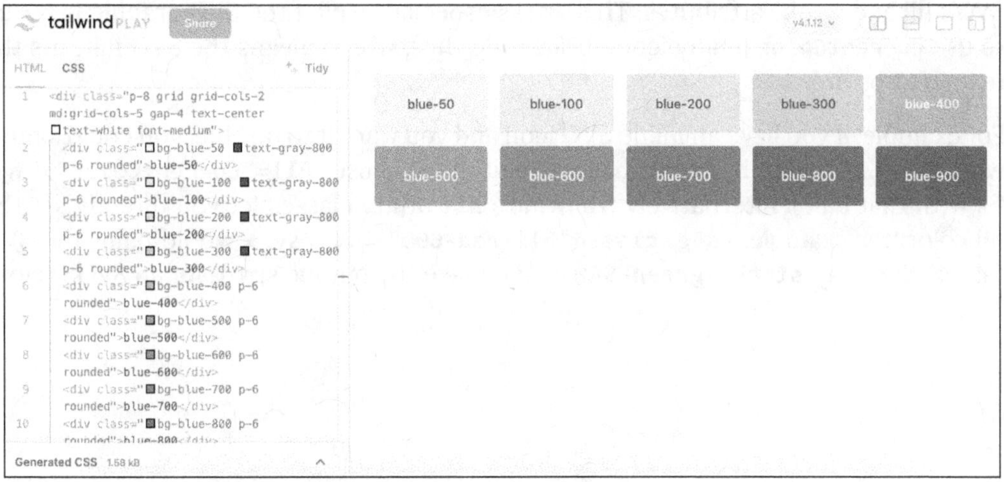

Figure 3.16: *Tailwind's Color Palette Sample – Showing a Range of Blue Color from 50 to 900*

Tailwind's default palette covers common needs, but you can **customize or extend it** via the theme configuration (more on that soon). This is useful if you have specific brand colors. By extending the theme's colors, you can generate new utility classes (for example, adding a `brandPurple` color gives you `bg-brandPurple`, `text-brandPurple`, and so on, automatically).

One really neat feature is the ability to adjust color opacity on the fly. You can append an **opacity modifier** to any color class using a slash syntax. For example, `bg-black/50` makes a 50% opaque black background (essentially `background-color: rgba(0,0,0,0.5)`), and `text-blue-500/80` would make slightly transparent blue text. Tailwind allows both percentage (0–100) and arbitrary opacity values using this `/<amount>` notation. This saves you from needing separate utility classes for every opacity variant – you just tack `/<number>` onto the color class.

Finally, note that Tailwind's palette and naming were chosen with accessibility in mind. The default shades (500-600 range for colors on contrasting backgrounds) often meet contrast guidelines for text, and so on. However, always test your specific combinations. For instance, `text-gray-500` on `bg-white` might be too low contrast for body text, whereas `text-gray-800` is much better. Tailwind's docs encourage using the numeric scale to find the right contrast (darker for text if on light backgrounds, lighter for text if on dark backgrounds).

Working with SVGs and Icons

SVG images and iconography are common in UIs (for icons, logos, and so on), and Tailwind provides utilities to style SVG elements as well. Notably, Tailwind treats SVGs like any other element when it comes to layout (you can `w-6 h-6` an inline SVG for sizing, for example). For colors, there are `fill-*` and `stroke-*` classes that apply to an SVG's fill and stroke attributes. This works especially well if the SVG graphic is set up to use `currentColor` (many icon libraries do this), which means the SVG inherits the text color by default.

For example, if you have an inline SVG icon and you want it to be blue, you could simply wrap it in a span that has `text-blue-500` (if the SVG uses `fill="currentColor"` it will fill with that blue). Alternatively, Tailwind's `fill` utility classes let you directly set the fill color: for example, `<svg class="fill-red-600">...</svg>` would paint the SVG fill red. Similarly, `stroke-green-500` would make the outline stroke of an SVG green.

Figure 3.17: *Example of SVG Icon with Different Tailwind Color Classes Applied to Its Fill and Stroke*

Since icons are often SVG, you might also use sizing utilities (**`w-4 h-4,`** and so on) to control their size, and perhaps **`inline-block align-middle`** to line up with text. Tailwind does not include an official icon set, but it pairs well with libraries such as **Heroicons**[4] (by the makers of Tailwind) which provide SVG icons you can easily drop in. Heroicons are designed to use Tailwind classes for styling – for instance, you add **`class="h-5 w-5 text-gray-600"`** on the SVG to get a 1.25rem icon in gray.

In summary, **Tailwind makes using SVGs straightforward** because you can treat icon SVGs almost such as text, controlling color and size with classes. The **`fill-current`** class (which Tailwind includes) sets the fill to the element's current text color (**`currentColor`** in CSS) – this is often used by default on SVG icons so that simply setting **`text-*`** on the parent container will color the icon. If you see your icons not inheriting color, ensure they have **`fill="currentColor"`** or use Tailwind's **`fill-*`** utilities.

Theme Configuration and Extending Tailwind

Tailwind's default design system (colors, spacing scale, fonts, breakpoints, and so on) is **highly customizable.** Every project can define its own theme in the **`tailwind.config.js`** file to override or extend the defaults. This is powerful for aligning Tailwind to your brand or design requirements.

For instance, if your brand has a custom purple color or you need an extra breakpoint, you can add those. The theme config lives in **`module.exports = { theme: { ... } }`** in the config file, with sub-keys for things such as **`colors`**, **`spacing`**, **`screens`** (breakpoints), and so on.

[4] https://github.com/tailwindlabs/heroicons

If you **extend** the theme, Tailwind will keep its defaults and just add yours on top. For example, to add a new color and a new breakpoint:

```
// tailwind.config.js
module.exports = {
  theme: {
    extend: {
      colors: {
        brandPurple: ‹#7e5bef›,
      },
      screens: {
        ‹xs›: ‹480px›, // extra-small breakpoint at 480px
      },
    },
  },
}
```

By doing this, you would get a utility class **`bg-brandPurple`** (and corresponding **`text-brandPurple`**, **`border-brandPurple`**, and so on) for your custom purple. And you would have a new **`xs:`** prefix to target min-width 480px. Extending is typically safer than overriding, because you do not lose the defaults you might still want to use.

On the other hand, you can also override values. If you set **`colors: { ... }`** without **`extend`**, you are replacing the entire palette with your specified ones. You might do that if you want to strip out all the default colors and only use a limited set, for example.

Why bother with the theme config? The benefit is **centralizing design tokens**. All developers (and AI code assistants) then use the same vocabulary of classes that map to your design system. As one blog noted, by encoding a custom design system into Tailwind's config, you ensure a unified style guide – "this consistency and predictability make it easier for tools such as Copilot or ChatGPT to suggest accurate code, since the AI can rely on a well-defined vocabulary of classes". In other words, if your project consistently uses classes such as **`text-brandPurple`** (because you added that color), an AI might pick up on it in context and use it correctly when suggesting the code.

Beyond simple theme tweaks, you can enable official **plugins** or write custom ones (which we will explore in much greater depth in *Chapters 4 and* 5). Tailwind has first-party plugins for things such as **forms** (to better style form controls), **typography** (we mentioned), **aspect-ratio** (for fixed aspect ratio boxes), and so on. Including a plugin (usually via **`npm install`** and adding it to the **`plugins: []`** array in your config) will add new utilities or components. For example, the forms plugin resets form element styles for better consistency, and the aspect-ratio plugin provides utilities such as **`aspect-w-16 aspect-h-9`** to make an element maintain a 16:9 aspect ratio.

You can even create your **own plugin** to introduce custom utilities or variants. This is more advanced, but Tailwind provides an API for it. A simpler route for tiny additions is to use the low-level **@apply** directive or custom CSS in the **@layer utilities** (discussed further) to define a utility class.

For example, say you often need a fancy text shadow that Tailwind does not include by default. You could add your own CSS:

```
@layer utilities {
  .text-glow {
    @apply text-white;
    text-shadow: 0 0 4px rgba(255,255,255,0.8);
  }
}
```

This snippet uses **@layer utilities** to inject a new utility class **.text-glow** which combines an existing utility (**text-white**) and a custom CSS rule (the glow shadow). Now, you can use **<h1 class="text-glow">Glowing Text</h1>** in your HTML. Tailwind will include it in the build, and you did not have to globally write a lot of CSS – just a little augmentation within Tailwind's system.

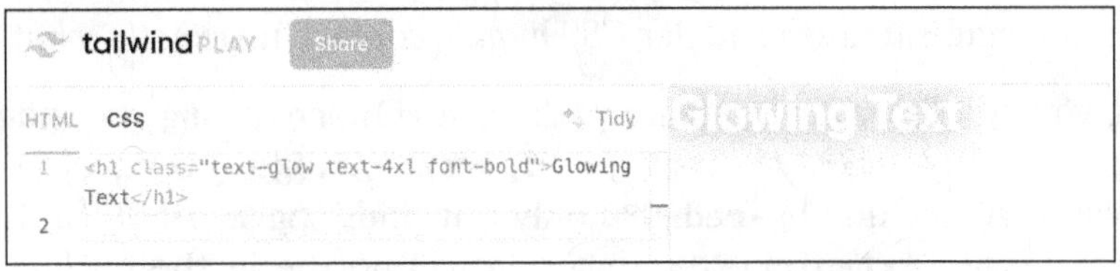

Figure 3.18: *Example of Custom Utility Class (Text-Glow)*

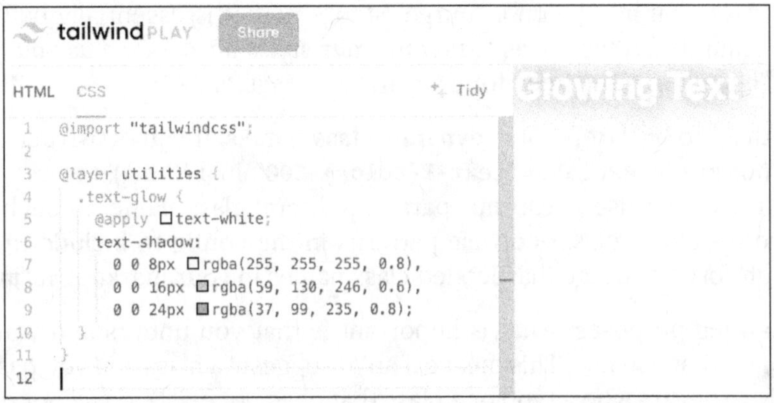

Figure 3.19: *The `.Text-Glow` Class is Defined within the `@Layer Utilities`*

The key takeaway is that Tailwind can grow with your needs. Out of the box, it covers a ton, but every design has unique aspects. By knowing how to extend the theme and add utilities, you ensure you will not hit a wall. AI tools might not be aware of your custom classes unless you document them (they will not magically know what **.text-glow** is unless told), but you can still describe to the AI what you want, and it might suggest the underlying CSS, which you then integrate. In later chapters or projects, we might explore writing a simple Tailwind plugin or using more first-party plugins as needed.

Removing Unused CSS (Purging with JIT)

One concern with utility-first frameworks is: If every possible utility class is generated in CSS, will not that file be huge? Tailwind addresses this by **purging unused CSS** – essentially removing styles for classes you never use in your HTML. In older Tailwind versions (v1/v2), you configured PurgeCSS to scan files and strip unused classes. In Tailwind v3+, this is mostly handled automatically by the **Just-in-Time (JIT) compiler**.

Tailwind's JIT mode generates CSS for a class only when it sees that class in your source files. This means during development, as you add classes to your HTML, Tailwind injects the corresponding CSS on the fly.

Note: *And for production, it scans all your content* (HTML, JS, JSX, *templates, and so on, as specified in the* `content` *array in your config) and only includes those classes in the final* CSS. *The result is a much smaller* CSS *bundle containing exactly what you used.*

Practically, you still list your template paths in **`tailwind.config.js`** under **`content: []`** (for example, **`"./src/**/*.html", "./src/**/*.{js,jsx}"`**, etc.). When you build, Tailwind will include **`bg-red-500`** only if it finds "bg-red-500" in those files. If you never use, say, **`text-pink-800`**, that rule will not be in the output. This keeps things lean.

In the old days, you might run a "purge" step – now it is essentially built-in via JIT. Tailwind's team describes JIT as "*generate your styles on-demand as you author your templates,*" eliminating the need for a separate purge step.

The main thing to be careful of is **dynamic class names**. If you construct class names in strings (for example, **`class="text-${color}-500"`** in a JS file), the compiler might not catch those because it can not parse the literal class name. In such cases, you might need to safelist classes or use patterns in the config to include them. But for most straightforward usage (hardcoded class names in your markup), it "just works."

For our learning purposes, what is important is that you understand your final CSS includes only what you use. This means if an AI suggests a class and you paste it in, but it is slightly wrong (maybe a typo or a class that does not exist), it will not do anything, because Tailwind will drop unknown classes or you will not see the effect. Always double-check unfamiliar classes (AI is pretty good thanks to Tailwind's consistency, but for example, it might suggest **`bg-light-blue-500`** if it was trained on an older Tailwind version that had a different color name). Those classes might have changed (in Tailwind 2, **`lightBlue`** was a color; in Tailwind 3, it was removed/renamed to just `sky`). If you use an incorrect class, you will find it does not work and will likely be purged.

Tip: *If you notice that some expected style is not applying in your project, it could be that the class was not recognized (perhaps due to a typo or because it only appears in a string the parser cannot see). In such cases, check your spelling and ensure the class is present in the built CSS. Tailwind's JIT will strip out truly unused or unknown classes, keeping your CSS efficient.*

Tailwind's CSS Directives and Functions (@ apply, `theme()`, and so on)

While most of your Tailwind usage will be writing classes in HTML, there are scenarios where writing a bit of CSS is still useful or necessary. Tailwind provides special **directives** (which you use in CSS files) and helper **functions** to assist in those cases. These include:

`@apply`: Arguably the most used directive. It allows you to *apply* a list of utility classes within a CSS selector. This is great for reducing repetition or when you want to create a semantic class name for reuse. For example, if you have multiple buttons in your HTML with the same combo of classes (**`px-4 py-2 bg-blue-500 text-white rounded font-semibold`**), you might prefer to define a **`.btn-primary`** class in your CSS and use **`@apply`** to give it those styles:

```
.btn-primary {
  @apply px-4 py-2 bg-blue-500 text-white font-semibold rounded;
}
.btn-primary:hover {
  @apply bg-blue-700;
}
```

Then, your HTML can just be **`<button class="btn-primary">...</button>`**. Under the hood, during your build, **`@apply`** will be expanded to the actual CSS rules for those utilities. This gives you the convenience of a single class without abandoning Tailwind's design system. **Keep in mind that using @apply too heavily might indicate you are fighting the framework (Tailwind's philosophy prefers using the utilities directly)**, but it is very handy for a few common patterns or when integrating Tailwind with third-party components that expect certain class names.

`theme()`: This function allows you to access values from your Tailwind config within CSS. For example, **`theme('spacing.12')`** would get the value for your spacing scale at key 12 (by default, spacing 12 = 3rem). You might use this to ensure a custom CSS rule still ties into Tailwind's design tokens. A simple case: if you want to set an element's width to 16rem (which is spacing 64 in the default config), you could write **`width: theme('spacing.64');`**. If you ever update the spacing scale, this will pull the new value.

Note: *In Tailwind v4,* ***theme()*** *is being deemphasized in favor of CSS variables, but it is still widely used in many projects and examples.*

@screen: A directive (historical, in JIT, you can often just use **@media**) that injects a media query for a given breakpoint. For instance, **@screen lg { ... }** would create a media query block for the lg breakpoint. Similarly, the function form **screen('md')** returns the min-width value for **md**.

This is useful if you need to write a custom media query in your CSS but want to use the same breakpoints as Tailwind's system. For example:

```
@media (min-width: ${theme('screens.md')}) {
  .sidebar { position: fixed; }
}
```

This ensures you did not hardcode "768px" in multiple places - it pulls from your config's md value. Usually, you will not need this often (since using md: in classes is simpler), but it is there if needed for more complex CSS.

Other Directives: Tailwind uses **@tailwind base**, **@tailwind components**, and **@ tailwind utilities** in your main CSS to include its layers. There is also **@layer**, which we saw for adding your own CSS to a specific layer (base, components, or utilities). Additionally, as of newer versions, you might encounter **@variants** or **@responsive** in older code, or **@config** to reference the config values. These are beyond our scope to deeply cover, but be aware that they exist. They allow advanced customization of how Tailwind generates classes (for instance, defining custom variant names).

For most learners, understanding **@apply** is the big one - it lets you create your own shortcuts when needed. We used it in the example above for a button class. **A good rule of thumb from the Tailwind community: Try to use utilities in HTML first, and reach for @apply only when you notice repetition or when a semantic class name would really help (such as styling something coming from a CMS where you cannot add lots of classes to the HTML).**

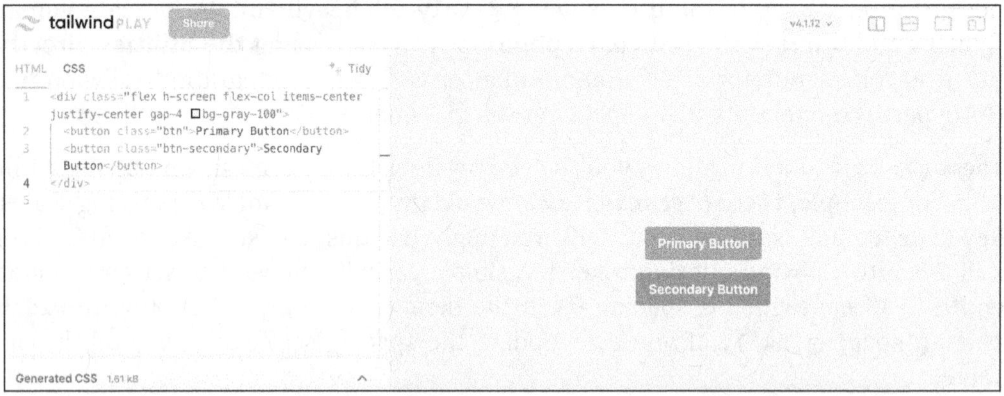

Figure 3.20: *Illustration of Two Buttons Using a .btn Class in the HTML*

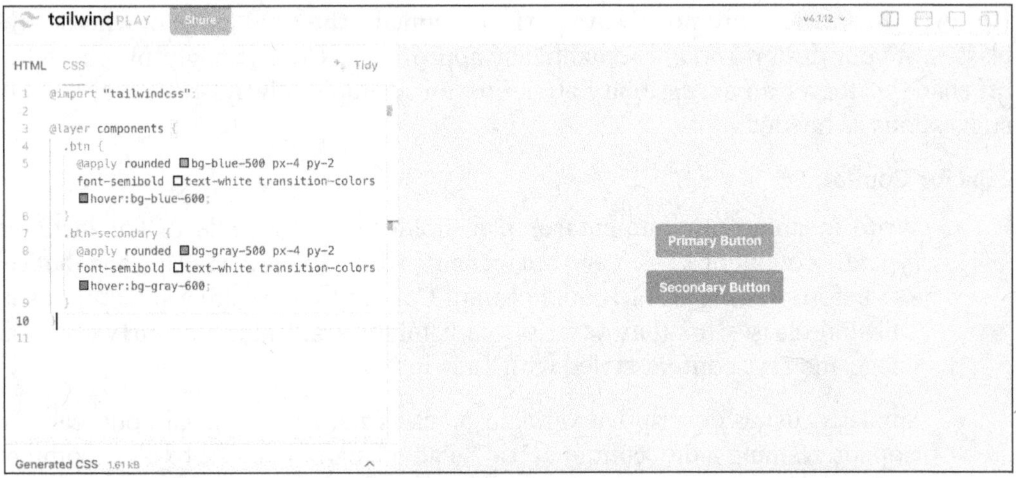

***Figure 3.21**: Illustration of the Usage of @apply in a CSS File to Create a .btn Class*

AI Integration as a Support Layer in Coding

With an understanding of Tailwind basics, let us discuss how AI can help you write and understand code faster. AI integration in development can take many forms – here we focus on using tools such as GitHub Copilot (an AI pair-programmer that suggests code in your IDE) and ChatGPT, Claude, Gemini, or similar models (where you explicitly prompt an AI for code or explanations). These tools are not a replacement for understanding fundamentals (you still need to know what classes such as **flex** or **mt-4** do!), but they can dramatically speed up routine tasks and provide inspiration or fixes when you are stuck.

AI-Powered Code Suggestions (Copilot, and so on)

GitHub Copilot (powered by OpenAI Codex, a derivative of GPT) can suggest Tailwind code as you write. For example, if you start typing an HTML snippet in VS Code such as **<div class="flex justify-...">**, Copilot might intelligently autocomplete it to **<div class=" flex justify-between ...">** based on context and common patterns. It has been trained on tons of code (including Tailwind usage across many projects), so it can make educated guesses.

If you write a comment such as **<!-- a red button -->** and then start typing a **<button** element, Copilot may even suggest a full button element with appropriate Tailwind classes (for example, **class="bg-red-500 text-white px-4 py-2 ...">**) without you explicitly asking. This can save time on boilerplate.

However, suggestions are not always perfect – **you are the final judge** of whether the classes fit your design and are semantically appropriate. Copilot might pick a slightly off shade or forget an accessibility attribute, for example. Always review and adjust suggestions as needed.

Tips for Copilot:

- Write meaningful comments or placeholder text to guide it. For instance, typing a comment **`<!-- Card component with image, title, and button -->`** before writing HTML could prompt Copilot to generate a structure using Tailwind classes for that description. It might scaffold a nice **`<div>`** with an image and text content styled with Tailwind.
- Similarly, using descriptive variable or class names in partial code can cue Copilot. Naming a div "container" or "header" might cause it to fill in common utility classes for those (such as **`max-w-screen-xl mx-auto`** for a container, perhaps).

In essence, Copilot is great for accelerating repetitive or standard chunks of UI code. It shines when there is ample context or prior usage patterns (which Tailwind, with its consistent approach, provides). Simply keep an eye out for subtle issues (wrong semantics, using an outdated class name, and so on) – though in practice, for Tailwind, Copilot's guesses are often on point, because Tailwind's API is so systematic.

AI Code Generation with ChatGPT

While Copilot works inside your editor as you type, **ChatGPT (or similar language models)** can generate larger blocks of code on demand via prompts. Instead of auto-completing your line, you ask for what you need in plain English (or any language) and get an answer. This is more flexible for bigger picture tasks or when you are brainstorming.

For example, you could ask:

"Give me the HTML for a responsive card component using Tailwind CSS. It should have an image at the top, a title, some text, and a button. Make it mobile-friendly."

A well-crafted prompt like that gives the AI a clear goal and context (Tailwind CSS, responsive card). ChatGPT might return a complete code snippet, perhaps something such as:

```
<div class="max-w-sm bg-white rounded-lg shadow-md overflow-hidden">
  <img class="w-full h-48 object-cover" src="image.jpg" alt="Card
image">
  <div class="p-6">
    <h2 class="text-xl font-bold mb-2">Card Title</h2>
    <p class="text-gray-700 text-base mb-4">This is a brief description
```

```
of the card content...</p>
    <button class="bg-blue-500 text-white font-semibold px-4 py-2
rounded hover:bg-blue-600">Learn More</button>
  </div>
</div>
```

This snippet is a plausible AI-generated answer for a basic card component (obviously, the actual output might vary). It includes a container with border-radius and shadow, an image that covers the full width, some text styling, and a button with a hover effect – all using Tailwind classes. That is a pretty good starting point!

The takeaway: ChatGPT can be like a "design partner" that provides boilerplate or frameworks to speed you up.

Effective Prompting: The key with these models is how you ask:

- **Be Specific** about the outcome and context. Mention "using Tailwind CSS" or even the version if you know it, to anchor the AI in the right toolkit.
- **Describe Functionality and Styling**. Instead of "give me a card," say "responsive card with image top, content below, use Tailwind classes."

If the answer is missing something (for example, no hover state or no dark mode variant), you can follow up: "*Include a hover state on the button*," or "*Also show how it would look in dark mode*." The iterative conversation lets you refine the output.

Sometimes, providing a brief hint of code can help, but often it is not needed if your description is clear. ChatGPT has "seen" a lot of Tailwind code, so it usually knows class names – but if you ask for something unusual, be prepared to correct it.

Finally, remember that **ChatGPT's knowledge has a cutoff**. If you are on Tailwind 3 and ask for something that changed from v2, it might occasionally give an outdated class name. Always test and verify the code in your environment.

Prompting AI for Tailwind Snippets – Examples

To illustrate how to communicate with the AI effectively, here are a few example prompts and what they aim to achieve:

1. **Generating a Component:**
    a. **Prompt:** "Create an HTML snippet for a responsive navigation bar using Tailwind CSS. It should collapse into a hamburger menu on small screens."
    b. **What We Expect:** The AI should produce a `<nav>` element with something such as **`class=" flex items-center justify-between"`** for

the nav bar on larger screens, a menu that has **`hidden md:block`** to hide it on mobile, and a hamburger button with **`md:hidden`** to show it only on mobile. Essentially, use Tailwind's responsive utilities to create a collapsible menu. If it forgets the JS for the toggle, we might need to ask for that separately. The important part is how the prompt specifies *responsive* and *Tailwind*, so the AI will likely use breakpoints (**`md:`** classes) rather than writing a media query in pure CSS.

2. **Including State Variants:**

    a. **Prompt:** "Give me a Tailwind-styled button with hover and active states, and a dark mode variant."

    b. **What We Expect:** A `<button>` element styled with base classes (background color, text color, padding, and so on), plus **`hover:`** classes (maybe a slightly darker background on hover), an **`active:`** class (perhaps scale down or even darker on click), and **`dark:`** classes to adjust colors when the parent has dark mode. A correct answer might include something such as: `<button class="bg-green-500 hover:bg-green-600 active:bg-green-700 text-white px-4 py-2 rounded dark:bg-green-700">...</button>` (just as an example). If the first answer omitted the dark mode or active state, we could prompt again: "Include an active state (such as a press effect) and ensure it has a different look in dark mode." The AI can then refine the classes.

3. **Converting the Existing Code:**

    a. **Prompt:** "Here is a simple card in HTML with some CSS. Convert it to use Tailwind CSS utility classes."

    b. **Usage:** This is great if you have legacy code or an example in another framework (such as Bootstrap) and you want to see the Tailwind approach. For instance, a blog prompt might say "*Convert the below code using Bootstrap to use Tailwind* CSS", then paste a snippet. The AI would then replace **`<div class="text-center mt-4">`** (if it were Bootstrap) with Tailwind equivalents (**`text-center mt-4`** are ironically the same class names in this case!), or convert a Bootstrap grid into Tailwind flex or grid classes, etc. This is a neat way to learn Tailwind by comparing how the same structure is done in different systems.

In all cases, **review the AI's output**. Tailwind's systematic naming helps the AI get it mostly right, but there could be minor mismatches:

- The AI might use a class that does not exist (for example, a typo such as **`bg-gry-500`** or an outdated **`bg-light-blue-500`**). If so, Tailwind will simply have no effect for that class. You would notice and should correct it (and maybe let the AI know it used the wrong class).

- If the AI suggests a combination that is suboptimal or non-standard, feel free to tweak. For example, if it sets excessive margins or does not use a responsive prefix where needed, you can adjust or ask, "How can I make this part responsive?" and so on.

One thing to highlight: Because Tailwind's naming is so systematic, **AI usually gets class names very close to correct**. You will not often see it hallucinate completely random names – it might miss the mark by using the wrong color name or forgetting a prefix, but for example, it will not invent **`bg-blue-6000`**. This reliability is why Tailwind + AI is a compelling combo.

AI for Fixing Styling Bugs

Another great use of AI is **debugging your styles**. Suppose you wrote some HTML with Tailwind classes, but the result is not what you expected – maybe a layout is off, or an element is not centered when it should be. You can actually paste that code into ChatGPT and ask something similar to:

"*I am using these Tailwind classes, but the div is not centered vertically – what am I doing wrong?*"

The AI can analyze the code and often pinpoint the issue. For instance, it might respond: "You have **`items-center`** on a flex container, but you need **`min-h-screen`** on the container or a parent with a defined height to truly center vertically." Or "You used **`mx-auto`** on an inline element; try making it **`block`** or wrapping it in a container." Essentially, it is similar to having a tutor or a rubber duck[5] that knows Tailwind.

If you encounter something like "*my dark mode classes are not taking effect*", you could ask:

"*Why is my dark mode class not working in Tailwind?*"

The answer might remind you of the basics: "Ensure you have **`darkMode: 'class'`** in your config and that an ancestor element (such as **`<html>`**) has the class **`dark`** applied. Without these, the **`dark:text-...`** utility will not activate". Or if using media strategy, ensure the OS is in dark mode, and so on. The AI draws from general knowledge of common pitfalls (it does not know your specific project config, but it knows typical things people forget).

Even for plain syntax errors, AI can help. If Tailwind classes are not applying, sometimes it is not a Tailwind issue at all – maybe you forgot a closing quote or angle bracket

[5] *Rubber duck debugging is a problem-solving technique where a developer explains their code line by line to an inanimate object (such as a rubber duck) or to another person. The act of verbalizing the logic often helps the developer notice mistakes or gaps in understanding, leading to solutions without external input. The name originates from the 1999 book "The Pragmatic Programmer," where one of the authors described carrying a rubber duck to debug code by explaining it to the duck.*

in your HTML, causing the classes to not be recognized properly. You can paste the snippet and ask if there is a syntax issue. Often, the AI will spot an unclosed tag or a missing quote. It is surprisingly good at this kind of quick code review.

Again, treat these suggestions as advice – sometimes the AI might assume one cause (such as a missing **`darkMode`** config) when in reality you perhaps misspelled a class. But it gives you a direction to investigate. Use it to supplement your own debugging: "Is there something obvious I am missing?" More often than not, it will mention the common gotchas.

AI for Refactoring and Optimization

Once you have a working code, AI can also assist in making it better. Tailwind makes it easy to rapidly build UI, but sometimes you end up with duplication or could organize things more cleanly (for example, extracting a component).

You can ask the AI for suggestions on refactoring. For example:

"*Here is my* HTML *for three cards with a similar structure. How can I avoid repeating the same classes for each? Can Tailwind help me simplify this?*"

The AI might suggest using a loop if you are in a templating context, or extracting a component partial, or even using **`@apply`** for common class groups. It might also point out where you could use a single utility instead of two (maybe you wrote **`p-4 pt-6`** on an element, and it suggests you could simplify to just adjust one value).

Another form of optimization is performance/size: "*Are there any Tailwind classes here that are unnecessary or could be combined?*" The AI might notice if you, say, added both **`px-4`** and **`pl-4 pr-4`** (redundant), or if you set a default that could be moved to a parent container.

Tailwind's philosophy encourages optimizing design in the browser (trying classes and seeing results). AI can complement this by quickly answering "W*hat classes would achieve a sticky footer layout?*" or "*How do I make this div scrollable only on small screens?*" (Maybe the answer: use **`overflow-auto md:overflow-visible`**, and so on.)

Finally, AI can help compare AI-generated versus human-written code. If you are curious whether a suggestion is idiomatic, you could ask: "Is *this how one would typically implement this in Tailwind? Any improvements?*" and the AI might refine the answer.

In summary, think of AI as a versatile assistant:

- **During writing,** it autocompletes and suggests.
- **When stuck,** it explains and debugs
- **When polishing,** it refactors and educates on best practices.

Throughout this chapter, we will use these strategies in a practical way – especially in the upcoming **Concept Walkthrough**, where we build a component with AI's help.

Concept Walkthrough: Building a Responsive Card Component (with AI Assistance)

To tie everything together, let us build a basic **mobile-first card UI** using Tailwind CSS, leveraging AI to help with the workflow. The card will include an image, a title, some descriptive text, and a call-to-action button. We will ensure it is fully responsive (stacking layout on narrow screens, maybe side-by-side on wider screens) and supports dark mode. This will demonstrate how we can go from a blank slate to a nice component by combining our Tailwind knowledge with AI-generated suggestions.

Step 1: Initial Structure – Base HTML and Styling

First, let us create the basic card structure. We prompt ChatGPT with something similar to: "*Generate a simple card component with an image at the top, title, text, and a button, using Tailwind CSS.*" As discussed, the AI might give us a snippet similar to the one earlier:

```
<div class="max-w-sm bg-white rounded-lg shadow-md overflow-hidden">
  <img class="w-full h-48 object-cover" src="https://placehold.
co/600x400/3b82f6/ffffff?text=Hello
" alt="Card image">
  <div class="p-6">
    <h2 class="text-xl font-bold mb-2">Card Title</h2>
    <p class="text-gray-700 text-base mb-4">
      This is a brief description of the card content. It provides an
overview and entices the user to learn more.
    </p>
    <button class="bg-blue-500 text-white font-semibold px-4 py-2
rounded hover:bg-blue-600">Learn More</button>
  </div>
</div>
```

Let us break down what we got (and indeed what we needed):

- The outermost **`<div>`** acts as the card container. The AI gave it **`max-w-sm`** (so the card will not stretch too wide) and essential styling: white background, rounded corners, a shadow, and **`overflow-hidden`** (so that the image's corners are clipped by the rounded border). This is a solid base, mobile-first (no media queries yet).

- Inside, an **<img> with w-full** makes it span the full width of the card, and **h-48 object-cover** sets a fixed height and crops the image (maintaining aspect cover). On small screens, it will be full width of the card (since the card is **max-w-sm** anyway). We might consider later making the image flexibly height or different on larger screens, but this is fine for now – a classic "image on top" card.
- The content **<div class="p-6">** adds padding inside the card for the text content.
- The title **<h2>** has **text-xl font-bold mb-2** – a reasonably large title, bold, with margin-bottom for spacing.
- The paragraph has **text-gray-700 text-base mb-4** – normal body text size, a gray color, and some bottom margin.
- The button has **bg-blue-500 text-white font-semibold px-4 py-2 rounded** and a hover class to darken it (**hover:bg-blue-600**). This is straightforward: a medium blue button, white text, slightly bold, padding, rounded corners, and a hover effect.

We should test this in our project (or a Tailwind Playground) to verify it looks good. At this point, we have a functional card component that works on mobile and up (it will be centered or left-aligned depending on the container, but the component itself is responsive in that it will naturally shrink on small screens due to the max-width).

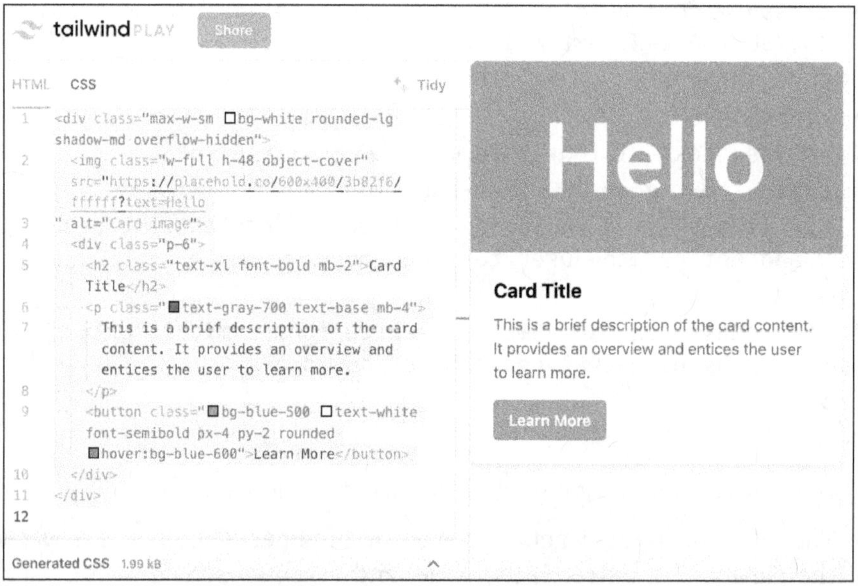

Figure 3.22: *First Version of Our Card Component*

Step 2: Enhancing with Responsive Behavior

Now, suppose we want the card to display differently on larger screens – maybe show the image on the left and content on the right (a horizontal layout) when there is room. This is a common pattern: Stack on mobile, side-by-side on desktop.

We can either code this manually or ask the AI to modify it. Let us try prompting the AI: "*Update the card to display horizontally (image on left, text on right) on large screens.*" The AI might modify the structure to use a flex layout at a certain breakpoint. One possible suggestion:

```
<div class="max-w-lg bg-white rounded-lg shadow-md overflow-hidden
lg:flex">
  <img class="w-full lg:w-1/3 h-48 object-cover" src="https://placehold.
co/600x400/3b82f6/ffffff?text=Hello" alt="Card image">
  <div class="p-6 lg:w-2/3">
<h2 class="text-xl font-bold mb-2">Card Title</h2>
    <p class="text-gray-700 text-base mb-4">
      This is a brief description of the card content. It provides an
overview and entices the user to learn more.
    </p>
    <button class="bg-blue-500 text-white font-semibold px-4 py-2
rounded hover:bg-blue-600">Learn More</button>  </div>
</div>
```

What changed?

- Added **`lg:flex`** on the container, turning it into a flex container on large screens (≥1024px). No **`flex`** on small screens means it will stack by default (which is what we want for mobile).
- Gave the **`<img>`** a **`lg:w-1/3`** and the content div **`lg:w-2/3`**. So on large screens, the image takes 33% of the card's width, and content takes 66%. On small screens, those **`w-1/3`** and **`w-2/3`** do not apply, so the image is full width of the card (as before) and the content is naturally full width below it.
- Also, making the container **`lg: flex`** implicitly makes it horizontal, placing the image and content side by side. We might also want to ensure alignment (they will top-align by default, which is fine in this case since the image has a fixed height).
- The card max width was changed to **`max-w-lg`** here, simply as an example to allow a slightly wider card on desktop, but that is optional. **`max-w-sm`** could still work; just the content area would wrap more.

We should verify this: On mobile, **`lg:flex`** does nothing, so it is just like before (image above text). On ≥1024px, **`lg: flex`** kicks in, making the card a horizontal flex layout. The

lg:w-1/3 on the image means the image will occupy one-third of the flex container's width, and **lg:w-2/3** means the content takes two-thirds. That sums to the full width of the card. We likely also want **object-cover** to ensure the image still covers its box, which we have.

This demonstrates how easily we can adapt the component with a few responsive classes. The AI was able to suggest the appropriate approach using Tailwind's breakpoints.

Step 3: Adding Dark Mode Support

Let us ensure our card looks good in dark mode. If the rest of our site supports dark mode (via the **dark** class on HTML), we should adapt the card. Likely, we would invert the colors: background becomes darker, text becomes lighter.

We can manually add dark classes or ask: "*Modify the card code to support dark mode.*" The AI might respond by adding **dark:** variants, for example:

```
<div class="max-w-lg bg-white dark:bg-gray-800 rounded-lg shadow-md
overflow-hidden lg:flex">
  <img class="w-full lg:w-1/3 h-48 object-cover" src="https://placehold.
co/600x400/3b82f6/ffffff?text=Hello" alt="Card image">
  <div class="p-6 lg:w-2/3">
    <h2 class="text-xl font-bold mb-2 text-gray-900 dark:text-gray-
100">Card Title</h2>
    <p class="text-gray-700 dark:text-gray-300 text-base mb-4">
      This is a brief description of the card content...
    </p>
    <button class="bg-blue-500 dark:bg-blue-600 text-white font-semibold
px-4 py-2 rounded hover:bg-blue-600 dark:hover:bg-blue-700">
      Learn More
    </button>
  </div>
</div>
```

Changes made:

- The container gets **dark:bg-gray-800** in addition to the default white. Now, when dark mode is active, the card background will be a dark gray.
- The title text gets **dark:text-gray-100** (making it near-white in dark mode).
- The paragraph text gets **dark:text-gray-300** (a lighter gray for dark mode).
- The button background in dark mode could be tweaked too; here it is used **dark:bg-blue-600** so it is a bit darker by default, and **dark:hover:bg-blue-700** for hover. The text on the button is already white, which works on

both blue-500 and blue-600, so that is fine. Alternatively, we might have left the button blue in dark mode – blue on gray is usually okay – but making it a slightly different shade in dark mode could match the aesthetic.

Now, our card **automatically adjusts for dark mode** (provided the page has the **`dark`** class on a parent). Always double-check contrast: gray-100 text on gray-800 background is usually good (it is white-ish on dark gray). Grey-300 on gray-800 is also fine for paragraph text (not too bright). If anything, blue-500 on a dark background might be a tad saturated; using blue-400 or blue-300 for the button in dark mode might even be considered to pop against dark. In our example, we went with a slightly darker blue for the dark mode button (blue-600) to differentiate it. These are design tweaks that you can adjust as needed, but the main point is the mechanics: we add **`dark:*`** classes to handle the switch.

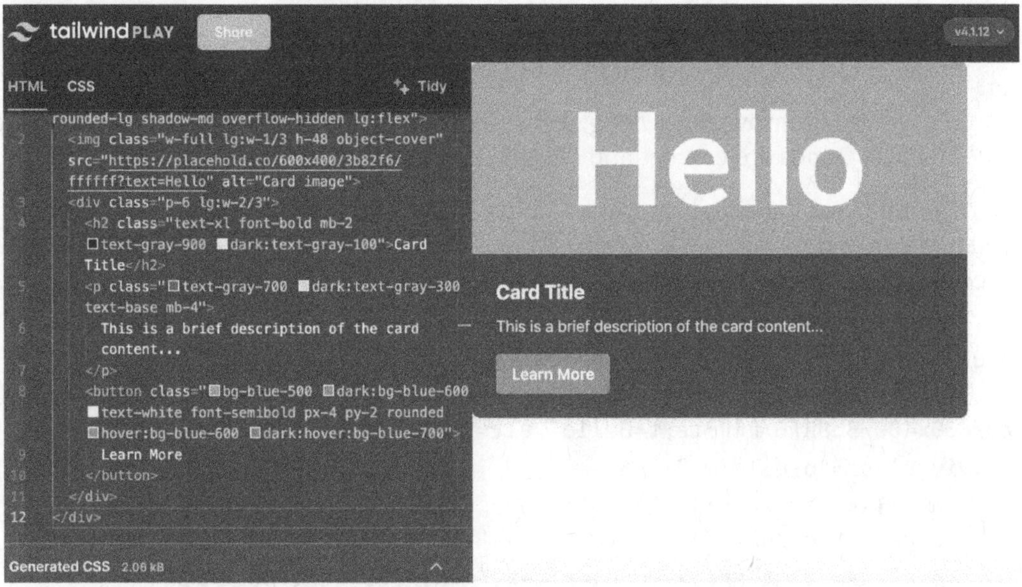

***Figure 3.23:** Card in Dark Mode Showing the New Dark Background and Light Text*

Step 4: Polish – Hover and Focus States, Accessibility

We have already included a hover state on the button. We might also consider adding a subtle hover effect on the card itself – for instance, maybe increase the shadow (**`hover:shadow-lg`**) or translate it up slightly (**`hover:-translate-y-1`**) to give a lift effect on hover. Tailwind makes that easy. If we wanted, we could add to the container:

```
<div class="... shadow-md hover:shadow-lg transition-shadow duration-300
...">
```

This would animate the shadow on hover for a nice touch (note: adding **`transition-shadow duration-300`** for smoothness). The AI could suggest this if asked: "*Add a hover effect to the card container.*" It might also mention adding **`cursor-pointer`** if the whole card is clickable (such as a link).

For completeness, ensure things such as the image have **`alt`** text (we did that), and the button has an accessible label (in our case, "Learn More" is fine).

We should also test how multiple cards would look in a grid or column. If we place two of these card components side by side in a flex container, do they responsively wrap? Usually yes, if the parent has **`flex flex-wrap`**. Or we could use a grid.

But that is beyond our single component scope. Our focus was the process:

1. We used AI to generate the initial markup and classes.
2. We then iteratively improved the component by describing changes (responsive layout, dark mode), which the AI suggested in Tailwind terms.
3. We used our own knowledge to verify and tweak those suggestions (ensuring class names are correct and design choices make sense).

At this point, we have built a pretty robust Tailwind component more quickly than coding from scratch thanks to AI assistance. We also understood each class that was used, which is crucial, because if something did not look right, we knew how to fix it.

```
<div class="max-w-lg bg-white dark:bg-gray-800 rounded-lg shadow-md
overflow-hidden lg:flex hover:shadow-lg transition-shadow duration-300">
  <img class="w-full lg:w-1/3 h-48 object-cover" src="https://placehold.
co/600x400/3b82f6/ffffff?text=Hello" alt="Card image">
  <div class="p-6 lg:w-2/3">
    <h2 class="text-xl font-bold mb-2 text-gray-900 dark:text-gray-
100">Card Title</h2>
    <p class="text-gray-700 dark:text-gray-300 text-base mb-4">
      This is a brief description of the card content...
    </p>
    <button class="bg-blue-500 dark:bg-blue-600 text-white font-semibold
px-4 py-2 rounded hover:bg-blue-600 dark:hover:bg-blue-700">
      Learn More
    </button>
  </div>
</div>
```

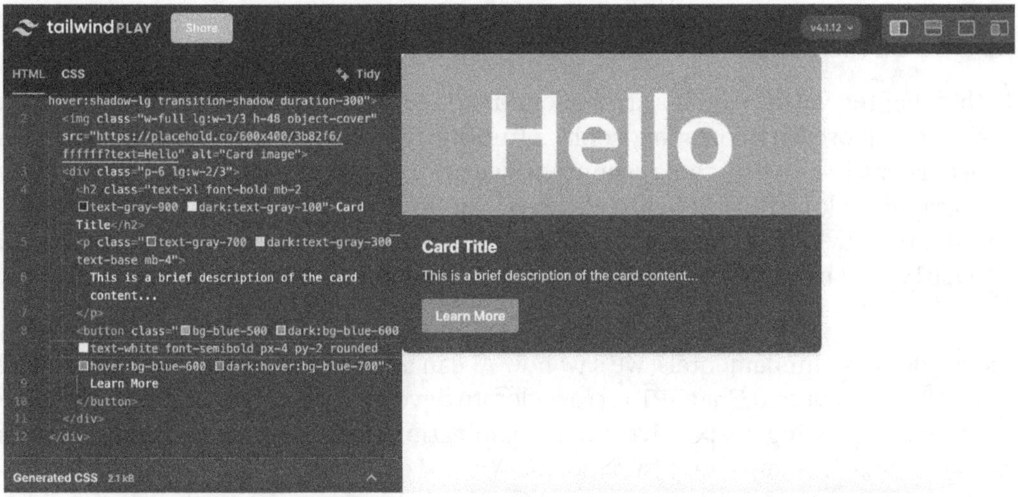

Figure 3.24: *Final Card Component Example Shown in Light Mode Default, and in Dark Mode When Toggled, with Hover States Visible on Button and Card Elevation*

As you can see, the light mode provides a crisp interface, with the hover effects adding a layer of interactivity to the button and the card container itself. Now, by simply toggling the system or browser theme, the dark: utility classes we added earlier will automatically take over. The component seamlessly inverts its color scheme to accommodate low-light environments without requiring any additional CSS logic.

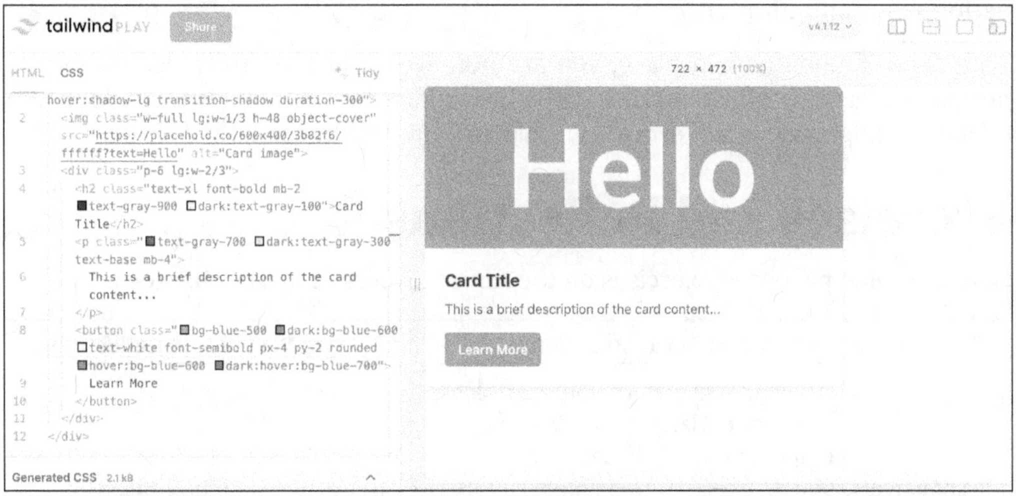

Figure 3.25: *Final Card Component Example Shown in Light Mode Default, and in Dark Mode When Toggled, with Hover States Visible on Button and Card Elevation*

Conclusion

In this chapter, we have built a strong foundation for working effectively with Tailwind CSS. We explored its core philosophy of utility-first styling and examined essential concepts such as Preflight, responsive design, pseudo-class variants, dark mode, typography, colors, SVG handling, flexbox, and grid utilities. We also discussed how to extend Tailwind through configuration and custom utilities using directives such as `@apply`, and how the framework's Just-in-Time compiler ensures efficient and lean CSS output.

Alongside these fundamentals, we saw how AI can act as a supportive layer. Tools such as GitHub Copilot and ChatGPT can accelerate development by generating boilerplate snippets, suggesting responsive class combinations, and even debugging common mistakes. Still, it is important to remember that AI assistance should complement, not replace, a developer's understanding of Tailwind. As we emphasized, always validate AI-generated output against the documentation and your project's needs.

By practicing with examples, interactive exercises, and the Tailwind Play environment, you have taken the first major step toward mastering responsive, mobile-first UI development with Tailwind CSS. This knowledge will empower you to approach more complex layouts and interactive components in future chapters. The principles learned here—clarity, modularity, and conscious use of utilities—will remain central as we move toward advanced prompt engineering, AI-assisted component building, and performance optimization.

With these foundations in place, you are now well-equipped to transition into the next stage: learning how to harness prompt engineering techniques to guide AI more effectively in producing high-quality, scalable Tailwind CSS code.

Exercises and Reflections

Here are some proposed exercises on the topics discussed in this chapter.

Exercise	Prompt Instructions	Code Review and Reflection
Responsive Button with Variants	Use an AI assistant (or your own skills) to generate a large, responsive button component in HTML using Tailwind. It should be full-width on mobile (`w-full` on small screens) and become an inline-block (auto width) on medium screens and up. Include a hover state that changes the background color, and ensure the button works in dark mode (for example, different colors).	After generating the code, manually identify what each class does and test the button in both light and dark themes.

Exercise	Prompt Instructions	Code Review and Reflection
Form Input Group	Prompt an AI like ChatGPT to create a simple form group – for example, a text input with a label and an error message below it. The output should use Tailwind classes for spacing, fonts, and colors (perhaps a `red-500` text for the error).	Inspect the AI's code for accessibility (does it associate the label with the input? Is the error text appropriately styled?). Adjust the classes as needed and try to improve it if something is missing
Navigation Bar	Without looking up code directly, ask an AI to generate a responsive navigation bar with Tailwind. It should have a logo on the left and some menu items on the right. On mobile, menu items should collapse into a hamburger menu.	Examine the solution – does it use a `<ul>` for the menu? Does it handle the hide/show of the menu (maybe using `hidden` and `md:block` classes)? Consider what JavaScript might be needed and whether the AI provided any (some might include a script or just leave it static). Modify the code to better suit what you envision for a nav.
AI Code Review	Take one of the above components (button, form, or nav) that you got from AI and pretend you are reviewing a teammate's code. Write down at least 3 comments: for example, "Is this class necessary?" "Could we simplify this by using a different utility or a common parent class?", or "This is good usage of `flex` for alignment."	This will help reinforce your ability to critically evaluate AI-generated code. (You can actually ask ChatGPT to critique its own output as well, which is an interesting exercise to see if it identifies issues.)
Build Without AI	As a comparison, try building a small component without any AI assistance – for instance, a simple alert box (with a message and a close "×" button). Use Tailwind classes to style it (background, text, padding, border, and so on). Then, after you are done, you could ask AI to do the same and compare results.	Reflect on which parts you found easy and which parts the AI may have handled differently. This will highlight where AI adds the most value for you.

Table 3.1: *Chapter 3 Prompting Exercises*

Multiple Choice Questions

1. Which of the following best describes the purpose of Tailwind's Preflight?
   a. It adds custom styles to all elements to create a unique design out of the box.
   b. It resets browser defaults (such as margins, font styles) to provide a consistent base for using utility classes.
   c. It automatically prefixes CSS for cross-browser compatibility.
   d. It generates additional color shades for the default color palette.
2. You see the following button code: `<button class="bg-green-500 hover:bg-green-600 text-white px-4 py-2 rounded"></button>`. What will happen on hover?
   a. The button will become smaller.
   b. The button's background will change to a lighter green.
   c. The button's background will change to a darker green.
   d. The text will change color.
3. Tailwind's default color classes (for example, `text-blue-500, bg-blue-500`) are organized by a number scale. What does a higher number generally mean?
   a. A lighter color.
   b. A darker or more saturated color.
   c. It indicates the opacity level.
   d. There is no consistent meaning; it is arbitrary.
4. If you want an element to be center-aligned horizontally within a container, which utility class would you likely use?
   a. `mx-auto` (with the element set to `block` or have a defined width).
   b. `text-center.`
   c. `justify-center.`
   d. `items-center.`
5. How do you enable Tailwind's dark mode using the class strategy?
   a. Add `darkmode=true` in tailwind.config.js.
   b. Use `dark:` classes in HTML; no config needed.
   c. Set `darkMode: 'class'` in tailwind.config.js and add a `class="dark"` on a parent element (such as, the `<html>` tag).
   d. It is on by default; Simply start using `dark:` classes.

6. Suppose you have a lot of repeated utility classes on several elements. What feature does Tailwind provide to help avoid repetition?
   a. Nothing – repetition is expected in Tailwind.
   b. The `@apply` directive in CSS to create a custom utility (for example, a `.btn` class) reusing those classes.
   c. Variables to store class lists.
   d. Special "combo" utility classes built-in for common patterns.
7. When using Tailwind's JIT mode (just-in-time compiler), what happens if you use a class that is not found in your HTML or other source files during build?
   a. It will still be included in the CSS, making it larger.
   b. It will not be included in the generated CSS, effectively purging that unused style.
   c. The build will throw an error.
   d. Tailwind will attempt to guess and include similar classes.
8. You ask an AI to generate a Tailwind snippet, and it gives you `<div class="col-span-6">`, but your project is using an older Tailwind version that does not have that utility. What is a likely outcome?
   a. `col-span-6` will be ignored if the class is not in your CSS (AI suggesting a class from a newer version).
   b. Tailwind will automatically add it because AI suggested it.
   c. The browser will interpret it as a standard CSS class with no effect unless defined.
   d. Both a and c are correct (it will be ignored since it is not in your CSS, which in practice means no effect).
9. In Tailwind, which utility would not by itself contribute to centering an absolutely positioned element within a container?
   a. `absolute` – because that merely sets positioning mode.
   b. `inset-0` – because that stretches the element to all sides of the container (not centering).
   c. `mx-auto` – because it centers block elements within a container, but is not used for absolute elements.
   d. `items-center` – because it works with a flex container to align items, not for an absolutely positioned element.

(Think carefully: absolute positioning requires using top/right/bottom/left or transforms to center, whereas the listed utilities have different purposes.)

10. Which is a good strategy when using AI assistance with Tailwind CSS?
    a. Rely on AI suggestions without understanding the classes – it usually knows best.
    b. Use AI to generate snippets, but always review the classes, check if they exist in the docs, and adjust for your design needs.
    c. Avoid using AI for Tailwind because class names are too inconsistent.
    d. Only use AI for HTML structure, not for Tailwind classes.

Answers

1. b
2. c
3. b
4. a
5. c
6. b
7. b
8. d
9. d
10. b

Chapter 4
Prompting Copilot and GPT for Smarter Code

Introduction

This chapter marks the transition from foundational Tailwind CSS concepts to more advanced techniques for building scalable and interactive user interfaces. You have already established proficiency in utility-first styling; now the focus shifts to the higher-level patterns that enable sophisticated layouts and component architectures. Modern AI assistants such as GitHub Copilot and GPT-based models play a central role here, acting as expert collaborators capable of accelerating development and reinforcing best practices when guided by precise prompts.

Each section pairs an advanced prompt-engineering strategy with a specific Tailwind CSS concept, offering a blend of theory, hands-on experimentation, and practical workflow patterns. By mastering these techniques, you will learn to articulate complex UI requirements to an AI assistant and transform vague ideas into refined, production-ready code. By the end of this chapter, you will be able to reliably prompt AI tools to generate responsive layouts, interactive component states, and optimized Tailwind patterns, while iteratively evaluating and improving the results.

Structure

In this chapter, we will cover the following topics:

- Part I: Mastering the Core Engine and Configuration
    - Advanced Theming with CSS Variables and `@Theme`
    - The JIT Engine and On-Demand Generation
- Part II: Advanced Selectors and State Management
    - Dynamic State Styling with Data and ARIA Attributes
    - Harnessing Modern CSS: Container Queries and `:has()`

- Part III: Building Scalable Architectures
  - Component Abstraction with `@Apply` and Scoped Styles
  - Authoring Custom Plugins
- Part IV: Ecosystem Integration for Interactive UIs
  - Building Accessible Components with Headless UI (`React/Vue`)
  - Lightweight Interactivity with `Alpine.js`
- Part V: Production Readiness
  - Production Optimization and Dynamic Class Safety

Part I: Mastering the Core Engine and Configuration

This initial part of the chapter moves beyond basic configuration to examine the foundational technologies that power Tailwind's most advanced features. A deep understanding of the modern theming engine and the Just-in-Time (JIT) compiler is essential for any developer seeking to master the framework. These core components are not merely implementation details; they represent a fundamental architectural philosophy that enables the flexibility and performance for which modern Tailwind is known.

Advanced Theming with CSS Variables and `@theme`

Note: *Tailwind Play does not support custom JavaScript or script-based logic. Some of the examples in this chapter, particularly those involving dynamic theming or attribute toggling, require a local development setup. To follow along successfully, please use the VSCode configuration we provided earlier in the book. You can find it at https://github.com/charlesribeiro/prompt-to-tailwind.*

The initial approach to theming in Tailwind CSS was centered within the **`tailwind.config.js`** file, a JavaScript-based configuration object. While functional, this created a separation between the styling logic (defined in JavaScript) and the styling language (CSS). The introduction of the **`@theme`** directive represents a significant evolution, moving theme definition directly into the CSS file and embracing modern, CSS-native features. This shift is more than syntactic as it aligns Tailwind's architecture with the web platform itself, enabling more powerful and dynamic theming capabilities.

The **`@theme`** directive allows developers to define design tokens as CSS Custom Properties (variables). These are not ordinary CSS variables. They are "theme variables" that instruct Tailwind to generate corresponding utility classes. For example, defining

--color-primary: oklch(0.72 0.11 221.19);[1] Within an **@theme** block, automatically makes utilities such as **bg-primary, text-primary**, and **border-primary** available for use in the markup.

This CSS-native approach makes theming dynamic at runtime. By scoping CSS variables within different selectors (for example, **[data-theme="dark"])**, one can create multiple themes—light mode, dark mode, or distinct brand palettes—that can be switched by simply changing an attribute on the <html> element, without requiring any JavaScript-driven re-renders or class replacements.

Prompting Strategy: Role-Playing and Contextual Prompting

To effectively generate a robust theming system, one can instruct an AI assistant to adopt the persona of a specialist, such as a "Design Systems Architect." This role-playing prompt, combined with rich context about the desired outcome, guides the AI to produce a more structured and comprehensive result than a generic request would.

Example Prompt:

Assume the role of a Design Systems Architect. I am building a SaaS application that requires a flexible theming system with support for a default 'light' mode, a 'dark' mode, and a 'high-contrast' accessibility mode.

Using the modern **@theme** directive in Tailwind CSS, generate the CSS code for my **input.css file**.

- Define a base set of semantic color tokens using CSS variables: **--color-primary**, **--color-secondary**, **--color-accent,** **--color-surface**, **--color-on-surface**, and **--color-border**.
- In the main **@theme** block, map these semantic tokens to specific color values from Tailwind's default palette (for example, **--color-primary: var(--color-blue-600);**). These will serve as the 'light' theme defaults.
- Within a **@layer base** rule, define CSS rules for **[data-theme="dark"]** and **[data-theme="high-contrast"]** selectors. Inside these rules, override the values of the semantic CSS variables to define the dark and high-contrast themes.
- Finally, provide an example HTML structure that uses these semantic utility classes (for example, **bg-surface**, **text-on-surface**, **bg-primary**) and includes buttons to demonstrate how to switch the **data-theme** attribute on the **<html>** tag with a small JavaScript snippet."

---

[1] **oklch()** is a modern CSS color function based on the **OKLab** color space, which is designed to be perceptually uniform. Unlike traditional RGB or HSL, **OKLCH** expresses colors with three components: L (Lightness): the perceived brightness (0 = black, 1 = white), C (Chroma): the colorfulness or intensity of the hue, H (Hue): the angle on the color wheel in degrees. Please refer to https://developer.mozilla.org/en-US/docs/Web/CSS/color_value/oklch

AI-Generated Output

```
@import "tailwindcss";

/* 1. Define semantic color tokens and map them to the default (light)
theme. */
@theme {
  --color-primary: var(--color-sky-600);
  --color-secondary: var(--color-slate-700);
  --color-accent: var(--color-teal-500);
  --color-surface: var(--color-white);
  --color-on-surface: var(--color-slate-800);
  --color-border: var(--color-slate-300);
}

/* 2. Define theme overrides within the 'base' layer. */
@layer base {
  [data-theme="dark"] {
    --color-primary: var(--color-sky-400);
    --color-secondary: var(--color-slate-300);
    --color-accent: var(--color-teal-400);
    --color-surface: var(--color-slate-900);
    --color-on-surface: var(--color-slate-100);
    --color-border: var(--color-slate-700);
  }

  [data-theme="high-contrast"] {
    --color-primary: oklch(100% 0 0); /* White */
    --color-secondary: oklch(0.8 0 0); /* Light Gray */
    --color-accent: oklch(0.88 0.19 256); /* Bright Purple */
    --color-surface: oklch(0% 0 0); /* Black */
    --color-on-surface: oklch(100% 0 0); /* White */
    --color-border: oklch(100% 0 0); /* White */
  }
}

<html lang="en" data-theme="light">
<head>
 <meta charset="UTF-8">
 <meta name="viewport" content="width=device-width, initial-
scale=1.0">
 <link href="./src/output.css" rel="stylesheet">
 <title>Theming Demo</title>
</head>
```

```
<body class=”bg-surface text-on-surface font-sans transition-colors
duration-300”>
 <div class=”p-8 max-w-2xl mx-auto”>
   <h1 class=”text-3xl font-bold text-primary”>Advanced Theming</h1>
   <p class=”mt-4 text-secondary”>
     Switch between themes by changing the <code>data-theme</code>
attribute on the root element.
   </p>
   <div class=”mt-6 p-6 border border-border rounded-lg”>
     This container uses semantic colors that adapt to the current
theme.
   </div>
   <div class=”mt-8 flex gap-4”>
   <div class=”mt-8 flex gap-4”>
<button id=”light-btn”
 class=”px-4 py-2 bg-primary text-on-surface rounded-md ring-1 ring-
border”>
 Light Theme
</button>

<button id=”dark-btn”
 class=”px-4 py-2 bg-primary text-on-surface rounded-md ring-1 ring-
border”>
 Dark Theme
</button>

<button id=”contrast-btn”
 class=”px-4 py-2 bg-accent text-on-surface rounded-md ring-1 ring-
border”>
 High Contrast
</button>
   </div>
   </div>
 </div>
<script>
 const lightBtn = document.getElementById(‘light-btn’);
 const darkBtn = document.getElementById(‘dark-btn’);
 const contrastBtn = document.getElementById(‘contrast-btn’);

 if (!lightBtn || !darkBtn || !contrastBtn) {
   console.warn(‘Theme buttons not found in the DOM.’);
 } else {
   lightBtn.addEventListener(‘click’, (e) => {
```

```
      console.log('Light clicked');
      document.documentElement.setAttribute('data-theme', 'light');
    });
    darkBtn.addEventListener('click', () => {
      console.log('Dark clicked');
      document.documentElement.setAttribute('data-theme', 'dark');
    });
    contrastBtn.addEventListener('click', () => {
      console.log('High contrast clicked');
      document.documentElement.setAttribute('data-theme', 'high-
contrast');
    });
 }
</script>
</body>
</html>
```

Figure 4.1 shows the output of this code.

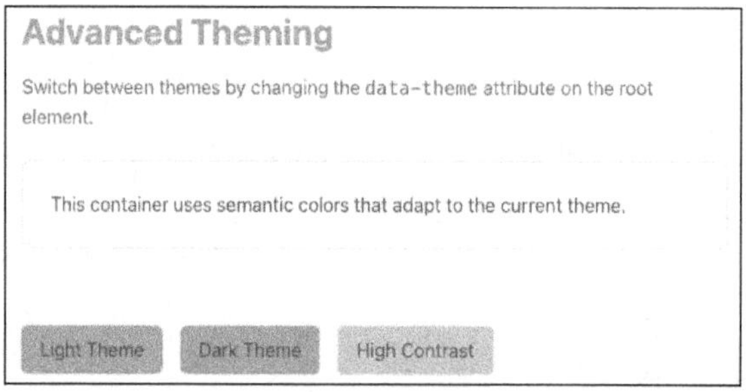

Figure 4.1: *The Card Displayed with the data-theme="light" Attribute. Semantic Colors Provide a Clean Surface Background, Dark Text, and a Balanced Visual Hierarchy Suitable for Standard Reading Conditions*

Figure 4.2 shows the implementation for the dark theme.

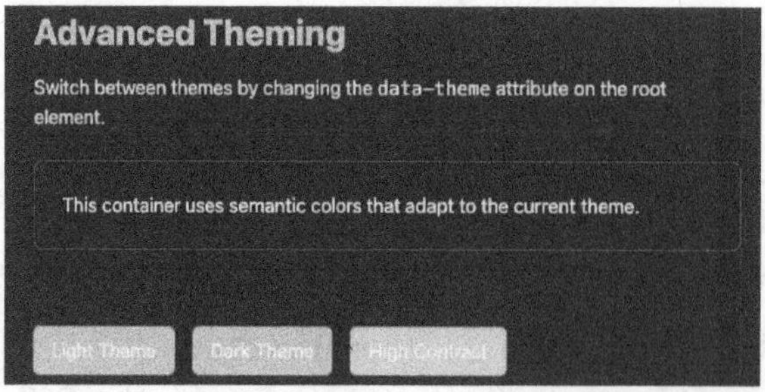

Figure 4.2: *The Same Card When the data-theme="dark" Attribute is Applied. The Background Shifts to a Dark Surface, with Lighter Text for Readability, Reducing Eye Strain in Low-Light Environments*

The high contrast mode (for accessibility) was also introduced, as in *Figure* 4.3.

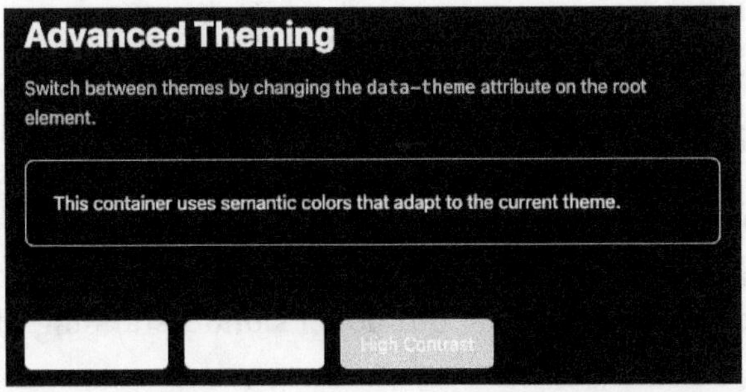

Figure 4.3: *A High-Contrast Variant Triggered by data-theme="high-contrast". Bold Accent Colors and Sharper Borders Enhance Visibility for Accessibility, Making the Interface Clearer for Users with Visual Impairments*

The JIT Engine and On-Demand Generation

The Just-in-Time (JIT) engine, introduced in Tailwind CSS v2.1, and represents the most significant architectural shift in the framework's history. It transformed Tailwind from a static utility generator into a high-performance, on-demand CSS compiler.

Before JIT, Tailwind generated a large CSS file containing every possible utility class and variant during development. This led to slow initial build times, particularly in complex projects or with bundlers such as Webpack, and required careful configuration to "purge" unused styles for production.

The JIT engine reverses this model. It scans project files (HTML, JS, Vue, and so on) for class names first and then generates *only* the CSS for the utilities that are actually being used. This process is exceptionally fast, reducing initial compile times from seconds (or even minutes) to milliseconds.

This fundamental change from a "generate-everything" to a "generate-on-demand" model is not merely a performance enhancement. It is the direct enabler of Tailwind's most powerful modern features. Because the generated CSS file is always minimal, the framework no longer suffers from the file-size constraints that previously limited its capabilities. This directly unlocked two critical features:

1. **Universal Variant** Activation: All variants (for example, **`focus-visible`**, **`disabled`**, **`aria-expanded`**) are enabled by default. Developers can stack them freely (for example, **`sm:dark:hover:disabled:opacity-50`**) without any configuration, as the corresponding CSS will only be generated if that specific combination is used.

2. **Arbitrary Value Support:** Developers can use hyper-specific, one-off values that are not part of the pre-defined theme. By using square bracket notation (for example, **`w-[513px]`**, **`top-[-113px]`**, **`text-`**), developers can achieve pixel-

perfect designs without needing to write custom CSS or extend the theme configuration.

Prompting Strategy: Chain-of-Thought and Constraint-Based Prompting

To leverage the full power of the JIT engine via an AI assistant, one can use a constraint-based prompt. By providing highly specific, non-standard design requirements, the developer forces the AI to use arbitrary value syntax. Pairing this with a Chain-of-Thought request (“`Explain your steps`”) encourages the AI to articulate *why* it chose this approach, reinforcing the developer’s understanding of the underlying JIT capabilities.

Example Prompt

I need to create a hero section component[2] for a marketing website. The design has very specific, pixel-perfect positioning requirements that do not align with my standard theme spacing.

Generate the HTML for a `div` that acts as a container for a background image and some text content.

The requirements are:

- The container must have a precise height of **`720px`**.
- It should have an inner padding of exactly **`37px`**.
- Inside the container, there should be a decorative background **`img`** element. This image must be positioned absolutely with **`top: -42px`** and **`right: 68px`**.
- The image must have a specific width of **`811px`**.
- On medium screens (the `md` breakpoint), the image’s top position should change to **`-55px`**.

After generating the HTML, provide a step-by-step explanation (**Chain-of-Thought**) of how you used Tailwind’s arbitrary value syntax to meet these precise constraints and why this is possible due to the JIT engine.

AI-Generated Output

```
<div class=”relative h-[720px] p-[37px] bg-gray-100 overflow-hidden”>
  <img class="absolute top-[-42px] right-[68px] w-[811px] md:top-[-55px]
opacity-20"
    src="/path/to/decorative-background.svg"
    alt="Decorative background element"
  />
  <div class="relative z-10">
```

[2] *A hero section is the large, visually prominent area at the top of a webpage, typically containing a headline, supporting text, and a call-to-action. Its purpose is to immediately capture attention, communicate the core message, and guide users toward the primary action on the site.*

```
    <h1 class="text-4xl font-bold">Pixel-Perfect Design</h1>
    <p class="mt-4">This layout uses arbitrary values for precise
control.</p>
  </div>
</div>
</div>
```

Figure 4.4 shows the output of the generated code.

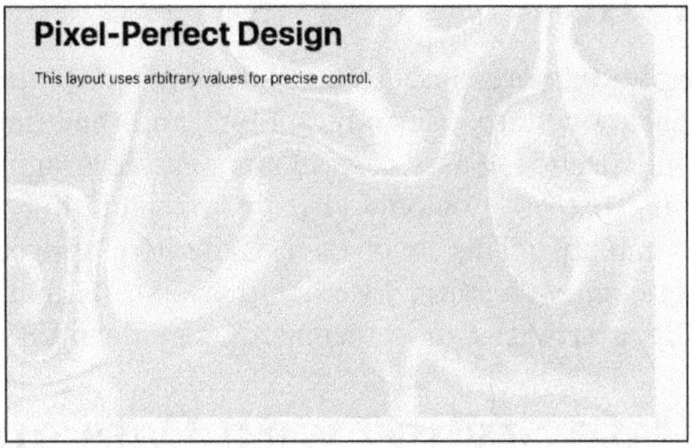

***Figure 4.4**: Output of a Layout That Uses Arbitrary Values for Sizing and Positioning. Background Image (Source: https://unsplash.com/photos/an-abstract-painting-of-blue-and-red-colors-uAvq7gFQecc)*

Chain-of-Thought Explanation:

Here is the step-by-step reasoning for the generated code:

- **Container Sizing (`h-[720px]` and `p-[37px]`):** The design required a height of 720px and padding of 37px. These values are not standard in the default Tailwind spacing scale. I used square bracket notation to generate these as arbitrary values. The JIT engine detects **`h-[720px]`** and compiles the exact CSS rule **`height: 720px;`** on demand. The same process applies to **`p-[37px]`**.
- **Absolute Positioning (`top-[-42px]` and `right-[68px]`):** To achieve the quirky, off-grid positioning for the background image, I used arbitrary values for the `top` and `right` properties. The JIT engine supports negative values and any unit, compiling **`top-[-42px]`** to **`top: -42px;`**.
- **Image Width (`w-[811px]`):** Similar to the container height, the image required a non-standard width of 811px. The utility **`w-[811px]`** was used to generate the corresponding **`width: 811px;`** CSS rule.
- **Responsive Arbitrary Value (`md:top-[-55px]`):** The JIT engine's capabilities extend to variants. The requirement was to change the top position at the **`md`** breakpoint. I combined the responsive variant **`md:`** with the arbitrary value **`top-[-55px]`** to create **`md:top-[-55px]`**. The JIT engine compiles this into a media query: **`@media (min-width: 768px) {.md\:top-\[-55px\] { top: -55px; } }`**.

This entire approach is only possible because the Just-in-Time (JIT) engine generates styles on demand by scanning the source files. Instead of being limited to a pre-generated set of utilities, it can create any utility needed, making it possible to achieve any design specification directly within the HTML without writing custom CSS.

Part II: Advanced Selectors and State Management

This part of the chapter explores how to build dynamic and interactive components that respond to application state, user interactions, and their surrounding layout. By moving beyond simple pseudo-classes, developers can leverage Tailwind's advanced variants to create UIs that are not only visually appealing but also more semantic, accessible, and maintainable. This involves a declarative approach where styling is directly linked to an element's state, whether that state is managed by **JavaScript**, driven by **accessibility attributes**, or determined by **modern CSS layout features**.

Dynamic State Styling with Data and ARIA Attributes

While basic state variants such as `hover:` and `focus:` are fundamental, modern web applications require styling based on more complex, application-defined states. For example, a dropdown menu can be "open" or "closed," an accordion item can be "expanded" or "collapsed," and a form input can be "invalid." Traditionally, managing these states involved JavaScript, manually adding and removing CSS classes.

Tailwind provides a more declarative and robust solution through its support for **`data-*`** and **`aria-*`** attribute variants. This approach creates a direct bridge between an application's state and its visual presentation, promoting a cleaner separation of concerns.

- **`data-*` Attributes:** These are used for custom, application-specific states. JavaScript's role is simplified to merely updating a data attribute on an element (for example, **`element.dataset.state = 'open'`**). Tailwind can then use variants such as **`data-[state=open]:opacity-100`** to style the element and its children declaratively.
- **`aria-*` Attributes:** These are used for accessibility states. By styling based on ARIA attributes (for example, **`aria-expanded="true"`**), developers are incentivized to build accessible components from the start. The same attribute that communicates the component's state to a screen reader also drives its visual styling. For example, **`aria-expanded:rotate-180`** can be used to rotate a chevron icon in an accordion.

This pattern significantly reduces the "glue code" required to synchronize application logic with UI styles, leading to more maintainable and semantic components.

To clarify the distinct use cases for Tailwind's various state management selectors, the following table provides a systematic comparison.

Variant Type	Example Syntax	Trigger Mechanism	Primary Use Case
Pseudo-class	`hover:bg-blue-500`	Direct user interaction (browser-defined).	Styling simple, transient states such as hover, focus, active, or checked states on the element itself.
Group/ Peer	`group-hover: opacity-100`	State of a designated parent (**group**) or sibling (**peer**).	Styling a child or sibling element based on the interaction state of a related element.
Data Attribute	`data-[state=open] :block`	Custom state managed by JavaScript.	Styling complex, custom component states (for example, open/closed, active/inactive) in a declarative way.
ARIA Attribute	`aria-expanded: bg-gray-100`	Accessibility state (often synced with JS state).	Styling components based on their accessibility status, ensuring visual design and accessibility are linked.

Table 4.1: *Comparison of State Management Variants*

Prompting Strategy: Few-Shot and Zero-Shot Prompting

A few-shot prompt can be used to teach the AI a pattern. By providing a simple example of a **data-*** variant, one can then ask it to apply the same logic to a more complex component in a zero-shot fashion. This guides the AI to generalize the pattern correctly.

Example Prompt:

I am building a set of accessible UI components. I want to use data and ARIA attributes to manage their visual states.

Example (Few-Shot): A simple toggle switch uses `data-state` to change its background color.

```
<button role="switch" data-state="checked" class="bg-gray-200 data-[state=checked]:bg-blue-600">...</button>
```

Task (Zero-Shot): Now, using this pattern, generate the HTML for an accessible accordion component with two items.

- The root element of each item should have a **`group`** class.
- The trigger button should have an `aria-expanded` attribute that controls the state.
- When the button's **`aria-expanded`** is 'true', a chevron icon inside the button should rotate 180 degrees. Use the **`group-aria-expanded:*`** variant for this.
- The content panel should be hidden by default and only show when **`aria-expanded`** is 'true'. Use the **`aria-expanded:*`** variant on a sibling or a **`group-aria-expanded:*`** variant to control its visibility.
- Style the active trigger button with a different background and text color.

AI-Generated Output:

```
<!DOCTYPE html>
<html lang="en">
<head>
  <meta charset="UTF-8" />
  <meta name="viewport" content="width=device-width, initial-
scale=1.0"/>
  <title>Accessible Accordion (Tailwind + ARIA)</title>
  <script src="https://cdn.tailwindcss.com"></script>
</head>
<body class="bg-gray-50 text-gray-900 font-sans p-8">
  <h1 class="text-2xl font-bold mb-6">Accessible Accordion</h1>

  <div class="w-full max-w-md mx-auto rounded-lg border border-gray-200
bg-white shadow">
    <div class="border-b border-gray-200">
      <button
        type="button"
        id="acc-btn-1"
        aria-controls="acc-panel-1"
        aria-expanded="true"
        class="accordion-trigger peer group flex w-full items-center
justify-between p-4 text-left font-medium text-gray-700 hover:bg-gray-50
aria-expanded:bg-gray-100 aria-expanded:text-blue-600"
      >
        <span>What is Tailwind CSS?</span>
        <svg
          class="h-5 w-5 shrink-0 transition-transform duration-200
```

```
group-aria-expanded:rotate-180"
          xmlns="http://www.w3.org/2000/svg"
          viewBox="0 0 20 20"
          fill="currentColor"
          aria-hidden="true"
        >
          <path fill-rule="evenodd" d="M5.293 7.293a1 1 0 011.414 0L10
10.586l3.293-3.293a1 1 0 111.414 1.414l-4 4a1 1 0 01-1.414 0l-4-4a1 1 0
010-1.414z" clip-rule="evenodd" />
        </svg>
      </button>
      <div
        id="acc-panel-1"
        role="region"
        aria-labelledby="acc-btn-1"
        class="accordion-panel p-4 hidden peer-aria-expanded:block"
      >
        <p class="text-gray-600">
          Tailwind CSS is a utility-first CSS framework for rapidly
building custom user interfaces.
        </p>
      </div>
    </div>

    <div>
      <button
        type="button"
        id="acc-btn-2"
        aria-controls="acc-panel-2"
        aria-expanded="false"
        class="accordion-trigger peer group flex w-full items-center
justify-between p-4 text-left font-medium text-gray-700 hover:bg-gray-50
aria-expanded:bg-gray-100 aria-expanded:text-blue-600"
      >
        <span>How do ARIA variants work?</span>
        <svg
          class="h-5 w-5 shrink-0 transition-transform duration-200
group-aria-expanded:rotate-180"
          xmlns="http://www.w3.org/2000/svg"
          viewBox="0 0 20 20"
          fill="currentColor"
          aria-hidden="true"
```

```
        >
          <path fill-rule="evenodd" d="M5.293 7.293a1 1 0 011.414 0L10
10.586l3.293-3.293a1 1 0 111.414 1.414l-4 4a1 1 0 01-1.414 0l-4-4a1 1 0
010-1.414z" clip-rule="evenodd" />
        </svg>
      </button>
      <div
        id="acc-panel-2"
        role="region"
        aria-labelledby="acc-btn-2"
        class="accordion-panel p-4 hidden peer-aria-expanded:block"
      >
        <p class="text-gray-600">
          ARIA variants let you style based on ARIA state. Here, the
panel displays when the
          trigger's <code>aria-expanded</code> is <code>true</code>.
        </p>
      </div>
    </div>
  </div>

  <script>
    const singleOpen = true;
    const triggers = Array.from(document.querySelectorAll('.accordion-
trigger'));

    function closeAll() {
      triggers.forEach(btn => {
        btn.setAttribute('aria-expanded', 'false');
      });
    }

    triggers.forEach(btn => {
      btn.addEventListener('click', () => {
        const wasExpanded = btn.getAttribute('aria-expanded') ===
'true';

        // If singleOpen is true, and we're about to open a new one,
close all others first.
        if (singleOpen && !wasExpanded) {
          closeAll();
        }
```

```
        // Toggle the state of the clicked button.
        btn.setAttribute('aria-expanded', String(!wasExpanded));

        // No need to manually toggle panel.hidden.
        // Tailwind's `peer-aria-expanded:block` class handles this
automatically.
      });
    });
  </script>
</body>
</html>
```

The output can be seen in *Figure* 4.5

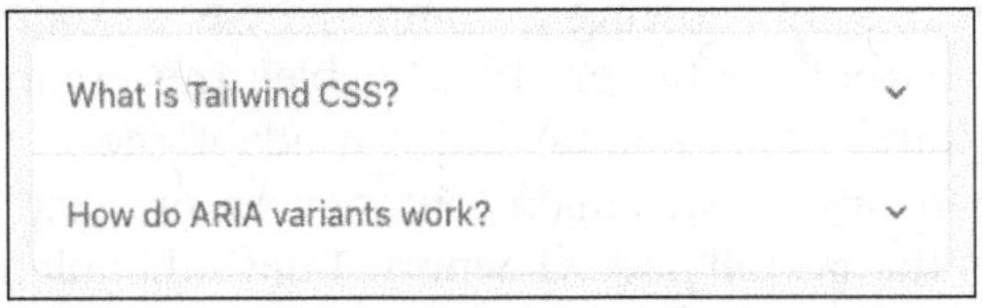

Figure 4.5: *Accordion That Uses ARIA Attributes*

Figure 4.6 shows the achieved behavior of the component. The selected items are highlighted, and the chevron shows the correct state.

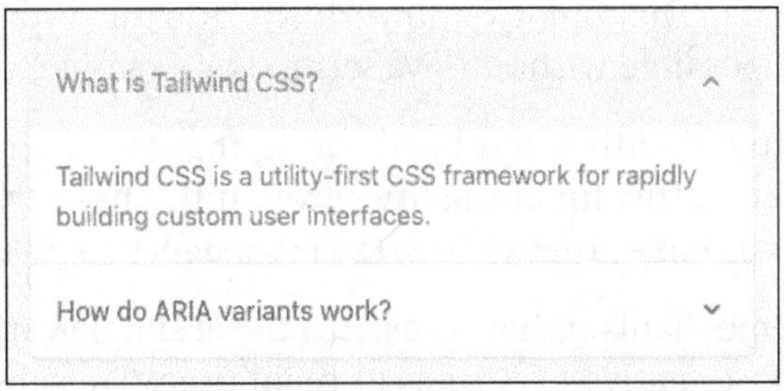

Figure 4.6: *First Item of the Accordion Expanded*

This applies to all sections of the accordion, like *Figure* 4.7 shows.

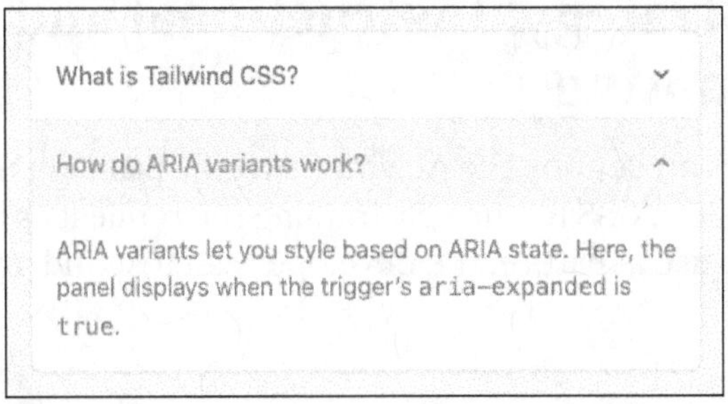

Figure 4.7: *Second Item of the Accordion Expanded*

Harnessing Modern CSS: Container Queries and `:has()`

Tailwind CSS excels at making modern and sometimes complex CSS features accessible through its simple and consistent variant syntax. This approach lowers the barrier to adoption for cutting-edge capabilities, allowing developers to use them ergonomically without needing to memorize new native CSS syntax. Two of the most powerful recent additions to the CSS specification are Container Queries and the **`:has()`** relational pseudo-class, both of which Tailwind supports through its variant system.

- **Container Queries (`@container`):** For years, responsive design was tied exclusively to the viewport size via media queries. Container queries revolutionize this by allowing a component to respond to the dimensions of its direct parent container. This enables the creation of truly modular, "container-aware" components that can adapt their layout to fit wherever they are placed—a sidebar, a main content area, or a grid column—without any knowledge of the overall page viewport. Tailwind implements this by marking a parent with the **`@container`** class and then using **`@*`** variants (for example, **`@lg:flex-row`**) on child elements[3].
- **The `:has()` Selector:** Often referred to as the "parent selector," **`:has()`** allows an element to be styled based on the presence, state, or number of its descendants. This unlocks powerful relational styling patterns that were previously impossible without JavaScript. For example, a form group.
- **`div`** can be styled with a red border if it **`:has()`** an `input` that is **`:invalid`**. Tailwind exposes this functionality through the **`has-*`** variants and arbitrary variants such as **`has-[input:invalid]:border-red-500`**.

The JIT engine is the mechanism that translates these simple variants into the correct, and often more verbose, native CSS rules at build time. This abstraction layer makes modern CSS development faster, more intuitive, and more consistent with the utility-first workflow.

Prompting Strategy: Instructional and Problem-Solving Prompting

This strategy involves presenting the AI with a specific problem that can only be solved efficiently with a modern CSS feature. By framing the request as a problem rather than a direct command to use a feature, the developer can test and guide the AI's problem-solving capabilities.

---

[3] *https://tailkits.com/blog/tailwind-container-queries/*

Example Prompt:

I need to build two distinct UI components that require advanced responsive and relational styling.

1. **Problem 1 (Container Queries):** Create a product card component. This card will be used in various places across a website, sometimes in a narrow sidebar and sometimes in a wide main content grid. The card's layout must adapt to its container, not the viewport. By default (in narrow containers), the card should have a vertical layout (image on top, text content below). When its immediate container is at least **`32rem`** wide, the card should switch to a horizontal layout (image on the left, text on the right). Generate the HTML for this component, using Tailwind's container query features.

2. **Problem 2 (`:has()` Selector):** Create a form field wrapper **`div`**. This wrapper should visually indicate when the **`input`** inside it is invalid. The **`div`** should have a default gray border. If the `div` contains an `input` element that is in an **`:invalid`** state, the **`div`**'s border color should change to red. Generate the HTML for this component, using Tailwind's **`has()`** selector variant.

AI-Generated Output

Solution 1 (Container Queries):

```
<div class="@container/card rounded-lg border border-gray-200 shadow-md">
  <div class="flex flex-col @[32rem]/card:flex-row">
    <img
      src="https://images.unsplash.com/photo-1517336714731-
489689fd1ca8?ixlib=rb-4.0.3&auto=format&fit=crop&w=800&q=80"
      alt="Product Image"
      class="aspect-[4/3] w-full object-cover @[32rem]/card:w-48 @
[32rem]/card:aspect-square"
    />
    <div class="flex flex-col p-4">
      <h3 class="text-lg font-semibold text-gray-800">Ergonomic Keyboard</h3>
      <p class="mt-2 text-sm text-gray-600">
        A high-quality mechanical keyboard designed for comfort and
productivity.
      </p>
      <button class="mt-4 ml-auto rounded-md bg-blue-600 px-4 py-2 text-
sm font-medium text-white">
        Add to Cart
      </button>
    </div>
  </div>
</div>
```

Figure 4.8: *Output of a Layout That Uses Container Queries (Image Provided by Unsplash.com)*

Commentary: The AI correctly identified the need for the `@container` class on the parent. It used an arbitrary container query variant, **`@[32rem]/card:flex-row`**, to apply the horizontal layout when the container's width reaches **`32rem`**. The **`/card`** suffix is a named container query, which scopes the variant to this specific container, preventing conflicts in nested scenarios.

Solution 2 (`:has()` Selector):

```
<div class="group rounded-md border border-gray-300 p-2 has-[input:invalid]:border-red-500 has-[input:invalid]:ring-1 has-[input:invalid]:ring-red-500">
  <label for="email" class="block text-sm font-medium text-gray-700">Email Address</label>
  <input
    type="email"
    id="email"
    name="email"
    required
    class="w-full border-0 p-1 focus:ring-0"
    placeholder="you@example.com"
  />
  <p class="hidden text-sm text-red-600 group-has-[input:invalid]:block">
    Please enter a valid email address.
  </p>
</div>
```

Figure 4.9 shows the rendered component.

Figure 4.9: *Output of a Layout That Uses the Has Selector for an Email Form*

The component validates the input, and displays an error message upon invalid emails.

Figure 4.10: *Output of a Layout That Uses the has Selector for an Email Form*

Commentary: The AI used the arbitrary variant **`has-[input:invalid]:border-red-500`** on the parent **`div`** to change its border color based on the state of its child. It also cleverly used **`group`** and **`group-has-[input:invalid]:block`** to conditionally display an error message, demonstrating a more complex relational styling pattern.

Part III: Building Scalable Architectures

As projects grow in complexity, the direct application of utility classes can lead to challenges in maintainability and readability. Long, repetitive strings of classes in the markup can become difficult to manage. This part of the chapter addresses these challenges by exploring strategies for creating abstractions. The focus shifts from simply *using* utilities to *composing* them into reusable, semantic, and scalable patterns, ensuring that a Tailwind CSS codebase remains clean and maintainable over the long term.

Component Abstraction with `@apply` and Scoped Styles

A frequent point of discussion in the Tailwind community revolves around the verbosity of utility classes. While co-locating styles in the markup is a core tenet of the utility-first philosophy for its directness and prevention of unintended side effects, it can lead to long and seemingly repetitive class lists in complex components.

The **`@apply`** directive is Tailwind's primary tool for addressing this issue. It allows developers to compose multiple utility classes into a single, semantic custom class within a CSS file. For example, a long string of utilities for a button can be abstracted into a **`.btn-primary`** class.

However, **the official Tailwind documentation advises caution against the overuse of `@apply`**, as it can lead developers back toward writing traditional, monolithic CSS and creating abstractions prematurely. A more nuanced and powerful approach, particularly within component-based frameworks such as Vue and Svelte, is to use **`@apply`** within component-scoped style blocks (**`<style scoped>`**). This strategy offers a compelling balance:

- **Clean Templates:** The component's template remains clean and readable, using semantic classes such as <button class="btn-primary">.
- **Encapsulation:** The styling logic, though abstracted from the template, remains co-located within the same single-file component, preserving encapsulation and preventing global scope pollution.
- **Maintainability:** All aspects of the component—template, logic, and styles—are contained in one place, making it easier to understand, modify, and maintain.

This surgical use of `@apply` is not a rejection of the utility-first approach but rather a pragmatic enhancement for component-level architecture. The ideal use case for `@apply` is restricted to highly reusable, globally consistent, and semantically meaningful components, or when overriding styles in third-party libraries where you cannot modify the HTML directly. To clarify when to extract utilities and when to keep them inline, consider the following guidelines:

Usage Scenario	Characteristics	Impact / Example
Ideal Usage	Globally consistent, highly reusable components. Overriding styles in inaccessible third-party HTML. Setting base styles for raw, unstyled content (for example, Markdown).	Maintains a single source of truth for global defaults without cluttering standard UI development. *Example*: Styling a mandatory external widget or setting base link colors.
Over-usage (Anti-pattern)	Creating custom classes just to make HTML look "cleaner." Abstracting single-use or highly specific layouts. Premature abstraction before a true pattern emerges.	Breaks the utility-first workflow, reintroduces naming fatigue, and forces constant context-switching between CSS and HTML files. Example: .hero-section `{ @apply flex flex-col p-8 bg-gray-100; }`

Table 4.2: *Comparison of Usage Scenarios for the @Apply Directive*

Prompting Strategy: Multi-Turn Refinement Prompting

This interactive prompting technique mimics the real-world process of code refactoring. A developer first asks for a functional piece of code and then, in a subsequent turn, requests a specific refinement to improve its structure or readability. This guides the AI through a logical progression from a direct implementation to a more abstract and maintainable one.

Example Prompt

Generate the HTML and CSS for a primary action button. The button should be styled using utility classes from a framework such as Tailwind CSS. It needs a solid blue background, white text, rounded corners, padding, a subtle shadow, and a transition for a slightly darker background on hover."

AI-Generated Output

Turn 1

This initial output is functional but places all the styling logic directly within the HTML, making it verbose and hard to maintain.

HTML

```
<button class="bg-blue-600 text-white font-semibold py-2 px-4 rounded-lg
shadow-md hover:bg-blue-700 focus:outline-none focus:ring-2 focus:ring-
blue-400 focus:ring-opacity-75 transition-colors duration-200">
  Click Me
</button>
```

"This is functionally correct, but the class list in the HTML is too long and difficult to read. Refactor this. Create a dedicated stylesheet and define a single, reusable **`.btn-`** primary class that encapsulates all the styling for the button and its states. Use the **`@ apply`** directive to compose the class from the existing utilities."

Turn 2: Refined

The AI now separates the structure (HTML) from the presentation (CSS), leading to a much cleaner and more reusable solution.

HTML (index.html)

HTML

```
<button class="btn-primary">
  Click Me
</button>
```

CSS (styles.css)

CSS

```
.btn-primary {
  @apply bg-blue-600 text-white font-semibold py-2 px-4 rounded-lg
shadow-md transition-colors duration-200;
}

.btn-primary:hover {
  @apply bg-blue-700;
}
```

```
.btn-primary:focus {
  @apply outline-none ring-2 ring-blue-400 ring-opacity-75;
}
```

We can see the recreated component in action in *Figure 4.11*

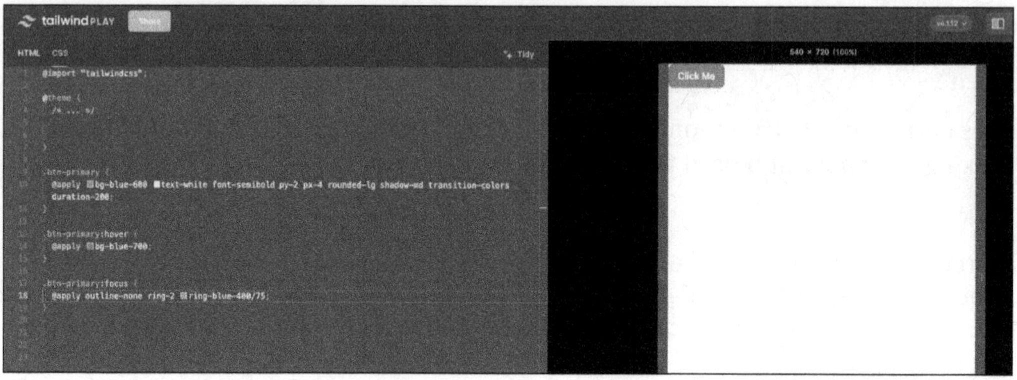

Figure 4.11: *Output of an Action Button That Uses a btn-primary Class*

Commentary: The AI successfully refactored the code. The **HTML is now clean and semantic**, using a single class name that describes the button's purpose rather than its appearance. The styling logic is **encapsulated in a separate CSS file**, using `@apply` to leverage the design tokens of the utility framework. This represents an ideal, maintainable structure for styling reusable elements in a large web application.

Authoring Custom Plugins

For the ultimate level of customization and scalability, Tailwind provides a powerful plugin API. While component abstractions and `@apply` are effective for reusing styles within a single project, plugins allow developers to extend Tailwind's core functionality in a distributable and deeply integrated way. A custom plugin can be shared as an `npm` package, enabling an entire organization to use a consistent, proprietary set of design system tools across all its projects.

The plugin API elevates Tailwind from a CSS framework to a design system *engine*. It provides a formal, programmatic interface for encoding design rules and patterns. Key functions in the plugin API include:

- `addUtilities()`: Registers new, static utility classes.
- `matchUtilities()`: Registers dynamic utilities that can accept values from the user's theme configuration (for example, `text-shadow-md` pulling from `theme.textShadow.md`) and support arbitrary values.
- `addComponents()`: Registers more complex, multi-rule component classes such as `.card` or `.btn`.

- **`addVariant()`**: Registers new custom variants (for example, **`hocus:`** for applying styles on both hover and focus).

A well-authored plugin integrates seamlessly with the user's `tailwind.config.js`, allowing its utilities to be customized via the `theme` object just like core utilities.

Prompting Strategy: Scaffolding and Instructional Prompting

Creating a plugin requires a specific structure and knowledge of the API. A scaffolding prompt provides the AI with a clear blueprint of the desired file structure and the specific API functions to use. This is highly effective for generating boilerplate code that the developer can then refine.

Example Prompt:

You are an expert Tailwind CSS plugin author. I need you to scaffold a custom plugin that adds backdrop-blur utilities to my project.

- Generate the code for a file named **`tailwind-plugins/backdrop-blur.js`**. This file should export a Tailwind plugin created with the **`plugin()`** function from **`tailwind.config /plugin`**.
- Inside the plugin, use the **`matchUtilities`** helper to register dynamic utilities for the **`backdrop-filter: blur(...)`** CSS property. The utilities should be named **`backdrop-blur-*`**.
- The **`matchUtilities`** function should pull its values from a new **`backdropBlur`** key in the user's theme configuration.
- The plugin should also provide a default set of **`backdropBlur`** values (**`sm`**, **`md`**, **`lg`**) in its configuration object.
- Finally, show me how to register this local plugin and extend its theme values in my **`tailwind.config.js`** file.

AI-Generated Output

```
tailwind-plugins/backdrop-blur.js

const plugin = require('tailwindcss/plugin');

module.exports = plugin(
  function ({ matchUtilities, theme }) {
    matchUtilities(
      {
        'backdrop-blur': (value) => ({
          backdropFilter: `blur(${value})`,
        }),
```

```
      },
      { values: theme('backdropBlur') }
    );
  },
  {
    theme: {
      backdropBlur: {
        sm: '2px',
        md: '4px',
        lg: '8px',
      },
    },
  }
);
```

tailwind.config.js

```
/** @type {import('tailwindcss').Config} */
module.exports = {
  content: [
    './src/**/*.{html,js,vue,jsx,ts,tsx}',
  ],
  theme: {
    extend: {
      backdropBlur: {
        xl: '12px',
      },
    },
  },
  plugins: [
    require('./tailwind-plugins/backdrop-blur.js'),
  ],
};
```

Note: *To fully grasp the value of authoring this custom plugin, consider how a developer would have to apply this specific 4px blur effect without the plugin, compared to the workflow with it:*

- **Before the Plugin (Arbitrary Values):** *To achieve a non-standard blur, a developer would have to rely heavily on JIT arbitrary values in the HTML, such as `<div class="backdrop-blur-[4px]">`. While functional, this hardcodes design tokens directly into the markup. If the design system updates the "medium" blur from 4px to 6px, developers must manually hunt down and update every instance of `[4px]` across the entire codebase.*

- **After the Plugin (Systematic Utility):** *The developer simply uses* `<div class="backdrop-blur-md">`*. The plugin dynamically pulls the md value directly from the centralized* `tailwind.config.js` *theme object. If the design token changes in the config, every component using that utility updates automatically.*

The Core Benefit: *Beyond centralizing design tokens, the plugin API deeply integrates the custom utility into Tailwind's engine. By using* `matchUtilities`*, Tailwind automatically generates responsive and state variants for your custom class. This means combinations such as* `hover:backdrop-blur-lg` *or* `md:backdrop-blur-sm` *will work out of the box with zero additional CSS, ensuring your proprietary design elements scale and behave exactly like native Tailwind utilities.*

```
<!DOCTYPE html>
<html lang="en">
<head>
  <meta charset="UTF-8">
  <meta name="viewport" content="width=device-width, initial-scale=1.0">
  <title>Backdrop Blur Plugin Comparison</title>
  <script src="https://cdn.tailwindcss.com"></script>
</head>
<body class="flex items-center justify-center min-h-screen bg-gray-900">
  <div class="grid grid-cols-1 md:grid-cols-2 gap-6 max-w-4xl w-full">

    <!-- Card without backdrop blur -->
    <div class="relative">
      <img
        src="https://images.unsplash.com/photo-1507525428034-b723cf961d3
e?auto=format&fit=crop&w=800&q=80"
        alt="Ocean Background"
        class="w-full h-64 object-cover rounded-xl"
      />
      <div class="absolute inset-0 flex items-center justify-center">
        <div class="bg-white/40 p-6 rounded-xl text-center">
          <h2 class="text-xl font-bold text-gray-800">Without Blur</h2>
          <p class="mt-2 text-gray-700">
            This card only has a semi-transparent background.
          </p>
        </div>
      </div>
    </div>

    <!-- Card with backdrop blur -->
    <div class="relative">
      <img
```

```
    src=”https://images.unsplash.com/photo-1507525428034-b723cf961d3
e?auto=format&fit=crop&w=800&q=80”
    alt=”Ocean Background”
    class=”w-full h-64 object-cover rounded-xl”
   />
   <div class=”absolute inset-0 flex items-center justify-center”>
    <div class=”backdrop-blur-md bg-white/40 p-6 rounded-xl text-
center”>
     <h2 class=”text-xl font-bold text-gray-800”>With Blur</h2>
     <p class=”mt-2 text-gray-700”>
      This card uses <code>backdrop-blur-md</code>.
     </p>
    </div>
   </div>
  </div>

 </div>
</body>
</html>
```

Figure 4.12 shows the output of the component.

Figure 4.12: *Example of Usage of Backdrop-Blur.*
(Source: *https://unsplash.com/photos/seashore-during-golden-hour-KMn4VEeEPR8*)

Part IV: Ecosystem Integration for Interactive UIs

While Tailwind CSS provides an exceptional styling layer, building modern, interactive web applications requires integration with JavaScript. This part of the chapter focuses on practical, real-world strategies for combining Tailwind with popular JavaScript libraries to create complex UI components. The following sections demonstrate how Tailwind's utility-first approach complements, rather than conflicts with, JavaScript-driven logic, state management, and accessibility, leading to the development of robust and maintainable interactive experiences.

Building Accessible Components with Headless UI (`React/Vue`)

Building complex interactive components such as modals, dropdowns, or comboboxes from scratch is notoriously difficult. Managing state, keyboard navigation, focus trapping, and the correct ARIA attributes requires significant effort and expertise to get right. While traditional UI component libraries (such as Bootstrap or Material-UI) solve this by providing pre-built, pre-styled components, they often introduce a new problem: Overriding their opinionated styles can be cumbersome and lead to specificity conflicts.

Headless UI[4], an official library from the Tailwind CSS team, offers an elegant solution to this dilemma. It provides completely unstyled, fully accessible UI components for React and Vue. The "headless" philosophy is to provide all the complex logic, state management, and accessibility hooks, but none of the visual styling. This cleanly separates the responsibility of behavior (handled by Headless UI) from the responsibility of presentation (handled by Tailwind CSS).

This separation allows developers to apply Tailwind utility classes directly to the Headless UI components without any friction, giving them complete creative control over the appearance while benefiting from the pre-built, accessible foundation. To further streamline this integration, the **`@headlessui/tailwindcss`** plugin provides **`ui-*`** variants (for example, **`ui-open`**, **`ui-active`**) that allow for styling the internal states of Headless UI components with the same variant syntax as native Tailwind states.

Prompting Strategy: Persona-Based and Few-Shot Prompting

Adopting a persona focused on accessibility encourages the AI to prioritize best practices. Combining this with a few-shot example that demonstrates the use of **`ui-*`** variants provides a clear pattern for the AI to follow when generating the more complex component.

Example Prompt:

Act as a senior front-end developer with a strong focus on accessibility and best practices. I am building a modal dialog component for a React application using Headless UI and Tailwind CSS.

Pattern to Follow (Few-Shot): I style Headless UI's `Menu.Item` using the `ui-active` variant like this:

```
<Menu.Item> <a className=”block px-4 py-2 text-sm text-gray-700 ui-active:bg-gray-100 ui-active:text-gray-900”> Your Profile </a> </Menu.Item>
```

[4] *https://headlessui.com/*

Task: Now, generate a complete, copy-pasteable React component for an accessible modal dialog.

- Use the **`Dialog`** and **`Dialog.Panel`** components from **`@headlessui/react`**.
- The modal should be triggered by a button and its state managed with **`useState`**.
- Include a **`Dialog.Title`** for accessibility.
- Style the modal overlay (backdrop) and the panel using Tailwind CSS classes.
- Use the **`Transition`** component from Headless UI to animate the modal's entrance and exit. Style the transitions using the **`data-*`** attributes that **`Transition`** provides (for example, **`data-[enter]:...`**, **`data-[leave]:...`**).
- Ensure that the modal is fully styled, including the panel's background, shadow, and rounded corners, and includes 'Confirm' and 'Cancel' buttons.

```
<!DOCTYPE html>
<html lang="en">
<head>
  <meta charset="UTF-8" />
  <meta name="viewport" content="width=device-width, initial-scale=1.0"
/>
  <title>Accessible Modal with React & Tailwind CSS</title>
  <script src="https://cdn.tailwindcss.com"></script>
  <script src="https://unpkg.com/@babel/standalone/babel.min.js"></script>
</head>
<body class="bg-gray-900">
  <div id="root"></div>

  <script type="importmap">
  {
    "imports": {
      "react": "https://esm.sh/react@18.3.1",
      "react-dom/client": "https://esm.sh/react-dom@18.3.1/client",
      "@headlessui/react": "https://esm.sh/@headlessui/react@2.0.0"
    }
  }
  </script>

  <script type="text/babel" data-type="module">
    import React, { Fragment, useState } from 'react';
    import ReactDOM from 'react-dom/client';
    import { Dialog, DialogPanel, DialogTitle, Transition,
TransitionChild } from '@headlessui/react';
```

```
function App() {
  let [isOpen, setIsOpen] = useState(false);

  function closeModal() {
    setIsOpen(false);
  }

  function openModal() {
    setIsOpen(true);
  }

  return (
    <div className="text-white min-h-screen flex items-center
justify-center font-sans">
      <div className="flex items-center justify-center">
        <button
          type="button"
          onClick={openModal}
          className="rounded-lg bg-blue-600 px-5 py-3 text-sm
font-medium text-white hover:bg-blue-700 focus:outline-none focus-
visible:ring-2 focus-visible:ring-white focus-visible:ring-opacity-75
transition-colors"
        >
          Open Dialog
        </button>
      </div>

      {/* Headless UI Transition component for managing enter/leave
animations */}
      <Transition appear show={isOpen} as={Fragment}>
        <Dialog as="div" className="relative z-10"
onClose={closeModal}>
          {/* The backdrop overlay */}
          <TransitionChild
            as={Fragment}
            enter="ease-out duration-300"
            enterFrom="opacity-0"
            enterTo="opacity-100"
            leave="ease-in duration-200"
            leaveFrom="opacity-100"
            leaveTo="opacity-0"
          >
            <div className="fixed inset-0 bg-black bg-opacity-50" />
          </TransitionChild>
```

```
            <div className="fixed inset-0 overflow-y-auto">
              <div className="flex min-h-full items-center justify-
center p-4 text-center">
                {/* The modal panel */}
                <TransitionChild
                  as={Fragment}
                  enter="ease-out duration-300"
                  enterFrom="opacity-0 scale-95"
                  enterTo="opacity-100 scale-100"
                  leave="ease-in duration-200"
                  leaveFrom="opacity-100 scale-100"
                  leaveTo="opacity-0 scale-95"
                >
                  <DialogPanel className="w-full max-w-md transform
overflow-hidden rounded-2xl bg-white p-6 text-left align-middle shadow-xl
transition-all">
                    <DialogTitle as="h3" className="text-lg font-
medium leading-6 text-gray-900">
                      Payment Successful
                    </DialogTitle>
                    <div className="mt-2">
                      <p className="text-sm text-gray-500">
                        Your payment has been successfully submitted.
We've sent you an email with all of the details of your order.
                      </p>
                    </div>

                    <div className="mt-5 flex justify-end gap-3">
                      <button
                        type="button"
                        className="inline-flex justify-center rounded-
md border border-transparent bg-gray-100 px-4 py-2 text-sm font-medium
text-gray-800 hover:bg-gray-200 focus:outline-none focus-visible:ring-2
focus-visible:ring-gray-500 focus-visible:ring-offset-2 transition-colors"
                        onClick={closeModal}
                      >
                        Cancel
                      </button>
                      <button
                        type="button"
                        className="inline-flex justify-center rounded-
md border border-transparent bg-blue-100 px-4 py-2 text-sm font-medium
text-blue-900 hover:bg-blue-200 focus:outline-none focus-visible:ring-2
```

```
focus-visible:ring-blue-500 focus-visible:ring-offset-2 transition-
colors"
                             onClick={closeModal}
                           >
                             Confirm
                           </button>
                         </div>
                       </DialogPanel>
                     </TransitionChild>
                   </div>
                 </div>
               </Dialog>
             </Transition>
           </div>
         );
       }

       // Render the App component into the #root div
       const container = document.getElementById('root');
       const root = ReactDOM.createRoot(container);
       root.render(<App />);
     </script>

</body>
</html>
```

The created component renders the dialog button correctly, as in *Figure* 4.13.

Figure 4.13: *Button Created with Headless UI*

Figure 4.14 shows that Upon clicking **`Open Dialog`**, the dialog appears.

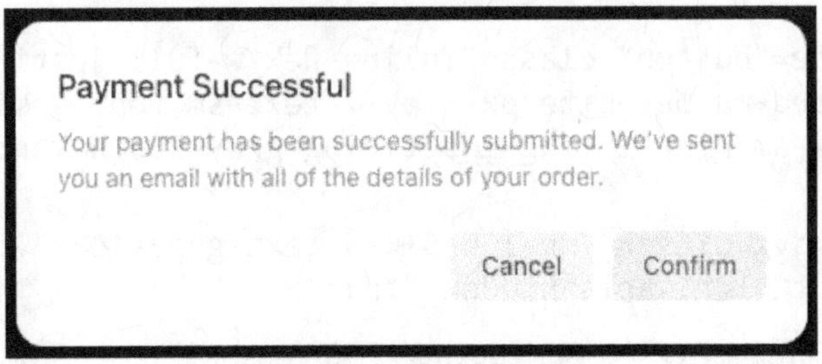

Figure 4.14: *Example of Our Dialog Component Built with React.js and TailwindCSS*

Lightweight Interactivity with `Alpine.js`

While frameworks such as React and Vue are powerful, they introduce a level of complexity, including build tools, virtual DOMs, and component lifecycle management, that is often unnecessary for content-focused websites, marketing pages, or applications built with server-side frameworks such as Laravel or Ruby on Rails.

For these scenarios, a "sprinkle of interactivity" is often all that is needed. Alpine.js is a rugged, minimal JavaScript framework designed for this exact purpose. It allows developers to add client-side interactivity directly within their HTML markup, using a declarative syntax that is heavily inspired by **`Vue.js`**. **`Alpine.js`** pairs exceptionally well with Tailwind CSS because both frameworks operate primarily within HTML, allowing for the creation of fully encapsulated, self-contained interactive components without separate JavaScript or CSS files.

The core of Alpine.js is the **`x-data`** directive, which defines a component's scope and its reactive state. Other directives, such as **`x-show`**, **`x-on:click`**, and **`x-bind,`** are then used to manipulate and react to this state. Tailwind's transition utilities integrate seamlessly with Alpine's **`x-transition`** directive, making it trivial to add sophisticated animations to components as they appear and disappear.

This combination provides a modern, powerful successor to the jQuery-era approach, enabling rich user interfaces while preserving the simplicity and performance of server-rendered HTML[5,6].

Prompting Strategy: Contextual and Fill-in-the-Blank Prompting

This strategy involves providing the AI with a static, styled HTML structure and asking it to augment that structure with the necessary interactivity. This is a highly effective way to quickly add behavior to the existing markup.

Example Prompt:

I have a static dropdown menu component styled with Tailwind CSS. I need to make it interactive using Alpine.js.

Here is the static HTML:

```
<div class=”relative inline-block text-left”>
  <div>
    <button type="button" class="inline-flex w-full justify-center
gap-x-1.5 rounded-md bg-white px-3 py-2 text-sm font-semibold text-
gray-900 shadow-sm ring-1 ring-inset ring-gray-300 hover:bg-gray-50">
      Options
      >       <svg class="-mr-1 h-5 w-5 text-gray-400" viewBox="0 0 20
20" fill="currentColor" aria-hidden="true">
```

[5] *https://dberri.com/lets-build-a-tab-navigation-with-alpine-js/*
[6] *https://www.jesper.dev/2020/01/27/creating-a-dropdown-with-alpinejs*

```
        <path fill-rule="evenodd" d="M5.293 7.293a1 1 0 011.414 0L10
10.586l3.293-3.293a1 1 0 111.414 1.414l-4 4a1 1 0 01-1.414 0l-4-4a1 1 0
010-1.414z" clip-rule="evenodd" />
      </svg>
    </button>
  </div>
  <div class="absolute right-0 z-10 mt-2 w-56 origin-top-right rounded-
md bg-white shadow-lg ring-1 ring-black ring-opacity-5 focus:outline-
none">
    <div class="py-1">
      <a href="#" class="text-gray-700 block px-4 py-2 text-sm">Account
settings</a>
      <a href="#" class="text-gray-700 block px-4 py-2 text-
sm">Support</a>
      <a href="#" class="text-gray-700 block px-4 py-2 text-
sm">License</a>
    </div>
  </div>
</div>
```

Task: Modify this HTML to add the necessary **`Alpine.js`** functionality.

- Add an **`x-data`** directive to manage an **`isOpen`** state, initialized to **`false`**.
- Use **`x-on:click`** on the button to toggle the **`isOpen`** state.
- Use **`x-show`** to conditionally display the dropdown menu panel based on the **`isOpen`** state.
- Add the **`x-transition`** directive to the panel to apply a smooth fade and scale animation. Use Tailwind's transition classes for this.
- Add functionality to close the dropdown when the user clicks outside of it (**`@click.outside`**) or presses the Escape key (**`@keydown.escape.window`**)."

AI-Generated Output:

HTML

```
<!DOCTYPE html>
<html lang="en">

<head>
  <meta charset="UTF-8">
  <meta name="viewport" content="width=device-width, initial-scale=1.0">
  <title>Alpine.js Dropdown</title>

  <!-- Tailwind CSS for styling -->
  <script src="https://cdn.tailwindcss.com"></script>
```

```
  <!-- Alpine.js -->
  <script src="https://cdn.jsdelivr.net/npm/alpinejs@3.14.8/dist/cdn.
min.js"></script>

  <style>
    /* This is a best practice for Alpine.js.
      It prevents elements with x-cloak from being shown until Alpine
has
      finished initializing, avoiding any flickering on page load.
    */
    [x-cloak] {
      display: none !important;
    }
  </style>
</head>

<body class="bg-gray-100 flex items-center justify-center min-h-screen
font-sans">

  <div class="w-72 p-8 bg-white rounded-lg shadow-md">
    <!--
      Refactored Alpine.js Dropdown Component
      - The main container for the dropdown state and logic.
      - @keydown.escape.window closes the dropdown if the Escape key is
pressed anywhere.
    -->
    <div x-data="{ isOpen: false }" @keydown.escape.window="isOpen =
false" class="relative inline-block text-left">

      <!-- Dropdown Button -->
      <div>
        <button
          @click="isOpen = !isOpen"
          type="button"
          class="inline-flex w-full justify-center gap-x-1.5 rounded-md
bg-white px-3 py-2 text-sm font-semibold text-gray-900 shadow-sm ring-1
ring-inset ring-gray-300 hover:bg-gray-50"
          id="menu-button"
          aria-haspopup="true"
          :aria-expanded="isOpen" <!-- REFACTOR: aria-expanded is now
dynamic and reflects the component's state for better accessibility. -->
        >
          Options
          <svg
            :class="{'rotate-180': isOpen}"
```

```
            class="-mr-1 h-5 w-5 text-gray-400 transition-transform
duration-200"
            viewBox="0 0 20 20"
            fill="currentColor"
            aria-hidden="true"
          >
            <path fill-rule="evenodd"
              d="M5.293 7.293a1 1 0 011.414 0L10 10.586l3.293-3.293a1 1
0 111.414 1.414l-4 4a1 1 0 01-1.414 0l-4-4a1 1 0 010-1.414z"
              clip-rule="evenodd" />
          </svg>
        </button>
      </div>

      <!--
        Dropdown Panel
        - x-show toggles the visibility of this element based on the
`isOpen` state.
        - @click.outside closes the dropdown when a click occurs outside
of this component.
        - x-cloak is added to prevent a "flash" of content on page load.
        - The inline 'style="display: none;"' has been removed as it's
redundant when using x-show.
      -->
      <div
        x-show="isOpen"
        @click.outside="isOpen = false"
        x-cloak
        x-transition:enter="transition ease-out duration-100"
        x-transition:enter-start="transform opacity-0 scale-95"
        x-transition:enter-end="transform opacity-100 scale-100"
        x-transition:leave="transition ease-in duration-75"
        x-transition:leave-start="transform opacity-100 scale-100"
        x-transition:leave-end="transform opacity-0 scale-95"
        class="absolute right-0 z-10 mt-2 w-56 origin-top-right rounded-
md bg-white shadow-lg ring-1 ring-black ring-opacity-5 focus:outline-
none"
        role="menu"
        aria-orientation="vertical"
        aria-labelledby="menu-button"
        tabindex="-1"
      >
        <div class="py-1" role="none">
```

```
          <a href="#" class="text-gray-700 block px-4 py-2 text-
sm hover:bg-gray-100" role="menuitem" tabindex="-1" id="menu-item-
0">Account settings</a>
          <a href="#" class="text-gray-700 block px-4 py-2 text-
sm hover:bg-gray-100" role="menuitem" tabindex="-1" id="menu-item-
1">Support</a>
          <a href="#" class="text-gray-700 block px-4 py-2 text-
sm hover:bg-gray-100" role="menuitem" tabindex="-1" id="menu-item-
2">License</a>
        </div>
      </div>
    </div>
  </div>

</body>
</html>
```

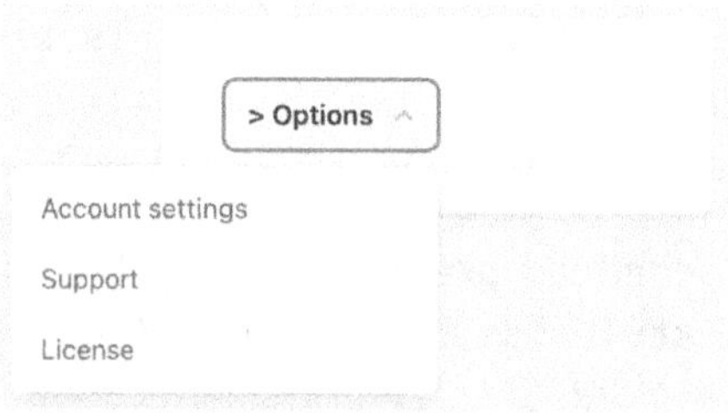

Figure 4.15: *Output of the Dropdown Menu Implemented with Alpine.js and TailwindCSS*

Part V: Production Readiness

The final stage of any development workflow is preparing the application for a production environment. For Tailwind CSS, this involves not only optimizing the final CSS bundle for performance but also ensuring that the way utility classes are used is compatible with Tailwind's build-time compilation process. This part of the chapter addresses these critical final steps, focusing on advanced optimization techniques and the crucial concept of "dynamic class safety" to prevent common and often perplexing production-only bugs.

Production Optimization and Dynamic Class Safety

Tailwind's performance is one of its defining features. By generating only the CSS that is actually used in a project, it produces exceptionally small bundles, often less than 10kB, even for large applications. This is achieved through a process of static analysis, where Tailwind scans all specified source files for class names at build time.

For the smallest possible production build, two main steps are crucial:

- **Minification:** The generated CSS should be minified to remove all unnecessary characters without changing its functionality. This is often handled automatically by frameworks, but can be done manually with tools such as `cssnano` or by using the `--minify` flag with the Tailwind CLI.
- **Compression:** The server should be configured to compress assets using methods such as Gzip or, preferably, Brotli, which can further reduce the file size delivered to the client.

However, the most critical aspect of production readiness with Tailwind is understanding the implications of its build-time static analysis. Because Tailwind scans for class names as complete, unbroken strings, it cannot detect classes that are dynamically constructed at runtime using string concatenation or interpolation.

A class name constructed such as **`const myClass = ‘bg-’ + color + ‘-500’`** will not be found by the build process. The scanner sees the parts (**`‘bg-’`**, **`‘-500’`**) but not the complete class name (for example, **`‘bg-blue-500’`**). As a result, the necessary CSS for **`‘bg-blue-500’`** is never generated, and the style will appear to be “broken” only in the production build, where unused styles have been purged. This is one of the most common and frustrating issues for developers new to Tailwind’s production workflow.

The correct and safe approach is to ensure that every potential class name exists in its entirety as a full string in the source files. This is typically achieved by mapping dynamic props or state to complete class strings.

Prompting Strategy: Explanatory and Corrective Prompting

This strategy involves providing the AI with a piece of “broken” or unsafe code and asking it not only to fix it but also to explain the underlying reason for the problem. This is an excellent way to use AI for learning and debugging, as it reveals the “why” behind the fix.

Example Prompt:

“I have a React component for a notification banner. It works perfectly in my local development environment, but when I deploy it to production, the background and text colors are missing.

Here is the unsafe code:

```
    JavaScript

function Notification({ type, message }) {
  // ‹type› can be ‹success›, ‹warning›, or ‹error›
  const bgColor = `bg-${type}-100`;
  const textColor = `text-${type}-800`;
  const borderColor = `border-${type}-400`;

  return (
```

```
    <div className={`p-4 border-l-4 ${bgColor} ${textColor}
${borderColor}`}>
      {message}
    </div>
  );
}
```

Task:

- Explain in detail why this pattern fails in a production Tailwind CSS build. Describe the role of static analysis and the purging process.
- Correct the code to follow best practices for dynamic classes, ensuring it will work correctly in production. Use a mapping object to associate the **`type`** prop with full, static class strings."

AI-Generated Output:

Explanation of the Problem:

"This pattern fails in production due to how Tailwind CSS optimizes its output. Here is a breakdown of the process:

- **Static Analysis:** During the production build, Tailwind's JIT engine scans your source files (such as **`.js`**, **`.jsx`**, **`.vue`**) for class names. It does this using regular expressions to find strings that look like Tailwind classes. It does not execute your JavaScript code or know the value of variables such as **`type`**.
- **Purging:** The engine builds a list of all the complete class names it finds. It then generates CSS *only* for those specific classes. Any potential class that is not found as a full, unbroken string in your files is considered "unused" and is purged from the final CSS bundle to keep it as small as possible.
- **The Failure Point:** In your code, you are dynamically creating class names with string concatenation, such as **`` `bg-${type}-100` ``**. The Tailwind scanner does not see **`'bg-success-100'`** or **`'bg-warning-100'`**. It only sees the fragments **`'bg-'`**, **`'-100'`**, and the variable **`type`**. Since no complete class names are found, the CSS for them is never generated. While this works in development (where Tailwind might generate all possible classes for convenience), these styles are absent from the optimized production file, causing the component to appear unstyled."

Corrected Code:

JavaScript

```
import clsx from 'clsx'; // Optional but recommended for cleaner class
joining

// Best practice: Map dynamic props to full, static class strings.
const typeVariants = {
```

```
  success: ‹bg-green-100 text-green-800 border-green-400›,
  warning: ‹bg-yellow-100 text-yellow-800 border-yellow-400›,
  error: ‹bg-red-100 text-red-800 border-red-400›,
};
function Notification({ type = 'success', message }) {
  // The full class strings are now present in the file and will be
detected by Tailwind.
  const variantClasses = typeVariants[type];
  return (
    <div className={clsx(‹p-4 border-l-4›, variantClasses)}>
      {message}
    </div>
  );
}
```

Commentary: The AI correctly identifies the root cause and provides a safe, statically analyzable solution. By using a mapping object (**`typeVariants`**), all possible class name strings (**`'bg-green-100'`**, **`'text-green-800'`**, and so on) are present in the source file. The Tailwind scanner can now find these strings, ensuring the necessary CSS is included in the final production build. The use of the **`clsx`** utility is also a best practice for conditionally combining class strings cleanly.

Conclusion

This chapter has shown that advanced Tailwind CSS is a comprehensive engine for building scalable and maintainable design systems. Powered by the Just-in-Time compiler, it makes modern CSS features such as container queries and the **`:has()`** selector accessible, while enabling declarative, state-based styling with **`data-*`** and **`aria-*`** attributes. For large-scale projects, abstraction strategies such as scoped **`@apply`** and custom plugins provide the necessary structure, and seamless integration with libraries such as Headless UI and Alpine.js connects styling with logic. A list of the prompting strategies used during this chapter is available in *Table* 4.3.

Prompting Strategy	Description and How it Works	Primary Use Case in Chapter
Role-Playing and Contextual	Instruct the AI to adopt a specific expert persona (for example, "Design Systems Architect") and provide rich context to generate structured, comprehensive results.	Generating a robust theming system using the `@theme` directive and CSS variables.
Chain-of-Thought and Constraint-Based	Provide highly specific, strict design constraints and ask the AI to explain its step-by-step reasoning for the solution it generates.	Forcing the use of arbitrary values to leverage the JIT engine for pixel-perfect designs.

Prompting Strategy	Description and How it Works	Primary Use Case in Chapter
Few-Shot and Zero-Shot	Teach the AI a pattern by providing a simple example (few-shot), then immediately ask it to apply that same logic to a new, more complex component (zero-shot).	Creating dynamic state styling using custom `data-*` and `aria-*` accessibility attributes.
Instructional and Problem-Solving	Frame the request as a specific UI problem to solve rather than a direct command to use a specific feature, guiding the AI's problem-solving capabilities.	Harnessing modern CSS features such as Container Queries and the `:has()` relational selector.
Multi-Turn Refinement	Mimic a code refactoring session: first ask for a functional piece of code, then follow up in a second turn to request structural or readability improvements.	Abstracting long utility lists into reusable component classes using `@apply`.
Scaffolding and Instructional	Provide a clear blueprint of the desired file structure and specific API functions to generate boilerplate code that can be refined later.	Authoring custom Tailwind plugins and integrating them into `tailwind.config.js`.
Persona-Based and Few-Shot	Adopt an accessibility-focused persona and pair it with a code example to ensure the AI prioritizes best practices while integrating complex UI logic.	Building accessible, interactive components (such as modals) using Headless UI for `React/Vue`.
Contextual and Fill-in-the-Blank	Provide the AI with a fully styled, static HTML structure and ask it to augment the existing markup with necessary interactive directives.	Adding lightweight client-side interactivity using `Alpine.js`.
Explanatory and Corrective	Provide the AI with "broken" or unsafe code and instruct it to not only fix the code but also explain the underlying reason why it failed.	Debugging dynamic class safety and explaining Tailwind's build-time static analysis/purging process for production.

***Table 4.3**: Overview of Prompting Strategies Used in This Chapter*

Mastering these principles is the foundation for effective AI prompting. A deep understanding of Tailwind's architecture allows developers to engage in a structured dialogue with AI, elevating it from a code completion tool to a true collaborator in creating sophisticated user interfaces.

In the next chapter, we build directly on these foundations by shifting from Tailwind's advanced capabilities to the art of **prompting AI effectively for Tailwind code generation**. You will learn how to structure prompts, supply context, and guide models such as Copilot, GPT, Cursor AI, and Claude Code to reliably produce high-quality, production-ready UI components. We will explore different prompting patterns, dissect real examples, and demonstrate how a strong understanding of Tailwind's architecture enables AI to produce cleaner, more scalable code. This chapter turns theory into practice, showing you how to collaborate with AI as a true development partner.

Multiple Choice Questions

1. Regarding advanced theming, what is the primary advantage of using the `@theme` directive in your CSS file?
   a. It allows for faster build times by pre-compiling all possible theme values.
   b. It is the only method for adding third-party plugins to a project.
   c. It moves theme definition into CSS, enabling dynamic, runtime theming with CSS variables that can be changed with selectors such as `[data-theme="dark"]`.
   d. It automatically generates JavaScript helper functions for accessing theme values.
2. The Just-in-Time (JIT) engine is a core part of modern Tailwind CSS. Which of the following features does it enable, allowing for pixel-perfect designs with non-standard values?
   a. The `@apply` directive for creating component classes.
   b. Automatic support for all Google Fonts without configuration.
   c. The use of arbitrary values with square bracket notation (for example, `w-[615px]`).
   d. Automatic conversion of CSS to inline styles for email templates.
3. When building an accessible component such as a dropdown menu, which variant is most appropriate for styling its open/closed state to ensure that the visual design is linked to its accessibility status?
   a. The `hover: variant`.
   b. The `aria-expanded:* variant`.
   c. The `first-child: variant`.
   d. The `group-focus: variant`.
4. How does Tailwind CSS allow a component to change its layout based on the width of its immediate parent container, rather than the entire browser viewport?
   a. By using standard responsive variants such as `lg:flex-row`.
   b. By writing custom JavaScript to measure the parent element's width.

   c. By marking the parent with the `@container` class and using `@* variants` (for example, `@md:flex-row`) on child elements.
   d. By using the `:has()` selector to detect the parent's width.

5. The chapter discusses abstracting long utility strings into reusable classes. What is the recommended, balanced approach for using `@apply` within a framework such as Vue?
   a. Creating a single, global stylesheet with all `@apply` rules for the entire application.
   b. Using `@apply` within a component's `<style scoped>` block to encapsulate styles while keeping the template clean and readable.
   c. Avoiding `@apply` entirely, as it is considered a legacy feature.
   d. Using `@apply` to create new, dynamic utility classes inside the `tailwind.config.js` file.

6. When authoring a custom Tailwind plugin to add new, dynamic utilities that can accept values from the theme (for example, `text-shadow-md` or `text-shadow-lg`), which plugin API function is the most appropriate choice?
   a. `addUtilities()`
   b. `addComponents()`
   c. `addBase()`
   d. `matchUtilities()`

7. What is the core philosophy of the Headless UI library, as described in the chapter?
   a. It provides fully styled, production-ready components that match Tailwind's default design system.
   b. It is a tool for converting Figma designs directly into styled React and Vue components.
   c. It provides completely unstyled, fully accessible component logic, cleanly separating a component's behavior from its visual presentation.
   d. It is a CSS-only library that extends Tailwind with more advanced utility classes.

8. When adding lightweight interactivity to a static HTML component with `Alpine.js`, which directive is used to initialize the component's scope and its reactive state?
   a. `x-show`
   b. `x-data`

   c. `x-on:click`
   d. `x-transition`

9. Why does a dynamically constructed class name, such as `` `text-${color}-500` ``, often fail in a production build of a Tailwind CSS project?
   a. Because template literals are not supported in production environments.
   b. Because the `--minify` flag removes all dynamically generated classes.
   c. Because the JIT engine's static analysis cannot find the complete, unbroken class string at build time, the class is purged as "unused."
   d. Because production builds do not support colors outside of the default palette.

10. What is the recommended "safe" pattern for applying conditional styles in a React component where the style depends on a prop (for example, `type="success"`) to ensure it works in production?
    a. Constructing the class name using string concatenation: `className={'bg-' + type + '-100'}`.
    b. Using inline styles with CSS variables instead of Tailwind classes.
    c. Creating a mapping object that links the prop value to full, static class strings that can be detected at build time.
    d. Using the `@apply` directive directly inside the JSX template

Answers

1. c
2. c
3. b
4. c
5. b
6. d
7. c
8. b
9. c
10. c

CHAPTER 5
Building Dynamic Web Components with Advanced Tailwind CSS

Introduction

The previous chapter explored the advanced architecture and capabilities of Tailwind CSS. Now, we transition from theory to practice. This chapter is dedicated to building the essential, interactive components that form the backbone of modern web applications. We will construct common UI patterns such as dropdowns, tabs, modals, and more, by combining Tailwind's styling prowess with the power of JavaScript.

Our goal is to solidify a component-first mindset: The practice of breaking down complex interfaces into small, reusable, and encapsulated pieces. To achieve this, we will explore two distinct but complementary paths for adding interactivity, each suited to different project needs.

Path 1: Lightweight Interactivity with `Alpine.js`. Often described as the "Tailwind for JavaScript," **`Alpine.js`** allows us to add declarative, reactive behavior directly within our HTML, making it the perfect companion for server-rendered applications or projects where a full Single-Page Application (SPA) framework would be overkill. We will spend the first half of this chapter mastering **`Alpine.js`**, as it will be our primary tool for the hands-on projects in the chapters that follow.

Path 2: Scalable Applications with `React.js`. For complex, state-heavy SPAs, React provides a robust component-based architecture. In the second half of this chapter, we will focus not on teaching React itself, but on the essential patterns for using Tailwind CSS effectively within a React ecosystem. We will cover best practices for managing dynamic classes, creating component variants, and integrating with accessibility-focused libraries.

By the end of this chapter, you will be equipped with the targeted prompt engineering strategies needed to transform an AI assistant from a simple code generator into an expert collaborator, helping you build accessible, maintainable, and production-ready components with confidence.

Structure

In this chapter, we will discuss the following topics:

- Part I: The "Tailwind for JavaScript" – Mastering Alpine.js
    - An Introduction to Alpine.js
    - Building an Accessible Dropdown Menu
    - Building an Accessible Tabs Component
    - Building an Accessible Modal
    - Mastering Forms with @tailwindcss/forms and Alpine.js
- Part II: Scaling up with React and Advanced Patterns
    - The "Do Not Concatenate" Rule: Safe Dynamic Classes
    - Bulletproof Conditional Classes with clsx and tailwind-merge
    - Component Variants with CVA
    - The Best of Both Worlds: Headless UI for React

Part I: The "Tailwind for JavaScript" – Mastering `Alpine.js`

The synergy between Tailwind CSS and **`Alpine.js`** (https://alpinejs.dev/) stems from a shared philosophy: Both frameworks are designed to live primarily within your HTML, allowing you to build fully functional and styled components in a single, co-located block of code. This declarative approach simplifies development, especially for projects that do not require a complex build step or a virtual DOM.

An Introduction to `Alpine.js`

`Alpine.js` is a rugged, minimal JavaScript framework that provides the reactive and declarative nature of larger frameworks such as Vue or React at a fraction of the cost. It is not intended for building SPAs but excels at "sprinkling" interactivity onto a page. This makes it an ideal choice for server-rendered applications (for example, using Laravel, Rails, and Django) or static sites where you need components such as dropdowns, modals, and tabs without pulling in a heavy framework.

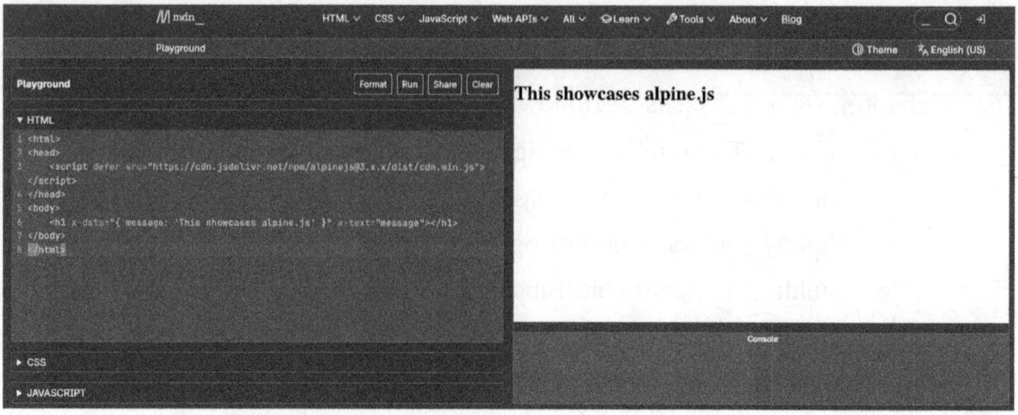

Figure 5.1: *A Simple Alpine.js Showcase Using Mdn Play*

At its core, Alpine works through a set of special attributes (called directives) that you add to your HTML. These directives are the bridge between your markup and your JavaScript logic.

Directive	Shorthand	Description
`x-data`		Declares a new component scope and its reactive data (state). This is the starting point for any Alpine component.
`x-on:[event]`	`@[event]`	Listens for a browser event (such as click or keydown) and runs a JavaScript expression when it occurs.
`x-show`		Toggles the visibility of an element (using display: none;) based on a Boolean expression.
`x-bind:[attribute]`	`:[attribute]`	Dynamically sets the value of an HTML attribute. Most commonly used for :class to apply styles conditionally.
`x-model`		Creates a two-way data binding between an input element's value and an x-data property.
`x-text`		Sets the textContent of an element to the value of a JavaScript expression.
`x-transition`		Applies CSS transitions when an element is shown or hidden with `x-show`.
`x-if`		Conditionally adds or removes an element from the DOM entirely. Must be used on a `<template>` tag.
`x-for`		Creates new DOM elements by iterating over an array. Must be used on a `<template>` tag.

Table 5.1: *Alpine.js Main Directives*

To better understand how these directives interact, consider the following HTML structure. This block demonstrates state initialization, event listening, visibility toggling, and dynamic attribute binding all in one place:

```
<!DOCTYPE html>
<html lang="en">

<head>
  <meta charset="UTF-8" />
  <meta name="viewport" content="width=device-width, initial-scale=1.0" />
  <title>Alpine.js Directives Showcase</title>

  <script src="https://cdn.jsdelivr.net/npm/@tailwindcss/browser@4"></
script>

  <script defer src="https://cdn.jsdelivr.net/npm/alpinejs@3.x.x/dist/
cdn.min.js"></script>
</head>

<body class="p-10 bg-gray-100">

  <div x-data="{ isSelected: false, statusText: 'Click to Activate' }"
class="text-center">

    <button @click="isSelected = !isSelected; statusText = isSelected ?
'Active' : 'Inactive'"
      :class="isSelected ? 'bg-green-600' : 'bg-blue-600'"
      class="rounded-lg px-6 py-2 font-medium text-white shadow-md
transition-all hover:opacity-90">
      <span x-text="statusText"></span>
    </button>

    <p x-show="isSelected" class="mt-4 text-green-700 font-semibold"
style="display: none;">
      The logic is working!
    </p>

  </div>
</body>

</html>
```

Prompting Strategy: Instructional Prompting

To begin, we can ask our AI assistant to generate a simple, annotated example that demonstrates the fundamental relationship between these core directives[1,2]. We will be use for many examples in this chapter Mozilla's Javascript playground (https://developer.mozilla.org/en-US/play), where we will be able to test the features.

---

[1] *https://hexshift.medium.com/designing-an-adaptive-settings-panel-with-tailwind-css-and-alpine-js-ccc3158f5fc0*

[2] *https://cruip.com/using-tailwind-css-and-alpine-js-to-create-animated-and-accessible-tabs/*

Example Prompt

"As a senior developer explaining **`Alpine.js`** to a junior, generate a simple 'Show/Hide' component.

1. Use the **`x-data`** directive to initialize a state variable **`isOpen`** to false.
2. Create a button that uses the **`@click`** directive to toggle the **`isOpen`** state.
3. Create a **`div`** that is conditionally displayed using the **`x-show`** directive based on the **`isOpen`** state.
4. Add the **`x-transition`** directive to the **`div`** to apply a smooth fade-in/fade-out animation.
5. Add comments in the HTML to explain what each **`Alpine.js`** directive is doing."

AI-Generated Output

```
<html>
  <head>
    <script
      defer
      src="https://cdn.jsdelivr.net/npm/alpinejs@3.x.x/dist/cdn.min.js"
    ></script>
    <script src="https://cdn.jsdelivr.net/npm/@tailwindcss/browser@4"></
script>
  </head>
  <body>
    <div x-data="{ isOpen: false }" class="p-8 bg-gray-100 rounded-lg">
      <button
        @click="isOpen =!isOpen"
        class="px-4 py-2 font-semibold text-white bg-blue-600 rounded-md"
      >
        Toggle Content
      </button>

      <div
        x-show="isOpen"
        x-transition
        class="p-4 mt-4 bg-white border rounded-md"
      >
        <p class="text-gray-700">This content can be shown or hidden!</p>
      </div>
    </div>
  </body>
</html>
```

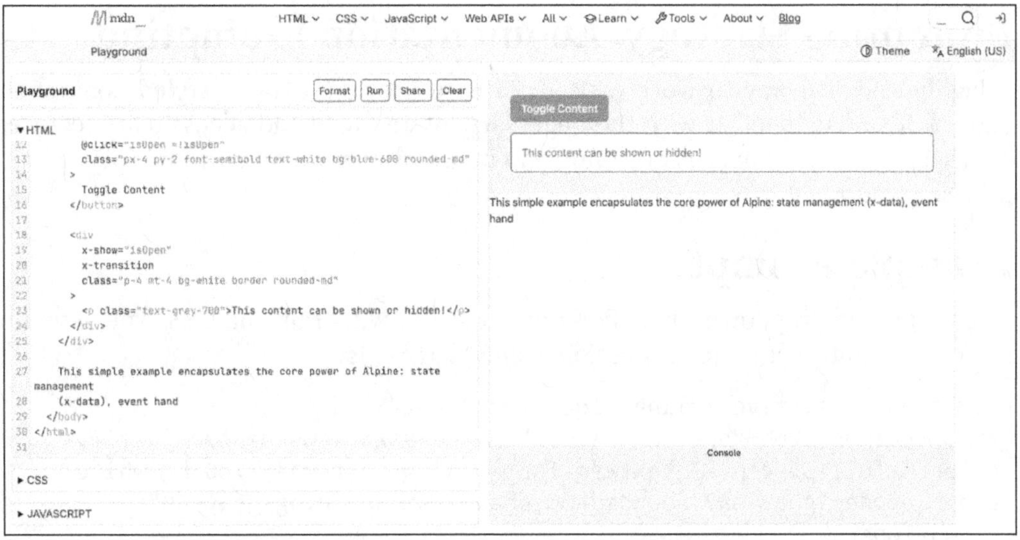

Figure 5.2: *Show/Hide Component Built with Alpine.js and Tailwind*

This simple example encapsulates the core power of Alpine: state management (**`x-data`**), event handling (**`@click`**), and DOM manipulation (**`x-show`**) are all handled declaratively within the HTML.

Building an Accessible Dropdown Menu

Dropdown menus are one of the most common interactive components on the web. Building one correctly involves managing its open/closed state, handling user interactions such as clicks and key presses, and ensuring that it is fully accessible to all the users.

A robust dropdown requires[3]:

- **State Management:** Tracking whether the menu is open or closed.
- **Event Listeners:** Toggling the menu on a button click.
- **Click Away:** Closing the menu when the user clicks outside of it.
- **Keyboard Navigation:** Closing the menu with the Escape key and navigating items with arrow keys
- **Accessibility (ARIA):** Using ARIA attributes such as aria-haspopup and aria-expanded to communicate the component's state to assistive technologies.

[3] *https://www.penguinui.com/components/dropdowns*

Prompting Strategy: Augmentation Prompting

A highly effective way to work with an AI is to provide a static, styled component and ask it to "augment" it with the necessary interactivity and accessibility features. This separates the concerns of styling and behavior, allowing for a more focused and precise prompt.

Example Prompt

"I have a static dropdown menu component styled with Tailwind CSS. I need you to make it fully interactive and accessible using **`Alpine.js`**. "

```
<div class="relative inline-block text-left">
  >   <button type="button" class="inline-flex items-center justify-
center w-full px-4 py-2 text-sm font-medium text-gray-700 bg-white
border border-gray-300 rounded-md shadow-sm hover:bg-gray-50">
    Options
    <svg class="w-5 h-5 ml-2 -mr-1" xmlns="http://www.w3.org/2000/svg"
viewBox="0 0 20 20" fill="currentColor">
      <path fill-rule="evenodd" d="M5.293 7.293a1 1 0 011.414 0L10
10.586l3.293-3.293a1 1 0 111.414 1.414l-4 4a1 1 0 01-1.414 0l-4-4a1 1 0
010-1.414z" clip-rule="evenodd" />
    </svg>
  </button>

  >   <div class="absolute right-0 w-56 mt-2 origin-top-right bg-white
rounded-md shadow-lg ring-1 ring-black ring-opacity-5">
    <div class="py-1">
      <a href="#" class="block px-4 py-2 text-sm text-gray-700">Account
settings</a>
      <a href="#" class="block px-4 py-2 text-sm text-gray-700">Support</a>
      <a href="#" class="block px-4 py-2 text-sm text-gray-700">License</a>
    </div>
  </div>
</div>
```

Task: Modify this HTML with the following **`Alpine.js`** functionality:

- Initialize an **`isOpen`** state variable to false using **`x-data`**.
- The button should toggle the **`isOpen`** state on click.
- The dropdown panel should only be visible when **`isOpen`** is true. Use **`x-show`** and add a smooth **`x-transition`**.
- The dropdown should close when the user clicks outside of it. Use the **`@click.outside`** modifier.
- The dropdown should close when the user presses the Escape key. Use the **`@keydown.escape.window`** modifier.

- Add the necessary ARIA attributes (aria-haspopup="true" and a dynamically bound :aria-expanded) to the trigger button for accessibility.
- Dynamically rotate the chevron icon 180 degrees when the dropdown is open **`using :class`**."

AI-Generated Output

```
<html>
  <head>
    <script
      defer
    src="https://cdn.jsdelivr.net/npm/alpinejs@3.x.x/dist/cdn.min.js"
    ></script>
    <script src="https://cdn.jsdelivr.net/npm/@tailwindcss/browser@4"></
script>
  </head>
  <body>
    <div x-data="{ isOpen: false }" @keydown.escape.window="isOpen =
false" class="relative inline-block text-left">
  <button
    @click="isOpen =!isOpen"
    type="button"
    class="inline-flex items-center justify-center w-full px-4 py-2 text-
sm font-medium text-gray-700 bg-white border border-gray-300 rounded-md
shadow-sm hover:bg-gray-50 focus:outline-none focus:ring-2 focus:ring-
offset-2 focus:ring-indigo-500"
    aria-haspopup="true"
    :aria-expanded="isOpen"
  >
    Options
    <svg
      :class="{ 'rotate-180': isOpen }"
      class="w-5 h-5 ml-2 -mr-1 transition-transform duration-200"
      xmlns="http://www.w3.org/2000/svg"
      viewBox="0 0 20 20"
      fill="currentColor"
    >
      <path fill-rule="evenodd" d="M5.293 7.293a1 1 0 011.414 0L10
10.586l3.293-3.293a1 1 0 111.414 1.414l-4 4a1 1 0 01-1.414 0l-4-4a1 1 0
010-1.414z" clip-rule="evenodd" />
    </svg>
  </button>
```

```
  <div
    x-show=”isOpen”
    @click.outside=”isOpen = false”
    x-transition:enter=”transition ease-out duration-100”
    x-transition:enter-start=”transform opacity-0 scale-95”
    x-transition:enter-end=”transform opacity-100 scale-100”
    x-transition:leave=”transition ease-in duration-75”
    x-transition:leave-start=”transform opacity-100 scale-100”
    x-transition:leave-end=”transform opacity-0 scale-95”
    class=”absolute right-0 w-56 mt-2 origin-top-right bg-white rounded-md shadow-lg ring-1 ring-black ring-opacity-5 focus:outline-none”
    style=”display: none;”
  >
    <div class=”py-1” role=”menu” aria-orientation=”vertical”>
      <a href=”#” class=”block px-4 py-2 text-sm text-gray-700 hover:bg-gray-100” role=”menuitem”>Account settings</a>
      <a href=”#” class=”block px-4 py-2 text-sm text-gray-700 hover:bg-gray-100” role=”menuitem”>Support</a>
      <a href=”#” class=”block px-4 py-2 text-sm text-gray-700 hover:bg-gray-100” role=”menuitem”>License</a>
    </div>
  </div>
</div>
  </body>
</html>
```

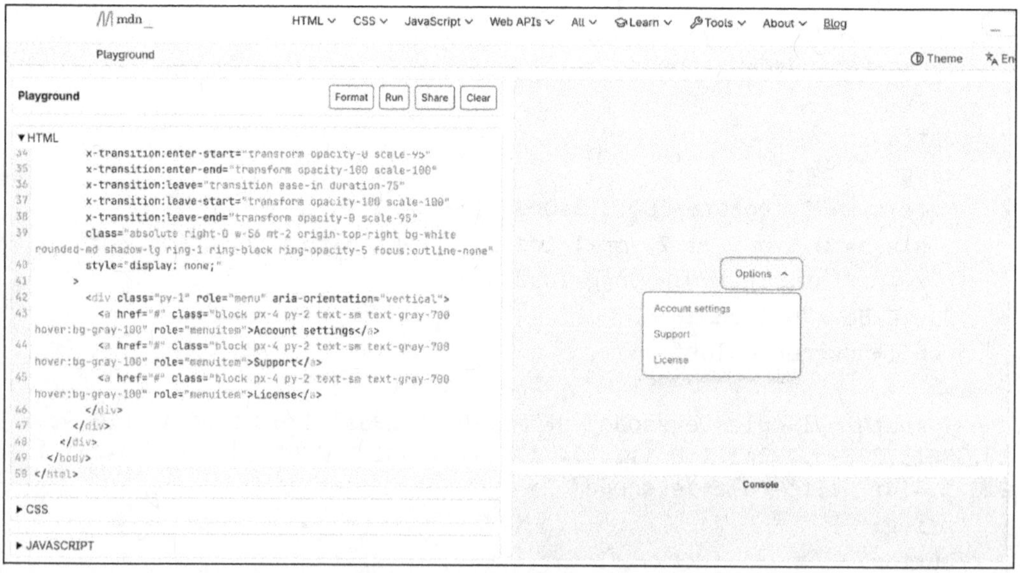

Figure 5.3: *Output of the Accessible Dropdown*

Building an Accessible Tabs Component

Tabs are a powerful pattern for organizing related content into distinct sections, allowing users to switch between them without navigating to a new page. A well-implemented tabs component requires careful management of state and a strong focus on accessibility, particularly the keyboard navigation.

Key requirements include[4]:

- **Active Tab State**: A mechanism to track which tab is currently selected[5].
- **Content Panels**: Displaying only the content panel that corresponds to the active tab[6].
- **Styling Active State**: Visually distinguishing the active tab from the others.
- **Accessibility (ARIA)**: Correctly using `role="tablist"`, `role="tab"`, `role="tabpanel"`, `aria-selected`, and `aria-controls` to create a semantic structure that screen readers can understand.
- **Keyboard Navigation**: Allowing users to switch between tabs using the arrow keys, as is standard for this pattern.

Prompting Strategy: Problem-Solving and Constraint-Based Prompting

For a more complex component such as tabs, we can frame the prompt as a problem to be solved, providing a clear set of functional and accessibility constraints. This guides the AI to generate a complete, robust solution.

Example Prompt

"Generate a complete, accessible tabs component using Tailwind CSS and `Alpine.js`.

Functional Requirements:

- The component should have three tabs: '`Profile`', '`Settings`', and '`Billing`'.
- Use `x-data` to manage an `activeTab` state, initialized to the first tab.
- Clicking a tab button should update the `activeTab` state.
- Only the content panel corresponding to the `activeTab` should be visible. Use `x-show` for this.
- The active tab button should have a distinct style (for example, different text and border color). Use `:class` to apply these styles conditionally.

---

[4] *https://www.penguinui.com/components/dropdowns*

[5] *https://lexingtonthemes.com/tutorials/how-to-create-persistent-tabs-with-tailwind-css-and-alpinejs/*

[6] *https://codepen.io/cruip/pen/gOZgMMd*

Accessibility Requirements:

- The list of tab buttons must have **role="tablist"**.
- Each button must have **role="tab"**.
- Each content panel must have **role="tabpanel"**.
- Each tab button must be linked to its panel via an aria-controls attribute that matches the panel's id.
- The active tab button must have **aria-selected="true"**, and inactive tabs must have **aria-selected="false"**. Bind this dynamically.
- Implement keyboard navigation using the Left and Right arrow keys to switch focus between tabs. The **Alpine.js** Focus plugin (**$focus**) can be used for this."

AI-Generated Output

```
<html>
  <head>
    <script
      defer
      src="https://cdn.jsdelivr.net/npm/alpinejs@3.x.x/dist/cdn.min.js"
    ></script>
    <script src="https://cdn.jsdelivr.net/npm/@tailwindcss/browser@4"></
script>
  </head>
  <body>

    <div x-data="{ activeTab: 'profile' }" class="w-full max-w-lg mx-auto">
  <div
    role="tablist"
    aria-label="User account tabs"
    class="flex p-1 space-x-1 bg-gray-200 rounded-xl"
    @keydown.right.prevent.stop="$focus.wrap().next()"
    @keydown.left.prevent.stop="$focus.wrap().prev()"
  >
    <button
      id="tab-profile"
      role="tab"
      @click="activeTab = 'profile'"
      :class="{ 'bg-white text-blue-600 shadow': activeTab === 'profile',
'text-gray-600 hover:bg-white/[0.6]': activeTab!== 'profile' }"
      class="w-full px-3 py-2 text-sm font-medium leading-5 text-
blue-700 rounded-lg focus:outline-none focus:ring-2 ring-offset-2 ring-
offset-blue-400 ring-white ring-opacity-60"
      :aria-controls="'panel-profile'"
      :aria-selected="activeTab === 'profile'"
    >
```

```
      Profile
    </button>

    <button
      id="tab-settings"
      role="tab"
      @click="activeTab = 'settings'"
      :class="{ 'bg-white text-blue-600 shadow': activeTab ===
'settings', 'text-gray-600 hover:bg-white/[0.6]': activeTab!== 'settings' }"
      class="w-full px-3 py-2 text-sm font-medium leading-5 text-
blue-700 rounded-lg focus:outline-none focus:ring-2 ring-offset-2 ring-
offset-blue-400 ring-white ring-opacity-60"
      :aria-controls="'panel-settings'"
      :aria-selected="activeTab === 'settings'"
    >
      Settings
    </button>

    <button
      id="tab-billing"
      role="tab"
      @click="activeTab = 'billing'"
      :class="{ 'bg-white text-blue-600 shadow': activeTab ===
'billing', 'text-gray-600 hover:bg-white/[0.6]': activeTab!== 'billing' }"
      class="w-full px-3 py-2 text-sm font-medium leading-5 text-
blue-700 rounded-lg focus:outline-none focus:ring-2 ring-offset-2 ring-
offset-blue-400 ring-white ring-opacity-60"
      :aria-controls="'panel-billing'"
      :aria-selected="activeTab === 'billing'"
    >
      Billing
    </button>
  </div>

  <div class="mt-4">
    <div
      id="panel-profile"
      x-show="activeTab === 'profile'"
      role="tabpanel"
      aria-labelledby="tab-profile"
      class="p-4 bg-white rounded-xl"
    >
      <p>Profile content goes here. Users can view and edit their
personal information.</p>
    </div>

    <div
```

```
      id=”panel-settings”
      x-show=”activeTab === ‘settings’”
      role=”tabpanel”
      aria-labelledby=”tab-settings”
      class=”p-4 bg-white rounded-xl”
      style=”display: none;”
    >
      <p>Settings content goes here. Users can manage their application
preferences.</p>
    </div>

    <div
      id=”panel-billing”
      x-show=”activeTab === ‘billing’”
      role=”tabpanel”
      aria-labelledby=”tab-billing”
      class=”p-4 bg-white rounded-xl”
      style=”display: none;”
    >
      <p>Billing content goes here. Users can view their subscription
and payment history.</p>
    </div>
  </div>
</div>

  </body>
</html>
```

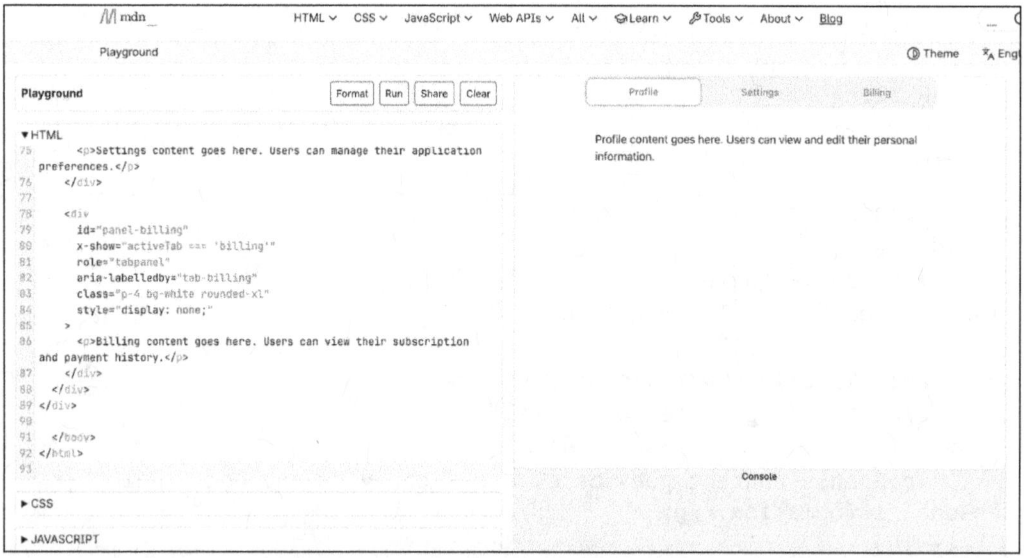

Figure 5.4: *Output of the Accessible Tabs Component*

Building an Accessible Modal

Modals (or dialogs) are used to present critical information or require user input by overlaying the main content. A correct implementation is vital for usability and accessibility.

Key requirements include[7,8,9]:

- **Overlay/Backdrop:** A semi-transparent layer that covers the page content.
- **Focus Trapping:** Once the modal is open, keyboard focus must be "trapped" within it, preventing users from accidentally tabbing to elements on the page behind it. This is a critical accessibility feature.
- **Dismissal:** The modal must be closable by clicking a close button, clicking the backdrop, or pressing the Escape key.
- **Accessibility (ARIA):** The modal container needs role="dialog", aria-modal="true", and an accessible name via aria-labelledby.

Prompting Strategy: Step-by-Step Instructional Prompting

Building a modal involves several distinct parts that must work together. A step-by-step prompt helps the AI construct the component logically, ensuring that all requirements are met.

Example Prompt

"Generate the code for a complete, accessible modal component using Tailwind CSS and `Alpine.js`. Follow these steps:

1. **State:** Create an Alpine component using `x-data` that manages an `isOpen` state, initialized to false.
2. **Trigger:** Add a button that sets `isOpen` to true when clicked.
3. **Container and Backdrop:** Create a fixed-position container that is shown with `x-show="isOpen"`. Inside it, create a semi-transparent backdrop `div`.
4. **Dismissal:** The main container should listen for the Escape key on the window to set `isOpen` to false. The backdrop `div` should also set `isOpen` to false when clicked.

---

[7] *https://lexingtonthemes.com/tutorials/how-to-create-an-animated-log-in-modal-with-tailwind-css-and-alpine-js/*
[8] *https://cruip.com/how-to-build-a-modal-video-with-html-tailwind-css-and-alpine-js/*
[9] *https://dberri.com/lets-build-an-accessible-modal-with-alpine-js/*

5. **Modal Panel:** Inside the container, create the modal panel div. It should have a white background, shadow, and rounded corners. Add a smooth entrance/exit animation using **`x-transition`**.
6. **Accessibility:** The main container must have role="dialog", aria-modal="true", and an aria-labelledby attribute pointing to the modal's title id.
7. **Implement Focus Trapping**: Add the **`x-trap="isOpen"`** directive to the main container (note that this requires the **`Alpine.js`** Focus plugin).
8. **Content:** The panel should contain a title (h2 with an id), some paragraph text, and a 'Close' button that sets **`isOpen`** to false."

AI-Generated Output

```
<html>
  <head>
    <script
      defer
      src="https://cdn.jsdelivr.net/npm/alpinejs@3.x.x/dist/cdn.min.js"
    ></script>
    <script src="https://cdn.jsdelivr.net/npm/@tailwindcss/browser@4"></
script>
  </head>
  <body>
<div x-data="{ isOpen: false }">
  <button @click="isOpen = true" class="px-4 py-2 text-white bg-
indigo-600 rounded-md">Open Modal</button>

  <div
    x-show="isOpen"
    style="display: none;"
    x-trap="isOpen"
    @keydown.escape.window="isOpen = false"
    class="fixed inset-0 z-50 overflow-y-auto"
    role="dialog"
    aria-modal="true"
    aria-labelledby="modal-title"
  >
    <div
      x-show="isOpen"
      x-transition:enter="ease-out duration-300"
      x-transition:enter-start="opacity-0"
      x-transition:enter-end="opacity-100"
```

```
      x-transition:leave="ease-in duration-200"
      x-transition:leave-start="opacity-100"
      x-transition:leave-end="opacity-0"
      class="fixed inset-0 bg-black bg-opacity-50"
      @click="isOpen = false"
    ></div>

    <div
      x-show="isOpen"
      x-transition:enter="ease-out duration-300"
      x-transition:enter-start="opacity-0 scale-95"
      x-transition:enter-end="opacity-100 scale-100"
      x-transition:leave="ease-in duration-200"
      x-transition:leave-start="opacity-100 scale-100"
      x-transition:leave-end="opacity-0 scale-95"
      class="relative w-full max-w-md p-6 mx-auto my-8 bg-white rounded-
lg shadow-xl"
    >
      <h2 id="modal-title" class="text-2xl font-bold text-gray-
900">Modal Title</h2>
      <p class="mt-2 text-gray-600">
        This is the content of the modal. Focus is trapped inside, and
you can close it by clicking the button, the backdrop, or pressing the
Escape key.
      </p>
      <div class="mt-6 text-right">
        <button @click="isOpen = false" class="px-4 py-2 text-sm font-
medium text-white bg-indigo-600 rounded-md">
          Close
        </button>
      </div>
    </div>
  </div>
</div>
  </body>
</html>
```

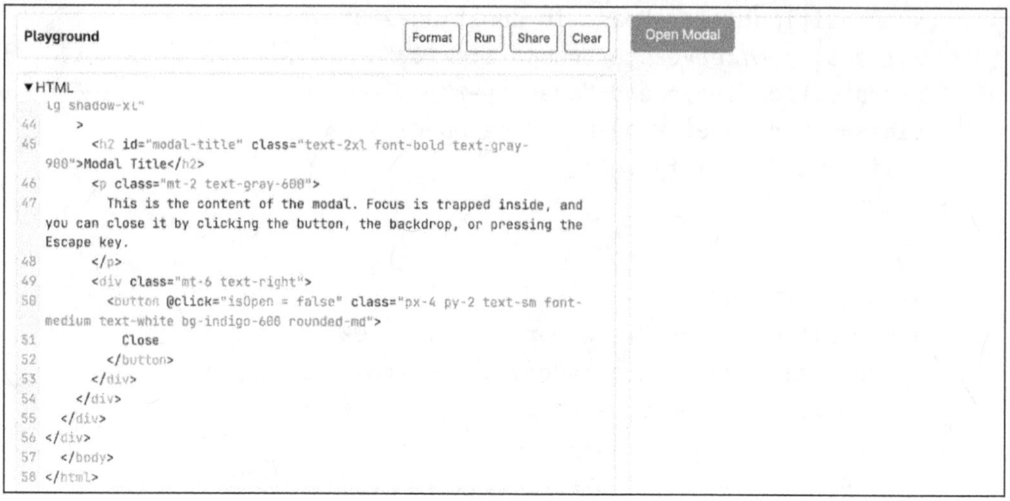

***Figure* 5.5:** *Output of the Component We Just Created*

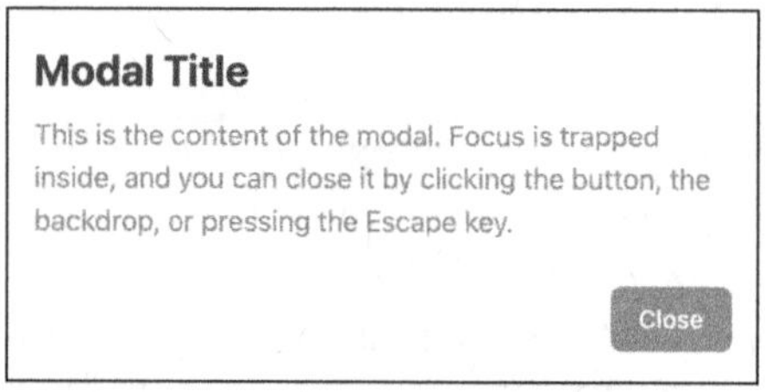

***Figure* 5.6:** *This is the Modal You Should Expect When Clicking on the "Open Modal" Button*

Mastering Forms with `@tailwindcss/forms` and `Alpine.js`

HTML forms are notoriously inconsistent across browsers and difficult to style. The official **`@tailwindcss/forms`** plugin solves this by applying a minimal reset to native form controls, making them easy to customize with utility classes. When combined with **`Alpine.js`**, you can create forms that provide real-time, client-side validation feedback without a full page refresh.

The `@tailwindcss/forms` Plugin

First, you need to install and configure the plugin.

Installation: **npm** install -D **`@tailwindcss/forms`**

Configuration: Add the plugin to your **`tailwind.config.js`** file.

```
// tailwind.config.js
module.exports = {
```

```
  //...
  plugins: [
    require('@tailwindcss/forms'),
  ],
}
```

Once enabled, the plugin normalizes the appearance of inputs, textareas, selects, checkboxes, and radio buttons, allowing you to style them consistently (for example, **`px-4 py-2 rounded-md border-gray-300`**).

Prompting Strategy: Role-Playing and Constraint-Based Prompting

To generate a complete form, we can ask the AI to adopt the persona of a UX-focused developer and provide it with a clear set of validation rules.

Example Prompt

"Act as a front-end developer focused on user experience. Generate the HTML for a user registration form styled with Tailwind CSS and made interactive with **`Alpine.js`**. The **`@tailwindcss/forms`** plugin is installed.

Form Fields:

- Full Name (text input)
- Email Address (email input)
- Password (password input)

`Alpine.js` Requirements:

- Use **`x-data`** to create an object to hold the form input values (name, email, and password) and another object to hold validation errors.
- Use **`x-model`** to bind the inputs to the data properties.
- Create a validate method in **`x-data`** that checks the following rules on form submission:
  - Name must not be empty.
  - Email must be a valid email format.
  - Password must be at least 8 characters long.
- The form should only submit if validation passes.

Styling and UX Requirements:

- Each input should be styled with a gray border.

- If an input has a validation error, its border should turn red. Use **:class** for this.
- An error message should appear below an input if it is invalid. Use **x-show** and **x-text** to display the correct message from the errors object."

AI-Generated Output

```
<html>
  <head>
    <script
      defer
      src="https://cdn.jsdelivr.net/npm/alpinejs@3.x.x/dist/cdn.min.js"
    ></script>
    <script src="https://cdn.tailwindcss.com/3.4.1"></script>
  </head>
  <body>
    <div
      class="w-full max-w-md p-8 mx-auto mt-10 space-y-6 bg-white
rounded-lg shadow-md"
      x-data="{
        form: {
          name: '',
          email: '',
          password: ''
        },
        errors: {},
        validate() {
          this.errors = {};
          let valid = true;
          if (!this.form.name) {
            this.errors.name = 'Full name is required.';
            valid = false;
          }
          const emailRegex = /^[^\s@]+@[^\s@]+\.[^\s@]+$/;
          if (!this.form.email ||!emailRegex.test(this.form.email)) {
            this.errors.email = 'Please enter a valid email address.';
            valid = false;
          }
          // Corrected the '||' operator here
          if (!this.form.password || this.form.password.length < 8) {
            this.errors.password = 'Password must be at least 8
characters long.';
            valid = false;
```

```
          }
          return valid;
        },
        submitForm() {
          if (this.validate()) {
            alert('Form submitted successfully! 🎉');
            // In a real app, you would submit the form data here.
            // e.g., fetch('/register', { method: 'POST', body: JSON.
stringify(this.form) });
            console.log('Submitting:', this.form);
          }
        }
      }"
    >
      <h2 class="text-2xl font-bold text-center text-gray-800">Create
Account</h2>
      <form @submit.prevent="submitForm" novalidate>
        <div>
          <label for="name" class="block text-sm font-medium text-gray-
700">Full Name</label>
          <input
            id="name"
            type="text"
            x-model="form.name"
            :class="{ 'border-red-500': errors.name, 'border-gray-
300':!errors.name }"
            class="block w-full mt-1 border rounded-md shadow-sm
focus:ring-indigo-500 focus:border-indigo-500"
          />
          <p x-show="errors.name" x-text="errors.name" class="mt-1 text-
xs text-red-600"></p>
        </div>

        <div>
          <label for="email" class="block text-sm font-medium text-gray-
700">Email Address</label>
          <input
            id="email"
            type="email"
            x-model="form.email"
            :class="{ 'border-red-500': errors.email, 'border-gray-
300':!errors.email }"
            class="block w-full mt-1 border rounded-md shadow-sm
```

```
focus:ring-indigo-500 focus:border-indigo-500"
          />
          <p x-show="errors.email" x-text="errors.email" class="mt-1
text-xs text-red-600"></p>
        </div>

        <div>
          <label for="password" class="block text-sm font-medium text-
gray-700">Password</label>
          <input
            id="password"
            type="password"
            x-model="form.password"
            :class="{ 'border-red-500': errors.password, 'border-gray-
300':!errors.password }"
            class="block w-full mt-1 border rounded-md shadow-sm
focus:ring-indigo-500 focus:border-indigo-500"
          />
          <p x-show="errors.password" x-text="errors.password"
class="mt-1 text-xs text-red-600"></p>
        </div>

        <div>
          <button type="submit" class="w-full px-4 py-2 font-bold text-
white bg-indigo-600 rounded-md hover:bg-indigo-700">
            Register
          </button>
        </div>
      </form>
    </div>
  </body>
</html>
```

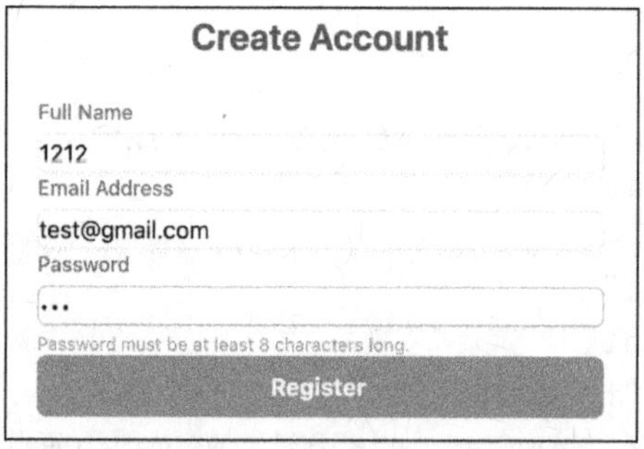

Figure 5.7: *The Component We Created has Built-in Forms. Notice the Validation is Working and Preventing the User from Entering a Password That Does Not Match the Requirements*

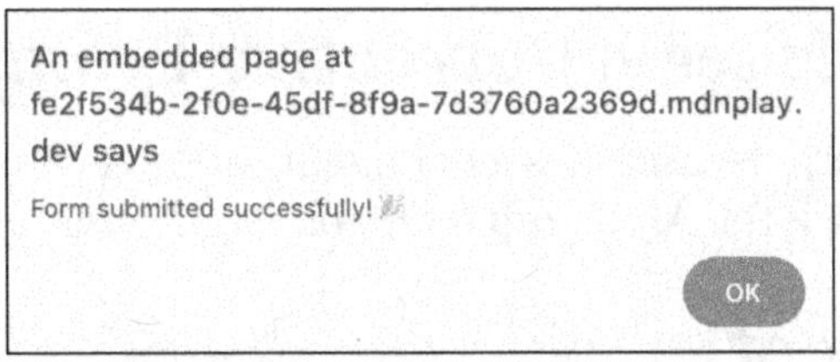

Figure 5.8: *The New Component Also has a Placeholder Function for the Successful Submission of the Form Data*

Part II: Scaling up with React and Advanced Patterns

While **`Alpine.js`** is perfect for adding targeted interactivity, complex single-page applications (SPAs) often benefit from the structured, component-based architecture of a framework such as React. When using Tailwind in a React project, the primary challenge shifts from writing CSS to effectively managing and composing utility classes in a way that is scalable, maintainable, and type-safe.

This section is not a React tutorial, there are many books and tutorials online (https://react.dev/learn) that cover React in depth. Instead, it focuses on the specific patterns and tools that enable a professional, large-scale workflow for combining React and Tailwind CSS.

The "Do Not Concatenate" Rule: Safe Dynamic Classes

As covered in *Chapter 4, Prompting Copilot and GPT for Smarter Code*, Tailwind's JIT engine works by statically analyzing your source files to find complete, unbroken class strings. This means that constructing class names dynamically with string concatenation will fail in production, because the compiler never sees the final class name.

Incorrect (Unsafe) Pattern:

```
// This will break in production!
function Alert({ type, children }) {
  // `type` could be ‘success’, ‘warning’, or ‘error’
  const bgColor = `bg-${type}-100`;
  const textColor = `text-${type}-700`;

  return <div className={`${bgColor} ${textColor} p-4 rounded-
md`}>{children}</div>;
}
```

Prompting Strategy: Corrective Prompting

This is a perfect scenario to use AI as a debugging and teaching tool. We can provide the broken code and ask the AI to both fix it and explain the underlying problem.

Example Prompt

"I have a React component that works in development, but the background and text colors disappear in the production build.

Broken Code:

```
function Alert({ type, children }) {
  const bgColor = `bg-${type}-100`;
  const textColor = `text-${type}-700`;
  return <div className={`${bgColor} ${textColor} p-4 rounded-
md`}>{children}</div>;
}
```

Task:

- Explain why this code fails in a production Tailwind build.
- Refactor the component to use a safe, statically analyzable pattern for applying dynamic classes based on the type prop."

AI-Generated Output

Explanation: "This code fails in production because of Tailwind's purging process. At build time, Tailwind scans your files for complete class names (such as **'bg-green-100'**). It does not execute your JavaScript, so it cannot resolve the template literal **`bg-${type}-100`** into its possible outcomes. Since it does not find the full class strings, it assumes they are unused and removes them from the final CSS file. This is why the styles work in development (where all utilities are often available) but disappear in the optimized production build."

Corrected Code:

```
// This pattern is safe for production.
function Alert({ type, children }) {
  const typeStyles = {
    success: 'bg-green-100 text-green-700',
    warning: 'bg-yellow-100 text-yellow-700',
    error: ‹bg-red-100 text-red-700›,
  };

  // The full class strings are now present in the file and will be
detected by Tailwind.
  const classes = `p-4 rounded-md ${typeStyles[type] || ''}`;
```

```
  return <div className={classes}>{children}</div>;
}
```

Bulletproof Conditional Classes with `clsx` and `tailwind-merge`

While mapping props to strings works, class lists can become complex when dealing with multiple conditional styles. This can lead to messy ternary operators and, more subtly, conflicting utility classes (for example, applying `p-2` and later overriding it with `p-4`). Two small utilities solve these problems elegantly:

- **`clsx:`** A tiny utility for conditionally constructing className strings. It allows you to use objects where keys are class names and values are Boolean conditions, making the logic much cleaner.
- **`Tailwind-Merge:`** A utility that intelligently merges Tailwind class lists, automatically resolving conflicts. For example, **`twMerge('p-2', 'p-4')`** will correctly output just **`'p-4'`**.

The standard best practice is to combine them into a single helper function, often called `cn`.

Prompting Strategy: Scaffolding Prompting

We can ask the AI to scaffold this essential utility function for us.

Example Prompt

*"Create a utility function named cn for a React project that uses Tailwind CSS. This function should combine the functionality of the **`clsx`** and **`tailwind-merge`** libraries to provide a robust way to handle conditional and conflicting class names. Provide the necessary npm install commands and the code for the utility file."*

AI-Generated Output

Installation:

```
npm install clsx tailwind-merge
```

- **`lib/utils.js:`**

  ```
  import { clsx } from "clsx";
  import { twMerge } from "tailwind-merge";

  export function cn(...inputs) {
    return twMerge(clsx(inputs));
  }
  ```

Usage Example:

```
import { cn } from './lib/utils';

function Button({ isPrimary, isDisabled, className }) {
  const buttonClasses = cn(
    'px-4 py-2 rounded font-semibold transition-colors', // Base classes
    {
      'bg-blue-500 text-white hover:bg-blue-600': isPrimary &&!isDisabled,
      'bg-gray-200 text-gray-800':!isPrimary &&!isDisabled,
      'bg-gray-100 text-gray-400 cursor-not-allowed': isDisabled,
    },
    className // Allow overriding with external classes
  );

  return <button className={buttonClasses} disabled={isDisabled}>Click
Me</button>;
}
```

Component Variants with CVA

For design systems and reusable component libraries, **Class Variance Authority (CVA)** is a game-changing tool. It provides a structured way to create components with multiple style variants, managed through props. Instead of writing complex conditional logic inside your component, you define all possible variants in a single, co-located configuration.

This approach offers several advantages[10]:

- **Readability:** All styling logic is centralized and declarative.
- **Type Safety:** When used with TypeScript, it provides autocompletion and ensures that you only pass valid variant props.
- **Reusability:** It is easy to define and apply consistent styles across your entire application.

Prompting Strategy: Persona-Based and Scaffolding Prompting

We can ask the AI to act as a Design Systems Engineer and provide it with a clear specification for a component with multiple variants.

Example Prompt

"Act as a Design Systems Engineer. I need to create a flexible Button component for my React design system using Tailwind CSS and the class-variance-authority (CVA) library."

[10] *https://konabos.com/blog/streamline-your-styling-with-cva-and-tailwind-css*

Requirements:

- Define a **buttonVariants** configuration using **cva**.
- The button should have a variant prop with three options: '**primary**', '**secondary**', and '**destructive**'.
- The button should have a size prop with three options: **'sm'**, **'md'**, and **'lg'**.
- Define a **defaultVariants** configuration for a medium-sized primary button.
- Create a **React** Button component that accepts these variants as props and applies the correct classes. It should also accept an additional **className** prop to allow for overrides. Use the **cn** utility for merging classes.
- Provide TypeScript types for the component's props."

AI-Generated Output

components/Button.jsx:

```
import * as React from "react";
import { cva } from "class-variance-authority";
import { cn } from "@/lib/utils"; // Assuming cn utility from previous
section
const buttonVariants = cva(
  // Base classes applied to all variants
  "inline-flex items-center justify-center rounded-md text-sm font-
medium transition-colors focus-visible:outline-none focus-visible:ring-2
focus-visible:ring-ring focus-visible:ring-offset-2 disabled:opacity-50
disabled:pointer-events-none",
  {
    variants: {
      variant: {
        primary: "bg-blue-600 text-white hover:bg-blue-600/90",
        secondary: "bg-gray-200 text-gray-900 hover:bg-gray-200/80",
        destructive: "bg-red-600 text-white hover:bg-red-600/90",
      },
      size: {
        sm: "h-9 px-3",
        md: "h-10 px-4 py-2",
        lg: "h-11 px-8",
      },
    },
    defaultVariants: {
      variant: "primary",
      size: "md",
    },
  }
);
```

```
const Button = React.forwardRef(
  ({ className, variant, size,...props }, ref) => {
    return (
      <button
        className={cn(buttonVariants({ variant, size, className }))}
        ref={ref}
        {...props}
      />
    );
  }
);
Button.displayName = "Button";

export { Button, buttonVariants };
```

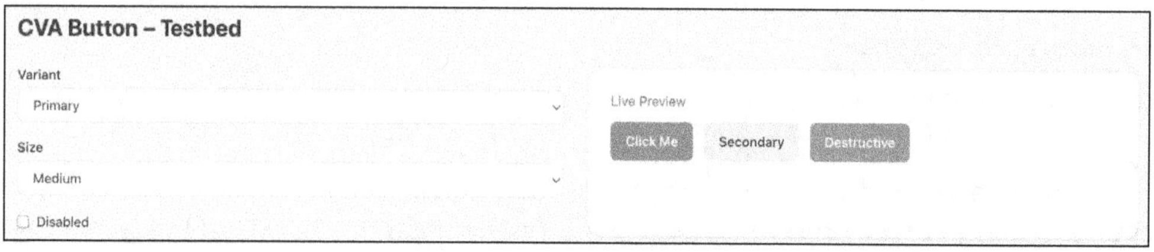

Figure 5.9: *Preview of Buttons Created with React, CVA, and Tailwind*

The Best of Both Worlds: Headless UI for React

Building truly accessible interactive components from scratch is hard. It requires managing focus, keyboard navigation, and dozens of ARIA attributes correctly.

Headless UI, from the makers of Tailwind CSS, solves this by providing completely unstyled, fully accessible component logic for React and Vue.

The philosophy is simple: Headless UI handles the complex behavior, and you handle the presentation with Tailwind CSS. This separation of concerns is incredibly powerful, giving you full design control without sacrificing accessibility.

You can style Headless UI components using **`data-*`** attributes that they expose for different states (for example, **`data-open`**, **`data-selected`**). The official **`@headlessui/tailwindcss`** plugin makes this even easier by providing **`ui-*`** variants (for example, **`ui-open:bg-gray-100`**).

Prompting Strategy: Persona-Based and Instructional Prompting

We can instruct the AI to act as an accessibility expert and guide it to build a component using Headless UI, ensuring that the best practices are followed.

Example Prompt

"Act as a senior front-end developer specializing in accessibility. Generate a complete, accessible modal dialog component for a React application using **`@headlessui/react`** and styled with Tailwind CSS.

Requirements:

- Use the **`Dialog`**, **`DialogPanel`**, and **`DialogTitle`** components from **`Headless UI`**.
- The modal's **`open/close`** state should be managed with **`React's useState`** hook.
- Use the Transition component from **`Headless UI`** to create a smooth fade and scale animation for the modal panel and a fade animation for the backdrop overlay.
- Style the component states using the **`data-*`** attributes that Headless UI's Transition component provides (for example, **`data-[enter]:...`**).
- The final component should be fully styled, accessible, and include a trigger button and a close button."

AI-Generated Output

```
import { Dialog, DialogPanel, DialogTitle, Transition, TransitionChild }
from '@headlessui/react';
import { Fragment, useState } from 'react';

export default function AccessibleModal() {
  let [isOpen, setIsOpen] = useState(false);

  return (
    <>
      <button
        onClick={() => setIsOpen(true)}
        className="px-4 py-2 text-sm font-medium text-white bg-black
rounded-md bg-opacity-80 hover:bg-opacity-90"
      >
        Open Dialog
      </button>

      <Transition appear show={isOpen} as={Fragment}>
        <Dialog as="div" className="relative z-10" onClose={() =>
setIsOpen(false)}>
          {/* Backdrop Overlay */}
          <TransitionChild
            as={Fragment}
            enter="ease-out duration-300"
```

```
            enterFrom="opacity-0"
            enterTo="opacity-100"
            leave="ease-in duration-200"
            leaveFrom="opacity-100"
            leaveTo="opacity-0"
          >
            <div className="fixed inset-0 bg-black bg-opacity-40" />
          </TransitionChild>

          <div className="fixed inset-0 overflow-y-auto">
            <div className="flex items-center justify-center min-h-full
p-4 text-center">
              {/* Modal Panel */}
              <TransitionChild
                as={Fragment}
                enter="ease-out duration-300"
                enterFrom="opacity-0 scale-95"
                enterTo="opacity-100 scale-100"
                leave="ease-in duration-200"
                leaveFrom="opacity-100 scale-100"
                leaveTo="opacity-0 scale-95"
              >
                <DialogPanel className="w-full max-w-md p-6 overflow-
hidden text-left align-middle transition-all transform bg-white shadow-
xl rounded-2xl">
                  <DialogTitle as="h3" className="text-lg font-medium
leading-6 text-gray-900">
                    Payment Successful
                  </DialogTitle>
                  <div className="mt-2">
                    <p className="text-sm text-gray-500">
                      Your payment has been successfully submitted.
We've sent you an email with all of the details of your order.
                    </p>
                  </div>
                  <div className="mt-4">
                    <button
                      type="button"
                      className="inline-flex justify-center px-4 py-2
text-sm font-medium text-blue-900 bg-blue-100 border border-transparent
rounded-md hover:bg-blue-200"
                      onClick={() => setIsOpen(false)}
                    >
```

```
                        Got it, thanks!
                      </button>
                    </div>
                  </DialogPanel>
                </TransitionChild>
              </div>
            </div>
          </Dialog>
        </Transition>
      </>
    );
}
```

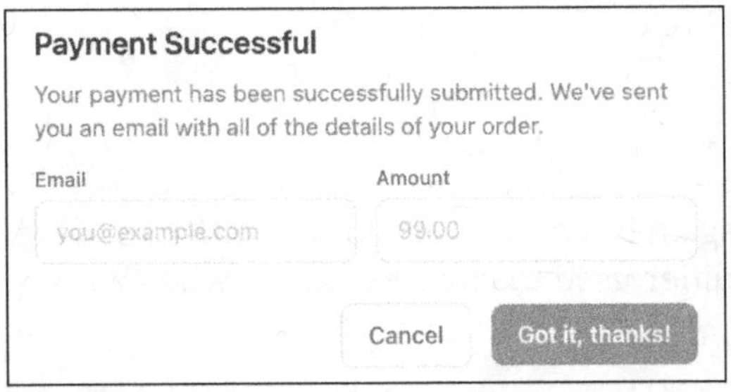

***Figure* 5.10:** *Output of the Modal Built with React.js, Headless and TailwindCSS*

Conclusion

This chapter has provided a practical roadmap for building the interactive components that power modern web applications. We have explored two powerful, yet distinct, approaches for integrating JavaScript with Tailwind CSS.

For projects that value simplicity, speed, and a markup-centric workflow, the combination of Tailwind and **`Alpine.js`** offers an unparalleled development experience. By keeping state and behavior co-located with our styles, we can rapidly build common UI patterns such as tabs, modals, and dropdowns without the complexity of a build step or virtual DOM.

For large-scale, state-intensive applications, **`React`** provides a robust and scalable architecture. Our focus here has been on the critical patterns that ensure maintainability such as: safely handling dynamic classes, managing conditional styles with utilities such as **`cn`**, creating variant-driven components with **`CVA`**, and offloading complex accessibility logic to **`Headless UI`**.

The common thread through both approaches is the power of a component-first mindset and the role of AI as a development partner. By mastering the prompting strategies demonstrated, from augmentation and correction to persona-based scaffolding, we can effectively translate complex requirements into clean, accessible, and production-ready code.

With these foundational component patterns now firmly established, we are fully equipped to move into the next chapter, where we will begin assembling these building blocks into complete, functional applications

Multiple Choice Questions

1. Which `Alpine.js` directive is essential for initializing a new component scope and declaring its reactive state?
   a. `x-show`
   b. `x-on:click`
   c. `x-data`
   d. `x-model`
2. When building an interactive dropdown with `Alpine.js`, what is the common directive modifier used to close the menu when a user clicks outside of it?
   a. `@click.self`
   b. `@keydown.escape.window`
   c. `@click.outside`
   d. `@click.prevent`
3. What is the primary purpose of the `@tailwindcss/forms` plugin?
   a. To provide complete, pre-styled form components like a login form.
   b. To add client-side validation logic to forms.
   c. To apply a minimal reset to native form controls, making them easier to style with utility classes.
   d. To automatically generate form submission endpoints.
4. What is the "Do Not Concatenate" rule when working with Tailwind CSS in a React application?
   a. You should never use more than one class on an element.
   b. You should avoid creating dynamic class names with string concatenation (for example, `` `bg-${color}-500` ``) because Tailwind's JIT engine cannot detect them at build time.
   c. You should use inline styles instead of dynamic classes.
   d. You must use the `clsx` library for all class strings.

5. When using a `cn` helper function that combines `clsx` and `tailwind-merge`, what specific problem does `tailwind-merge` solve?
    a. It minifies the final CSS bundle.
    b. It automatically adds vendor prefixes to CSS properties.
    c. It intelligently resolves conflicting Tailwind utility classes, ensuring the last class applied takes precedence.
    d. It converts Tailwind classes into TypeScript types.
6. What is the primary benefit of using CVA (Class Variance Authority) in a React and Tailwind CSS project?
    a. It replaces the need for a `tailwind.config.js` file.
    b. It provides a structured way to create components with multiple style variants (for example, size, intent) that are managed through props.
    c. It is a state management library similar to Redux.
    d. It automatically writes unit tests for your components.
7. What is the core philosophy of the Headless UI library?
    a. It provides fully styled, production-ready components that match Tailwind's design system.
    b. It is a tool for converting Figma designs directly into styled React and Vue components.
    c. It provides completely unstyled, fully accessible component logic, separating a component's behavior from its presentation.
    d. It is a CSS-only library that extends Tailwind with more advanced utility classes.
8. In an accessible `Alpine.js` tabs component, what is the purpose of dynamically binding the aria-selected attribute on a tab button?
    a. To change the font size of the tab's text.
    b. To programmatically communicate to assistive technologies which tab is currently active.
    c. To prevent the tab from being clicked.
    d. To store the tab's content in local storage.

9. According to the chapter, for which type of project is `Alpine.js` generally a better fit than React?
    a. Large-scale, complex Single-Page Applications (SPAs) with heavy state management.
    b. Server-rendered applications or static sites that need "sprinkles" of interactivity.
    c. Mobile application development.
    d. Projects that require a virtual DOM for maximum performance.
10. When styling a Headless UI component, what is the recommended way to apply styles for different states (for example, open, active) using the official plugin?
    a. Using inline styles with JavaScript logic.
    b. Writing custom CSS with the `@apply` directive.
    c. Using the `@headlessui/tailwindcss` plugin, which provides `ui-*` variants (like `ui-open:*`).
    d. Manually adding and removing classes with useEffect or watchers.

Answers

1. c
2. c
3. c
4. b
5. c
6. b
7. c
8. b
9. b
10. c

CHAPTER 6
Build a Calculator, a Web Scraper, and More

Introduction

In this chapter, we dive into **complete, real-world projects** that showcase how AI (especially GitHub Copilot) can accelerate development with Tailwind CSS. These projects range from beginner to intermediate complexity and mirror tasks often requested on freelance platforms such as Upwork and Workana. We will build a variety of applications – from a simple calculator to a data dashboard – emphasizing **practical utility** and **AI-assisted workflows**. Each project includes an overview, the tech stack, how AI prompts were used, key Tailwind concepts, a walkthrough of the final result, and reflections (with prompt engineering tips and AI-vs-human code insights). Throughout these projects, we focus on getting things working with Tailwind and Copilot's help, deferring deep optimizations or accessibility audits to later chapters.

Structure

In this chapter, we will cover the following topics:

- Project 1: Simple Calculator (Alpine.js + Tailwind CSS)
- Project 2: Creating a Web Scraper
- Project 3: Creating a Responsive Landing Page
- Project 4: Designing a Data Dashboard

Project 1: Simple Calculator (`Alpine.js + Tailwind CSS`)

This first project is a basic calculator web app built with a lightweight stack: Tailwind CSS for styling and Alpine.js for interactivity. The calculator allows users to input numbers and operations, then displays the computed result – essentially replicating a standard calculator's functions (addition, subtraction, and so on).[1]

Such a component might be simple, but it is a great starting point to learn AI-assisted development, and small calculation tools are occasionally needed in freelance projects (for example, ROI calculators or finance calculators embedded in websites). We will demonstrate how GitHub Copilot can assist both in building the front-end UI (using Tailwind utility classes for a neat layout) and the logic (implementing the arithmetic operations).

Tech Stack and Tools

For this first project, we will use the following technologies:

- **`Alpine.js`**: Handles the client-side logic and state (button clicks, updating the display) within the HTML, avoiding the need for a heavy framework.
- **Tailwind CSS**: Provides utility classes to quickly style the calculator interface (for layout, spacing, colors, and so on).
- **Visual Studio Code + GitHub Copilot**: Our AI pair-programmer. Copilot is used through its VSCode extension to scaffold the HTML/CSS and even some JS logic. We will leverage Copilot's suggestions as we type Tailwind classes and write Alpine.js functions.

Here, our focus is on the front-end, with any "backend" logic (the arithmetic) done in Alpine for simplicity.

Refresher: Setting up a Tailwind + `Alpine.js` Project

Before diving into the projects, let us review how to quickly set up a basic environment using **Tailwind CSS** and **`Alpine.js`**.

- **Open Visual Studio Code** and create a new folder for your project.
- Inside it, create a **`src`** folder to hold your files.
- **Initialize Tailwind CSS** by running the following commands in your terminal:

```
npm install tailwindcss @tailwindcss/cli
npx tailwindcss init
```

- This installs Tailwind and its CLI. Now
- create the Tailwind build script in your **`package.json:`**

```
"scripts": {
```

[1] *https://www.geeksforgeeks.org/javascript/how-to-create-calculator-card-using-tailwind-css-javascript/*

```
«dev": «npx @tailwindcss/cli -i ./src/input.css -o ./src/
output.css --watch"
}
```

This script watches for changes in your source CSS and automatically recompiles.

- Set up your CSS input file at **`src/input.css`** with the following content:

```
@import “tailwindcss”;
```

- **Create the main HTML file** at **`src/index.html`**, and include **`Alpine.js`** via **CDN**:

```
<!doctype html>
<html lang=”en”>
<head>
<meta charset=”UTF-8”>
<meta name=”viewport” content=”width=device-width, initial-
scale=1.0”>
<link href=”./output.css” rel=”stylesheet”>
<script defer src=”https://cdn.jsdelivr.net/npm/alpinejs@3.x.x/
dist/cdn.min.js”></script>
<title>Tailwind + Alpine Starter</title>
</head>
<body class=”min-h-screen flex items-center justify-center bg-gray-50”>
<h1 class=”text-3xl font-bold text-gray-800”>Tailwind + Alpine.js
Setup Complete!</h1>
</body>
</html>
```

- Run the development build:

```
npm run dev
```

  Tailwind will compile your styles into `src/output.css` and keep watching for changes as you build. Go live using an extension such as Live Server.

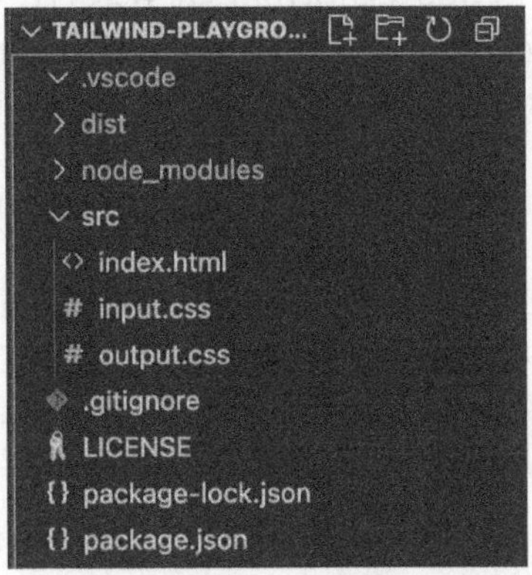

Figure 6.1: *Your Project Structure Will Look Something Like This*

Development with AI Prompts

We begin by creating the basic HTML structure. Copilot's scaffolding ability shines here: by writing a comment or a partial snippet (for instance, typing **<!-- Calculator container -->** or a starting **<div>** with some classes), Copilot can suggest the boilerplate for a centered calculator layout. For example, as soon as we create a **<body>** tag, Copilot might suggest adding Tailwind classes such as **bg-gray-100 flex justify-center items-center h-screen** to center our calculator on a gray background – a combination a human might also use, but Copilot provides it instantly.

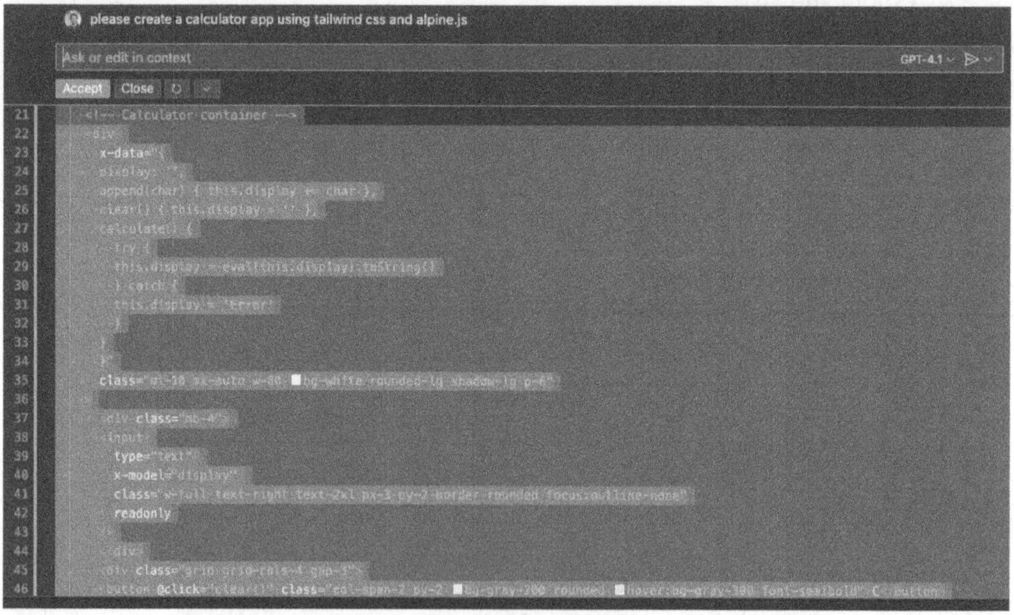

Figure 6.2: *A Simple Prompt Like 'Please Create a Calculator App Using Tailwind.css and Alpine.js' Already Created a Skeleton of Our App*

We then prompt Copilot (pressing a shortcut such as *ctrl* + I for Windows, or *command* + I for macOS, via code comments or just by starting to write HTML) to generate the calculator UI: A display input and a grid of buttons. Because calculators follow a predictable pattern of buttons (digits 0–9, operators, equals, clear, and so on), Copilot recognizes this pattern and can autocomplete much of the repetitive HTML. For instance, after we manually create one button (say the "7" button with styling), Copilot suggests the next buttons "8", "9", and so on, each with the same Tailwind styling (**bg-gray-300 hover:bg-gray-400 text-gray-800 font-bold py-2 px-4 rounded**) and appropriate **onclick** handlers for Alpine or JS. This saves us from typing similar lines over and over.

On the **Alpine.js** side, we use an **x-data** object to store the current input and result, and methods for clearing, appending characters, and evaluating the expression.

Copilot aids here as well: we write a comment such as **`// Function to evaluate the expression`** inside a **`<script>`** tag, and Copilot suggests an implementation (and so on, using **`eval()`** for simplicity or a safer approach using a parsing function). We do need to be cautious - Copilot might naively suggest using **`eval()`** on raw strings, which works but could be risky. As a rule, always review AI-generated logic for correctness and security. In our case, because we know the domain (simple arithmetic) and for learning purposes, using **`eval()`** on a controlled input may be acceptable, but we note to the reader that a more secure parser or backend validation might be needed in real freelance projects.

Utility-Class Suggestions: While styling the calculator, Copilot also helps with Tailwind classes. For example, when we start writing a class name such as text-, Copilot can often suggest completions (such as **`text-center mb-4 text-3xl font-bold`**) based on common UI patterns. Tailwind's utility-first approach lends itself well to AI suggestions, since the names are very descriptive (for example, **`rounded-lg shadow-lg border-2 border-green-500`** for a card-style panel). In fact, developers note that UI development with Tailwind CSS is an area where Copilot excels, because the self-contained utility classes follow standard patterns. Copilot "knows" many Tailwind utility classes, so it can autocomplete them correctly or even suggest a combination of classes to achieve a certain layout without the developer explicitly writing each one.

Final Result Walkthrough

```
<!doctype html>
<html lang="en">
  <head>
    <meta charset="UTF-8">
    <meta name="viewport" content="width=device-width, initial-
scale=1.0">
    <link href="./output.css" rel="stylesheet">
    <title>Tailwind + AlpineJS Hello World</title>
    <script defer src="https://cdn.jsdelivr.net/npm/alpinejs@3.x.x/dist/
cdn.min.js"></script>
  </head>
  <body class="flex h-screen items-center justify-center bg-gray-100">
    <!-- Calculator container -->
    <div
      x-data="{
      display: '',
      append(char) { this.display += char },
      clear() { this.display = '' },
      calculate() {
        try {
```

```
          this.display = eval(this.display).toString()
          } catch {
          this.display = 'Error'
          }
        }
        }"
        class="mt-10 mx-auto w-80 bg-white rounded-lg shadow-lg p-6"
    >
        <div class="mb-4">
        <input
          type="text"
          x-model="display"
          class="w-full text-right text-2xl px-3 py-2 border rounded
focus:outline-none"
          readonly
        />
        </div>
        <div class="grid grid-cols-4 gap-3">
        <button @click="clear()" class="col-span-2 py-2 bg-gray-200
rounded hover:bg-gray-300 font-semibold">C</button>
        <button @click="append('0')" class="py-2 bg-gray-100 rounded
hover:bg-gray-200 font-semibold">0</button>
        <button @click="append('/')" class="py-2 bg-blue-500 text-white
rounded hover:bg-blue-600 font-semibold">/</button>
        <button @click="append('7')" class="py-2 bg-gray-100 rounded
hover:bg-gray-200 font-semibold">7</button>
        <button @click="append('8')" class="py-2 bg-gray-100 rounded
hover:bg-gray-200 font-semibold">8</button>
        <button @click="append('9')" class="py-2 bg-gray-100 rounded
hover:bg-gray-200 font-semibold">9</button>
        <button @click="append('*')" class="py-2 bg-blue-500 text-white
rounded hover:bg-blue-600 font-semibold">*</button>
        <button @click="append('4')" class="py-2 bg-gray-100 rounded
hover:bg-gray-200 font-semibold">4</button>
        <button @click="append('5')" class="py-2 bg-gray-100 rounded
hover:bg-gray-200 font-semibold">5</button>
        <button @click="append('6')" class="py-2 bg-gray-100 rounded
hover:bg-gray-200 font-semibold">6</button>
        <button @click="append('-')" class="py-2 bg-blue-500 text-white
rounded hover:bg-blue-600 font-semibold">-</button>
        <button @click="append('1')" class="py-2 bg-gray-100 rounded
hover:bg-gray-200 font-semibold">1</button>
```

```
        <button @click=”append(‘2’)” class=”py-2 bg-gray-100 rounded
hover:bg-gray-200 font-semibold”>2</button>
        <button @click=”append(‘3’)” class=”py-2 bg-gray-100 rounded
hover:bg-gray-200 font-semibold”>3</button>
        <button @click=”append(‘+’)” class=”py-2 bg-blue-500 text-white
rounded hover:bg-blue-600 font-semibold”>+</button>
        <button @click=”append(‘.’)” class=”py-2 bg-gray-100 rounded
hover:bg-gray-200 font-semibold”>.</button>
        <button @click=”calculate()” class=”col-span-3 py-2 bg-green-500
text-white rounded hover:bg-green-600 font-semibold”>=</button>
        </div>
      </div>
   </body>
</html>
```

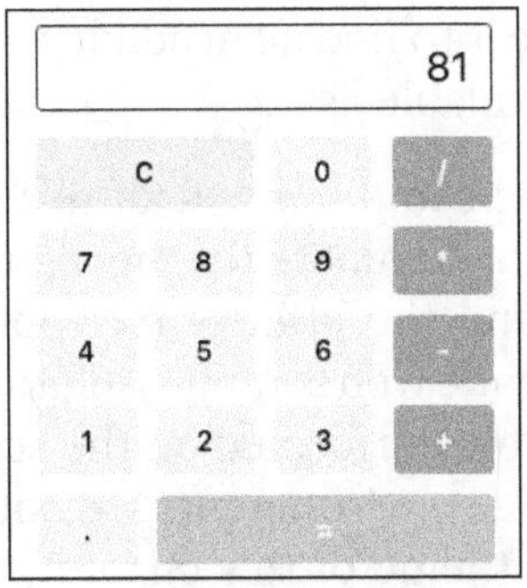

Figure 6.3: *Example of a Tailwind + Alpine.js Calculator Interface. The Design is Centered on the Page with a Clear Display at the Top and a Grid of Styled Buttons for Digits and Operations*

When the calculator is opened, the user sees a **calculator card** centered on a gray backdrop. The card has a title “Basic Calculator” and an output display area initialized to “0”. The number and operator buttons are laid out in a 4x5 grid. Using the app feels just like a small calculator: The user clicks digits and operation buttons, and the expression builds up in the display. When the user presses “=”, the result of the computation is shown in the display. For example, clicking “7”, “+”, “5”, then “=” will display “12”. There is also a clear “C” button that resets the display. Thanks to **`Alpine.js`**, the buttons update a reactive state (**`x-data`**), so the display updates immediately as characters are appended. Tailwind’s responsive design ensures that if we resize the browser or use the calculator on a mobile device, the grid layout still looks good (buttons wrap appropriately and remain touch-friendly in size).

Behind the scenes, **Copilot accelerated our development** at several points. It helped generate repetitive button elements and suggested correct Tailwind classes for styling, allowing us to focus on the app’s functionality. The end result is a neat-looking calculator built much faster than hand-coding everything from scratch.

Project 2: Creating a Web Scraper

This chapter embarks on a practical project to build a simple yet functional web application: A client-side information extractor. The goal is to create a tool that can fetch the contents of a public webpage and extract specific pieces of information, such as headlines, directly within the user's browser. This exercise serves as a powerful vehicle for exploring core concepts in modern frontend development, from managing asynchronous data to building responsive, state-aware user interfaces.

What We are Building (and What We are Not)

The application will feature a clean, minimalist interface: A single input field for a URL, a button to initiate the process, and a display area for the extracted results. When a user enters a URL and clicks "Fetch and Extract," the application will retrieve the HTML of the target page, parse it to find all headline elements (for example, `<h2>` tags), and render them as a clean, readable list.

It is essential to define the scope and purpose of this project from the outset. This is an educational tool designed to illuminate the mechanics of client-side data handling, state management in React, and the utility-first approach of TailwindCSS. It is not intended to be a production-grade web scraping solution. Robust, scalable, and reliable web scraping is almost invariably performed on the server-side using languages such as Python or Node.js. Server-side environments are not bound by the browser security restrictions that are a central theme of this chapter, making them far more suitable for large-scale data extraction. This project, by contrast, operates entirely within the browser, providing a unique opportunity to understand and navigate its inherent security features.

To keep the logic clear as we combine the React state with asynchronous web scraping, think of the application flow in these four distinct stages:

1. Stage 1: The Request (React State): **We capture the user's URL and store it in a React state variable.**
2. Stage 2: The Handshake (CORS Proxy): **Because of browser security restrictions, we send that URL to a "middleman" server (`AllOrigins`) that fetches the data on our behalf.**
3. Stage 3: The Extraction (DOMParser): **We take the raw text returned by the proxy and use the browser's built-in tools to "find" the specific `<h2>` tags we want.**
4. Stage 4: The Presentation (Tailwind CSS): **Finally, we take that list of headlines and style them into a clean, responsive UI using Tailwind utility classes.**

About React.js

React.js is a declarative, component-based JavaScript library for building user interfaces. React's state management capabilities, particularly the **`useState`** hook, are ideal for handling the dynamic nature of our application. It allows the UI to reactively update based on the current status of the data-fetching process—whether it is loading, has encountered an error, or has successfully retrieved the data.

The Fundamental Challenge: The Browser's Sandbox and CORS

Before a single line of code is written, it is crucial to understand the principal technical obstacle that defines this project: The browser's security model. Web browsers operate as a "sandbox," a restricted environment where code from one website is strictly limited in its ability to interact with resources from another. This security architecture is fundamental to a safe web experience, but it presents a direct challenge to our goal of fetching data from an arbitrary URL. The next section will delve into this core problem and the mechanisms that govern it.

The primary reason client-side web scraping is challenging is a security feature, not a bug. Browsers enforce a strict policy to protect users from malicious scripts. To build our application, this gatekeeper must first be understood.

Imagine a web application as an employee working inside a secure corporate building. This building represents the application's "origin." An origin is defined by the combination of the protocol (for example, **`https`**), domain (for example, **`example.com`**), and port (for example, **`:443`**) of a URL. Inside their own building, the employee can freely access any file, room, or resource. This is a same-origin request, and it is always permitted.

The Same-Origin Policy dictates that this employee cannot simply pick up the phone, call a different corporation's secure building, and ask for their internal documents. The browser, acting as a security guard, will block this request. This is a cross-origin request. This policy is a cornerstone of web security. Without it, a malicious script on a seemingly harmless website could make requests to your online banking portal, your email, or other private services using your logged-in credentials, potentially compromising your personal data.

CORS: The Official Visitor Pass System

While the Same-Origin Policy is essential, there are many legitimate reasons for web applications to request resources from different origins, such as fetching data from a public API or loading web fonts. To accommodate these use cases, a mechanism called Cross-Origin Resource Sharing (CORS) was created.

CORS is an HTTP-header-based system that allows a server to relax the Same-Origin Policy and specify which origins are permitted to access its resources. It acts as an official visitor pass system. When a browser makes a cross-origin request, the destination server can include a special HTTP header in its response, **`Access-Control-Allow-Origin`**. If this header's value matches the origin of the requesting application (or is a wildcard *), the browser's security guard checks the "visitor pass" and allows the application to access the response. If the server does not send this header, or if the origin does not match, the browser blocks the request and throws an error.

The crucial takeaway is that the power to grant access lies entirely with the server hosting the resource. The client-side application can only ask for permission; it cannot force its way in. This server-side opt-in model is fundamental. The challenge for our scraper is that most websites do not include permissive CORS headers, as they are not designed to be used as public APIs.

To witness this security mechanism in action, one can perform a simple experiment. On any website, open the browser's developer tools and navigate to the console. Then, type and execute the following JavaScript command:

```
fetch('https://www.github.com');
```

Almost instantly, the console will display an error message similar to this:

```
Access to fetch at 'https://www.github.com/' from origin '...' has been
blocked by CORS policy: No 'Access-Control-Allow-Origin' header is
present on the requested resource.
```

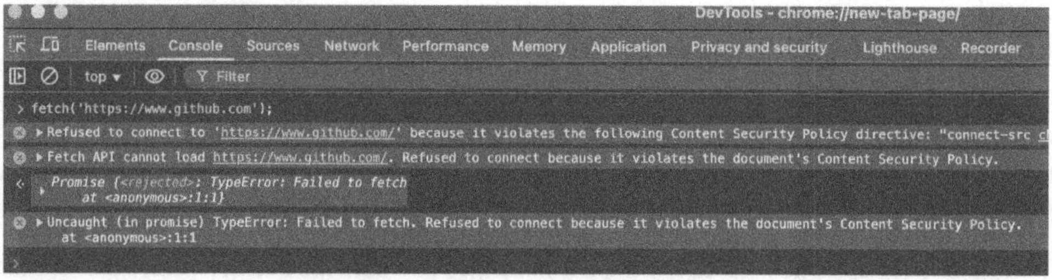

Figure 6.4: *Example of CORS Error*

This demonstrates the problem perfectly. The JavaScript code itself only receives a generic network error; the specific details of the CORS failure are only visible in the developer console for security reasons. The browser has successfully blocked the cross-origin request because the GitHub server did not return the required **`Access-Control-Allow-Origin`** header. This is the exact hurdle our application must overcome.

The Key to the City: Using a CORS Proxy

Since the target server cannot be forced to send the correct CORS headers, a different approach is needed. The solution involves introducing a middleman that can make the request on our application's behalf—a CORS proxy.

About the CORS Proxy

A CORS proxy is a server that acts as an intermediary between a client-side application and a target server. The workflow is as follows:

- **Request:** The React application makes a request not to the target website (for example, `https://example.com`), but to the CORS proxy, embedding the target URL within the proxy's URL (for example, `https://proxy.example/https://example.com`).
- **Forwarding:** The CORS proxy server receives this request. Because this is a server-to-server request, it is not subject to the browser's Same-Origin Policy or CORS restrictions. The proxy forwards the request to the actual target website.
- **Response:** The target website sends the HTML response back to the proxy server.
- **Enrichment and Return:** The proxy server takes the response from the target website and adds the crucial permissive CORS header, such as `Access-Control-Allow-Origin: *`. It then sends this modified response back to the original React application.

From the browser's perspective, it made a successful cross-origin request to the proxy server, which kindly returned the necessary headers. It remains unaware of the subsequent server-to-server hop. This technique effectively bypasses the browser's security constraint for our specific use case.

Choosing Your Proxy: A Double-Edged Sword

While one could build and host a personal CORS proxy, the objective of this project is to minimize backend work. Therefore, a free, public CORS proxy will be used. These services are often run by students, open-source enthusiasts, or as free tiers of commercial products, and they provide a convenient way to get a project running quickly.

However, this convenience comes with significant caveats. Public proxies can be unreliable, with potential for downtime or sudden discontinuation. They often have strict rate limits to prevent abuse. Most importantly, they present a security risk. All data sent to and received from the target website passes directly through the proxy server. This means the proxy operator can read the full contents of the request and response.

For this reason, a critical security rule must be followed: **Never send sensitive information, such as API keys, passwords, cookies, or personal data, through a public CORS proxy**. For this project, which only deals with fetching publicly available, unauthenticated HTML, the risk is minimal. However, this technique is strictly for development and prototyping and is not suitable for production applications.

The existence of this ecosystem of free, often fragile, public proxies highlights a fundamental friction in web development. The browser's robust security model, designed for large-scale application safety, can be cumbersome for developers building small prototypes or personal tools that need to aggregate public data. These proxies fill a niche by providing a "gray market" solution. Using them responsibly means understanding their limitations and treating them as a temporary development aid, not a permanent architectural component.

A Curated List of Public Proxies for Development

To ensure the project is resilient to the potential downtime of any single service, here is a curated list of public proxies suitable for this tutorial. The application will be built using **`AllOrigins`**, but the others serve as excellent alternatives.

Proxy Service	Example URL Format	Rate Limit (approx.)	Notes
`AllOrigins`	`https://api.allorigins.win/raw?url={URL}`	20/min	Reliable for simple GET requests. Returns raw HTML.
`CodeTabs CORS Proxy`	`https://api.codetabs.com/v1/proxy?quest={URL}`	5/s	Supports GET only.
`cors-anywhere`	`https://cors-anywhere.herokuapp.com/{URL}`	50/3 mins	Often requires a temporary demo activation click on its homepage. Good for quick tests.

Table 6.1: *Comparison of Proxy Tools*

Getting Your Code Started

For this project, a pre-configured starter template using **`Vite`**, **`React`**, and **`TailwindCSS`** is the ideal starting point. **`Vite`** is a modern frontend build tool known for its extremely fast startup time and Hot Module Replacement (HMR), which makes for a seamless development experience.

On your terminal, type

```
npm create vite@latest headline-extractor -- --template react
npm install tailwindcss @tailwindcss/vite
```

Create **`vite.config.js`** at the project root (or edit the one **`Vite`** created):

```
// vite.config.js
import { defineConfig } from 'vite'
import react from '@vitejs/plugin-react'
import tailwindcss from '@tailwindcss/vite'

export default defineConfig({
```

```
  plugins: [react(), tailwindcss()],
})
```

A Quick Tour of the Files

The key files of interest are:

- **index.html**: The root HTML file of the application. The React application will be injected into the **<div id="root">** element within this file.
- **src/main.jsx**: The entry point of the application. This file is responsible for rendering the main **App** component into the DOM.
- **src/App.jsx**: The main application component. For this project, all of the logic and markup will be contained within this single file to keep things simple.
- **src/index.css**: The main CSS file. It imports Tailwind's base styles, components, and utilities.
- **tailwind.config.js**: The configuration file for TailwindCSS. While the defaults are sufficient for this project, this is where one could customize the framework's design system (for example, colors, fonts, and spacing).

With the environment set up, the next step is to begin crafting the user interface.

Crafting the Interface: Layout and Styling with TailwindCSS

This section focuses on building the application's user interface piece by piece using TailwindCSS. The emphasis will be on explaining the semantic meaning behind the utility class combinations to foster a deeper understanding of the utility-first workflow. All changes will be made within the **src/App.jsx** file.

The Main Application Shell

First, the root **div** of the **App** component will be styled to serve as the main container. This will establish the background color and center the content both vertically and horizontally.

```
// In src/App.jsx
function App() {
  return (
    <div className="bg-slate-100 min-h-screen flex items-center justify-
center p-4 font-sans">
      {/*... content will go here... */}
    </div>
  );
}
```

- **bg-slate-100**: Sets a light, neutral gray background color from Tailwind's default color palette.
- **min-h-screen**: Ensures the container's minimum height is 100% of the viewport height, so that the background color always fills the screen.
- **flex items-center justify-center**: This is a classic flexbox pattern. **flex** establishes a flex container, **items-center** aligns children vertically in the center, and **justify-center** aligns them horizontally in the center.
- **p-4**: Adds padding around the container to prevent content from touching the screen edges on small devices.
- **font-sans**: Sets a default sans-serif font stack for the application.

The Scraper's Control Panel

Inside the main shell, a container will be created to act as the main "card" for the application's controls. This card will have a white background, rounded corners, and a subtle shadow to lift it off the page.

```
<div className="bg-white rounded-xl shadow-lg p-6 w-full max-w-lg
space-y-6">
  {/*... form elements will go here... */}
</div>
```

- **bg-white rounded-xl shadow-lg**: These classes work together to create the card's visual appearance. **bg-white** sets the background, **rounded-xl** applies large, soft rounded corners, and **shadow-lg** adds a pronounced drop shadow.
- **p-6**: Adds a generous amount of internal padding to give the content inside the card room to breathe.
- **w-full max-w-lg**: This combination is key to responsive design. **w-full** makes the card take up the full width of its parent on small screens. **max-w-lg** constrains its width to a maximum of **32rem** on larger screens, preventing it from becoming too wide and unreadable.
- **space-y-6**: This is a powerful layout utility. It automatically adds vertical margin between all direct child elements, ensuring consistent spacing without needing to manually add margin to each one.

The Input Form

Next, the **form** element containing the URL input field is added inside the card. The input field will be styled to be clean and provide clear visual feedback to the user when it is active.

```
<form>
  <label htmlFor="url-input" className="block text-sm font-medium text-
```

```
slate-700 mb-1">
    Enter URL to Extract Headlines
  </label>
  <input
    id="url-input"
    type="text"
    placeholder="https://example.com"
    className="w-full px-4 py-2 border border-slate-300 rounded-md
focus:ring-2 focus:ring-blue-500 focus:border-blue-500 outline-none
transition-all"
  />
</form>
```

- **Label Styling:** The **`label`** is styled to be a slightly smaller, medium-weight text in a dark gray color, with a small margin at the bottom.
- **Input Base Styling: `w-full`** makes the input fill the width of the card. **`px-4 py-2`** sets horizontal and vertical padding for a comfortable text entry area. **`border border-slate-300 rounded-md`** creates a standard, light gray border with medium rounded corners.
- **Input State Styling:** The **`focus:`** variants are crucial for user experience. **`focus:ring-2 focus:ring-blue-500`** adds a blue "ring" outline around the input when it is focused, providing a clear visual indicator of the active element. **`focus:border-blue-500`** changes the border color to match.
- **Input Polish: `outline-none`** removes the default browser focus outline, allowing the custom **`ring`** to take precedence. **`transition-all`** ensures that the changes in border color and ring visibility are smoothly animated.

The Action Button

Finally, the "**`Fetch and Extract`**" button is added. Its styling will communicate its function and provide feedback across different interaction states: Default, hover, active, and disabled.

```
<button
  type="submit"
  className="w-full bg-blue-600 text-white font-bold py-3 px-4 rounded-
md hover:bg-blue-700 active:bg-blue-800 focus:outline-none focus:ring-2
focus:ring-blue-500 focus:ring-opacity-50 transition-colors disabled:bg-
slate-400 disabled:cursor-not-allowed"
>
  Fetch & Extract
</button>
```

- **Base Styling:** `w-full` makes it a block-level button. `bg-blue-600 text-white font-bold py-3 px-4 rounded-md` defines its primary appearance: A strong blue background, white text, bold font, generous padding, and rounded corners.
- **Interaction States:** `hover:bg-blue-700` darkens the button slightly when the mouse hovers over it. `active:bg-blue-800` darkens it further when the button is being clicked.
- **Accessibility:** `focus:outline-none focus:ring-2...` provides a visible focus ring for keyboard navigation, similar to the input field.
- **Disabled State:** `disabled:bg-slate-400 disabled:cursor-not-allowed` is critically important. These classes will automatically apply when the button's `disabled` attribute is true. They change the background to a muted gray and set the cursor to "not-allowed," providing clear feedback that the action is temporarily unavailable, such as during a data fetch.

With the static UI complete, the next step is to bring it to life with React's state management.

Wiring the Engine: State Management and Data Fetching

With the static interface built, the focus now shifts to the application's logic. This involves using React's `useState` hook to manage the application's state and implementing the function that will fetch and process the data.

Introducing `useState`

The `useState` hook allows functional components to hold and manage state. Four distinct pieces of state are required to track the application's lifecycle:

- `url`: A string to store the current value of the URL input field.
- `loading`: A boolean that will be `true` while a network request is in progress and `false` otherwise. This is used to disable the form and show a loading indicator.
- `error`: A string to hold any error message that occurs during the fetching process.
- `data`: An array that will store the successfully extracted headline objects.

These are initialized at the top of the `App` component:

```
import React, { useState } from 'react';

function App() {
```

```
  const [url, setUrl] = useState('');
  const [loading, setLoading] = useState(false);
  const [error, setError] = useState(null);
  const = useState();

  //... rest of the component
}
```

The **handleSubmit** Function

An **async** function named **handleSubmit** will orchestrate the entire data-fetching process. This function will be attached to the **onSubmit** event of the **form** element.

The function begins by preventing the default form submission behavior, which would cause a page reload. It then enters a "loading" state by setting **loading** to **true** and clearing any previous data or errors.

```
const handleSubmit = async (e) => {
  e.preventDefault();
  setLoading(true);
  setError(null);
  setData();
  //... fetching logic will go here
};
```

Fetching Data through the Proxy

The core of the **handleSubmit** function is the network request. This is where the CORS proxy is used. The URL from the state is encoded to ensure it is safe to be used as a query parameter, and then it is appended to the **AllOrigins** proxy URL.

The entire fetching operation is wrapped in a **try...catch...finally** block. This is a robust pattern for handling asynchronous operations that might fail.

- The **try** block contains the "happy path": making the **fetch** request, checking if the response was successful (for example, status code 200), and parsing the response body as text.
- The **catch** block will execute if the **fetch** call itself fails (for example, due to a network issue or if the proxy is down). It sets an error message in the state.
- The **finally** block will always execute, regardless of whether the **try** block succeeded or the **catch** block was triggered. This is the perfect place to set **loading** back to **false**, ensuring that the UI becomes interactive again after the operation is complete.

```
const handleSubmit = async (e) => {
  //... (state setup from before)
```

```
  try {
    const proxyUrl = `https://api.allorigins.win/
raw?url=${encodeURIComponent(url)}`;
    const response = await fetch(proxyUrl);

    if (!response.ok) {
      throw new Error(`HTTP error! Status: ${response.status}`);
    }

    const htmlString = await response.text();
    //... parsing logic will go here

  } catch (err) {
    setError(`Failed to fetch data. Please check the URL or try again.
(Error: ${err.message})`);
  } finally {
    setLoading(false);
  }
};
```

With the raw HTML string successfully fetched, the next step is to parse it and extract the desired information.

Sifting for Gold: Parsing HTML with `DOMParser`

The response from the proxy is a single, large string of HTML text. To extract information from it programmatically, this string must be converted into a structured Document Object Model (DOM) tree, similar to the one the browser maintains for the current page.

From String to Document

While various third-party libraries exist for HTML parsing, many, such as Cheerio, are designed primarily for Node.js environments. For a purely client-side application, the most efficient and direct solution is to use the browser's built-in **`DOMParser`** Web API.

This API requires no external dependencies, adding zero weight to the application bundle, and is universally supported in modern browsers. This choice exemplifies a key principle of efficient frontend development: Leveraging native browser capabilities before reaching for external libraries.

The **`DOMParser`** interface provides a **`parseFromString()`** method that takes a string and a MIME type as arguments. It returns a complete, queryable **`Document`** object.

The implementation is straightforward. A new **`DOMParser`** instance is created, and its **`parseFromString`** method is called with the fetched HTML string and the MIME type **`'text/html'`**.

```
// Inside the 'try' block of handleSubmit, after getting htmlString
const parser = new DOMParser();
const doc = parser.parseFromString(htmlString, 'text/html');
```

The **`doc`** variable now holds a DOM document created in memory, which can be manipulated and queried without affecting the visible page.

Querying for Elements

With the HTML string converted into a **`Document`** object, standard DOM traversal methods such as **`querySelector`** and **`querySelectorAll`** can be used to find specific elements. To extract all level-two headlines, **`doc.querySelectorAll('h2')`** is used.

```
// Inside the 'try' block, after creating the doc
const headlines = doc.querySelectorAll('h2');
```

This method returns a **`NodeList`**, which is an array-like collection of all matching **`<h2>`** elements found within the parsed document.

Extracting and Cleaning the Data

The final step in the parsing process is to iterate over the **`NodeList`** and transform it into a clean array of objects suitable for storing in the React state. This involves three steps:

1. **Convert to Array:** The **`NodeList`** is converted into a true JavaScript array using **`Array.from()`** to enable the use of array methods such as **`.map()`**.
2. **Map and Extract:** The array is mapped over. For each headline element, an object is created containing its **`textContent`**. The **`.trim()`** method is called to remove any leading or trailing whitespace.
3. **Filter Empty Results:** Some **`<h2>`** tags on a page might be empty or contain only whitespace. The **`.filter()`** method is used to remove any items that have no text content, ensuring that the final data is clean.

```
// Inside the 'try' block, after querying for headlines
const extractedData = Array.from(headlines)
  .map(el => ({
    text: el.textContent.trim(),
  }))
  .filter(item => item.text);
```

```
if (extractedData.length === 0) {
    setError('No h2 headlines found on the page.');
} else {
    setData(extractedData);
}
```

This cleaned array, **extractedData**, is then set into the application's state using **setData()**. If no headlines are found, a user-friendly error message is set instead. The application's core logic is now complete. The final task is to render the results, errors, and loading states in the UI.

Presenting the Findings: Dynamically Rendering Results

The final implementation step is to connect the application's state to the user interface. The UI should dynamically change to reflect whether the application is loading, has encountered an error, or has successfully retrieved data. This is achieved through conditional rendering in JSX.

Conditional Rendering

Using JavaScript's logical **&&** operator and ternary expressions within JSX provides a concise way to render elements based on the current state.

- **Loading Indicator:** A simple loading message or spinner can be shown when the **loading** state is **true**.
- **Error Message:** A styled error box is displayed if the **error** state contains a message.
- **Results:** The list of extracted data is rendered only if the **data** array is not empty.

These conditional blocks are added below the form in **App.jsx**.

```
// Inside the main card div, below the form
<div className="mt-6">
  {loading && (
    <div className="text-center text-slate-500">
      <p>Fetching and parsing data...</p>
    </div>
  )}

  {error && (
    <div className="bg-red-100 border border-red-400 text-red-700 px-4
py-3 rounded-md" role="alert">
```

```
      <strong className="font-bold">Error:</strong>
      <span className="block sm:inline ml-2">{error}</span>
    </div>
  )}

  {/*... data mapping will go here... */}
</div>
```

Mapping and Displaying the Data

When the **data** array contains items, the **.map()** function is used to iterate over it and render a list item (**<li>**) for each extracted headline. This is a standard pattern in React for rendering lists of data.

Each list item must have a unique **key** prop. React uses this key to efficiently update the list when items are added, removed, or reordered. While using the array **index** as a key is acceptable for this simple, static list, a more stable unique identifier (such as an ID from the data) is preferred in more complex applications.

```
{data.length > 0 && (
  <div>
    <h2 className="text-lg font-semibold text-slate-800 mb-3">Extracted
Headlines:</h2>
    <ul className="space-y-3 max-h-96 overflow-y-auto pr-2">
      {data.map((item, index) => (
        <li
          key={index}
          className="bg-slate-50 p-3 rounded-md border border-slate-200
text-slate-700"
        >
          {item.text}
        </li>
      ))}
    </ul>
  </div>
)}
```

The list is styled with Tailwind utilities. **space-y-3** adds vertical spacing between list items. **max-h-96 overflow-y-auto** constrains the height of the list and makes it scrollable if the content overflows, preventing the page layout from breaking with a large number of results. With this final piece in place, the application is fully functional.

While the scraping logic is a powerful addition to your toolkit, the real 'gold' of this project is learning how to use **Tailwind's space-y-3 and max-h-96** to handle a dynamic list of unknown length while maintaining a clean, scrollable layout.

The Final Assembly: Complete Code and Live Demonstration

This chapter has walked through the theory and practice of building a client-side information extractor, from understanding browser security to implementing a reactive UI. This final section provides the complete code for the application, allowing for easy testing in the online IDE.

The Complete `App.jsx`

The following code is the final, complete version of the **`App.jsx`** component. It can be copied and pasted directly to our project or even a Stackblitz page, replacing the existing content of **`src/App.jsx`**.

Think of the following **`fetchHtmlThroughProxies`** function as a **Utility Helper**. You do not need to master the inner workings of proxy chains yet; simply understand that this is a robust 'black box' that ensures our data successfully reaches our React application.

```
import React, { useState } from "react";

export default function App() {
  const [url, setUrl] = useState("");
  const [loading, setLoading] = useState(false);
  const [error, setError] = useState(null);
  const [data, setData] = useState([]);

  const buildProxyChain = (targetUrl) => [
    // returns raw HTML
    `https://api.codetabs.com/v1/
proxy?quest=${encodeURIComponent(targetUrl)}`,
    // expects the raw URL appended (don't encode)
    `https://cors.isomorphic-git.org/${targetUrl}`,
    `https://thingproxy.freeboard.io/fetch/${targetUrl}`,
    `https://yacdn.org/proxy/${targetUrl}`,
    // AllOrigins JSON variant (as last resort)
    `https://api.allorigins.win/
get?url=${encodeURIComponent(targetUrl)}#json`,
  ];

  async function fetchHtmlThroughProxies(targetUrl) {
    const candidates = buildProxyChain(targetUrl);

    for (const proxy of candidates) {
      try {
        const res = await fetch(proxy, { method: "GET" });
        if (!res.ok) continue;
```

```
        // Handle the AllOrigins JSON variant (we tagged with #json)
        if (proxy.endsWith("#json")) {
          const json = await res.json();
          if (json && json.contents) return json.contents;
          continue;
        }

        // Others return raw HTML
        const text = await res.text();
        if (text && text.length) return text;
      } catch (_err) {
        // try next proxy
      }
    }
    throw new Error("All proxy attempts failed or were blocked.");
  }

  const handleSubmit = async (e) => {
    e.preventDefault();
    if (!url) {
      setError("Please enter a URL.");
      return;
    }
    setLoading(true);
    setError(null);
    setData([]);

    try {
      // Free CORS proxy — some sites may still block scraping
      const proxyUrl = `https://api.allorigins.win/
raw?url=${encodeURIComponent(
        url
      )}`;
      const response = await fetch(proxyUrl);

      if (!response.ok)
        throw new Error(`HTTP error! Status: ${response.status}`);

      const htmlString = await fetchHtmlThroughProxies(url);
      const parser = new DOMParser();
      const doc = parser.parseFromString(htmlString, "text/html");

      const headlines = doc.querySelectorAll("h2");
      const extractedData = Array.from(headlines)
        .map((el) => ({ text: el.textContent.trim() }))
```

```
        .filter((item) => item.text);
      if (extractedData.length === 0) {
        setError("No h2 headlines were found on the specified page.");
      } else {
        setData(extractedData);
      }
    } catch (err) {
      setError(
        `Failed to fetch data. Please check the URL or try again.
(Error: ${err.message})`
      );
    } finally {
      setLoading(false);
    }
  };

  return (
    <div className="flex items-center justify-center min-h-screen bg-
slate-100 font-sans">
      <div className="w-full max-w-lg bg-white rounded-xl shadow-lg p-6">
        <h1 className="text-2xl font-bold text-slate-800 mb-4 text-center">
          Headline Extractor
        </h1>

        <form onSubmit={handleSubmit} className="space-y-4">
          <div>
            <label
              htmlFor="url-input"
              className="block text-sm font-medium text-slate-700 mb-1"
            >
              Enter URL to Extract Headlines
            </label>
            <input
              id="url-input"
              type="text"
              value={url}
              onChange={(e) => setUrl(e.target.value)}
              placeholder="https://example.com"
              className="
      w-full
      px-4 py-2
      border border-slate-300
      rounded-md
      bg-white
```

```
      text-slate-800
      placeholder-slate-400
      focus:ring-2 focus:ring-blue-500 focus:border-blue-500
      outline-none transition-all
    "
              disabled={loading}
            />
          </div>

          <button
            type="submit"
            className="w-full bg-blue-600 text-white font-bold py-3
px-4 rounded-md hover:bg-blue-700 active:bg-blue-800 focus:outline-none
focus:ring-2 focus:ring-blue-500 focus:ring-opacity-50 transition-colors
disabled:bg-slate-400 disabled:cursor-not-allowed"
            disabled={loading}
          >
            {loading ? "Extracting..." : "Fetch & Extract"}
          </button>
        </form>

        <div className="mt-6">
          {loading && (
            <div className="text-center text-slate-500">
              <p>Fetching and parsing data...</p>
            </div>
          )}

          {error && (
            <div
              className="bg-red-100 border border-red-400 text-red-700
px-4 py-3 rounded-md"
              role="alert"
            >
              <strong className="font-bold">Error:</strong>
              <span className="block sm:inline ml-2">{error}</span>
            </div>
          )}

          {data.length > 0 && (
            <div>
              <h2 className="text-lg font-semibold text-slate-800 mb-3">
                Extracted Headlines:
              </h2>
              <ul className="space-y-3 max-h-96 overflow-y-auto pr-2
border-t pt-4">
```

```
                {data.map((item, index) => (
                  <li
                    key={index}
                    className="bg-slate-50 p-3 rounded-md border border-
slate-200 text-slate-700"
                  >
                    {item.text}
                  </li>
                ))}
              </ul>
            </div>
          )}
        </div>
      </div>
    </div>
  );
}
```

With the code pasted into the IDE of our choice, the application in the preview window should update automatically. It is now ready for testing. One can try various URLs, such as news sites or blogs, to see the results. It is important to note that this simple extractor will work best on websites with a straightforward HTML structure. It may fail or return no results for highly dynamic, JavaScript-heavy Single-Page Applications (SPAs) where the content is rendered client-side after the initial HTML load.

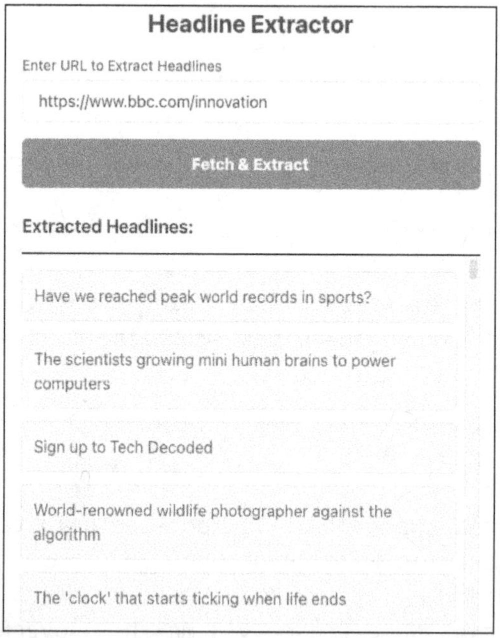

Figure 6.5: *The Final Output of Our Headline Extractor*

Project 3: Creating a Responsive Landing Page

Building a landing page is a perfect use case for AI assistance. The structure of such pages often follows established patterns (`header`, `hero`, `features`, and `footer`), which the Copilot recognizes and can generate quickly[2].

Our workflow will be to build the page section by section, starting with the HTML structure and applying Tailwind classes for styling. We will then add the necessary Alpine.js directives to bring the interactive elements to life.

Initial Setup

One of the biggest advantages of this stack is the near-instant setup. We begin with a standard HTML file and include the CDN links for both Tailwind CSS and `Alpine.js` in the `<head>`, just like we did in the start of this chapter in project 1.

```
<head>
  <meta charset="UTF-8" />
  <meta name="viewport" content="width=device-width, initial-scale=1.0"
/>
  <title>Responsive Landing Page</title>

  <!-- Tailwind CSS (Play CDN) -->
  <script src="https://cdn.tailwindcss.com"></script>
  <!-- Alpine.js for lightweight interactivity -->
  <script src="https://unpkg.com/alpinejs" defer></script>
</head>
```

With this boilerplate, we are ready to start building. The defer attribute on the Alpine.js script ensures that it runs after the HTML has been parsed, allowing it to properly initialize our components.

Building the Header and Mobile Navigation

The header is often the most complex part of a landing page because it needs to adapt its layout significantly between the desktop and mobile views.

AI Prompt Strategy: A good prompt for Copilot would be: `Create a header for my landing page app that uses Tailwind.css and Alpine.js. You should create a responsible menu containing Home, About and Contact links`.

---

[2] *https://github.blog/ai-and-ml/github-copilot/from-prompt-to-production-building-a-landing-page-with-copilot-agent-mode/#:~:text=Instead%20of%20repeatedly%20adding%20this,quality%20responses*

Copilot will likely generate a structure that uses:

- **Flexbox** (**flex**, **items-center**, and **justify-between**) for alignment.
- **Responsive Utilities** (**hidden**, **md:flex**) to toggle the visibility of the desktop navigation and the mobile menu button based on screen size.

The key piece of interactivity is the mobile menu. This is where **Alpine.js** comes in.

- **x-data="{ open: false }"**: We place this directive on the **<header>** tag. This initializes an Alpine component, creating a piece of reactive state called open and setting its initial value to false.
- **@click="open =!open"**: This event listener is added to the mobile menu **<button>**. When clicked, it toggles the value of open.
- **x-show="open"**: This directive is placed on the mobile navigation menu. The menu will only be visible when the open property is true.

This simple combination of directives creates a fully functional mobile menu with just three lines of Alpine-specific code.

```
<!-- Header -->
  <header x-data="{ open: false }" class="bg-white shadow">
    <div class="max-w-7xl mx-auto px-4 py-4 flex items-center justify-
between">
      <a href="#" class="text-2xl font-bold text-blue-600">BrandName</a>
      <!-- Desktop Nav -->
      <nav class="hidden md:flex space-x-6">
        <a href="#" class="text-gray-600 hover:text-blue-600">Home</a>
        <a href="#" class="text-gray-600 hover:text-blue-600">About</a>
        <a href="#" class="text-gray-600 hover:text-blue-600">Contact</a>
      </nav>
      <!-- Mobile Menu Button -->
      <button @click="open = !open" class="md:hidden text-gray-600
focus:outline-none">
        <svg class="w-6 h-6" fill="none" stroke="currentColor" viewBox="0
0 24 24">
          <path stroke-linecap="round" stroke-linejoin="round" stroke-
width="2"
                d="M4 6h16M4 12h16M4 18h16"/>
        </svg>
      </button>
    </div>

    <!-- Mobile Menu -->
    <nav x-show="open" class="md:hidden bg-white border-t border-gray-100">
      <a href="#" class="block px-4 py-2 text-gray-600 hover:text-blue-
```

```
600">Home</a>
      <a href="#" class="block px-4 py-2 text-gray-600 hover:text-blue-
600">About</a>
      <a href="#" class="block px-4 py-2 text-gray-600 hover:text-blue-
600">Contact</a>
    </nav>
  </header>
```

Crafting the Hero and Features Sections

For the static sections of the page, we rely heavily on Tailwind's utility classes.

- **Hero Section**: We will create a two-column layout. On mobile, the columns will stack vertically (**flex-col**), and on medium screens and up, they will sit side-by-side (**md:flex-row**). Copilot is excellent at suggesting common typography classes (**text-4xl**, **font-bold**, **text-lg**) and button styles (**bg-blue-600**, **text-white**, **rounded-lg**, **hover:bg-blue-700**).
- **Features Section**: This section uses Tailwind's grid system. A prompt such as `` will guide Copilot to use classes such as **grid**, **grid-cols-1**, **sm:grid-cols-2**, **md:grid-cols-3**, and **gap-8**. This creates a grid that automatically reflows from one column on small screens to three on larger screens.

```
<!-- Hero Section -->
  <section class="bg-gray-50 py-12">
    <div class="container mx-auto px-4 flex flex-col md:flex-row items-
center">
      <!-- Text Content -->
      <div class="md:w-1/2">
        <h1 class="text-4xl font-bold mb-4">Welcome to Our Product</h1>
        <p class="text-lg mb-6">A brief description or subtitle goes
here to entice users.</p>
        <a href="#"
          class="inline-block px-6 py-3 bg-blue-600 text-white rounded-
lg hover:bg-blue-700 transition-colors">
          Get Started
        </a>
      </div>
      <!-- Hero Image (Unsplash) -->
      <div class="md:w-1/2 mt-6 md:mt-0">
        <img
          src="https://images.unsplash.com/photo-1521737604893-d14cc237f
11d?auto=format&fit=crop&w=900&q=80"
          alt="Dashboard preview on a laptop screen"
          class="w-full rounded-lg shadow-lg"
```

```
        >
      </div>
    </div>
  </section>

  <!-- Features Section -->
  <section class="bg-white py-12">
    <div class="max-w-7xl mx-auto px-4">
      <h2 class="text-3xl font-bold text-center mb-8">Our Features</h2>
      <div class="grid gap-8 grid-cols-1 sm:grid-cols-2 md:grid-cols-3">
        <div class="bg-gray-50 p-6 rounded-lg shadow hover:shadow-lg
transition">
          <h3 class="text-xl font-semibold mb-2 text-blue-600">Feature
One</h3>
          <p class="text-gray-600">Description of the first feature,
highlighting its benefits.</p>
        </div>
        <div class="bg-gray-50 p-6 rounded-lg shadow hover:shadow-lg
transition">
          <h3 class="text-xl font-semibold mb-2 text-blue-600">Feature
Two</h3>
          <p class="text-gray-600">Description of the second feature
with some details.</p>
        </div>
        <div class="bg-gray-50 p-6 rounded-lg shadow hover:shadow-lg
transition">
          <h3 class="text-xl font-semibold mb-2 text-blue-600">Feature
Three</h3>
          <p class="text-gray-600">Description of the third feature and
why it stands out.</p>
        </div>
      </div>
    </div>
  </section>
```

Assembling the Footer

- The footer follows a similar pattern, using flexbox for layout. We will use **flex-col** and **md:flex-row** to ensure the layout adapts nicely to different screen sizes. Styling text for a dark background (**bg-gray-800**) is as simple as applying classes such as **text-gray-300** and **hover:text-white**.

```
  <footer class="bg-gray-800 text-gray-300">
    <div class="max-w-6xl mx-auto px-4 py-8 flex flex-col md:flex-row
justify-between">
```

```
      <!-- Contact Info -->
      <div class=”mb-4 md:mb-0”>
        <h4 class=”font-bold mb-2 text-white”>Contact Us</h4>
        <p>Email:
          <a href=”mailto:hello@example.com”
            class=”text-blue-400 hover:underline”>hello@example.com</a></p>
        <p>Phone: (123) 456-7890</p>
      </div>
      <!-- Social Links -->
      <div>
        <h4 class=”font-bold mb-2 text-white”>Follow Us</h4>
        <div class=”flex space-x-4”>
          <a href=”#” class=”text-gray-300 hover:text-white”>Facebook</a>
          <a href=”#” class=”text-gray-300 hover:text-white”>Twitter</a>
          <a href=”#” class=”text-gray-300 hover:text-white”>LinkedIn</a>
        </div>
      </div>
    </div>
    <div class=”text-center text-gray-500 text-sm py-4 border-t border-
gray-700”>
      &copy; 2025 Company Name. All rights reserved.
    </div>
  </footer>
```

Figure 6.6: *Screenshot of the Generated Landing Page. Image Provided by Unsplash.com (Source: https://unsplash.com/photos/selective-focus-photography-of-people-sits-in-front-of-table-inside-room-sggw4-qDD54)*

Remember:

When using any tool such as GitHub Copilot or ChatGPT, do not ask for everything at once.

Break your process into focused prompts that build progressively:

- **Structure Prompt:**

  "Generate a responsive landing page layout using Tailwind CSS and Alpine.js. Include a header, hero, features section, and footer."

- **Hero Refinement Prompt:**

  "Replace the placeholder image with a professional tech-themed Unsplash photo. Add rounded corners and a drop shadow."

- **Responsiveness Prompt:**

  "Ensure all sections use mobile-first responsive classes (`flex-col`, `md:flex-row`, `grid-cols-1`, and so on)."

- **Visual-Polish Prompt:**

  "Add hover transitions to buttons and cards for a modern feel."

- **Each Step Narrows the Output.**

  Think of prompt engineering as pair-programming with the AI: You design the intent, and the AI handles the boilerplate.

Project 4: Designing a Data Dashboard

This section provides a definitive guide to creating modern, interactive data visualizations using a lightweight, build-free technology stack. By leveraging the power of Content Delivery Networks (CDNs), this report will demonstrate how to seamlessly integrate Tailwind CSS for styling, Alpine.js for interactivity, and Chart.js for powerful data rendering. This approach is ideal for rapid prototyping, small-scale applications, and any scenario where the overhead of a traditional build process is undesirable. Each subsection provides detailed explanations and code snippets ready for direct implementation.

```
<head>
  <meta charset="UTF-8" />
  <meta name="viewport" content="width=device-width, initial-scale=1.0"/>
  <title>Title goes here</title>
  <link rel="stylesheet" href="./output.css">
  <script src="https://cdn.jsdelivr.net/npm/chart.js@4.4.3/dist/chart.
umd.min.js"></script>
</head>
```

With the foundational environment established, this section details the construction of a first complete component. This example will be static, with hardcoded data, serving to validate the setup and demonstrate the fundamental principles of styling a Chart.js canvas within a Tailwind CSS layout.

A Statically-Styled Chart

Before diving into dynamic and data-driven configurations, it is helpful to first understand the visual structure of a chart component; how it is styled and framed using Tailwind CSS.

Crafting the Chart Container

`Chart.js` renders its visualizations onto an HTML **`<canvas>`** element. For responsiveness and styling, it is a best practice to wrap the canvas in a container **`<div>`**. **`Chart.js`** will automatically adapt the canvas to the dimensions of its parent container, ensuring that the chart scales correctly on different screen sizes.[3]

The container **`<div>`** is styled using Tailwind's utility classes. This is where the "chrome" or frame of the component is defined—its background color, padding, shadow, and border radius. This clear separation of concerns, where Tailwind styles the container and Chart.js controls the canvas rendering, is a hallmark of this stack.

```
<div class="container mx-auto p-8">
    <div class="bg-white p-6 rounded-lg shadow-md">
        <h2 class="text-xl font-semibold mb-4 text-gray-800">Static Bar
Chart</h2>
        <canvas id="myBarChart"></canvas>
    </div>
</div>
```

Initializing a Bar Chart

The chart itself is initialized with JavaScript. A **`<script>`** block, placed just before the closing **`</body>`** tag, contains the logic to find the canvas element and instantiate a new Chart.js object.

The Chart constructor takes two arguments: The 2D rendering context of the canvas and a configuration object. This object defines every aspect of the chart, including its type (for example, **`'bar'`**, **`'line'`**), the data to be displayed, and various options for customization.

```
<script>
    const barChartCtx = document.getElementById('myBarChart');

    new Chart(barChartCtx, {
```

[3] https://taildashboards.com/

```
        type: 'bar',
        data: {
            labels: ['January', 'February', 'March', 'April', 'May', 'June'],
            datasets:,
                borderWidth: 1
                // Styling will be added in the next step
            }]
        },
        options: {
            responsive: true,
            maintainAspectRatio: false,
            scales: {
                y: {
                    beginAtZero: true
                }
            }
        }
    });
</script>
```

Applying Custom Styles from the Tailwind Theme

This step connects the inline Tailwind theme from the Project 4 - Designing a Data Dashboard setup to the Chart.js configuration. A common mistake is to attempt to style the chart's internal elements (such as bars or lines) with Tailwind classes on the **<canvas>** tag; this is ineffective because the chart is rendered programmatically. Instead, styling properties such as **backgroundColor** and **borderColor** must be passed into the datasets array of the configuration object.

To maintain design consistency, colors should not be hardcoded as hex values. Instead, they can be dynamically retrieved from the CSS custom properties defined in the **@theme** block. This is achieved using the **getComputedStyle** browser API. This approach creates a robust and maintainable design system: if the primary brand color is updated in the single **<style type="text/tailwindcss">** block, every chart on the site will automatically adopt the new color without any changes to the JavaScript code.

The following script demonstrates this powerful pattern.

```
<script>
    // Helper function to get CSS variables
    const getThemeColor = (variableName) => {
        return getComputedStyle(document.documentElement).
getPropertyValue(variableName).trim();
    };

    const barChartCtx = document.getElementById('myBarChart');

    new Chart(barChartCtx, {
```

```
        type: 'bar',
        data: {
            labels: ['January', 'February', 'March', 'April', 'May',
'June'],
            datasets:,
                backgroundColor: getThemeColor('--color-primary'),
                borderColor: getThemeColor('--color-primary'),
                borderWidth: 1
            }]
        },
        options: {
            responsive: true,
            maintainAspectRatio: false,
            scales: {
                y: {
                    beginAtZero: true
                }
            }
        }
    });
</script>
```

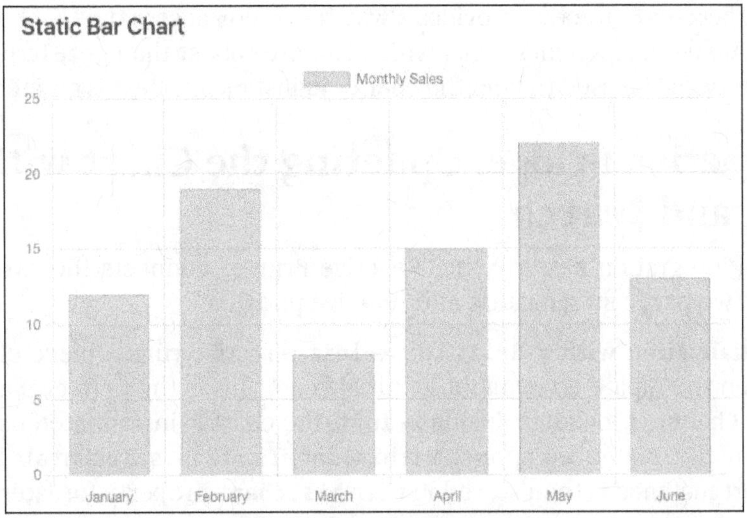

***Figure 6.7**: Static Dashboard Built with Alpine.js and TailwindCSS*

Bringing Charts to Life with `Alpine.js`

This section refactors the static chart into a fully interactive component, demonstrating the core pattern for making **`Chart.js`** reactive using **`Alpine.js`**. This involves building a bridge between Alpine's declarative, data-driven nature and **`Chart.js`**'s imperative, method-based API.

Managing State with `x-data`

The first step is to declare an Alpine component by adding the **`x-data`** directive to the chart's container **`<div>`**. This directive initializes a component and defines its reactive data. The chart's labels and data, previously hardcoded in the **`<script>`** tag, are moved into this **`x-data`** object. This makes them part of Alpine's reactivity system.

```
<div
    x-data="{
        labels: ['January', 'February', 'March', 'April', 'May', 'June'],
        salesData: ,
        chart: null
    }"
    class="bg-white p-6 rounded-lg shadow-md"
>
    <h2 class="text-xl font-semibold mb-4 text-gray-800">Interactive Bar
Chart</h2>
    <canvas x-ref="canvas"></canvas>
    </div>
```

Note the addition of **`x-ref="canvas"`** to the **`<canvas>`** element and a chart: Null property in **`x-data`**. The **`x-ref`** directive provides a way to directly access the DOM element from within the Alpine component's logic, which is more robust than **`getElementById`**. The chart property will be used to hold the **`Chart.js`** instance once it is created.

The Reactive Bridge: Updating the Chart with `x-init` and `$watch`

The central integration pattern, the "Reactive Bridge," connects the two libraries. It consists of two parts: initialization and reactive updates.

1. **Initialization with `x-init`:** The **`x-init`** directive runs a piece of code once, when the Alpine component is initialized.7 This is the perfect place to create the **`Chart.js`** instance. Inside **`x-init`**, the chart is instantiated using the data from the Alpine component (**`this.labels`**, **`this.salesData`**). The created chart instance is then stored in the **`this.chart`** property for later access.

2. **Reactivity with `$watch`**: Alpine's **`$watch`** magic property allows a callback function to be executed whenever a specific piece of data changes By watching the **`salesData`** property, we can trigger an update to the chart whenever that data is modified. Inside the **`$watch`** callback, the imperative **`chart.update()`** method is called. This is the core of the bridge: A declarative data change in Alpine triggers an imperative update in **`Chart.js`**.

This pattern is a universal and reusable model for integrating any third-party, imperative JavaScript library into a declarative **`Alpine.js`** component. By formalizing this approach—using **x-init** for setup, storing the instance, and using **$watch** for updates—it becomes a transferable mental model for developers.

The following code adds the **x-init** and **$watch** logic to the component's root **<div>**:

```
<div
    x-data="{
        labels: [‹January›, ‹February›, ‹March›, ‹April›, ‹May›, ‹June›],
        salesData: ,
        chart: null
    }"
    x-init="
        const chartData = {
            labels: labels,
            datasets:
        };
        chart = new Chart($refs.canvas, {
            type: ‹bar›,
            data: chartData,
            options: { responsive: true, scales: { y: { beginAtZero:
true } } }
        });

        $watch(‹salesData›, (newData) => {
            chart.data.datasets.data = newData;
            chart.update();
        });
    «
    class="bg-white p-6 rounded-lg shadow-md"
>
    </div>
```

User Interaction with @click

To demonstrate the reactivity, UI controls are added. These are simple buttons, styled with Tailwind CSS, that use Alpine's **x-on:click** directive (shorthand **@click**) to modify the **salesData** property.

When a user clicks a button, the following sequence occurs:

- The **@click** directive executes, assigning a new array to **salesData**.
- Alpine's reactivity system detects the change.
- The **$watch('salesData',...)** callback is triggered.
- Inside the callback, the new data is assigned to the **Chart.js** instance, and **chart.update()** is called.

- **`Chart.js`** re-renders the canvas with the new data, displaying an animated transition.

```
<div class=”mt-4 flex space-x-2”>
    <button @click=”salesData = “ class=”bg-[var(--color-primary)] text-white px-4 py-2 rounded-md hover:opacity-80 transition”>Data Set 1</button>
    <button @click=”salesData = “ class=”bg-[var(--color-secondary)] text-white px-4 py-2 rounded-md hover:opacity-80 transition”>Data Set 2</button>
</div>
```

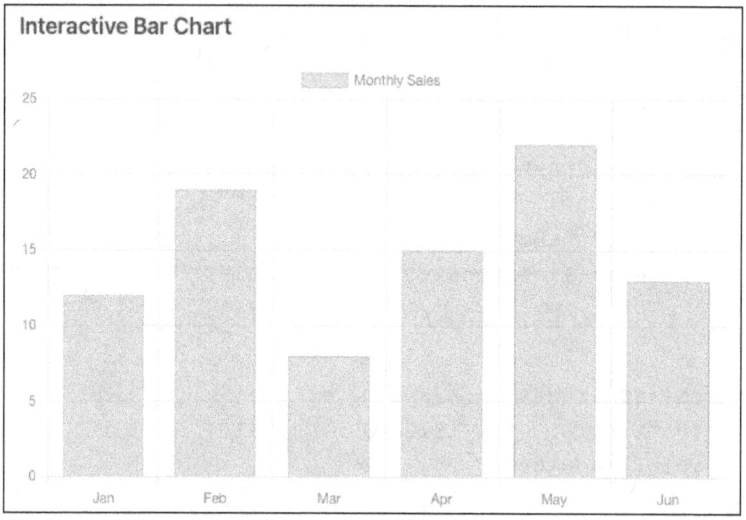

Figure 6.8: *Output of the Interactive Bar Chart*

Assembling an Advanced Dashboard Component

Building on the established patterns, this section constructs a more complex, realistic dashboard component. It features multiple charts that respond to a single, global control, demonstrating how the T.A.C. stack scales from simple widgets to interconnected UIs.

Designing a Multi-Chart Layout

A professional dashboard often requires multiple visualizations arranged in a grid. Tailwind CSS's grid utilities are ideal for this task. By using classes such as **`grid`**, **`grid-cols-1`**, **`md:grid-cols-2`**, and **`gap-6`**, a responsive layout can be created that stacks charts on small screens and places them side-by-side on medium screens and larger.

```
<div class="container mx-auto p-8">
    <div class="grid grid-cols-1 md:grid-cols-2 gap-6">
        <div class="bg-white p-6 rounded-lg shadow-md">
            </div>
        <div class="bg-white p-6 rounded-lg shadow-md">
            </div>
    </div>
</div>
```

Componentizing with `Alpine.js` and `Alpine.data`

To avoid duplicating the chart initialization and update logic for each chart, the logic can be abstracted into a reusable component using **`Alpine.data`**. This function allows for the registration of a named constructor **`forx-data`** objects. This promotes cleaner, more modular, and maintainable code, even within a single HTML file.

A **`<script>`** tag is added to the page (before the closing **`</body>`**) to define these reusable components.

```
<script>
    document.addEventListener('alpine:init', () => {
        Alpine.data('barChart', (initialData) => ({
            data: initialData,
            chart: null,
            init() {
                this.chart = new Chart(this.$refs.canvas, {
                    type: 'bar',
                    data: {
                        labels: this.data.labels,
                        datasets:
                    },
                    options: { responsive: true, scales: { y: {
beginAtZero: true } } }
                });

                this.$watch('data.values', (newValues) => {
                    this.chart.data.datasets.data = newValues;
                    this.chart.update();
                });
            }
        }));
    });
</script>
```

With this in place, initializing a chart in the HTML becomes much cleaner:

```
<div x-data="barChart({ labels: [...], values: [...], label: 'Sales',
color: '--color-primary' })">
```

```
    <canvas x-ref="canvas"></canvas>
</div>
```

Global State and Inter-Chart Communication with `Alpine.store`

The primary challenge in a dashboard is synchronizing state between components. **`Alpine.store`** provides a simple yet powerful solution by creating a global, reactive data store that can be accessed from any component using the **`$store`** magic property.

This allows for a clean decoupling of components. A global control, such as a dropdown menu, only needs to interact with the store. The chart components also only need to interact with the store. They do not need to be aware of each other's existence. This promotes a scalable, event-driven architecture typically associated with larger frameworks.

First, the global store is defined:

```
<script>
    document.addEventListener('alpine:init', () => {
        Alpine.store('dashboard', {
            timeRange: '7d',
            salesData: {
                '7d': ,
                '30d': [/*...30 days of data...*/],
                '90d': [/*...90 days of data...*/]
            },
            //... other data sets
        });

        //... Alpine.data definitions
    });
</script>
```

Next, a global UI control is created to modify the store:

```
<div class="mb-6">
    <label for="timeRange" class="block text-sm font-medium text-gray-
700">Time Range</label>
    <select x-model="$store.dashboard.timeRange" id="timeRange"
class="mt-1 block w-full pl-3 pr-10 py-2 text-base border-gray-300
focus:outline-none focus:ring-indigo-500 focus:border-indigo-500
sm:text-sm rounded-md">
        <option value="7d">Last 7 Days</option>
        <option value="30d">Last 30 Days</option>
        <option value="90d">Last 90 Days</option>
    </select>
</div>
```

Finally, the chart components are refactored to source their data from and watch the global store.

```
<div x-data=”barChart({
        labels: [...], // Labels might also come from the store
        values: $store.dashboard.salesData,
        label: ‘Sales’,
        color: ‘--color-primary’
     })”
     x-init=”$watch(‘$store.dashboard.timeRange’, (newRange) => {
        data.values = $store.dashboard.salesData;
     })”
>
    <h3 class=”text-lg font-medium”>Sales</h3>
    <canvas x-ref=”canvas”></canvas>
</div>
```

Polishing the User Experience

To enhance the user experience, visual feedback during state changes is essential. A simulated loading state can be added using **`x-show`** to display a spinner overlay while data is updated. Furthermore, **`x-transition`** can be used to smoothly fade chart elements in and out, providing a more polished feel to the interactions.

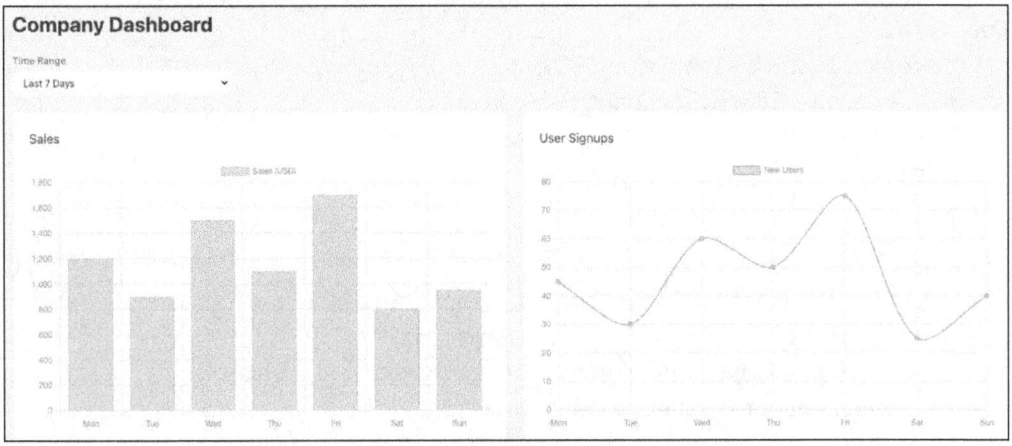

Figure 6.9: *Output of the Multi-Chart Layout*

Appendix

This appendix contains the complete, final HTML source code for the major examples developed in this chapter. These snippets are ready for immediate copy-and-paste into a code editor such as VS Code.

Complete Static Bar Chart

```
<!DOCTYPE html>
<html lang="en">
<head>
  <meta charset="UTF-8">
  <meta name="viewport" content="width=device-width, initial-scale=1.0">
  <title>Static Bar Chart</title>
  <link rel="stylesheet" href="./output.css">
  <script src="https://cdn.jsdelivr.net/npm/chart.js@4.4.3/dist/chart.
umd.min.js"></script>
  <style type="text/tailwindcss">
    @theme {
      --color-primary: #4f46e5;
    }
  </style>
</head>
<body class="bg-gray-100">

  <div class="container mx-auto p-8">
    <div class="bg-white p-6 rounded-lg shadow-md max-w-2xl mx-auto">
      <h2 class="text-xl font-semibold mb-4 text-gray-800">Static Bar
Chart</h2>
      <div class="relative h-96">
        <canvas id="myBarChart"></canvas>
      </div>
    </div>
  </div>

  <script>
    // Helper to get color from Tailwind theme
    const getThemeColor = (variableName) => {
      return getComputedStyle(document.documentElement)
        .getPropertyValue(variableName)
        .trim();
    };

    const barChartCtx = document.getElementById('myBarChart');

    new Chart(barChartCtx, {
      type: 'bar',
      data: {
        labels: ['January', 'February', 'March', 'April', 'May', 'June'],
        datasets: [
```

```
        {
          label: 'Monthly Sales',
          data: [12, 19, 8, 15, 22, 13],
          backgroundColor: getThemeColor('--color-primary'),
          borderColor: getThemeColor('--color-primary'),
          borderWidth: 1,
        },
      ],
    },
    options: {
      responsive: true,
      maintainAspectRatio: false,
      scales: {
        y: {
          beginAtZero: true,
        },
      },
    },
  });
 </script>
</body>
</html>
```

Complete Interactive Bar Chart with `Alpine.js`

```
<!DOCTYPE html>
<html lang="en">
<head>
  <meta charset="UTF-8">
  <meta name="viewport" content="width=device-width, initial-scale=1.0">
  <title>Interactive Bar Chart</title>
  <link rel="stylesheet" href="./output.css">
  <script src="https://cdn.jsdelivr.net/npm/chart.js@4.4.3/dist/chart.
umd.min.js"></script>
  <script defer src="https://cdn.jsdelivr.net/npm/alpinejs@3.14.0/dist/
cdn.min.js"></script>
  <style type="text/tailwindcss">
    @theme {
      --color-primary: #4f46e5;
      --color-secondary: #10b981;
    }
  </style>
```

```
</head>
<body class="bg-gray-100">

  <div class="container mx-auto p-8">
    <div
      x-data="chartComponent()"
      x-init="initChart()"
      class="bg-white p-6 rounded-lg shadow-md max-w-2xl mx-auto"
    >
      <h2 class="text-xl font-semibold mb-4 text-gray-800">Interactive
Bar Chart</h2>

      <div class="relative h-96">
        <canvas x-ref="canvas"></canvas>
      </div>

      <div class="mt-6 flex space-x-2">
        <button
          @click="updateData([12, 19, 8, 15, 22, 13])"
          class="bg-[var(--color-primary)] text-white px-4 py-2 rounded-
md hover:opacity-80 transition text-sm"
        >
          Q1/Q2 Data
        </button>
        <button
          @click="updateData([5, 25, 18, 10, 14, 20])"
          class="bg-[var(--color-secondary)] text-white px-4 py-2
rounded-md hover:opacity-80 transition text-sm"
        >
          Q3/Q4 Data
        </button>
      </div>
    </div>
  </div>

  <script>
    const getThemeColor = (variableName) => {
      return getComputedStyle(document.documentElement)
        .getPropertyValue(variableName)
        .trim();
    };

    function chartComponent() {
      return {
```

```
        labels: ['Jan', 'Feb', 'Mar', 'Apr', 'May', 'Jun'],
        salesData: [12, 19, 8, 15, 22, 13],
        chart: null,

        initChart() {
          const ctx = this.$refs.canvas.getContext('2d');
          this.chart = new Chart(ctx, {
            type: 'bar',
            data: {
              labels: this.labels,
              datasets: [
                {
                  label: 'Monthly Sales',
                  data: this.salesData,
                  backgroundColor: getThemeColor('--color-primary'),
                  borderColor: getThemeColor('--color-primary'),
                  borderWidth: 1,
                },
              ],
            },
            options: {
              responsive: true,
              maintainAspectRatio: false,
              scales: { y: { beginAtZero: true } },
            },
          });
        },

        updateData(newData) {
          const color = newData.length > 6
            ? getThemeColor('--color-secondary')
            : getThemeColor('--color-primary');
          this.chart.data.datasets[0].data = newData;
          this.chart.data.datasets[0].backgroundColor = color;
          this.chart.data.datasets[0].borderColor = color;
          this.chart.update();
        },
      };
    }
  </script>
</body>
</html>
```

Complete Multi-Chart Dashboard with Global State

```
<!DOCTYPE html>
<html lang="en">
<head>
  <meta charset="UTF-8" />
  <meta name="viewport" content="width=device-width, initial-scale=1.0"/>
  <title>Multi-Chart Dashboard</title>
  <link rel="stylesheet" href="./output.css">
  <script src="https://cdn.jsdelivr.net/npm/chart.js@4.4.3/dist/chart.
umd.min.js"></script>
  <script defer src="https://cdn.jsdelivr.net/npm/alpinejs@3.14.0/dist/
cdn.min.js"></script>
</head>
<body class="bg-gray-100">
  <div class="container mx-auto p-8">
    <h1 class="text-3xl font-bold mb-6 text-gray-900">Company
Dashboard</h1>

    <!-- Time range selector -->
    <div class="mb-6 max-w-xs" x-data>
      <label for="timeRange" class="block text-sm font-medium text-gray-
700">Time Range</label>
      <select
        x-model="$store.dashboard.timeRange"
        id="timeRange"
        class="mt-1 block w-full pl-3 pr-10 py-2 text-base border-gray-300
               focus:outline-none focus:ring-indigo-500 focus:border-
indigo-500
               sm:text-sm rounded-md"
      >
        <option value="7d">Last 7 Days</option>
        <option value="30d">Last 30 Days</option>
      </select>
    </div>

    <div class="grid grid-cols-1 lg:grid-cols-2 gap-6">
      <!-- Sales (Bar) -->
      <div
        x-data="chartComponent({
          type: 'bar',
          label: 'Sales (USD)',
          dataKey: 'salesData',
```

```
          colorVar: '--color-primary'
        })"
        x-init="initChart()"
        class="bg-white p-6 rounded-lg shadow-md"
      >
        <h3 class="text-lg font-medium text-gray-800">Sales</h3>
        <div class="relative h-96 mt-4">
          <canvas x-ref="canvas"></canvas>
        </div>
      </div>

      <!-- User Signups (Line) -->
      <div
        x-data="chartComponent({
          type: 'line',
          label: 'New Users',
          dataKey: 'userData',
          colorVar: '--color-secondary'
        })"
        x-init="initChart()"
        class="bg-white p-6 rounded-lg shadow-md"
      >
        <h3 class="text-lg font-medium text-gray-800">User Signups</h3>
        <div class="relative h-96 mt-4">
          <canvas x-ref="canvas"></canvas>
        </div>
      </div>
    </div>
  </div>

  <script>
    // Read a CSS custom property from the :root
    const getThemeColor = (variableName) =>
      getComputedStyle(document.documentElement)
        .getPropertyValue(variableName)
        .trim();

    document.addEventListener('alpine:init', () => {
      // Global store with labels and datasets for each range
      Alpine.store('dashboard', {
        timeRange: '7d',
        labels: {
          '7d':  ['Mon', 'Tue', 'Wed', 'Thu', 'Fri', 'Sat', 'Sun'],
```

```
          '30d': ['W1', 'W2', 'W3', 'W4']
        },
        salesData: {
          '7d':  [1200, 900, 1500, 1100, 1700, 800, 950],
          '30d': [5200, 6100, 5800, 6400]
        },
        userData: {
          '7d':  [45, 30, 60, 50, 75, 25, 40],
          '30d': [180, 210, 195, 240]
        }
      });

      // Reusable chart component for bar/line with live updates on
range change
      Alpine.data('chartComponent', (config) => ({
        chart: null,

        initChart() {
          const store = Alpine.store('dashboard');
          const labels = store.labels[store.timeRange];
          const values = store[config.dataKey][store.timeRange];
          const color = getThemeColor(config.colorVar);

          const dataset =
            config.type === 'line'
              ? {
                  label: config.label,
                  data: values,
                  borderColor: color,
                  backgroundColor: color,
                  borderWidth: 2,
                  pointRadius: 3,
                  tension: 0.3,
                  fill: false
                }
              : {
                  label: config.label,
                  data: values,
                  backgroundColor: color,
                  borderColor: color,
                  borderWidth: 1
                };

          const ctx = this.$refs.canvas.getContext('2d');
```

```
          this.chart = new Chart(ctx, {
            type: config.type,
            data: {
              labels,
              datasets: [dataset]
            },
            options: {
              responsive: true,
              maintainAspectRatio: false,
              scales: { y: { beginAtZero: true } }
            }
          });

          // React to timeRange changes
          this.$watch('$store.dashboard.timeRange', () => this.
refreshFromStore());
        },

        refreshFromStore() {
          const store = Alpine.store('dashboard');
          const labels = store.labels[store.timeRange];
          const values = store[config.dataKey][store.timeRange];
          const color = getThemeColor(config.colorVar);

          this.chart.data.labels = labels;
          this.chart.data.datasets[0].data = values;

          // Keep colors in sync (useful if you swap dataset type or
theme later)
          if (this.chart.config.type === 'line') {
            this.chart.data.datasets[0].borderColor = color;
            this.chart.data.datasets[0].backgroundColor = color;
          } else {
            this.chart.data.datasets[0].borderColor = color;
            this.chart.data.datasets[0].backgroundColor = color;
          }

          this.chart.update();
        }
      }));
    });
  </script>
</body>
</html>
```

Conclusion

In this chapter, we transformed theory into practice by building complete, real-world applications with the assistance of AI tools such as GitHub Copilot. Through the calculator, web scraper, landing page, and data dashboard projects, we demonstrated how generative AI can accelerate both front-end and back-end development, reducing boilerplate, improving consistency, and expanding creative possibilities.

Each project illustrated a key principle: the most effective developers are those who collaborate with AI, not depend on it blindly. By learning to guide Copilot with clear prompts, verify its outputs, and refine its suggestions, we combined human intent with AI efficiency. These workflows mirror real freelance and production environments where speed, accuracy, and maintainability matter equally.

Having now built functional apps from concept to completion, you are ready to take the next step—optimizing, debugging, and enhancing these AI-assisted projects to production quality. In the next chapter, we will explore how to use AI for debugging, performance tuning, and refinement, ensuring that every line of code not only works, but works well.

Multiple Choice Questions

1. Which JavaScript library was used in this chapter to add lightweight reactivity without a full framework?
   a. `React`
   b. `Vue.js`
   c. `Alpine.js`
   d. `Svelte`
2. In the calculator project, what is the primary risk of using the `eval()` function?
   a. It slows down arithmetic operations.
   b. It cannot handle decimals.
   c. It can execute arbitrary or malicious code.
   d. It requires a backend to function.
3. When setting up a Tailwind CSS + Alpine.js project, which command continuously rebuilds styles as you edit files?
   a. `npm run build`
   b. `npx run watch`

c. `npx @tailwindcss/cli -i ./src/input.css -o ./src/output.css --watch`

d. `npx tailwindcss build`

4. In the web scraper project, which Node.js library is commonly paired with Axios to parse HTML content?

   a. Cheerio

   b. Express

   c. Lodash

   d. Moment

5. What is the main purpose of GitHub Copilot in these projects?

   a. Version control

   b. AI-assisted code generation and suggestions

   c. Error logging

   d. Performance benchmarking

6. In the landing page project, which Tailwind utilities are most relevant for building responsive grids?

   a. `border-2` and `rounded-lg`

   b. `grid, grid-cols-*`, and responsive prefixes like `md:`

   c. `text-center` and `italic`

   d. `bg-gradient-to-r` and `from-indigo-500`

7. What Tailwind utility combination centers a card vertically and horizontally on the screen?

   a. absolute `inset-0`

   b. flex `justify-center` `items-center` `h-screen`

   c. grid `place-items-start`

   d. relative `mx-auto`

8. In the data dashboard project, which library was used to display visual charts?

   a. `D3.js`

   b. `Chart.js`

   c. `Highcharts`

   d. `ApexCharts`

9. Which `Alpine.js` directive is used to reference a DOM element inside a component?
    a. `x-if`
    b. `x-for`
    c. `x-ref`
    d. `x-bind`
10. According to the reflection sections, what is the best practice when working with AI-generated code?
    a. Accept it `as-is` to save time
    b. Review, test, and refine the AI's output before using it in production
    c. Disable Copilot once code compiles
    d. Copy only from online tutorials instead

Answers

1. c
2. c
3. c
4. a
5. b
6. b
7. b
8. b
9. c
10. b

CHAPTER 7

Debugging and Optimization with AI Help

Introduction

In this chapter, we explore how Artificial Intelligence (AI) can supercharge the debugging and optimization of Tailwind CSS user interfaces. Rather than treating them as focal solutions, we will frame modern AI tools, such as GPT-4, GitHub Copilot, and Cursor AI, as supportive examples within a broader, human-led debugging strategy. By integrating these tools into your workflow, you can identify bugs, suggest fixes, and generate tests with greater precision.

We will evaluate the impact of AI-assisted workflows using specific analytical criteria, including maintainability of the resulting code, the final UX impact on the end user, and the scalability of the solution across large projects. We will prioritize strategies for crafting effective queries to trace errors and refactor messy code while reinforcing that human judgment remains central to the process.

Common Tailwind issues, ranging from redundant utility classes to critical accessibility (a11y) and responsive edge cases, are addressed with AI-assisted guidance. We will also walk through the newest AI features inside Chrome DevTools and compare a traditional human-led session with an AI-assisted one to analyze the pros and cons of each approach. Finally, a hands-on challenge will allow you to apply these concepts to a faulty code snippet. By the end, you will be equipped to leverage AI as a sophisticated "debugging partner" that supports your technical expertise, making your development process faster, more insightful, and more resilient.

Structure

In this chapter, we will cover the following topics:

- The AI Debugging Toolkit for Tailwind CSS
    - GPT-4: Your AI Pair Programmer for Debugging

- GitHub Copilot: Real-Time Suggestions in Your Editor
- Cursor AI: Context-Aware Code Analysis and Review
- Chrome DevTools and Lighthouse: Baseline Debugging and Audits

- Prompt Engineering Strategies for Debugging and Optimization
  - Crafting Prompts for Error Analysis and Bug Hunting
  - Prompting AI to Generate Tests for Your UI Components
  - Refactoring and Clean-up: Prompts for Code and CSS Optimization
  - Performance Tuning Prompts - Lighthouse Optimization
- Common Tailwind CSS Pitfalls and AI Solutions
  - Redundant or Conflicting Utility Classes
  - Accessibility and Contrast Issues - A11y Pitfalls
  - Excessive DOM Depth and Unnecessary Markup
  - Layout Breakpoints and Responsive Design Issues
- Human-Led versus AI-Assisted Debugging: Pros and Cons
- Hands-on Challenge: Debug and Optimize with AI

The AI Debugging Toolkit for Tailwind CSS

AI-powered assistants have become invaluable tools for web developers, especially in diagnosing and fixing UI issues. These tools can analyze code, spot patterns, and suggest solutions at a speed and scale that complement human expertise. In the context of Tailwind CSS, AI specifically leverages the framework's structured utility-first approach to improve debugging precision. Because Tailwind uses a predictable, finite set of classes, AI can more accurately pinpoint styling conflicts, propose optimizations, and even write code on your behalf.

However, it is essential to clarify that while these tools provide powerful suggestions, they complement **(but do not replace!)** human architectural and UX judgment. This section introduces the key AI and automation tools we will use for debugging and optimizing Tailwind UIs, focusing on three distinct pillars of optimization: performance (for example, bundle size and rendering speed), maintainability (for example, clean and readable class structures), and visual consistency (for example, adhering to design systems and accessibility).

GPT-4: Your AI Pair Programmer for Debugging

GPT-4 (such as the ChatGPT interface or similar AI chatbots) acts like a supportive on-demand assistant that can answer questions, explain errors, and suggest code changes. It has demonstrated an impressive ability to identify and fix bugs in code, sometimes even outperforming traditional automated debugging methods. For example, if a Tailwind-styled component is not behaving as expected, you can paste relevant code or error messages into GPT-4 and ask for insight. The model can analyze the code for logical issues or wrong class usage and recommend fixes in natural language.

One strength of GPT-4 is speed: it can scan through a snippet and propose a solution GPT-4 (such as the ChatGPT interface or similar AI chatbots) acts like a supportive on-demand assistant that can answer questions, explain errors, and suggest code changes. It has demonstrated an impressive ability to identify and fix bugs in code, sometimes even outperforming traditional automated debugging methods. For example, if a Tailwind-styled component is not behaving as expected, you can paste relevant code or error messages into GPT-4 and ask for insight. The model can analyze the code for logical issues or wrong class usage and recommend fixes in natural language.

In practice, you might use GPT-4 to:

- **Identify Styling Issues**: For example, "Why is my **`<div>`** not centered despite using `mx-auto`?"[1] – GPT-4 can remind you to ensure the parent has a set width or suggest the correct utility class.
- **Resolve Exceptions**: If your build or console throws an exception (perhaps a misconfiguration of Tailwind or a runtime error in your React+Tailwind app), you can feed the error log to GPT-4. It can often trace the root cause (such as a missing plugin, incorrect import, and so on) and outline steps to fix it.[2]
- **Suggest Improvements**: GPT-4 can provide recommendations on how to rewrite a piece of code or markup for better clarity or performance. For instance, it might suggest consolidating redundant classes or using a different layout approach (flexbox versus grid) to achieve a design.

---

[1] *Centering in CSS, and by extension, Tailwind, is highly dependent on the broader layout context. While **`mx-auto`** is a powerful utility, its effectiveness relies on the element being a **block-level container** with a **defined width or max-width**, as well as the constraints imposed by its **parent element**. AI tools like GPT-4 are particularly helpful here because they can identify these missing structural requirements that go beyond just the utility classes themselves.*

[2] *Error logs can occasionally contain sensitive details, such as local file paths or environment variables, which should be redacted before sharing with an AI. Additionally, because AI models do not have access to your live environment, you must always validate their diagnosis against your project's exact dependency versions and configuration.*

Overall, think of GPT-4 as an ever-available senior developer who can debug and explain code. It excels at quick Q&A-style interactions and generating code snippets on demand. However, it is important to remember that while AI accelerates the process of applying fixes, it does not replace the need for deliberate debugging analysis or high-level architectural decision-making. Furthermore, any AI-suggested refactors, such as layout changes or the addition of aria-label attributes, must be manually validated against established accessibility and UX standards to ensure the final product remains high-quality and inclusive. In combination with prompt engineering techniques, GPT-4 becomes a powerful ally, provided the human developer retains final ownership and authority over all changes to ensure that they fit the project's unique constraints.

GitHub Copilot: Real-Time Suggestions in Your Editor

While GPT-4 is conversational, **GitHub Copilot** integrates AI assistance directly into your coding workflow (inside editors such as VS Code). As you write code, Copilot uses an AI model to suggest the next lines, or even entire functions, based on the context. For debugging and optimization, Copilot can help by proactively completing code in a way that avoids errors or by recommending best practices as you type. For example, if you start writing a Tailwind class name and often misuse a breakpoint prefix, Copilot might auto-complete it correctly. It is like an **AI pair programmer that works in real-time**.

How Copilot aids in debugging Tailwind UIs:

- **Preventing Mistakes**: Copilot's suggestions are informed by countless examples. If you accidentally try to use a non-existent Tailwind class or a wrong syntax, Copilot often will not suggest it, effectively warning you before you even run the code.
- **Quick Fixes**: When you encounter a bug and start coding a solution, Copilot can suggest the rest of the fix. For instance, suppose you realize a container needs to be made responsive. If you begin typing a media query utility (such as md:), Copilot might suggest the appropriate class completions (for example, turning a single-column layout into `md:grid-cols-2` for larger screens).
- **Refactoring Hints**: As you refactor markup, Alpine.js, or React components, Copilot can spot patterns. If it has seen similar code, it may suggest a more concise or idiomatic way to achieve the same result. For example, if you have multiple `<div>` wrappers, Copilot might help reorganize them or comment them for clarity as you edit.

Copilot is particularly helpful for boilerplate code and repetitive fixes; it can fill in the tedious parts, letting you focus on high-level decisions. In the context of debugging, it will not magically know there is a bug unless you prompt it via your code changes, but once you decide on a fix, Copilot accelerates applying that fix consistently (for example, adding an aria-label to multiple buttons, or renaming a class across many components). The upcoming Copilot X "agent" modes even promise conversational debugging inside the editor, where you can ask "Why is this section not showing up?" and get answers within VS Code. While such features are cutting-edge, this chapter will show how even today's Copilot can reduce debugging time by hinting at solutions and preventing new bugs during the fix.

Cursor AI: Context-Aware Code Analysis and Review

Cursor AI is an AI-enhanced Integrated Development Environment (IDE) designed to deeply understand your entire project. Think of Cursor as an AI code reviewer and navigator that can analyze multiple files, track dependencies, and find root causes of bugs that span across modules.[3] In a Tailwind CSS context, especially in large projects or complex dashboards, an issue may not be isolated to a single component. For example, a style might not apply because the CSS build omitted a class (maybe due to a dynamic class name not being picked up by the compiler). Cursor can help by scanning project-wide information and identifying such patterns.

To illustrate how Cursor's interface aligns closely with mainstream development environments, *Figure* 7.1 shows its visual similarity to VS Code.

***Figure* 7.1:** *Cursor is Derived from VSCode, Which Resembles It Closely in Terms of Appearance and General Features*

[3] *While Cursor's project-wide analysis is a powerful diagnostic tool, it is crucial to remember that architectural decisions and the scope of refactoring should always be validated by human review. Because changes that span multiple modules can have far-reaching effects, manual verification is necessary to prevent unintended regressions and ensure alignment with the project's overarching design standards.*

Figure 7.2 demonstrates how Cursor integrates conversational AI directly into the editor, allowing developers to access its chat panel with a simple keyboard shortcut.

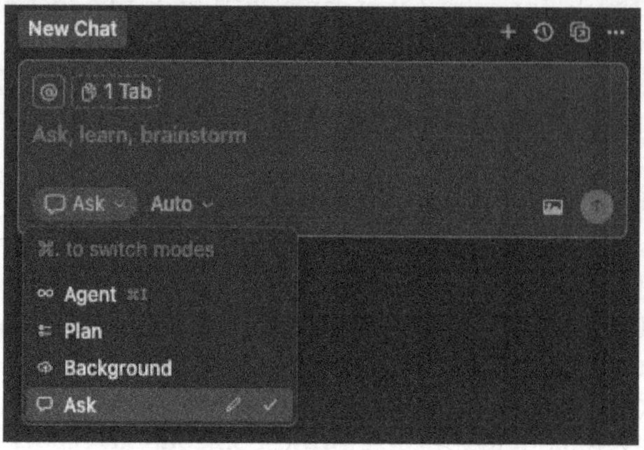

Figure 7.2: *Cursor's Chat Panel is Easily Accessible via Ctrl + I/Command + I*

Key Capabilities of Cursor AI for Debugging and Optimization:

- **Automated Root Cause Analysis**: Cursor can attempt to locate where in the codebase a bug originates. For instance, if a Tailwind class is not working, Cursor might scan the Tailwind config file and content paths to see if the class is being purged or if there is a misconfiguration. It accelerates bug detection. For example, missing await in async code is an error that Cursor can catch quickly by analyzing function usage across files. In our UI focus, that might translate to catching something such as a missing import or a logic error affecting state.

- **Multi-File, Project-Wide Insight**: Unlike GPT-4 (which you typically use on one snippet at a time), Cursor has context of the entire codebase. It prevents "fragmented fixes" by understanding how different pieces interact. Say your dashboard UI's layout is broken due to a CSS specificity issue introduced by a third-party stylesheet; the Cursor could trace that by looking at all loaded CSS and pointing out the conflict. This holistic view means it can suggest changes that account for the rest of your project, reducing the chance of regressions.

- **Automatic Test Generation and Running**: Cursor can generate tests for your code changes and even run them. For example, after debugging a component, you could ask Cursor to create a small unit test or UI snapshot test to ensure the issue is fixed and stays fixed. In fact, Cursor advertises an "automate test generation" feature to achieve near 100% pass rates, running tests after each change to keep code rock-solid. In a UI scenario, this could mean generating a Jest test that mounts a component and checks that a certain Tailwind class is present or that a conditional render works.

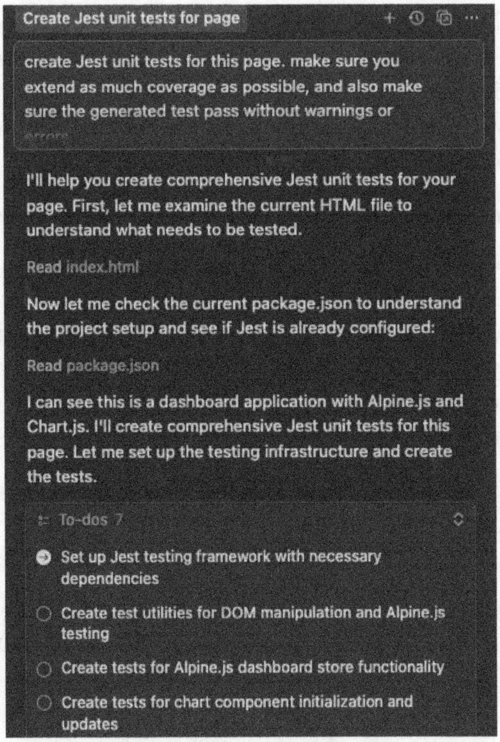

Figure 7.3: *You Can Use the Agent Mode of Cursor for Creating Unit Tests*

In essence, Cursor AI brings together editing, debugging, and testing in one AI-driven workflow. It is like having an AI project engineer that not only points out the bug but also prepares a patch and verifies it. Throughout this chapter's examples, we will note where a tool such as Cursor could streamline the process, especially in larger applications. Even if you do not use Cursor specifically, its capabilities illustrate what is possible when AI has full context: less time spent on trivial debugging and more on high-level problem solving. However, as you leverage these project-wide AI insights, you must ensure that any suggested changes or refactors strictly align with your existing design systems and UI consistency standards. While the AI can see the code, the human developer must ensure the output maintains the specific visual language and component governance of the application.

Chrome DevTools and Lighthouse: Baseline Debugging and Audits

No debugging toolkit is complete without mentioning the built-in browser developer tools. Chrome DevTools (and similar tools in Firefox, Edge, and so on) are not AI, but they are essential companions for any UI debugging session, even an AI-assisted one. DevTools (which you can open inside Chrome by pressing F12 on Windows/Linux or *command* + *option* + I on macOS) provides the ground truth of what is happening in your application: the HTML elements, applied CSS styles, the computed layout, console errors, network activity, and performance metrics. In this chapter, we treat DevTools as a first-line diagnostic tool: use it to inspect the problem, then use AI to analyze and solve the problem.

Key DevTools Features for Tailwind CSS Debugging:

- **Element Inspector and CSS Styles Panel**: This lets you select any element on the page and see all CSS rules affecting it. If a Tailwind class is not working, the styles panel will often reveal why. For example, you might see a rule crossed out (indicating it was overridden by a later rule or one with higher specificity). DevTools shows the order of styles and which ones prevail, helping you catch conflicting utility classes or a case where a custom CSS is taking precedence.

  Tip: *In the Styles panel, rules with a line through them are overridden; this visual cue immediately tells you if, say, your flex class got overridden by a display: grid from another class.*

- **Responsive Design Mode and Computed Styles**: You can simulate different screen sizes in DevTools. If a layout works on desktop but breaks on mobile, toggle the device toolbar to a small width and inspect how classes such as `sm:` or `md:` are behaving. If a responsive Tailwind class is not applied, ensure you use the correct breakpoint prefix and remember Tailwind is mobile-first (unprefixed classes apply to all sizes by default). The Computed tab shows the final calculated CSS properties on an element, which helps verify if a utility class had any effect. For instance, if you add **`bg-red-500`** but the computed background-color is different, something is off – perhaps a more specific rule or the class was not generated due to purge.

- **Console and Network Tabs**: JavaScript errors or failed network requests can also lead to UI issues. A React component might fail to render (showing a blank area in the UI) because of a runtime error, and the Console will log it. Or a CSS file might not load, meaning none of your Tailwind styles apply. DevTools helps catch these non-CSS bugs that nonetheless affect the interface.

- **Lighthouse Audits**: Lighthouse is an automated auditing tool built into Chrome (available under DevTools "Lighthouse" panel or via Chrome's developer website). It checks your page for performance, accessibility, best practices, and SEO. For our purposes, the performance and accessibility audits are goldmines for optimization guidance. Lighthouse can flag issues such as "excessive DOM size", low contrast text, missing ARIA attributes, long load times, unused CSS, and so on. For example, Lighthouse will warn if your page's DOM exceeds ~1,500 elements, as that can slow down rendering. It may say something like "Avoid an excessive DOM size" if you have thousands of nodes. It also reports the maximum depth of nesting and the element with the most children, which can pinpoint where your HTML structure might be too complex. On accessibility, Lighthouse checks color contrast and will list elements that do not meet WCAG guidelines, often with screenshots of the offending elements. This is incredibly useful to catch, say, light gray text on a light background introduced by some Tailwind class combination that looked fine to you but is not accessible.

By utilizing these tools, you establish the ground truth of your application's state. It is critical to use DevTools to verify the actual data, such as which styles are truly applied or why an element is failing a contrast check, before inviting an AI to interpret the situation. Ultimately, these technical Lighthouse metrics (such as LCP or DOM size) serve as proxies for real-world user experience and product quality. A high accessibility score translates to an inclusive product, while optimized performance metrics directly impact user retention and business outcomes. Use the data from DevTools to set the stage, and then use AI to strategize the best path forward.

Debugging with AI Assistance in Chrome DevTools

Chrome DevTools now integrates Google's Gemini AI directly into the browser, providing error explainers, AI-generated suggestions, and interactive bugfix workflows.[4]

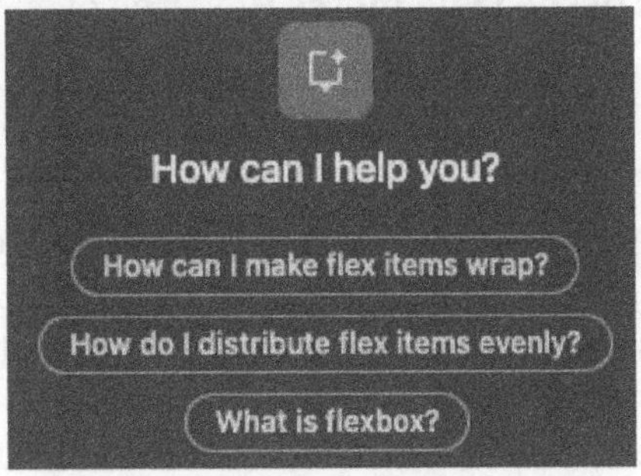

Figure 7.4: *This is What You Will Find in the AI Assistance Tab of Chrome Devtools When You Open a New AI Chat*

For example, the Console Insights feature adds a lightbulb next to each console error or warning; clicking "Understand this error" that asks Gemini to explain the issue in plain English.

[4] *As of early 2026, many AI features in Chrome DevTools, such as Console Insights and the AI Assistance panel, are still considered experimental and may require manual activation via the AI innovations or Experimental flags in DevTools settings. Consequently, these tools may experience occasional stability issues, and their capabilities or user interface may change significantly between browser versions. Always rely on DevTools' standard diagnostic data as your primary source of truth, using the AI as a high-level interpretive layer rather than a finalized solution.*

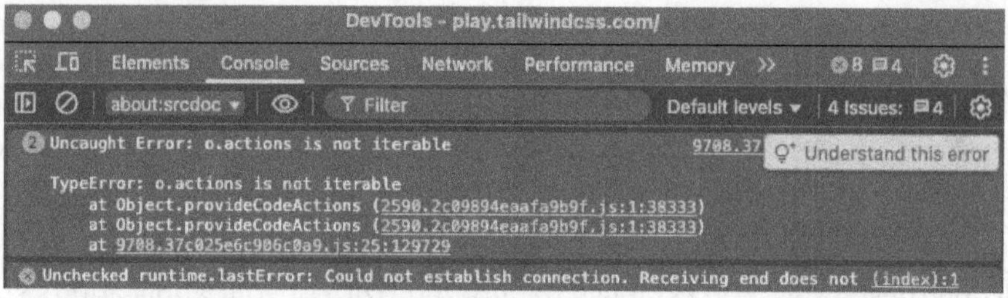

Figure 7.5: *The New DevTools Console Insights Feature Shows a Lightbulb Next to Errors. Click It to See an AI-Generated Explanation below the Error*

This can instantly clarify cryptic messages such as CORS or JavaScript errors without leaving DevTools.

Key AI Features

Before exploring concrete debugging workflows, it is helpful to understand the core AI capabilities built directly into DevTools. The following key features illustrate how the environment integrates real-time analysis, contextual styling guidance, and performance insights.

- **Console Insights (Issue Explainers)**: Hovering over console errors or warnings reveals a lightbulb icon. Clicking it prompts Gemini to analyze the message and stack trace, then provide a natural-language explanation and suggested fixes. This makes it easy to diagnose runtime errors on the spot.
- **AI Assistance Panel (Styling)**: A new "AI assistance" drawer (via More Tools or by right-clicking an element and choosing Ask AI) lets you chat with the AI about the current element. It knows the element's CSS (including Tailwind classes and computed styles) and can "understand a website's layout and get AI-generated fixes for CSS bugs". For instance, you can ask "Can you center this element?" or "Why is this element invisible?" and get step-by-step help.
- **Other Panels**: Similar AI helpers are available for network and performance debugging. You can ask questions such as "Why does this request fail?" or "Help me optimize my LCP score," and Gemini will explain headers or performance data. There are even prompts for auto-generating bug reports or investigating page performance.

These features streamline debugging by keeping context in DevTools. The AI sees the live DOM, Tailwind classes, and computed layout, so the advice is specific to your page. You do not have to copy code into an external chat. Instead, DevTools can highlight an element and let you ask about that exact element's styles or issues.

To begin using these AI-powered debugging capabilities, Chrome first requires you to authorize DevTools to access experimental AI features. The following figure shows the prompt that appears when opening the `AI Assistance` tab for the first time.

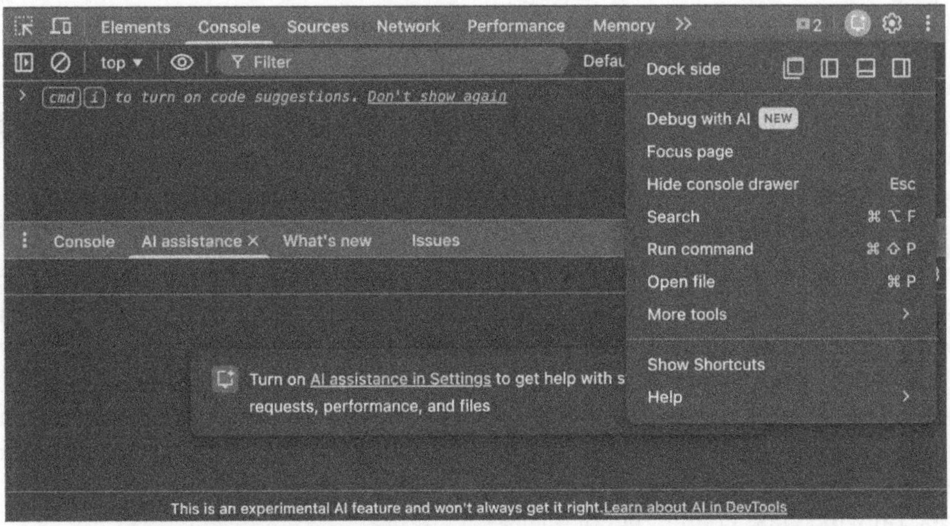

Figure 7.6: *Upon Clicking the AI Assistance Tab from Chrome Devtools (Shown Here in the Debug with AI Dropdown Menu), You will Find This Authorization Button That will Take You to the Settings of Chrome*

Before accessing any of the AI-driven debugging tools, Chrome requires you to enable the corresponding experimental flags. *Figure* 7.7 highlights the specific settings that must be activated for AI Assistance and Console Insights to function.

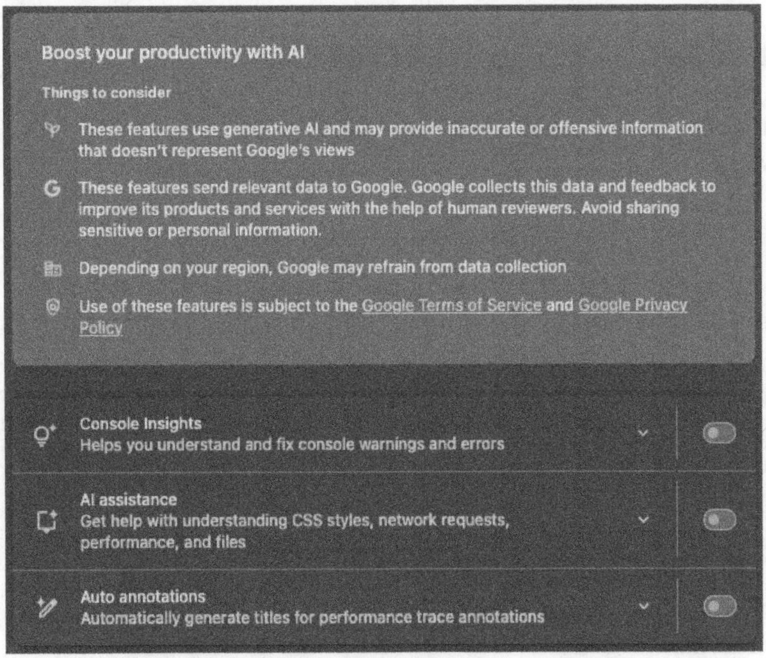

Figure 7.7: *Make Sure You Check Console Insights and AI Assistance so That You Can Take Advantage of the AI-Powered Devtools*

Benefits for Tailwind Developers

Integrating AI directly into the browser significantly enhances the developer experience by reducing the mental overhead of switching between the code editor, the live application, and external AI chat interfaces. In a real-world frontend workflow, this in-browser assistance allows you to maintain focus on the problem at hand, as the AI has immediate access to the "ground truth" of the rendered DOM and active styles.

For Tailwind users, Gemini can parse utility classes and layout context. If a flexbox is not aligned or an element is hidden, you can simply ask about it. For example, asking "Why is not this button centered?" might lead the AI to notice a missing justify-center on the parent. Because the AI panel grabs the selected element's classes and computed styles, it effectively knows you are using Tailwind and can suggest the right utilities. This can greatly speed up common fixes: instead of guessing and reloading, the AI explains the cause (say, "overflow-hidden is clipping this element") and suggests the exact Tailwind class change needed.

Example: Fixing an Overflow Issue

Try this Tailwind HTML snippet in Tailwind Play (it includes the Tailwind CDN script for convenience):

```
<html>
<head><script src="https://cdn.tailwindcss.com"></script></head>
<body>
  <div class="w-64 h-32 overflow-auto bg-gray-200">
    <div class="h-48 bg-blue-500">
      This tall div overflows its container.
    </div>
  </div>
</body>
</html>
```

The following figure shows the tall **<div>** rendered inside Tailwind Play before opening DevTools:

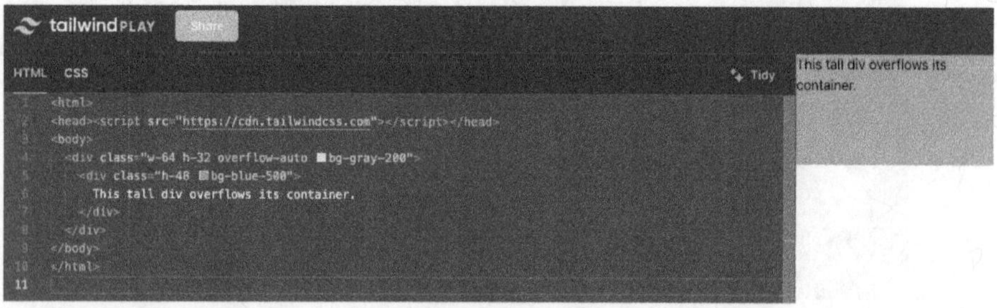

Figure 7.8: *This is What TailwindPlay and the Tall Div We Created Look Like. Paste the Code to TailwindPlay, and Then Open Your Devtools*

Once the component is rendered in Tailwind Play, the next step is to inspect the specific element you want to analyze so the AI panel can retrieve the correct context. The following figure illustrates this selection process inside DevTools.

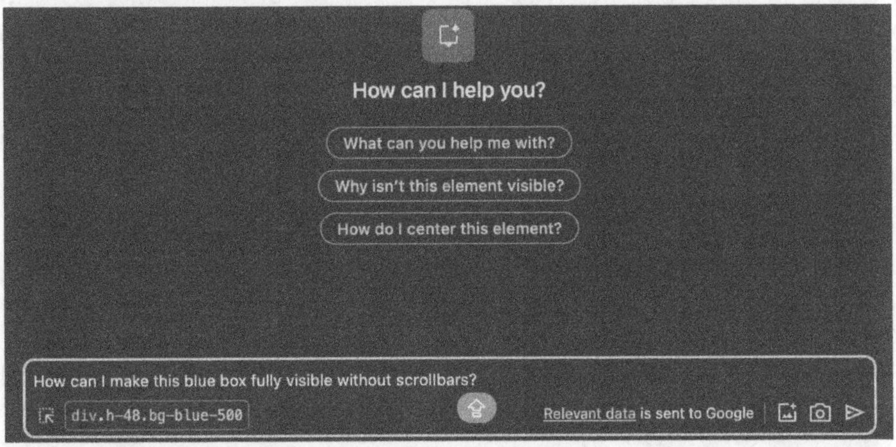

Figure 7.9: *Make Sure You Select the UI Element You Want to Debug and Start the Chat (in This Case, It is the Div with the bg-blue-500 Class)*

In this example, the blue box is taller than its gray container, causing a scrollbar. In DevTools, select the gray container `<div>`, open the AI assistance panel, and ask: "How can I make this blue box fully visible without scrollbars?" The AI will examine the element's CSS (noting h-32 and overflow-auto) and likely suggest removing the fixed height or changing the overflow. For instance, it may recommend deleting **`overflow-auto`**, or using **`overflow-visible`**, or increasing/removing the **`h-32`** class so the container fits the child. It might output an explanation like: "The container has a fixed height of **`8rem (h-32)`** and **`overflow-auto`**. Increasing its height or removing overflow will prevent clipping." You can then click "Apply the suggested change" to update the CSS live. This demonstrates how DevTools AI identifies the specific Tailwind classes causing overflow and fixes them without manual trial-and-error.

After enabling the AI features, Chrome DevTools can provide targeted suggestions based on the live DOM and computed styles of the selected element. *Figure* 7.10 illustrates how these AI-generated insights appear during a real debugging session.

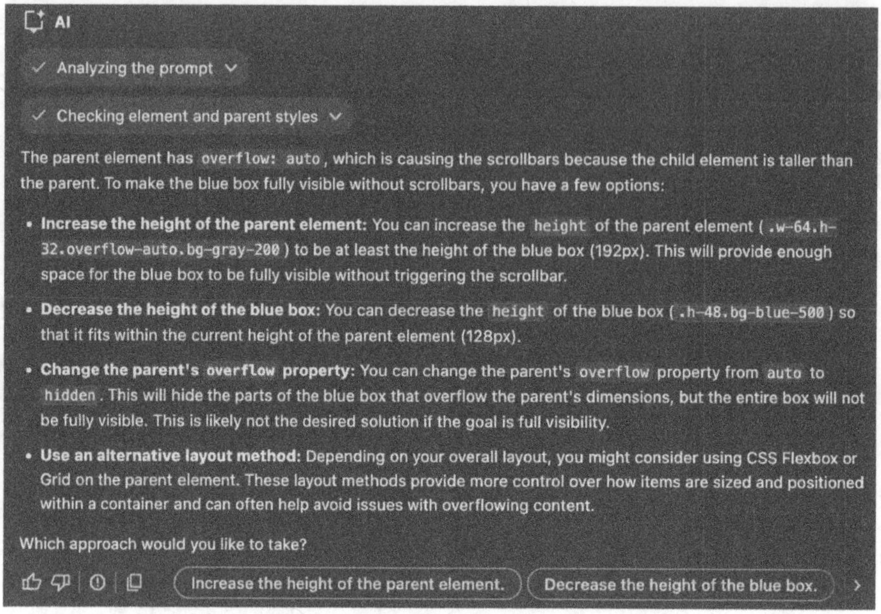

Figure 7.10: *The AI Suggestions Powered by the Chrome DevTools AI Indeed Found the Problem*

Figure 7.11 showcases the UI Working Properly.

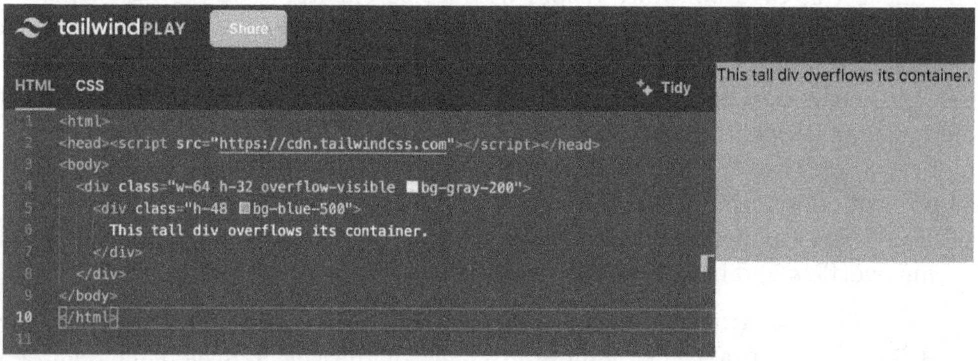

Figure 7.11: *The UI Behaves Correctly Now*

Example: Debugging a Hidden Element

Another common issue is negative margins or hidden overflow. Consider:

```
<html>
<head><script src="https://cdn.tailwindcss.com"></script></head>
<body>
  <div class="w-48 p-4 bg-gray-200 overflow-hidden">
```

```
    <div class="-ml-8 bg-green-300 p-2">
      This box is partially hidden due to negative margin.
    </div>
  </div>
</body>
</html>
```

Here, the green box is pushed left by `-ml-8` and gets cut off by the parent's overflow-hidden. In DevTools, select the green `<div>`, launch the AI panel, and ask, "Why is part of this box cut off?" The AI will analyze the layout and explain that the negative margin (`-ml-8`) is causing the overflow. It might suggest removing or adjusting that class, or changing `overflow-hidden` to `overflow-visible`. It could even propose a corrected HTML/CSS snippet. This makes it easy to spot the culprit (negative margin) and apply the Tailwind fix (for example, delete `-ml-8` or remove `overflow-hidden`). Again, the AI ties the symptom to the specific Tailwind utilities involved.

Prompt-Writing Strategies

Before relying on AI-generated fixes, it is important to craft prompts that give the model enough context to produce accurate and actionable suggestions. The following strategies outline how to write effective prompts when using Chrome's AI-assisted DevTools.

- **Be Specific and Descriptive**: Mention the element or classes and the exact problem. Instead of "Fix layout", try "Why is the sidebar not visible?" or "Center this green box". The more context (text, classes, and layout) you give, the better the AI can target its answer.
- **Use the Inspected Element Context**: Always start the AI chat from the DevTools Elements panel on the problematic element (**`right-click → Ask AI`**). This attaches the correct context so the AI knows what part of the page you mean.
- **Leverage Screenshots**: Use the camera icon in the AI panel to capture the current viewport and include it with your prompt. A visual can help the AI see spacing or layout issues that are hard to describe in words.
- **Iterate with Follow-ups**: If the first answer is not perfect, ask follow-ups or rephrase. For example, "What if I keep the height and instead change overflow?" or "Can you show the HTML after the change?" The panel even offers suggested follow-up prompts to refine the solution.

Note: *To get the most out of AI during a debugging session, your prompts should be specific and context-rich. Compare these two approaches:*

Poor Prompt: "My Tailwind layout is broken on mobile, help me fix it."

Improved Prompt: "My three-column grid using `grid-cols-3` is overflowing on small screens. I want it to stack vertically on mobile but remain three columns on lg screens. Here is my current markup: [code snippet]. Why is the responsive prefix not triggering as expected?"

The improved version provides the specific utility classes, the desired behavior (UX intent), and the technical context, allowing the AI to identify issues such as missing mobile-first logic or conflicting styles immediately.

DevTools AI versus GPT/Copilot

When deciding between these tools, it is helpful to evaluate them across four key criteria: context-awareness, scalability, workflow integration, and reliability.

- **Context-Awareness and Workflow Integration**: The built-in DevTools AI is superior for immediate, in-context fixes because it is tightly integrated with the live page. It has real-time access to the live DOM, CSS styles (including Tailwind classes), and even network data. It understands exactly which classes are present via Web APIs, allowing it to give precise advice and even apply changes back to your live page without you having to manually describe or paste code.
- **Scalability and Reliability:** In contrast, GPT-4 and GitHub Copilot offer better scalability for project-wide concerns. While they do not "see" the rendered page and require manual input, they provide more comprehensive language assistance and can generate larger code snippets or architectural plans outside the browser. However, because they are more mature than the experimental DevTools AI, they often provide more reliable results for complex logic or broader planning tasks.

For step-by-step debugging of a specific element or layout, use the DevTools AI—it is more convenient and often more accurate because it "sees" the ground truth. Use general LLMs such as GPT or Copilot for broader planning, code generation, and complex refactors that span multiple files.

Prompt Engineering Strategies for Debugging and Optimization

Getting useful help from AI often comes down to how you ask your questions. Prompt engineering is the craft of phrasing queries or instructions to AI in a way that yields the best answers. In the context of debugging Tailwind CSS and front-end issues, effective prompts can mean the difference between a vague response and a pinpoint solution. This section covers strategies for creating prompts aimed at four scenarios:

tracing errors, generating tests, refactoring code, and enhancing performance. Each scenario requires a slightly different approach in how you "talk" to the AI.

Crafting Prompts for Error Analysis and Bug Hunting

When an error occurs, be it a build error, a console stack trace, or simply a visual glitch, you should formulate a prompt that provides the AI with enough context to reason about the problem. Here are some tips[5]:

- **Include the Error Message or Description of the Visual Bug**: For example, if you see an error such as "TailwindCSS class not found: **`bg-prple-500`**" (a typo in class), your prompt to GPT-4 could be: "I have an error: '**`bg-prple-500`** not found'. Why might this Tailwind CSS class not be applying?". By quoting the error, you let the AI identify the core issue (in this case, a likely typo causing Tailwind to purge the class or simply a misspelling).
- **Provide Relevant Code Snippets**: If an element is not rendering correctly, include the HTML/JSX for that element in your prompt. For example, "The following Tailwind HTML is not working as expected. The box should be centered but is not. **`<div class='mx-auto flex flex-col items-center ...'>...</div>`**. What could be wrong?". GPT-4 can then analyze the snippet. Perhaps it notices you applied **`mx-auto`** to a flex item that is not within a container of fixed width, and it will explain that **`mx-auto`** centers only block elements with a set width (so if the parent is full width, it will not visibly center). By giving code context, you enable the AI to be specific. **Always double-check you have copied enough surrounding code; sometimes the issue is simply above or following the snippet you think is relevant.**
- **Ask for Probable Causes and Solutions**: Phrase your prompt to encourage not just identification of the bug, but also how to fix it. For instance: "In my React component using Tailwind, the toggle button does not change appearance on click. Here is the relevant code [...]. What are possible reasons and how can I fix it?". This invites the AI to enumerate potential causes (maybe a state issue or a missing: active class style) and to suggest specific remedies. A good AI answer might say, "Possible reason 1: the state is not updating, ensure **`onClick`** is wired. Possible reason 2: Tailwind's JIT did not generate the **`bg-blue-500:active class`** because it is not in the source. Solution: add it explicitly or use **`active:bg-blue-500`** in your JSX so that it is recognized."

[5] *When using AI to diagnose bugs, prioritize prompts that ask the model to explain the "why" behind an error. The goal of AI-assisted debugging is not just to receive a suggested fix, but to reinforce your understanding of core CSS and Tailwind principles, such as the cascade, specificity, and the mobile-first approach. By analyzing these explanations, you build the long-term debugging intuition necessary to identify similar issues independently in the future.*

Prompt Template - Error/Bug: A useful pattern is: "I am seeing [describe the unexpected behavior or error]. I expected [describe the desired outcome]. Here is the code snippet/config related to this. [Insert code]. Can you help me identify what is wrong and how to fix it?". This structure gives the AI a clear picture: symptom, expected behavior, and the evidence (code). By explicitly stating what you expected, the AI can focus on why reality diverged from expectation.

Prompting AI to Generate Tests for Your UI Components

Testing is an important part of debugging; writing tests can help catch bugs early or prevent regressions. AI can assist by generating test cases or testing code based on your description of a feature. Tailwind CSS primarily affects presentation, so tests might be about checking the presence of classes or verifying layout under conditions (in combination with your framework).[6]

When asking AI to generate tests:

- **Specify the Framework and Testing Library:** For example, if you are using React and Jest with Testing Library, your prompt should mention that: "*Write a Jest + React Testing Library test for the following component. It should verify that when the component is in error state, a red background (via Tailwind class* ***`bg-red-500`****) is present.*" Being specific ensures the AI writes the correct kind of test code (for example, it will use **`render()`** from Testing Library and queries such as **`getByText`** or **`getByTestId`** if you mention them).

- **Describe the Scenarios to Test:** AI can generate a lot, but you should guide it on what scenarios are important. For a Tailwind UI, scenarios could include responsive behavior (for example, "simulate a small screen and ensure the menu becomes vertical"), interactive states (hover/focus), or conditional rendering. You might prompt: "*Generate test cases for a TailwindCSS-based NavBar component. Test that: (1) it renders a mobile menu button on small screens (simulated), (2) clicking the button adds the class* *`block`* *to the dropdown (making it visible), (3) on large screens, the menu is horizontal and the button is hidden (dropdown has class* **`hidden`**). This way, the AI will likely produce multiple **`it()`** blocks covering each point.

- **Use AI for Edge Cases:** If you fixed a bug, ask the AI to write a test proving that the bug is resolved. For example: "I fixed an issue where the card component overflowed its container when too many items were added. Write a test to

[6] *When using AI to diagnose bugs, prioritize prompts that ask the model to explain the "why" behind an error. The goal of AI-assisted debugging is not just to receive a suggested fix, but to reinforce your understanding of core CSS and Tailwind principles, such as the cascade, specificity, and the mobile-first approach. By analyzing these explanations, you build the long-term debugging intuition necessary to identify similar issues independently in the future.*

ensure that in such a case, the card now adds `flex-wrap` and no overflow occurs.". Cursor AI, in particular, emphasizes generating tests after a fix to lock in the correctness. The AI might produce a test that mounts several card items and then checks the computed style or class list for `flex-wrap`. Even if the test is not perfect, it gives you a starting template that you can refine.

Prompt Template: Test Generation: "Create a [unit/integration/E2E] test for [component/module]. It should simulate [state or interaction] and assert [the expected outcome]. Use [framework/testing library]. Here is the component code for reference: [optional snippet]." By clearly stating what to simulate and assert, the AI knows the goal of the test. This approach can save time writing boilerplate test code and ensure you think through the expected behavior.

Refactoring and Clean-up: Prompts for Code and CSS Optimization

Refactoring involves improving the internal structure of code without changing its external behavior. Tailwind CSS encourages a certain way of structuring HTML with many classes; over time, this can become unwieldy (long class strings, repeated patterns, and so on). AI can assist in refactoring by analyzing patterns and suggesting simplifications or more maintainable solutions.

Effective Refactoring Prompts:

- **Ask for a More Concise or Clearer Version:** If you have a piece of markup with a very long list of utility classes or nested elements, you can ask GPT-4: *"Refactor the following code for clarity and maintainability. Use Tailwind best practices. [insert code]"*. The AI might respond by splitting classes into multiple lines (for readability), or by suggesting extractions (for example, "consider using a custom CSS class with `@apply` for these repeated utilities").
- **Target Redundant or Conflicting Classes:** Mention if you suspect redundancy. For example, "*The following* HTML *has some redundant or conflicting Tailwind classes. Identify them and refactor the code to remove any no-ops or conflicts. [code]*". Tailwind's documentation notes that you should never have two classes targeting the same property on an element (such as `flex` and `grid` together, or `text-xl` and `text-sm` on the same tag). GPT-4 can spot these conflicts and either remove one or restructure the code. It might answer: "You have `w-full` and `w-1/2` on the same element, which conflict. I will remove `w-full,` assuming you want half width," and provide the cleaned snippet. Similarly, it could point out unnecessary wrappers that serve no purpose.
- **Request Performance-Related Refactors:** Sometimes code works but is not optimal. You can prompt for specific improvements: "*Refactor the following component to reduce its DOM depth and improve performance*," or "Optimize

this Tailwind CSS markup for smaller HTML without changing the design." This nudges the AI to remove extraneous **<div>**s or consolidate multiple nested elements using flex/grid appropriately. For instance, an AI might combine two nested flex containers into one with more classes, reducing DOM nodes. It may also suggest enabling PurgeCSS (in your build config) if it sees a lot of unused classes - though that is more of a build step optimization.

- **Use AI to Enforce Best Practices:** You might not recall every best practice, but the AI has been trained on many. Prompt it directly: "*Apply Tailwind CSS best practices to this code.*" It could suggest things such as using semantic HTML (replace a **<div>** with a **<header>** or **<button>** where appropriate), adding **sr-only** classes for hidden accessible labels, or grouping classes in a logical order. While Tailwind does not enforce class order, some teams sort classes by category (display -> spacing -> color, and so on) for readability. AI can do this sorting for you as a refactor, making the code cleaner to read.

Prompt Template - Refactoring: "Here is some code: [code]. Refactor it to improve [readability/maintainability/performance]. Specifically, [optional hints, for example, 'remove any duplicate Tailwind classes or unnecessary wrappers']. Provide the refactored code and explain the changes." Including 'explain the changes' is useful for learning; the AI will tell you what it did (for example, "Removed **bg-white** because the parent already had it, so it was redundant"). This helps to ensure that you agree with the refactoring.

Performance Tuning Prompts: Lighthouse Optimization

Performance optimization often involves broader changes: minifying assets, reducing DOM size, tuning images, and so on. AI can offer advice for performance if you describe the scenario or provide tool output. It is important to remember that metrics such as LCP, DOM size, and bundle size are not just technical benchmarks; they directly correlate to perceived user experience and business impact. A faster site reduces bounce rates and improves conversion, while a lean DOM ensures that the application remains responsive on low-end devices.

How to Prompt for Performance Help:

- **Feed Lighthouse Results or Specific Metrics:** If Lighthouse flags, for instance, "Largest Contentful Paint (LCP) is 4s" or "Avoid enormous network payloads: total ~3 MB", include those in your prompt. "Lighthouse says my LCP is 4s on mobile and total download is 3MB. Using Tailwind CSS and lots of images. How can I improve performance?" The AI might recommend techniques such as enabling PurgeCSS to strip unused Tailwind classes (which can **dramatically** cut CSS size, for example, from megabytes down to a few kilobytes), compressing images, using **lazyload** for offscreen images, splitting long pages, and so on. If you specifically mention Tailwind, it will likely bring up Purge (or the built-in `content` purge in Tailwind v3+), as well as perhaps using CDN for assets or deferring scripts.

- **Ask for Architectural Changes:** Sometimes, performance improvements require rethinking how something is built. For example, "The dashboard feels slow due to many charts in the DOM. Any ideas to improve responsiveness?". An AI could suggest using virtual scrolling if there is a huge list, or splitting the dashboard into tabs so not everything loads at once, or using Tailwind's `collapse` classes to only render certain elements when needed. It might also point out if you have too many DOM nodes (remember, >1500 nodes can degrade performance). Perhaps it suggests removing an overly nested structure or template that repeats too many times.

- **Profile and Then Prompt:** For advanced cases, you might use Chrome's Performance Profiler to record a timeline, then describe the findings to the AI. "Profiling shows a layout thrash caused by constantly adding DOM nodes. How can I mitigate this?". While GPT-4 cannot see your performance trace, describing it can yield suggestions: it might mention "excessive DOM insertion" and advise techniques such as debouncing updates, or using CSS **will-change** for animations, and so on. Not all will be Tailwind-specific, but it is useful nonetheless.

- **Focus on Tailwind-Specific Performance Settings:** Tailwind itself can be optimized via configuration. For instance, enabling JIT mode (which is the default in newer versions) ensures classes are generated on the fly. Prompt for "Tailwind CSS production optimizations" and the AI should mention Purge (tree-shaking unused styles), possibly CSS minification, and using CDN for the Tailwind CSS file if applicable. Another example: "How to reduce the CSS bundle size in a Tailwind project?" - Answer would likely include purging unused classes, limiting the color palette or font sizes in the config (to generate fewer classes), and so on. Indeed, developers report huge reductions, such as going from **5.5 MB of CSS down to 3.5 KB** by purging unused classes, a massive improvement that eliminates Lighthouse complaints about oversized CSS.

Prompt Template - Performance: "My web app is slow in [area]. [If known, provide metric or tool warnings.] I am using Tailwind CSS and [mention framework if any]. What steps can I take to optimize performance and loading times?" This open question invites a list of suggestions. If the AI's answer is too generic, you can follow up with specifics: "It suggested reducing DOM nodes. Here is my DOM structure for a typical page: [outline or code]. What could be removed or simplified?". Iteratively, you can drill down to concrete changes (for example, remove an extra **<div>** used solely for styling - instead, apply that styling to the parent). The AI's broad knowledge, combined with your project specifics, can yield a tailored performance tuning plan.

By mastering these prompt strategies, you make the AI a far more effective assistant. In the next section, we will apply these techniques to real Tailwind CSS problems, demonstrating how the AI responds and how we can implement its suggestions.

Common Tailwind CSS Pitfalls and AI Solutions

Tailwind CSS, despite its utility-first power, comes with its own set of common issues and mistakes developers encounter. These include using classes incorrectly, ending up with bloated markup, or overlooking accessibility. Here, we highlight some frequent Tailwind-specific pitfalls in real-world projects and discuss how to identify and fix them, with the help of AI tools where appropriate. The focus will be on:

- **Redundant or Conflicting Utility Classes**: These not only clutter the HTML but also threaten design system governance by creating unpredictable styling outcomes.
- **Accessibility (a11y) Issues, Especially Insufficient Color Contrast**: Specifically insufficient color contrast, which impacts product quality and inclusivity.
- **Excessive DOM Depth or Unnecessary Markup Bloat**: This degrades performance and reflects architectural decisions that can impact perceived responsiveness on low-end devices.
- **Responsive Layout Problems and Breakpoint Misuse**: This degrades performance and reflects architectural decisions that can impact perceived responsiveness on low-end devices.

For each issue, we will describe the symptoms, why they matter, and how to debug/optimize the situation. You will see how AI assistants and Devtools can be used to quickly spot these problems and suggest fixes.

Redundant or Conflicting Utility Classes

The issue: In Tailwind, it is possible (especially as a project grows or when multiple developers touch the same code) to apply multiple utility classes to the same element that either overlap in functionality or outright conflict with each other. For example, an element might have `class="w-full w-1/2"` or `class="text-sm text-xl font-bold"`. These classes target the same CSS properties (width and font-size in these examples) with different values, so one of them will "win" and the other will do nothing. This is essentially redundant code because it does not break the site (the browser will apply one of the classes), but it is confusing and may indicate a mistake in logic. Tailwind's official guidance is clear: "never add two conflicting classes to the same element, only add the one you want to take effect". If both are present, which one wins depends on the order of CSS in the final stylesheet, which in turn depends on Tailwind's build order (not necessarily the order in your HTML). This uncertainty can lead to bugs when you upgrade Tailwind or change your config.[7]

Identifying Conflicts: Chrome DevTools is your friend. If you inspect an element with overlapping classes, the Styles panel will show one set of rules crossed out. For instance, with **`<div class="w-full w-1/2">`**, DevTools might display something such as:

- **`.w-full { width: 100% }`** (crossed out)
- **`.w-1/2 { width: 50% }`** (applied)

This tells you that **`w-1/2`** is overriding **`w-full`** (because Tailwind's generated CSS probably placed **`.w-1/2`** later in the file, or simply because it is a more specific rule in how Tailwind is structured). Similarly, if you had **`text-sm text-xl`**, one of the font-size utilities would be crossed out.

How AI can help: If you are unsure which classes conflict, you can literally ask an AI. For example: "I have a Tailwind class string: **`bg-red-500 bg-teal-500!`**. Is there a conflict?". GPT-4 might recall that the ! in Tailwind makes a utility important (which forces it to override others), so **`bg-teal-500!`** will win over **`bg-red-500`**. It would explain that normally, two background color classes would conflict, and the latter in CSS wins, but the bang makes one definitely win with !important. The AI can also suggest using tools such as **`twMerge`** if you are merging class lists in code – this library (or similar) will automatically remove conflicting classes, keeping only the one with the greatest "specificity" in Tailwind terms. In fact, if you prompt GPT-4 with "How do I handle conflicting Tailwind classes in a React component that merges props?", it might suggest using tailwind-merge to programmatically resolve duplicates, citing how **`merge("text-sm text-xl")`** yields "**`text-xl`**".

Solution Approach: The fix for conflicting classes is straightforward: remove the ones you do not want. The challenge is finding them. Here is where an AI code review (such as Cursor) can shine: it can scan your project for any instances of multiple utility classes that set the same property. For example, it could search for known pairs (such as any occurrence of both **`w-`** and another **`w-`** in the same class attribute). Alternatively, running a simple regex search in your IDE for patterns such as w-full and seeing if **`w-`** appears again on that line could catch some. But AI could do it more intelligently by actually understanding that **`max-w-lg`** and **`max-w-sm`** conflict even though their text is not obviously similar. Cursor's "bug finder" might catch such logical issues by comparing changes or looking at patterns.

---

[7] *It is important to recognize that many class conflicts originate from complex conditional rendering logic (for example, ternary operators in React or* **`x-bind:class`** *in Alpine.js). When debugging these conflicts, reviewing your component's state management and the logic that toggles these classes is often as important as simply removing the duplicate utilities from the markup.*

When you find a conflict, decide which class is intended. Remove the other, or adjust your conditional logic (if classes are conditionally added via code). If indeed you intended two different states (for example, one class for mobile, one for desktop), ensure one is wrapped in a responsive prefix (such as `w-full sm:w-1/2` instead of `w-full w-1/2` without prefixes). That way, they no longer conflict because they apply at different breakpoints.

Redundant classes (not exactly conflicting, but duplicate usage) are another issue. Sometimes you might inadvertently include the same class twice, or include a class that has no effect because it is the default. For instance, adding flex to an element that is already flex via parent or by default does not harm, but it clutters HTML. Tools such as Tailwind IntelliSense in VSCode warn about duplicates or unknown classes. An AI tool reading your code could point out, "You have `mt-4` applied twice; it only needs to be there once." Removing redundancies will not only clean up code but could marginally improve performance (less HTML to parse). Purging unused CSS will take care of duplicates in output (it does not generate two copies), but better not to have them in the first place.[8]

In summary, avoid conflicting utilities by design. Use one utility per CSS property per element, or use responsive/variant prefixes to make them context-specific. Lean on AI to detect these patterns across a large codebase, and use DevTools to confirm when debugging a specific element.

Accessibility and Contrast Issues - A11y Pitfalls

The issue: Tailwind CSS makes it easy to apply colors and hide elements, which is great for development speed, but developers must be mindful of accessibility. Two frequent a11y concerns are **color contrast** and **screen reader invisibility**:

1. **Color Contrast**: Ensuring that the text is readable against its background. With Tailwind's palette, it is easy to pick a combination that looks pretty but fails accessibility guidelines (WCAG). For example, using `text-gray-500` on a `bg-gray-200` might result in a contrast ratio that is too low for normal text. Lighthouse will flag this: "*Background and foreground colors do not have a sufficient contrast ratio.*" It might highlight an element: say, a button with yellow text on a white background, and so on. In fact, developers report that Lighthouse heavily penalizes such issues and explicitly lists elements with poor contrast, even providing screenshots for reference. Another aspect is forgetting to consider dark mode variants: if you set `dark:text-gray-400` on

---

[8] *Beyond simple code cleanliness, eliminating conflicting utilities is a matter of design system governance and token discipline. Allowing overlapping utilities to exist weakens the "source of truth" provided by your design tokens, making it difficult to maintain a consistent visual language as the application scales.*

a **`dark:bg-gray-800`**, is that contrast sufficient? Tailwind default colors are not all made to be AA or AAA contrast compliant at certain combinations.

2. **Focus Indicators and `sr-only`**: Tailwind provides utility classes such as `outline-none`, which some devs use to remove focus rings, but doing so without providing an alternative visual indicator is an a11y **`no-no`**. Similarly, hiding content with **`hidden`** or **`sr-only`** is fine for sighted users, but one must ensure that important information is not completely inaccessible. A common mistake is hiding an element that has no visible counterpart (for example, hiding an error message without any indicator that an error occurred). Conversely, using **`sr-only`** appropriately (to hide labels visually but keep them for screen readers) is a best practice that some forget.

Identifying a11y Issues: Automated tools are extremely helpful. **Lighthouse (Accessibility audit)** will catch a lot: - Contrast issues: as mentioned, it will call out text that does not meet at least AA contrast. Tailwind's mid-range grays (500 on 200, and so on) often fail AA for small text. - Missing alt attributes on images (not Tailwind-specific, but common). - Missing form labels or inputs not associated with labels. - Improper heading order or empty buttons/links (if you use an icon with no **`aria-label`**). It also flags using only color to indicate state (for example, "required fields in red" without another indicator).

Chrome's **Elements panel** also has an Accessibility sub-panel, which can show contrast ratio for selected text elements and whether it passes. You can click an element and see its contrast stats and even get suggested colors to improve contrast.

How AI can help: Once you know an accessibility problem, AI can help solve it:

- **Contrast Fixes:** If Lighthouse says your **`#FFD500`** yellow star icon on white is failing contrast, you can ask GPT-4: "*Tailwind: I have yellow text on white (using **`text-yellow-400`** on **`bg-white`**). It fails contrast. Suggest a fix.*" The AI might suggest using a darker shade for the text (maybe **`text-yellow-600`** or **`text-yellow-700`**) or adding a subtle shadow or outline. It could even note the WCAG contrast requirements (4.5:1 for normal text AA) and propose a color that meets it. If you give it the exact hex values, it could calculate or recall approximate contrast. Another prompt: "My *Lighthouse audit says contrast ratio is too low for `gray-500` on `gray-200`. What Tailwind color should I use instead of **`gray-500`** for text to meet* AA?" likely answer: use a darker gray such as **`gray-700`** or increase background lightness difference. The Accreditly article on Tailwind a11y specifically recommends using the Tailwind color palette's lighter or darker variants to ensure sufficient contrast and to **check contrast ratios with tools**[9].

[9] https://accreditly.io/articles/make-the-web-accessible-with-tailwind-css#:~:text=Maintaining%20sufficient%20color%20contrast%20is,contrast%20design%20choices

AI might echo such advice, for example, "Use **text-gray-800** on **bg-gray-200** for better contrast."[10]

- **Adding Accessibility Attributes:** If you suspect an issue (such as an interactive element missing attributes), you can ask, "*Is this code accessible? <button class='... '>🔍</button>*". GPT-4 would likely respond that the button has no text or label, which is a problem for screen readers, and suggest adding an **aria-label** or including visible text (or an **sr-only** span inside). It might mention Tailwind's **sr-only** class usage for hiding text visually while keeping it for screen readers. For instance, it could say: "*Wrap a descriptive word in <span class='sr-only'>Search</span> inside the button so screen readers know what the 🔍 icon means.*" We saw in the Accreditly resource that **sr-only** is recommended for icon-only buttons.

- **Accessibility Checklist via AI:** You can also have AI act as an auditor. Try a prompt such as: "*Review the following Tailwind UI code for accessibility issues.*" The AI will likely output a list of potential concerns – missing alt on images, low contrast if it recognizes color classes known to be problematic, usage of **role** or ARIA if needed, keyboard navigation issues (for example, if something is **hover:** only, mention adding focus styles). It is not perfect, but it can simulate an audit, and you can cross-check its points. This is handy as a learning tool, too, to see what common mistakes to avoid.

Solution Approach: Once identified, the fixes are typically:

- **Increase Contrast**: Choose color combos that meet guidelines (often just darker text or a darker background). Tailwind has many shades; use them wisely. Some developers opt to create a custom Tailwind theme with guaranteed contrast ratios for certain **text-on-bg** combinations.

- **Ensure Every Interactive Element is Reachable and Understandable for Assistive Tech**: Use focus styles (Tailwind's default focus outlines are usually okay; avoid removing them unless replaced), use **hover:** paired with **focus:** for any visual cue (so keyboard users get the effect too), and use **aria-** attributes or screen reader text for icons.

- **Check Semantic HTML**: Make sure you are not using a **<div>** when a **<button>** should be used (Tailwind does not prevent misuse of semantics). AI can remind you of this, too – for example, if you show GPT-4 a nav built with **<div>** and clickable spans, it will likely advise using proper **<nav>**, **<ul>/<li>**, and **<a>** or **<button>** tags for better accessibility and semantics.

---

[10] To prevent recurring contrast issues at scale, it is highly recommended to integrate accessible color tokens directly into your Tailwind configuration or design system. By defining semantic colors that are pre-validated for accessibility (for example, `text-primary-accessible`), you ensure that developers choose compliant combinations by default, reducing the need for manual debugging later.

Accessibility is a big topic, but the main takeaway is that you should not solely rely on AI or tools. Use them to augment your own understanding. Run Lighthouse audits regularly; use AI to interpret and fix the findings. In doing so, you will ensure that your Tailwind UI is not just pretty, but also usable by everyone.

Excessive DOM Depth and Unnecessary Markup

The issue: A complex UI (such as a dashboard with many widgets, modals, nested layouts) can lead to a very large DOM tree – lots of elements nested deeply. This can hurt performance: the browser takes longer to render and update the layout, memory usage goes up, and certain operations (such as query selectors or DOM mutations) slow down on lower end devices. Lighthouse defines some thresholds: it warns if you have more than ~800 DOM nodes on initial load and gives an outright "Excessive DOM size" error above ~1,400 nodes. It also flags if any element has a very large number of children or if the nesting level goes beyond a certain depth (commonly, >32 levels deep is considered too much nesting).[11] In Tailwind projects, this can happen if you wrap elements unnecessarily or use too many divisions for layout. For instance, using a **`<div>`** for purely stylistic reasons around every small component, or not simplifying the structure when possible.

Symptoms: Aside from a Lighthouse audit warning, you might notice sluggishness in the UI (especially on slower devices) when manipulating a large DOM. Scrolling could be janky if the DOM is huge. If your Tailwind UI is just a static site, you might not feel it until you benchmark, but in web apps, a big DOM can slow down diffing (in React, and so on) and DOM updates.

DevTools can help by showing the **DOM Tree** – you can count elements or just see visually if it is very nested. There is also a feature in Chrome (Rendering tab) to show the DOM element count live. If you suspect an area is overly nested, you can inspect that subtree and count children.

How AI can help: Optimization of the DOM structure is a design problem that AI can advise on when given context:

Reviewing HTML structure: You could copy a chunk of your HTML (or the JSX template) and ask GPT-4: "*Is there a way to simplify this HTML structure without changing the layout?*". The AI will try to remove extra wrappers. For example, if you have:

[11] *It is important to recognize that excessive DOM depth often reflects high-level component architecture decisions rather than just poor markup habits. Deeply nested trees are frequently a byproduct of over-componentization or the "wrapper-hell" that occurs when every small piece of logic is encapsulated in its own nested div. When optimizing, consider whether your underlying component structure can be flattened to improve both technical metrics and the perceived responsiveness of the UI.*

```
<div class="p-4">
  <div class="flex"><div class="mr-2">Label:</div><div>Value</div></div>
</div>
```

It might suggest that the outer **<div class="p-4">** could perhaps be merged with the inner flex container by applying **p-4** to that inner container instead, removing one level of nesting. Or it might suggest using a **<span>** for the label if appropriate, instead of two divs. Essentially, AI can point out, "*You have a container just to apply padding. You could put that padding on the flex parent and drop one <div>.*" It might also detect patterns such as a list that could be a **<ul>** with list items rather than multiple **<div>**s (improving both semantics and possibly structure).

Identifying Unnecessary Tailwind Wrappers: Sometimes, we wrap elements to apply background or borders. But Tailwind allows pseudo-elements and relative positioning that could eliminate wrappers (for decorative elements). AI might or might not get that advanced, but at least it can highlight obvious, unnecessary wrappers.

Alternate Layouts: If you have deep nesting because of certain layout choices, an AI might suggest a different Tailwind layout technique. For instance, maybe you nested a lot of divs to achieve a grid-like layout with some spacing. GPT-4 could suggest using Tailwind's **grid** utilities instead, flattening the structure. It could say, "*Use **grid grid-cols-3 gap-4** on a parent rather than writing a separate **<div>** for each column wrapper.*" This reduces both depth and number of elements.

Summarizing Lighthouse Suggestions: The Chrome Lighthouse documentation itself suggests creating DOM nodes only when needed, and destroying them when not in use. It also hints at simplifying CSS selectors if you cannot reduce the DOM size. An AI reading a Lighthouse report might reiterate: "*Remove offscreen elements from initial load, break long pages into multiple pages, or use virtualization, and* so *on.*" In a Tailwind context, virtualization might be beyond scope, but if you had a long list rendered, an AI could mention, "consider using pagination or infinite scroll to not load 1000 items at once."

Solution Approach: Start by removing what you do not need:

- **Eliminate Wrapper <div>s That only Serve Styling**: Tailwind utilities can often be combined so that one element can carry multiple responsibilities. For example, instead of **<div class="rounded-md"><img class="rounded-md"/></div>** (wrapping an image just to round the corners), you can simply apply **rounded-md** to the **<img>** itself.
- **Use Semantic Container Elements**: If you have many layers of generic containers, think in terms of meaningful groupings. A navigation bar might have **<nav>** containing a **<ul>** for items – you do not need an extra **<div>** inside the **<nav>** just to apply flex; apply **flex** to the **<nav>** or **<ul>**. Tailwind does not restrict which elements you put classes on.

- **Watch out for Copy-Pasted Code**: Many times, large DOMs come from copying a block of elements multiple times (for example, cards in a grid). If each card has unnecessary inner elements, that multiplies. Refactoring one card's structure to be lighter will benefit all.
- **Leverage Tailwind's Grid and Flex to the Fullest**: These layout systems can often replace extra markup. For example, instead of:

  ```
  <div class="flex">
    <div class="w-1/2">Column1</div>
    <div class="w-1/2">Column2</div>
  </div>
  ```

  You do not necessarily reduce elements here, but if you had more complex nested rows and columns, a CSS Grid could flatten some of that. - Use ***`::before`*** *and* ***`::after`*** *for decorative elements*: Tailwind allows styling of pseudo-elements via the **`before:`** and **`after:`** prefixes combined with **`content-['']`** and other utilities. If you have an extra **`<div>`** solely to, say, render a little badge or an icon, consider if it could be a pseudo-element of a parent.

AI can propose these ideas, but as a developer, you will apply them carefully. Always test after refactoring to ensure that you did not break anything visually. Tools such as **Percy** or simply taking before/after screenshots are useful for verifying the UI remains the same after removing elements.

One more angle: **Memory and JavaScript Performance.** A huge DOM not only impacts initial render, but also runtime. If you query the DOM or update styles, the cost grows with the DOM size. This might be outside what AI can directly help with, but by reducing the DOM, you inherently improve those aspects. If using a framework such as React or Vue, the *virtual* DOM diffing cost also increases with more components/ nodes, so trimming is beneficial all around.

In conclusion, **keep your HTML lean.** Tailwind's utilities should empower you to style efficiently, not tempt you into divitus (the condition of too many **`<div>`**s). Use AI to review and suggest cuts, but also use your judgment. And remember, Lighthouse's metric is a guide: try to stay below that ~1500 node mark for pages. It is not a hard rule, but a signal. If an AI refactor can remove 200 unnecessary elements, that is a win for performance.

Layout Breakpoints and Responsive Design Issues

The Issue: Tailwind CSS makes responsive design straightforward with its mobile-first breakpoints (for example, **`sm:`**, **`md:`**, **`lg:`** prefixes). However, developers can still run into problems where layouts "break" on certain screen sizes:

- Sometimes a responsive class is used incorrectly or not at all, resulting in elements that look fine on desktop but overflow or stack poorly on mobile.
- Or the inverse: too many `sm:` prefixes without understanding that base classes apply to all sizes (leading to something always being in the small-screen style even when it should not).
- Conflicting responsive utilities can also be an issue, though Tailwind's methodology usually avoids that if used correctly.

Common Examples:

- Forgetting to add a breakpoint prefix, for example, you intended a sidebar to be hidden on mobile, but wrote **`hidden md:block`**. On mobile, **`hidden`** applies (since no prefix means all sizes), and on md and up, **`block`** applies – this is correct. But if you flipped them (**`block md:hidden`**), on mobile it would be **`block`** (no prefix) and on md it becomes hidden, which likely is wrong logic. Misordering responsive intents can break layouts.
- Using a too-large fixed width that does not adapt: for example, an element with **`w-1/2`** but no smaller breakpoint handling could overflow on really small screens. Or images are not set to **`max-w-full`** and are causing overflow on mobile.
- Not testing intermediate breakpoints: maybe it looks okay at 375px and at 1200px, but at 800px, something odd happens because you had an **`md:`** but needed an **`lg:`** for a certain change.

Identifying Responsive Issues: The best way is to test at various widths (DevTools device mode, or simply dragging the browser to different sizes). Look for elements that get cut off or are too small, text that overlaps, or layouts that jump awkwardly. DevTools can show which CSS rules are active at a given width. If you inspect an element on a mobile and see that a **`sm:`** class is not yet active (because you are below that breakpoint), you confirm that the mobile style is the base class.

AI can help in a few ways:

- **Explaining Tailwind's Mobile-First Approach:** If a developer is confused why their design is not responsive, an AI explanation can clarify: "*Remember that an unprefixed class applies to all screen sizes unless overridden by a larger breakpoint. So, if you want an element to be one column on mobile and two columns on desktop, you might do* ***`grid-cols-1 md:grid-cols-2`****. The* ***`grid-cols-1`*** *applies always (mobile and up), then from medium upwards, it switches to 2 columns.*" This concept – that smaller breakpoints override the base style only when you go larger – is critical. Tailwind's philosophy: define default (mobile) styles, then layer on changes. An AI such as GPT-4 often reiterates, "Tailwind is mobile-first; unprefixed = all screens, so that higher breakpoints override."

- **Debugging a Specific Case:** If something is not working at a certain size, you can describe it: "*At 600px width, my layout looks wrong: the sidebar is supposed to be hidden, but it is visible overlapping content. I used* `hidden md:block` *on the sidebar.*". The AI might simulate the logic: 600px is just under Tailwind's default md (768px) breakpoint, so at 600px, `hidden` (base) applies, and `md:block` does not yet apply. Thus, the sidebar *should* be hidden. If it is visible, maybe the issue is that the sidebar is not actually using that class, or there is another rule making it visible (such as an inline style or `!important`). The AI could then suggest checking if maybe the class name is wrong or if some parent element's display is affecting it. In any case, describing the scenario + code will let the AI pinpoint what is off.

- **Recommending Proper Breakpoint Usage:** Suppose the AI detects that you used the wrong breakpoint. For example, you wanted a change at 1200px but used `lg:` (which is 1024px) instead of `xl:` (1280px). It could catch that if you mention screen sizes. "*My 1280px wide layout still stacks items that should be side by side at that width.*" AI: "Tailwind's `xl` breakpoint is 1280px. If you only used `lg:grid-cols-2`, that stops taking effect above 1279px since xl and above might require an `xl:grid-cols-2`. Consider using `xl:` if you need to extend that behavior or ensure that your container is not exceeding the breakpoint."

- **Edge-Case: JIT Mode Issues:** Tailwind's Just-In-Time mode (now standard) generates classes on the fly. If you dynamically apply classes (such as `className={isOpen ? 'block' : 'hidden'}` or combine strings), you must ensure those class names exist in the compiled CSS. If you see a responsive class not working, perhaps the string was not picked up by Tailwind (such as building a class name dynamically incorrectly). GPT-4 can remind: "*If using JIT, writing classes as concatenated strings can fail. Always include the full class in your source or in a safelist.*" For example, writing `"{size}-text-left"` with a variable might not be recognized; you should list possible values or use a safelist in config. An AI might or might not deduce this from a prompt, but if you mention "my classes are generated dynamically," it could.

Solution Approach: For responsive issues:

- **Use Correct Breakpoints and Test Them:** Know Tailwind's breakpoints (by default: `sm: 640px, md: 768px, lg: 1024px, xl: 1280px, 2xl:1536px`). Ensure you use them in ascending order properly. If something should change at 768px, use `md:`. If at 1024px, use `lg:`, and so on.

- **Do Not Forget Base Styles:** Provide a reasonable mobile style as the default (no prefix). Then add prefixes for changes. For example, if a menu should be horizontal on wide screens but vertical (stacked) on narrow, you might do: `<ul class="flex flex-col md:flex-row">...</ul>`

Here, `flex-col` is the default (mobile, vertical list), and `md:flex-row` kicks in at medium screens to make it horizontal. If you mistakenly did the opposite (put `flex-row` as base and `md:flex-col`), you would start with horizontal on mobile, which might overflow, then weirdly switch to vertical at md, which is probably unintended.

- **Use `max-w-full` on Images and Containers:** A very practical tip: images and iframes, and so on., by default can overflow their container. Tailwind has `max-w-full` (sets the element's max-width to 100%) and `overflow-x-hidden` on the parent to help avoid horizontal scroll on mobile. If you see horizontal scroll, use DevTools to find the culprit element (it will show an element exceeding width). Then, apply appropriate classes to fix (often `w-full` on that element or `max-w-full` if it has an intrinsic width).
- **Media Queries beyond Tailwind:** Occasionally, you might need a custom breakpoint (maybe a specific tablet width). Tailwind allows custom `screens` in config. If AI sees you struggling with a gap at, say, 700px (between `sm` and `md`), it might suggest introducing a custom breakpoint or using the `@media (min-width:700px){...}` via Tailwind's `@screen` or using an arbitrary breakpoint (`<div class="min-[700px]:bg-red-500">` as of Tailwind 3).
- **Responsive Testing**: It is not directly AI's role, but you can use AI to generate CSS if needed. However, a better usage is asking for verification: "*Will the classes `p-4 sm:p-2 md:p-8` work as I expect (4px padding default, 2px at >=640px, 8px at >=768px)?*". The AI can confirm the cascade: actually, `sm:p-2` applies at 640px+, and then `md:p-8` at 768px+, so at 800px, p-8 is in effect (overriding the smaller padding). This could catch a logical mistake if you meant something else.

In summary, debugging responsive issues is about understanding which classes apply when. DevTools shows you live, and AI can clarify any misunderstandings. The solution is often just adding or adjusting the breakpoint prefix on your utility classes. Remember that you can combine multiple breakpoints too (for example, `sm:text-sm md:text-base lg:text-lg` for gradually increasing text size). If you find yourself writing very complex responsive rules, consider if a simpler design or using container queries (new CSS) is applicable – though Tailwind's support for container queries is emerging, AI might even mention it if asked about modern responsive techniques.

With these common pitfalls covered, we have armed ourselves with knowledge and strategies to tackle them. Next, let us put it all together in a realistic **debugging walkthrough**, where we use AI and tools in concert to diagnose and fix a broken Tailwind UI.

Human-Led versus AI-Assisted Debugging: Pros and Cons

Debugging is traditionally a manual, sometimes tedious aspect of development. Introducing AI changes the dynamic. Let us analyze how a human-only debugging session might differ from an AI-assisted one, and what the advantages and disadvantages of each approach are. We can compare them on several aspects: speed, accuracy, thoroughness, learning curve, and reliability.

Aspect	Human-Led Debugging (No AI)	AI-Assisted Debugging (GPT-4, Copilot, and so on)
Speed of identifying issues	Relies on the developer's experience and meticulous checking of DevTools, logs, and so on. Might take longer to pinpoint issues in unfamiliar areas.	Can be significantly faster in spotting common patterns or errors. AI can quickly analyze logs or suggest likely causes (for example, missing `await` or a typo). For known bug types, AI often gives near-instant hints.
Accuracy of diagnosis	High for well-understood problems. A skilled dev can accurately diagnose complex issues, but might miss subtle multi-file interactions or be misled by assumptions.	AI is very good at known failure patterns and can catch subtle issues, such as a misuse of a Tailwind class or a logical error that a single developer might overlook. However, AI might sometimes misdiagnose if context is incomplete or if it "guesses" wrong, so oversight is needed.
Thorough-ness and scope	A human can systematically test the UI, but it is time-consuming to cover all combinations (responsive states, different user roles, and so on). Some issues might be left undiscovered until reported by users or QA.	AI (especially tools such as Cursor) can analyze the entire project scope at once, potentially catching issues across files or side effects that a human might not see initially • AI can also generate tests, improving coverage. • However, AI's suggestions are only as thorough as the prompts – it answers what you ask, so if you forget to ask about a certain aspect, it will not volunteer it unprompted.

Aspect	Human-Led Debugging (No AI)	AI-Assisted Debugging (GPT-4, Copilot, and so on)
Learning and knowledge	Humans draw on their personal knowledge and past experiences. They might not recall every detail (such as exact Tailwind config rules or new CSS specs) and might spend time researching. But the process of debugging manually can deepen the developer's understanding of the system.	AI brings a vast collective knowledge (documentation, best practices) instantly. It can remind you of Tailwind specifics (such as the mobile-first rule or class precedence) and suggest solutions you did not know. This can be a great learning aid – the developer learns from AI explanations. On the flip side, over-reliance could mean the dev does not deeply learn the problem if they accept answers blindly. Ideally, AI-assisted debugging should be a learning opportunity, with the dev reviewing and customizing suggestions.
Creativity in problem-solving	Humans excel at creative thinking and can devise novel solutions or workarounds that are not in any knowledge base – especially for design or UX issues that are subjective. They also better understand project-specific context (what the client or user expects).	AI is good at *algorithmic creativity* – recombining known solutions. It might not have true innovative capacity, but it can provide a wide range of suggestions (some of which the human might not have considered). For example, it might propose a different UX pattern or CSS approach drawn from another context. Still, it lacks the holistic understanding of user needs; the human has to curate which AI-suggested solution fits best.
Reliability and correctness of fixes	A human-written fix is implemented with understanding and can be tested by intuition. But humans can introduce new bugs inadvertently, or fix symptoms rather than the root cause if rushed. Code style and consistency depend on the individual.	AI-generated fixes often work for the specific scenario given (especially simple bug fixes) and can do so with a clean style (following best practices). For example, AI can automatically add tests to verify the fix or suggest a refactor that improves overall code quality. However, AI might produce code that does not fit the project's conventions or has hidden issues. Human oversight is crucial: you should review AI's code and run tests. AI may occasionally output syntactically correct but logically incorrect solutions if it misunderstood the problem.

Aspect	Human-Led Debugging (No AI)	AI-Assisted Debugging (GPT-4, Copilot, and so on)
Efficiency in repetitive tasks	Humans get fatigued or bored by repetitive debugging or refactoring (such as removing dozens of redundant classes manually, or renaming a utility across many files). This can lead to errors or just slow progress.	This is where AI shines – automating the drudgery. It can refactor across multiple occurrences swiftly (for example, remove all instances of `text-sm text-xl` conflicts by scanning the codebase). Multi-file edits that would take a person an afternoon can be done by AI in seconds (with verification) • The development cycle becomes 3-5× faster in such mechanical tasks. • The con is ensuring nothing is mistakenly changed; tests or careful code review are needed.
Team collaboration	In human-led debugging, communication among team members (for example, in a stand-up or code review) helps spread knowledge of the bug and its fix. It is a social process too; asking a colleague can be part of debugging.	AI can act as another "collaborator." Tools such as Cursor even allow sharing AI findings in real-time with the team, which can improve collective understanding. However, if only one person uses the AI and does not share the insights, the team might miss out on the learning. It is important to document AI-suggested changes (for example, in commit messages: "Fixed contrast per Lighthouse and GPT-4 suggestion"). Also, AI does not get annoyed by questions, and it is available 24/7, which is great for solo devs without immediate team support.

Table 7.1: *Comparison of Human-Led versus AI-Assisted Debugging*

From the preceding table, we see a pattern: AI-assisted debugging can greatly enhance speed and breadth, but it does not replace human judgment. The best outcomes arise from a partnership: the AI handles brute-force analysis and provides options, as well as the human makes decisions, adds creative insight, and ensures that the solution aligns with project goals[12].

[12] *To ensure consistency and knowledge sharing, it is highly recommended that organizations establish formal team guidelines for AI-assisted debugging. These guidelines should clarify that while AI is a powerful collaborator, human developers remain accountable for the final code. Encouraging team members to document AI-suggested fixes in pull requests helps spread insights and ensures that AI-driven decisions align with the team's long-term architectural standards.*

Some pros of AI assistance:

- Faster turnaround on identifying and fixing issues (bugs that might have taken hours can sometimes be fixed in minutes with the right prompt).
- Higher confidence in fixes, since AI often encourages writing tests and considering edge cases.
- **Continuous Learning**: developers can learn best practices and new techniques from AI explanations (it is like having a vast mentor library).
- **Reduced Frustration**: AI can reduce the time spent stuck, which is great for morale and meeting deadlines.

Some cons or cautions:

- AI is Not Infallible: If given ambiguous info, it might suggest something wrong or not perfectly suited. Blindly trusting it could cause new bugs.
- Need for Validation: One should treat AI suggestions as a strong hint, then test and verify just as you would your own code.
- **Context Limitations**: AI might not have access to your live running app or full codebase unless you provide it. Tools such as Cursor mitigate this by integrating deeply, but generic ChatGPT only knows what you paste. Missing context can lead to irrelevant suggestions.
- **Security/Privacy**: Not a focus of this chapter, but sending code to an external AI needs to be done with consideration of privacy and licenses. Self-hosted solutions or careful use of GitHub Copilot (which works on your code but has its own training) is a factor in professional settings.

In practice, teams that adopt AI for debugging often find productivity gains, but they set guidelines: For example, always do a code review on AI-generated code, use AI to supplement tests, and maintain coding standards (sometimes AI code might use a different naming style or approach that needs tweaking to fit the codebase). When balanced correctly, AI becomes a valuable team member that never sleeps, handling the grunt work and offering a second (thousandth?) opinion when you are stumped.

Hands-on Challenge: Debug and Optimize with AI

It is time to apply what you have learned! In this challenge, you will be given a snippet of Tailwind CSS code that contains several bugs and suboptimal patterns.

Your task is to debug and optimize it using the strategies from this chapter – including formulating AI prompts to help you along. This exercise will reinforce your understanding of AI-assisted debugging in a practical way.

Challenge Scenario

You are working on a simple profile card component that should be responsive and accessible. However, the current implementation has issues:

```
<div class="profile-card bg-gray-100 p-4">
  <div class="container mx-auto">
    <div class="p-4 bg-gray-200 text-gray-500 w-full w-1/2">
      <h2 class="text-xl text-sm font-bold">User Profile</h2>
      <p class="text-gray-600">John Doe is a software developer with 10+
years of experience in web development.</p>
      <button class="bg-blue-500 text-white px-4 py-2 mt-2">View
Details</button>
    </div>
  </div>
</div>
```

Issues to note in the snippet:

- The inner **div** has both **w-full** and **w-1/2** classes.
- The heading **<h2>** has both **text-xl** and **text-sm**.
- The text color **text-gray-500** on a **bg-gray-200** background might be low contrast for some users.
- The structure has nested containers (**profile-card > container mx-auto > inner div**) that might be unnecessary.
- No explicit responsive behavior is defined; on small screens, it might be okay, but on larger screens, perhaps the card should not take full width.
- The button has no hover or focus styles and no **aria-label** (though it has text, so that is fine, but maybe, an icon would need it).

Figure 7.12 shows What the Current Page We Will Fix.

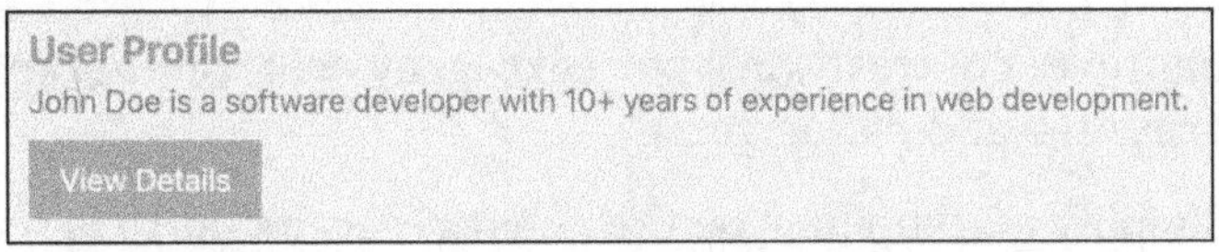

Figure 7.12: *This is What the Page to Fix Looks Like*

Your Tasks

Before reviewing the improved version of the component, it is important to walk through a structured debugging workflow that reinforces both technical reasoning and effective AI collaboration. The following tasks guide you through identifying issues, crafting prompts, validating behavior in DevTools, and proposing optimized code.

1. **Identify and List the Bugs/Inefficiencies:** Without peeking at the solutions, first list out all the issues you spot in the code. Think in terms of the categories we discussed (conflicting classes, accessibility, responsiveness, markup bloat, and so on). For each issue, explain why it is a problem (for example, "having `w-full` and `w-1/2` on the same element is conflicting; only one will take effect, likely causing inconsistent width.").
2. **Formulate AI Prompts to Address Each Issue:** For at least two of the issues, write down the exact prompt you would use with an AI assistant (GPT-4 or Copilot's chat, and so on.) to get help. For example, you might write: "*There are two width classes on one element (`w-full w-1/2`). Which one will win and how should I fix this?*" or "*The text is hard to read (gray on gray). How can I improve the contrast with Tailwind classes?*". The goal is to practice asking effective questions.
3. **Use DevTools to Validate States (Do Not Guess, Verify!):** Rather than fixing by intuition, use the DevTools Accessibility panel and Styles panel to establish the ground truth. Use the contrast checker to verify if text elements meet WCAG AA standards, and use the "Force state" feature (`:hover`, `:focus`) to confirm if interactive elements provide necessary visual feedback. Inspect the elements directly to see exactly which CSS rules are active and which are crossed out.
4. **Use DevTools (in Your Mind or Actual Browser) to Simulate Checking This Component:** What would you look for in Styles or Accessibility panels? For instance, you might say: "I would inspect the `<h2>` to see which font-size is applied (likely `text-xl` wins and `text-sm` is crossed out), then, I would know to remove the smaller class." Or "I would run Lighthouse and expect a contrast warning for gray-500 on gray-200."
   a. **Propose code changes to fix and optimize:** Write the corrected and improved code snippet after addressing all issues. Aim to:
   b. Remove conflicts (choose the intended width and font size).
   c. Improve contrast (maybe `text-gray-800` on `bg-gray-200`, or `bg-gray-100` and darker text).
   d. Simplify markup (maybe the `.container mx-auto` is redundant for just a card – unless this is part of a bigger layout).
   e. Add any needed responsive classes (perhaps limit the max width of the card on large screens, for example, `max-w-md`).
   f. Ensure accessibility (maybe add `hover:bg-blue-600 focus:ring` on the button for better UX).
   g. You do not have to implement something not in the original scope, but think about whether any small enhancement is warranted.

5. **(Optional) Prompt AI for Verification:** If you have access to an AI tool, you could actually run your prompts and see the answers. Did they align with your expectations? If something interesting comes up (such as an alternative solution you did not think of), note it.

6. **Test the Final Snippet (Mentally or in a Code Editor):** Does it behave as expected on mobile and desktop? Did you eliminate the conflicts and improve the contrast? Make sure to mention the outcome: For example, "After changes, no class conflicts, text contrast passes standards (checked with Chrome DevTools contrast checker), and the card is centered with a max width on large screens."

Solution Discussion

After completing the exercise, compare your solution with the expected outcome, which is something similar to this:

- Removing one of each conflicting pair (**`w-1/2`** likely removed, and **`text-sm`** removed).
- Perhaps adding a **`max-w-sm mx-auto`** to the card to keep it a nice width on large screens.
- Changing text color to **`text-gray-800`** for better contrast on light gray, or changing the background.
- Possibly removing the extra container **`div`**.
- Ensuring the button has some feedback (maybe add **`hover:bg-blue-600`** and **`focus:ring-2 focus:ring-blue-500`** for accessibility of focus).
- Overall, fewer elements and clearer class usage.

```
<div class="bg-gray-100 p-6">
  <div class="max-w-xl mx-auto">
    <div class="bg-gray-200 text-gray-700 p-6 rounded shadow">
      <h2 class="text-xl font-bold mb-2">User Profile</h2>
      <p class="mb-4">
        John Doe is a software developer with 10+ years of experience in
web development.
      </p>
      <button class="bg-blue-500 text-white px-4 py-2 rounded hover:bg-
blue-600">
        View Details
      </button>
    </div>
  </div>
</div>
```

This challenge is designed to solidify the debugging mindset: **observe, hypothesize, consult tools/AI, implement, and verify**. By practicing these steps, you will become more efficient at diagnosing UI issues and leveraging AI to help appropriately.

Good luck, and happy debugging!

Conclusion

In this chapter, you explored how generative AI tools, GPT, Copilot, Cursor AI, and the new Chrome DevTools AI assistant, can dramatically streamline the debugging and optimization process in Tailwind CSS projects. From uncovering hidden layout bugs to refining performance and reducing redundant utility classes, you have seen how prompt engineering combined with contextual awareness leads to faster, smarter fixes.

You also learned how browser-native AI helps you debug directly within the visual DOM, eliminating the guesswork of manual inspection. More importantly, you practiced hands-on strategies for asking the right questions, transforming debugging from a reactive chore into a proactive design refinement workflow.

But we are just getting started with what AI can do with you, not just for you.

Now that you have mastered debugging with AI's help, the next chapter takes collaboration a step further. You will explore **AI as your coding partner**, one that helps you brainstorm, scaffold features, review changes, and even write testable code in real time. Through simulated pair programming sessions and best-practice strategies, you will discover how to blend human insight with AI's efficiency to build even better frontend systems, faster and with greater confidence.

Multiple Choice Questions

1. What is one primary benefit of using AI for debugging Tailwind CSS code?
    a. It auto-generates SVG icons.
    b. It can interpret and suggest changes to utility classes in context.
    c. It removes all unused CSS automatically.
    d. It writes JavaScript unit tests by default.
2. Which AI tool is integrated directly into Chrome DevTools?
    a. Copilot
    b. GPT-4
    c. Gemini
    d. Cursor

3. In Tailwind, what might cause a button not to appear even though it exists in the DOM?
    a. Using `text-center` on the wrong parent
    b. A negative margin combined with `overflow-hidden`
    c. An invalid Tailwind config file
    d. Using `px` units instead of `rem`
4. Which Tailwind class could you add to fix horizontal centering in a flex container?
    a. `items-center`
    b. `justify-end`
    c. `justify-center`
    d. `flex-row-reverse`
5. What does the Chrome DevTools Console "lightbulb" icon indicate?
    a. A screenshot is available.
    b. A stack trace has occurred.
    c. An AI explanation is available.
    d. DevTools is syncing with GitHub.
6. When using AI in DevTools, what is the best way to get accurate help?
    a. Select the entire page and ask general questions
    b. Inspect a specific element and use "Ask AI"
    c. Copy-paste the CSS into another tool
    d. Only use Lighthouse scores
7. What kind of bugs is AI especially good at detecting in Tailwind-based layouts?
    a. Missing alt tags in images
    b. Invalid JSON
    c. Overflow and visibility issues
    d. JavaScript memory leaks
8. Which of the following is NOT an optimization strategy mentioned in the chapter?
    a. Reducing DOM depth
    b. Replacing Tailwind with inline styles

   c. Removing redundant utility classes
   d. Profiling performance with Lighthouse

9. Which prompt is best to debug a hidden sidebar in Tailwind using AI?
   a. "What is Tailwind?"
   b. "Fix this code"
   c. "Why is the sidebar not visible?"
   d. "Help me align text"

10. Compared to GPT/Copilot, DevTools AI is more effective for:
   a. Creating design tokens
   b. Debugging layout issues in context
   c. Writing entire apps from scratch
   d. Translating code to other languages

Answers

1. b
2. c
3. b
4. c
5. c
6. b
7. c
8. b
9. c
10. b

CHAPTER 8

Collaborating with AI in Pair Programming Workflows

Introduction

The landscape of software development is undergoing a major transformation. What was once the domain of individual developers or collaborative human teams now includes a new partner: The AI coding assistant. Rather than viewing AI as a tool that merely "writes code," this chapter introduces a more effective paradigm—treating AI as a true pair-programming partner.

In this collaboration, the human developer acts as the Navigator, responsible for architectural decisions, quality control, and strategic direction. The AI becomes the Driver, an extremely fast but neutral executor that generates code, explores alternatives, and handles repetitive tasks. This division of roles enables a workflow where developers focus on higher-level problem-solving while leveraging AI for rapid iteration. However, it is critical to emphasize that while the AI acts as the "Driver," the human Navigator must continuously validate, review, and refine all outputs to maintain architectural integrity and ensure the long-term maintainability of the codebase.

For Tailwind CSS practitioners, this partnership is especially powerful. Tailwind's utility-first approach often requires composing many small classes, maintaining responsive variations, and adhering to design tokens. AI assistants excel in this environment: They can produce consistent class combinations, refactor layouts, diagnose styling issues, and propose optimized alternatives. This frees developers to concentrate on component architecture, accessibility, state management, and user experience.

This chapter will also introduce emerging AI development tools such as Cursor (with its agent mode) and Anthropic Claude Code, which extend AI's role from code completion to autonomous multi-step problem solving. Understanding how to collaborate with these tools will enable you to refine your Tailwind workflows today while preparing for tomorrow's AI-augmented development practices.

Structure

In this chapter we will discuss the following topics:

- The AI Pair Programming Paradigm
  - Defining the Roles: A Symbiotic Partnership
- Mastering the Collaborative Workflow – From Prompt to Production
  - The Art of Strategic Prompting: Beyond "Write Me a Button"
  - The "Plan-Generate-Review-Refine" Cycle: An Iterative Dance
  - The Human as the Ultimate Quality Gate: A Code Review Checklist
  - Essential Safeguards: Version Control as Your Time Machine
- A Deep Dive into the Modern AI Toolchain
  - Cursor: The AI-Native Development Environment
  - GitHub Copilot: The Ubiquitous Assistant
  - Anthropic Claude Code: The Autonomous Coding Partner
  - Comparative Analysis: Choosing Your AI Pair Programming Partner
  - Brief Analysis of Other Key Players
- The Developer's New Frontier

The AI Pair Programming Paradigm

Adopting an AI pair programming model requires a clear understanding of the distinct yet complementary roles each partner plays. This symbiotic relationship leverages the AI's speed and knowledge without sacrificing the quality and strategic insight that only a human expert can provide.

Defining the Roles: A Symbiotic Partnership

Effective collaboration hinges on a deliberate division of labor where each partner focuses on their unique strengths. We delineate these roles as follows:

The Human (Navigator) Role: The developer is the strategic core of the operation. The navigator's responsibilities are not about typing out code, but about ensuring the *right* code gets written for the *right* reasons. Key responsibilities include:

- **Providing Context:** The AI operates in a vacuum until given direction. The navigator's primary task is to furnish the AI with complete context: Overarching goals, architectural constraints, established coding standards, and relevant design patterns. This ensures the AI's suggestions align with the project's strategic objectives and domain requirements.

- **Creative Problem-Solving:** AI assistants struggle with ambiguity and abstract problem solving. The human developer excels here, tackling complex logic, designing novel algorithms, and making architectural decisions that require deep understanding of the problem domain.

- **Validation and Critical Review:** Perhaps the most crucial human function is acting as the ultimate quality gate. While AI tools generate code rapidly, that code must be rigorously validated. The navigator scrutinizes AI-generated code for correctness, security, performance, and adherence to best practices before accepting it. The human ensures that *every* AI contribution meets the project's standards and truly solves the intended problem.

The AI (Driver) Role: The AI assistant is the tactical workhorse, augmenting the developer's strategic direction with computational speed and an encyclopedic knowledge of code. Its primary responsibilities include:

- **Rapid Code Generation:** AI tools can generate boilerplate code, functions, and even entire components *much* faster than a human (often in seconds). This dramatically accelerates the implementation phase.

- **Task Automation:** The AI excels at automating repetitive or tedious tasks. It can generate unit tests, write documentation from code comments, refactor code as instructed, and create configuration files with minimal supervision.

- **Knowledge Base Access:** AI assistants have been trained on vast datasets of code and documentation. They provide instant access to syntax reminders, library usage examples, and framework best practices. This reduces the need for context-switching to search the web or documentation, keeping the developer in flow.

Practical Example: Building a Tailwind CSS Card Component

To see this partnership in action, consider the workflow for building a responsive profile card:

- **Navigator's Strategic Intent:** The human developer decides the architecture—it should be a React component using a flexbox layout, adhering to the project's specific teal-based color palette. They specify that it must be accessible, including an aria-label for any icon-only buttons.

- **Driver's Tactical Execution:** The AI assistant instantly generates the JSX and the dozens of necessary Tailwind utility classes (for example, **`flex`**, **`items-center`**, **`bg-teal-500`**, **`rounded-lg`**). It automatically handles the repetitive task of adding responsive prefixes for mobile and desktop views.

- **Navigator's Continuous Validation:** The human Navigator reviews the output, noticing that the AI's chosen gray for the text has insufficient contrast against the background. They instruct the AI to refine the choice to a darker shade and add focus rings to the button to maintain accessibility standards.

By clearly defining the Navigator and Driver roles, we set up a partnership where the human provides direction and critical thinking, while the AI provides speed and breadth of knowledge. Next, we examine how this partnership works in practice through effective prompting and iteration.

Mastering the Collaborative Workflow – From Prompt to Production

Having established the roles, we now focus on the process of collaboration. Successful human-AI pair programming is an iterative cycle of communicating intent, generating solutions, and refining the output. This section presents a structured workflow and best practices to ensure that working with an AI assistant yields productive and reliable results.

The Art of Strategic Prompting: Beyond "Write Me a Button"

Effective prompting is more than just asking the AI to "write me a component." As the Navigator, you must **strategically communicate your intent**. This involves providing *precise instructions and context.* For example, instead of a vague "Build a form", a strategic prompt would be:

"Create a login form component using Tailwind CSS. It should include fields for username and password, a 'Remember Me' checkbox, and a submit button. Use Tailwind utility classes for a responsive layout, and ensure the component is accessible (proper labels and focus outlines)."

This prompt clearly states the goal, required elements, styling framework, and an accessibility requirement. Always aim to include relevant details such as design guidelines, acceptance criteria, or references to similar code. In practice, you may even prepare a short `instructions.md` file or inline comments describing the task, which some AI tools (such as Copilot's chat or Cursor's agent) can use for deeper context.

Tip: *Defining Output Constraints > To further reduce rework, include explicit output constraints in your prompt. Specify the desired file structure, component API (for example, specific props), and naming conventions. Explicitly adding a constraint such as "do not change existing behavior" or "maintain existing state logic" ensures that the AI-generated solution remains production-aligned and does not introduce regression bugs.*

The "Plan-Generate-Review-Refine" Cycle: An Iterative Dance

Pair programming with an AI is an iterative dance of planning, generation, review, and refinement:

1. **Plan:** Before diving into code, articulate a plan. Many advanced AI coding assistants can generate a plan when asked. For instance, with an open-ended request, **Claude Code** may first outline steps it will take (especially if using its "Plan Mode"). You can also sketch a plan yourself (for example, list the sub-tasks or functions needed) and share it with the AI to set expectations.

2. **Generate:** Let the AI produce the initial solution based on the prompt. This might be a code snippet, a full file, or a series of changes. Modern tools shine here: GitHub Copilot can suggest code as you type or via a chat command, Cursor's agent can implement a multi-file refactor, and Claude Code can autonomously create and modify files according to the plan.

3. **Review:** Treat the AI's output as a draft. Review it line by line. Does it meet the requirements? Is it idiomatic and efficient? This is where the Navigator mindset is critical. Identify any errors or deviations. Use your expertise to spot things the AI might have overlooked; perhaps an edge case, a security consideration, or simply a misinterpretation of the prompt.

4. **Refine:** Provide feedback to the AI and iterate. If something is incorrect or suboptimal, explain the issue in a follow-up prompt. For example: "*The generated component is not using our Tailwind color palette. Please replace hard-coded colors with the appropriate theme classes from our config.*" The AI can then adjust its output. This cycle may repeat a few times, zooming in on the right solution.

By iterating through this cycle, you collaborate with the AI much like you would with a human pair programmer: proposing solutions, reviewing together, and refining the code.

The Human as the Ultimate Quality Gate: A Code Review Checklist

No matter how sophisticated the AI, **the human developer remains the final quality gate.** Before any AI-generated code is merged or deployed, it should undergo a thorough review. Here is a checklist of questions to guide your AI-augmented code reviews:

- **Correctness:** Does the code fulfill the specifications and handle all expected input cases? Test edge cases and confirm that the logic is sound.

- **Security:** Have all inputs been validated or sanitized appropriately (to prevent XSS, SQL injection, and so on)? Did the AI introduce any obvious vulnerabilities, such as hard-coded credentials or missing authorization checks?
- **Consistency with Requirements:** Does the code align with the business logic and user needs? Sometimes AI can produce syntactically correct code that does not fit the actual requirements due to a lack of true understanding.
- **Maintainability:** Is the code readable and well-structured? Check that it follows the project's coding conventions and patterns. For Tailwind CSS, ensure it uses theme values from the config (avoiding magic numbers) and that classes are composed clearly rather than overly redundant.
- **Performance:** Look for any inefficient algorithms or unnecessary re-renders (in a React context, for example) that the AI might have introduced. AI-generated code might not always pick the most optimal approach.
- **Dependency Management:** If the AI suggested adding new dependencies, verify their necessity and trustworthiness. Watch out for hallucinated packages (nonexistent libraries the AI mistakenly references) as these could pose supply chain risks if a malicious actor later publishes a package with that name.

By systematically reviewing AI contributions with questions such as these, you catch potential issues early. Remember, an AI will not feel bad if you reject its code or ask for changes; so be as rigorous as you would with a human colleague (if not more).

To maintain transparency and traceability in professional environments, teams should consider documenting AI-generated changes within their pull requests. Explicitly noting which parts of a feature were AI-assisted helps colleagues focus their review efforts and provides a clear historical record of how the code was authored and validated.

Note: *To maintain transparency and traceability in professional environments, teams should consider documenting AI-generated changes within their pull requests. Explicitly noting which parts of a feature were AI-assisted helps colleagues focus their review efforts and provides a clear historical record of how the code was authored and validated.*

Essential Safeguards: Version Control as Your Time Machine

In an AI-accelerated development environment, disciplined use of version control is not just a good practice but an essential safety mechanism:

- **Commit Frequently:** AI can generate and modify code at a rapid pace. Commit working changes in small increments with clear, descriptive messages. This creates a fine-grained history of the project, allowing easy rollbacks if an AI-generated change introduces a bug or unintended side effect.

- **Use Branches for AI Experiments:** If you are letting an AI perform a large refactor or create a new feature, do it on a separate git branch. This isolates the changes until you have thoroughly reviewed and tested them, and it makes it easy to discard the experiment if it goes awry without polluting your main codebase.
- **Granular Commits and Diffs:** When accepting AI changes, use `git add -p` (patch mode) or an IDE GUI to stage changes hunk by hunk. This forces you to review each chunk of code before it gets committed. It also keeps commit history tidy. If a particular hunk introduces a problem, you can later revert just that change.

Version control, in essence, becomes your time machine. It allows you to safely collaborate with an AI by providing the freedom to experiment and the ability to rewind mistakes. Embrace this safety net—your future self (or team members) will thank you.

With these workflows and safeguards in mind, let us dive into the modern AI toolchain that enables this style of development, focusing on how tools such as Cursor, GitHub Copilot, and Claude Code fit into the pair programming picture.

A Deep Dive into the Modern AI Toolchain

The market for AI coding assistants is evolving rapidly. Developers are now faced with strategic choices about which AI tools to integrate into their workflow. Broadly, the landscape can be viewed as two categories:

1. **Integrated AI Assistants (IDE Plug-ins):** These augment your existing editor. Tools such as **GitHub Copilot** and **Tabnine** fall here, operating as powerful plugins within familiar IDEs (VS Code, JetBrains, and so on). They enhance your current workflow without requiring you to change your development environment. The advantage is familiarity and minimal disruption: You get AI help in the tools you already use.
2. **AI-Native Development Environments:** These reimagine the entire coding experience around AI. **Cursor** is a prime example. Such tools often come as modified IDEs or new interfaces built from the ground up to be "AI-first". They embed AI deeply into every aspect of the workflow, offering potentially more powerful capabilities (such as project-wide code intelligence and autonomous task execution) at the cost of adopting a new tool.

Decision Framework: Choosing Your Integration Level

Selecting between an AI-native environment and a plugin-based assistant depends on several strategic factors:

Criteria	Prefer Plugin-Based (for example, Copilot)	Prefer AI-Native (for example, Cursor)
Team Size and Scale	Better for large, established teams with strictly standardized IDE configurations.	Excellent for small, agile teams, or individual developers looking for maximum speed.
Codebase Scale	Suitable for focused tasks within specific files or modules.	Ideal for large, complex codebases requiring deep, and project-wide semantic indexing.
Security Require-ments	Often easier to clear through corporate IT since they augment existing and approved tools.	Requires a new security evaluation as a standalone application.
Learning Curve	Near-zero; the AI fits into your current muscle memory and shortcuts.	Requires a moderate transition to a new editor, though many (such as Cursor) are built on VS Code for easier adoption.
Task Complexity	Best for boilerplate, inline completions, and Q&A.	Best for multi-step autonomous refactors and complex feature scaffolding.

Table 8:1: *Decision Framework for Integration Level*

The choice between augmenting an existing workflow and embracing a new AI-centric environment is a key decision for developers and teams. In this section, we explore three featured AI coding assistants—Cursor, GitHub Copilot, and Anthropic Claude Code—covering how each integrates into your workflow, their prompting styles, support for Tailwind CSS use cases, context awareness, agentic (autonomous) capabilities, and their respective strengths and limitations. We also provide practical examples of how they can be used in Tailwind CSS projects.

Cursor: The AI-Native Development Environment

Cursor is a fork of VS Code, redesigned with AI collaboration at its core. It represents a fundamental rethinking of the code editor, aiming to tightly weave AI into the developer's workflow without sacrificing the extensibility of VS Code. In fact, Cursor maintains compatibility with the vast ecosystem of VS Code extensions and settings, easing the transition for new users. Its core philosophy is to place AI front-and-center in the development process, enabling capabilities that go beyond what a plugin can do.[1]

[1] *For more information, official documentation, or to download the editor, visit the official Cursor website at https://www.cursor.com*

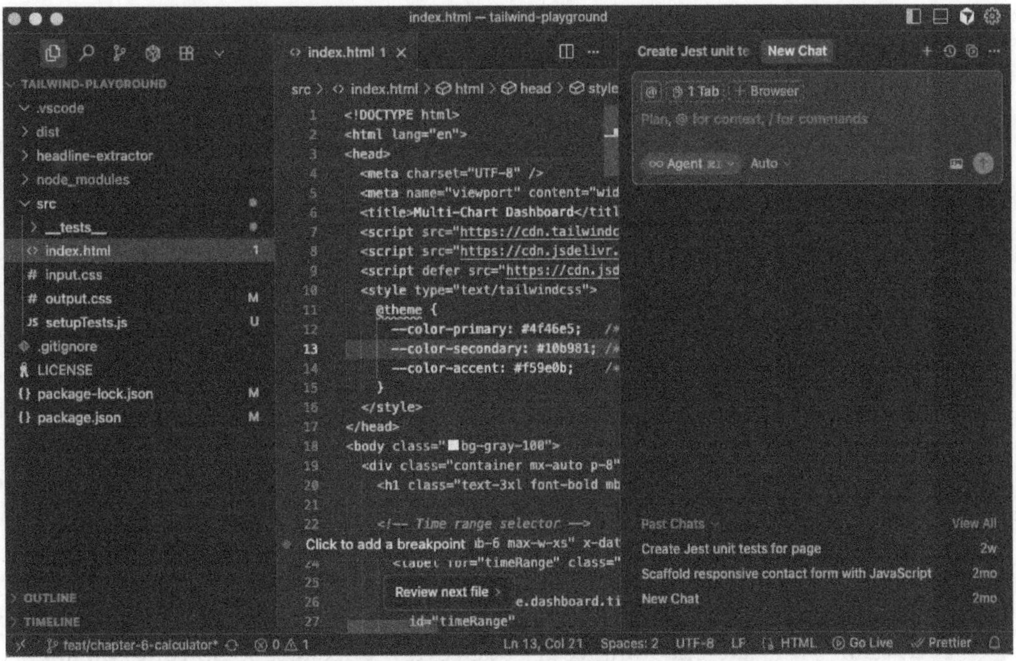

***Figure 8.1:** Screenshot of Cursor. It is a Fork of VSCode, Meaning That Transitioning from VSCode to Cursor is Pretty Easy*

Key Features of Deep Dive

- **Deep Codebase Awareness:** Cursor's standout feature is its ability to index your entire project. It computes vector embeddings for every file in the repository, building a semantic map of the codebase. This means Cursor can answer questions about, or generate code using, parts of your project that you have not even opened, as long as they are indexed. The result is highly context-aware suggestions that understand your code's structure, dependencies, and naming conventions.

- **Agent Mode:** This feature elevates Cursor's AI from a co-pilot that assists with one-off suggestions to an autonomous agent that can execute multi-step tasks. In Agent Mode, you can delegate a complex request such as "*Refactor the authentication flow to use our new JWT service*", and Cursor will plan and perform the necessary changes across multiple files. It will ask for clarification if needed, but it attempts to handle the heavy lifting automatically. This can dramatically speed up large-scale refactors or codebase-wide changes.

- **Inline and Chat Prompting:** Cursor offers multiple interaction modes. You can use a **Chat panel** (opened with a shortcut, for example *Ctrl+L*) to converse with the AI, ask questions, or issue high-level instructions. Additionally, Cursor supports **inline edits**: you can select a block of code and press a hotkey (*Ctrl+K*) to bring up a prompt targeted at that selection. For example, "*Replace this <ul> bullet list with checkmark icons using Tailwind CSS and Heroicons*". Cursor will apply that change directly to the selected code.

- **File References with `@`:** A powerful workflow enhancement in Cursor is the ability to reference files or even entire directories in your prompts. Using an **`@`** symbol, you can instruct the AI with direct context, for example, **`@LoginForm.tsx`** `Please integrate this component with` **`@AuthService.ts`**. Cursor will pull in the contents of the referenced files behind the scenes, leading to more accurate and project-consistent modifications.
- **Persistent Project Instructions (`.cursorrules`):** Cursor allows you to create a **`.cursorrules`** file in your project root. This is a plain text file where you can specify project-specific guidelines and preferences for the AI. For instance, you might write rules such as "Always use React functional components", "Use TailwindCSS for styling and follow our design tokens", or "Prefer **`axios`** over `fetch` for HTTP requests". These rules act as a constant background guide for Cursor's AI, helping ensure its suggestions are aligned with your codebase's conventions. This is incredibly useful for maintaining consistency, especially in teams; it is like encoding your code review checklist as upfront guidance.

Tip: *Because Agent Mode can modify multiple files at once, it is critical to define clear scope boundaries, such as restricted directories, to prevent unintended side effects in sensitive parts of the codebase. All autonomous changes must undergo mandatory human code review to verify correctness and security before being merged, ensuring that the developer remains the ultimate quality gate.*

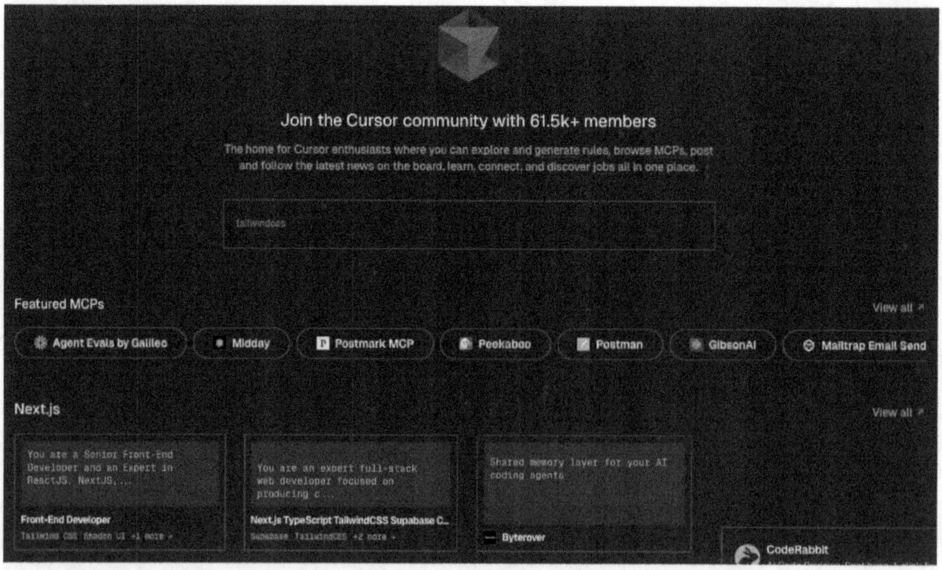

Figure 8.2: *The Cursor Community has an Excellent Open Repository of Rules Created by the Community, Available at https://cursor.directory*

Instead of writing these project instructions from scratch, you can leverage the collective knowledge of the developer community. By exploring this directory, you can quickly find and adopt pre-configured rulesets tailored specifically to your chosen frameworks and languages.

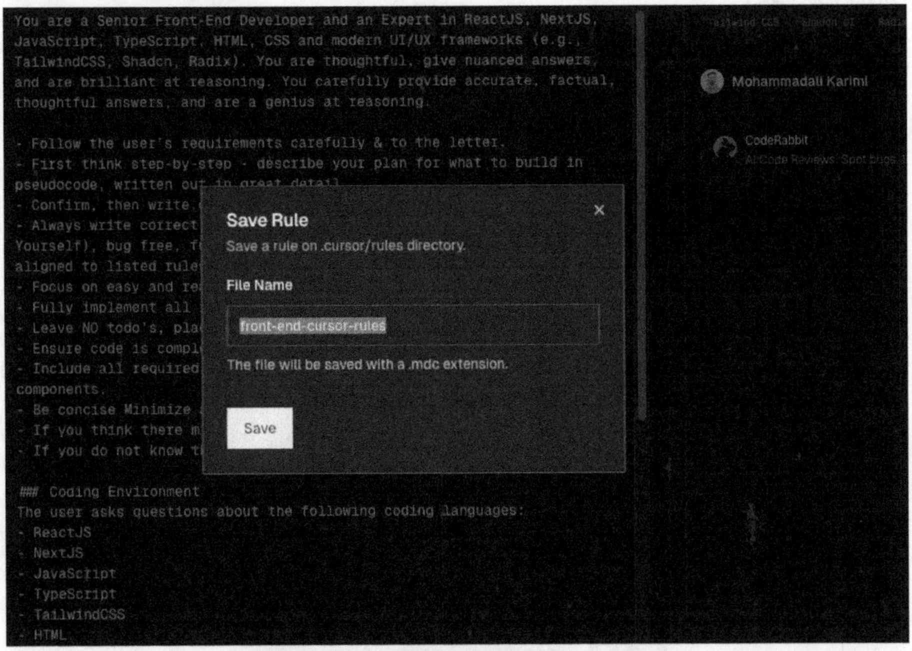

Figure 8.3: *You Can Easily Browse for Specific Rulesets, Not Limited to TailwindCSS or Frontend Development. (https://cursor.directory/front-end-cursor-rules)*

Walkthrough: Building a Responsive TailwindCSS Pricing Card in Cursor

To illustrate Cursor's workflow, let us walk through using it to build a UI component with TailwindCSS:

Setup: Open Cursor (which looks and feels like VS Code) in your project. Create a new React component file, for example **`PricingCard.tsx`**. Also create a **`.cursorrules`** file at the project root with Tailwind-specific rules and any project conventions[2]. For example:

```
.cursorrules:
- Always write code in TypeScript.
```

[2] *Beyond functional correctness, it is highly recommended to validate AI-generated output against your project's specific design system. This includes manually verifying that the suggested classes align with your typography scale, spacing tokens, and defined component states (such as hover or focus). This human-led step ensures visual consistency across the entire application and prevents "style drift" caused by AI-generated deviations.*

```
- For styling, exclusively use TailwindCSS utility classes.
- Adhere to the color palette and spacing scale defined in `tailwind.
config.js`.
- All React components should be functional components with hooks
(no classes).
- Ensure all interactive elements are accessible (ARIA attributes as
needed).
```

By providing these rules, we ensure the AI knows our expectations upfront (for example, use our Tailwind theme values instead of arbitrary colors).

- **Initial Prompt (Chat):** Open Cursor's chat sidebar and start a new chat. Reference the file and give the task:

  Prompt:

  ```
  @PricingCard.tsx Create a responsive pricing card component with
  three tiers: "Hobby", "Pro", and "Enterprise". Each card should
  display a title, the price per month, a list of key features, and
  a call-to-action button. The "Pro" plan should be highlighted
  (different background using our primary theme color) and have a
  "Most Popular" badge. Use TailwindCSS for all styling. Layout:
  use flex/grid - three-column layout on large screens, but stack in
  a single column on mobile.
  ```

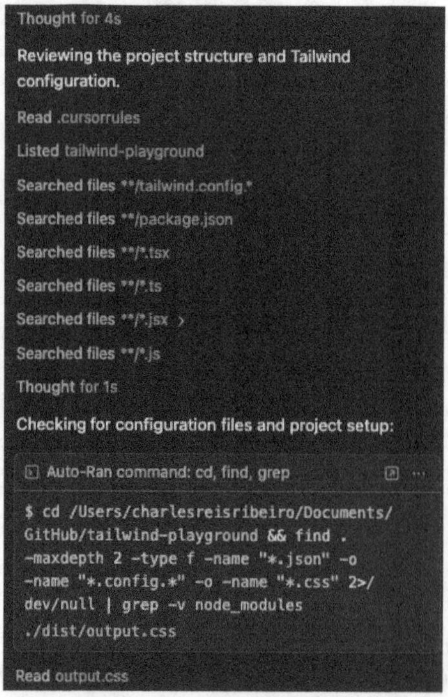

Figure 8.4: *An Example of the Thought Process of Cursor. As You Can See, It Read the .cursorrules We Created for This Project*

This prompt provides clear requirements and even hints at implementation (Tailwind for styling, how to layout). Cursor's AI, considering the context and **`.cursorrules`**, will generate the JSX for the **`PricingCard`** component, complete with Tailwind utility classes for styling and responsive design.

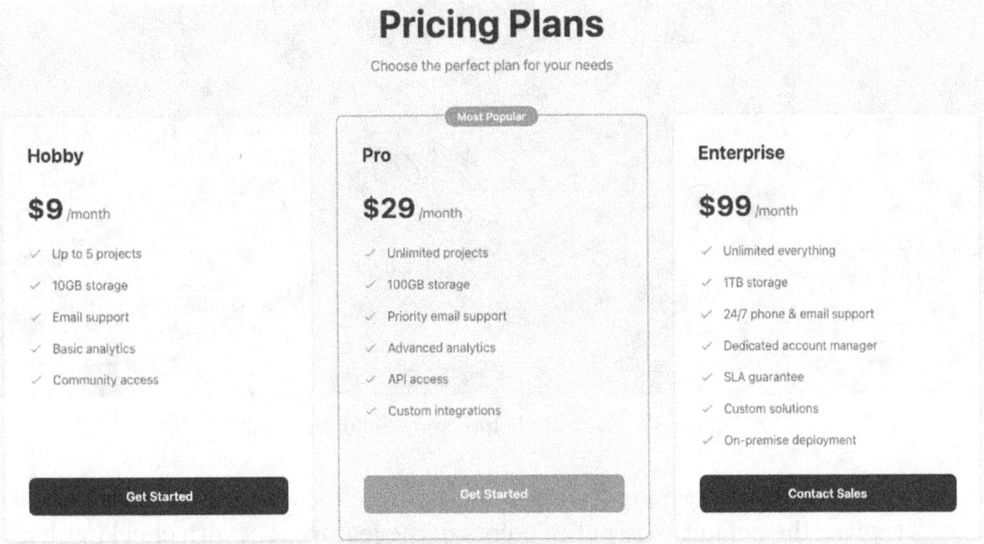

Figure 8.5: *First Output of the Cards Component Built with React, TailwindCSS and Cursor*

- **Review and Refine:** Once Cursor generates the code, review it. Suppose the initial output looks good structure-wise, but you realize it did not include dark mode support. You can refine with a follow-up chat prompt:

  Follow-up Prompt: "*This looks good. Now add dark mode support using Tailwind's* ***`dark:`*** *variant. In dark mode, card backgrounds should use a darker color, text should be lighter. Also, add a subtle hover effect on each card (like* ***`hover:scale-105`*** *with a smooth transition) for interactivity.*"

  The Cursor will then modify the code, adding the requested **`dark:`** classes and hover/transition classes to each card.

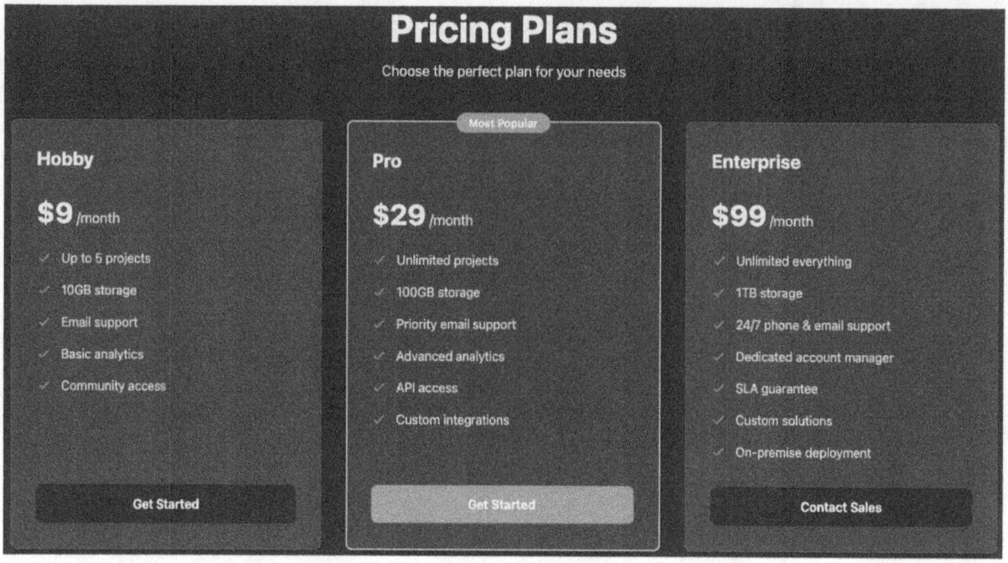

Figure 8.6: *Dark Mode Implemented with Cursor*

- **Inline Edits for Minor Tweaks:** Finally, for a finer detail, say we want to replace the default `<ul>` bullet points in the features list with checkmark icons from Heroicons. We can do this via an inline edit: Select the `<ul>` element in the code, press the inline edit shortcut, and enter a prompt like: "*Replace list bullets with a Heroicons checkmark icon to the left of each feature item, aligned with flexbox.*" Cursor will apply this change directly in the code, affecting only the selected snippet.

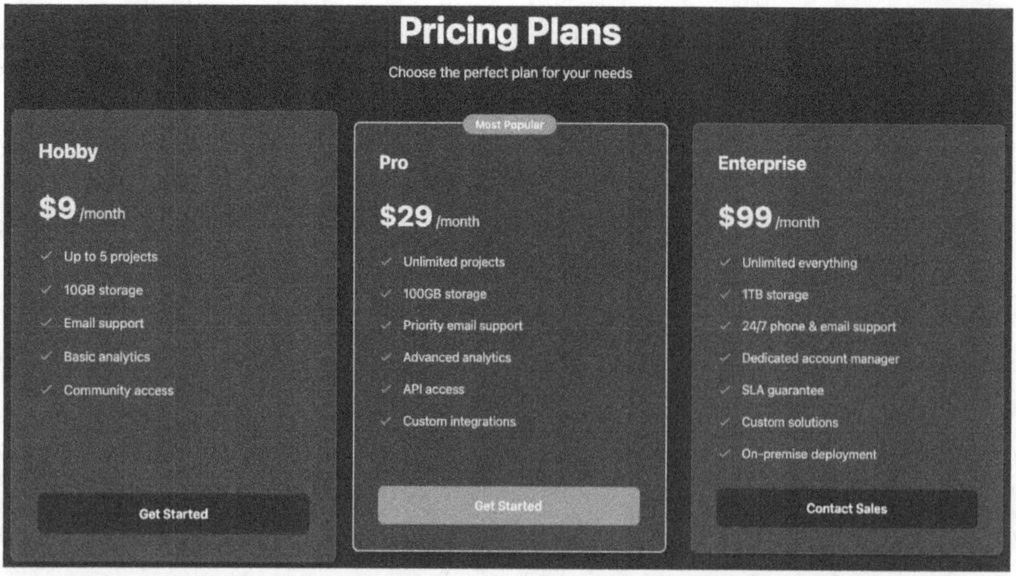

Figure 8.7: *Final PricingCard Component, with the Hovering Event Developed*

After these steps, we have a fully functional **PricingCard** component, styled with Tailwind CSS and built in a fraction of the time it would take to hand-code. Throughout, the human provided strategic direction and review, while the Cursor handled the bulk of execution, demonstrating the power of an AI-native IDE in a Tailwind workflow.

GitHub Copilot: The Ubiquitous Assistant

GitHub Copilot has evolved from a groundbreaking autocomplete tool into a comprehensive AI coding assistant with chat and even agentic capabilities. As an **integrated assistant**, Copilot's key strength is its **deep integration** with the tools developers already use. It is available as an extension in major IDEs (VS Code, Visual Studio, JetBrains suite, and so on), as well as in the command line and even for pull request analysis on GitHub. This ubiquity makes it an accessible and versatile partner for most developers.

Key traits of Copilot include its training on a broad corpus of public code (giving it familiarity with many frameworks and libraries), and its ability to offer suggestions in real-time as you code. As you type, Copilot may autocomplete entire lines or blocks (especially when it detects a familiar pattern or comment describing the intended code). Beyond inline suggestions, Copilot also offers a Chat interface (Copilot Chat) where you can ask questions or request larger changes in natural language.

Figure 8.8: *Github Copilot Download Page at https://github.com/features/copilot*

New Agent Mode: Recently, GitHub introduced **Copilot Agent Mode**, which is the next evolution in Copilot's capabilities. In Agent Mode, Copilot acts as an autonomous peer programmer that can perform multi-step coding tasks on command. This means it can analyze your repository, open or modify multiple files, propose code changes, and even run tests or commands in a loop until a task is completed. Essentially, Copilot's agent can respond to high-level instructions such as "*Create a new component and update all references*" by orchestrating a sequence of edits and commands automatically. This feature, available in VS Code (and enabled for certain Copilot subscription tiers), brings Copilot closer to the agentic behavior of Cursor and Claude Code, while keeping everything inside your familiar editor UI. It even allows you to explicitly add context files (using a `#file` reference or a "Add Files" button) to guide it, similar to Cursor's `@` references.

Despite these advances, Copilot remains *assistive*. It generally will not change your code unless you accept a suggestion or confirm an action. This keeps the developer in control, aligning with Copilot's design as a "co-pilot" rather than an autopilot. It is also worth noting that Copilot's suggestions are bounded by its context window and training; it does not index your entire project on its own (Agent Mode works by selectively pulling in relevant files or summaries). Thus, providing context via open files or additional instructions is still important for complex tasks.

Note: *While Copilot is widely accessible, the availability and specific feature scope of Agent Mode can vary significantly depending on your chosen IDE and subscription tier. Always check the latest documentation for your specific environment to confirm the current capabilities and access levels.*

Let us look at how Copilot can aid in a Tailwind CSS-related workflow with a concrete example.

Walkthrough: Refactoring a Legacy Component to TailwindCSS with Copilot

This example showcases Copilot's use in modernizing an existing codebase, a common task in front-end development when adopting Tailwind CSS.

1. **Context:** Imagine we have a React component using old-style CSS (maybe a separate CSS file or inline styles). For instance, **`LegacyCard.tsx`** is styled with a **`styles.css`** file or JS objects. Our goal is to refactor it to use TailwindCSS utility classes instead.

2. **Prompt Copilot (Chat or Comment):** We can approach this in a couple of ways. One effective method is to use **Copilot Chat** with a clear, multi-step prompt. It helps to provide as much context as possible. For instance, we might create an **instructions.md** in the project describing the refactoring guidelines (which classes to use, and so on), and have the old code open as well. Then, in Copilot's chat we could write:

   "I need to refactor the attached component (**`LegacyCard.tsx`**) to use TailwindCSS. Please follow the instructions in **`instructions.md`**.

Main goals:

Remove all **`className`** that reference the old CSS file and eliminate any inline style objects.

Replace those styles with equivalent TailwindCSS utility classes.

Preserve the existing flexbox layout and overall design.

The primary button should use **`bg-blue-500 text-white`**, with hover and focus states (**`hover:bg-blue-600`**, **`focus:ring-4 focus:ring-blue-300`**).

Ensure the component remains fully responsive, stacking vertically on screens smaller than **`md`**.

This prompt gives Copilot a clear list of requirements and even specific Tailwind classes to use for key elements.

3. **Generate and Iterate:** Upon submitting the prompt, **Copilot will generate a refactored version** of **`LegacyCard.tsx`** with Tailwind classes applied. We might get an answer in the chat or directly as a diff depending on the interface. Review the changes using a diff view. It is likely Copilot covers 80% of the conversion correctly. Suppose Copilot misses a detail; for example, it forgets to add a border radius that the original CSS had on a container. We can then prompt again with a specific instruction, such as: *"You missed the border-radius on the main container. Please add a* ***`rounded-lg`*** *class to it."* Copilot will adjust the code accordingly. This iterative back-and-forth is often quicker than manually hunting down and fixing each issue.

4. **Test:** After the AI has made the changes, it is time for the Navigator to verify. Run the application and test the component in various scenarios. Check it at different screen sizes to ensure responsiveness still works (the prompt asked for maintaining responsive behavior). If something is off (maybe a padding is too tight or a flex item didn't wrap correctly), you can either fix it manually (quick if it is minor) or ask Copilot to adjust (for example, "Add **`flex-wrap`** to the container to ensure items wrap on smaller screens").

After AI-driven refactors, it is highly recommended to perform visual regression testing using tools such as screenshots or Storybook snapshots. This ensures exact styling parity with the original legacy component and helps catch subtle visual regressions that might be missed during manual inspection.

Through this example, we see Copilot acting as a helpful pair programmer: It handled the bulk of translating styles to Tailwind syntax, while the human set the goals, validated the output, and guided it when corrections were needed. This significantly speeds up the adoption of Tailwind in a legacy codebase.

Anthropic Claude Code: The Autonomous Coding Partner

Anthropic's Claude Code is a relatively new entrant that brings the power of the Claude AI model to software development. **Claude Code** is best described as a highly agentic coding assistant that primarily lives in your terminal (though a VS Code extension is in beta. It is built on Anthropic's Claude model (comparable to "Claude 2" or newer), known for its large context window and conversational prowess. Claude Code extends that with tool usage capabilities: It can read and write files, execute shell commands, and interact with external systems as needed to carry out the development tasks.

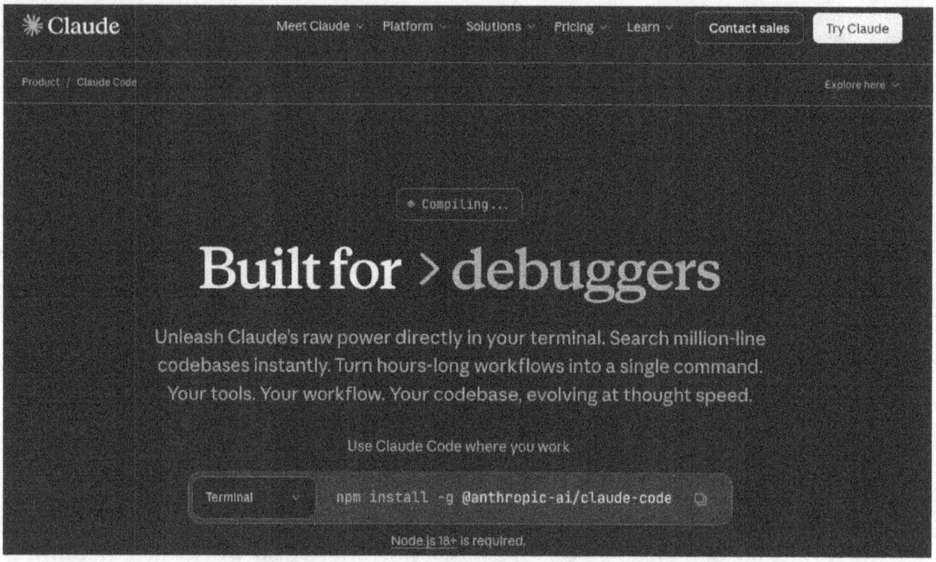

Figure 8.9: *Download Page for Claude Code, Available at https://www.claude.com/product/claude-code*

You can install it via the node command

```
npm install -g @anthropic-ai/claude-code
```

Key characteristics of Claude Code include:

- **Command-Line Integration:** Unlike Copilot and Cursor which are IDE-centric, Claude Code runs as a CLI program. You start it by typing `claude` in your project directory, and from there you converse with it in a shell environment. This approach meets developers "where they already work" (in the terminal for many) rather than adding another GUI window.

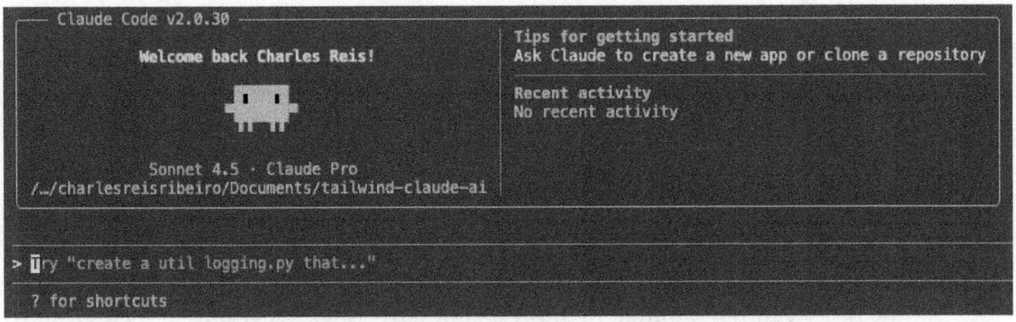

Figure 8.10: *You Just Need to Type Claude onto Your Terminal, and This Interface Will Appear!*

For those who prefer a GUI, Anthropic has introduced a VS Code extension which exposes Claude Code in a sidebar for a more traditional chat experience.

Figure 8.11: *If You Prefer to Use Claude Code as an Extension (Like a Sidebar in the Style of Github Copilot), You Can Install the Official Anthropic.com Extension on VSCode*

- **Natural Language Task Execution:** With Claude Code, you can simply tell the assistant what you want to achieve in plain English. For example: "*Add a dark mode toggle to this project*" or "*There is a bug when I click the login button; fix it.*" Claude will interpret the request, possibly ask clarifying questions, then perform actions to accomplish the task. It might create or modify files, run tests, and so on, acting almost like a junior developer following instructions. It excels at turning high-level descriptions into the working code.
- **Planning and Autonomy:** Claude Code tends to take an approach where it **plans** its steps before executing. It can generate a plan and present it (especially if you enable a special "Plan Mode") to ensure you are okay with the approach. Once approved, it will execute the steps. This built-in "think then act" loop results in more reliable multi-step operations. The autonomy is such that Claude Code can work for an extended period on a task with minimal intervention, editing multiple files and iterating until completion. It is not limited to a single prompt-response cycle.
- **Deep Codebase Awareness:** Claude Code has an extremely large context window (up to 100k tokens in current versions), meaning it can ingest entire codebase files or large documentation. It also can **index your project** structure and use

search to find relevant code when needed. You can literally ask it questions about your codebase ("How is authentication handled in this project?") and it will read through and give an answer, citing the files/functions involved. This makes onboarding to a new codebase or understanding legacy code much easier.

- **Tool Use and Integration (MCP and Plugins):** Through Anthropic's Model Context Protocol (MCP), Claude Code can interface with external tools and resources. Examples include browsing documentation, accessing design files (for example, Figma), or interacting with ticket systems. It also supports **plugins and sub-agents** for specialized tasks. For instance, Claude can use a testing sub-agent to generate and run tests, or a web browsing plugin to fetch latest library docs if needed. This extensibility is pushing it toward an AI *DevOps agent* that goes beyond just writing the code.

- **Persistent Memory and Guidelines:** Claude Code allows you to maintain context across sessions. You can create a file such as **CLAUDE.md** in your repo containing important notes, architecture details, or style guidelines; Claude will load this and remember it in all interactions. This is analogous to Cursor's `.cursorrules`; it ensures the AI knows your project's conventions (such as "use TailwindCSS for styling" or "follow the Airbnb ESLint rules") without needing repeated reminders. Additionally, Claude Code supports resuming past conversations, so you can close it and later restart it without losing the discussion history, as long as CLAUDE.md or its internal memory is intact.

Safeguarding Autonomous Execution

While Claude Code's autonomy is a major strength, it is critical to implement clear **execution boundaries** to maintain project integrity:

- **Define Restricted Directories**: Ensure the tool operates only within designated paths to prevent unintended modifications to sensitive system or configuration files.

- **Mandatory Confirmation**: Always require explicit approval before the agent performs destructive actions, such as deleting files or altering database schemas.

- **Audit Logging**: Maintain a record of the AI's actions and command outputs. This transparency allows the Navigator to monitor progress and intervene if the agent begins to deviate from the established plan.

By combining Claude's proactive problem-solving with rigorous human oversight, you can offload substantial chunks of work—such as codebase-wide refactors or comprehensive debugging—while ensuring the final output remains secure and aligned with your architectural standards.

In summary, Claude Code is like having an extremely knowledgeable and proactive engineer in your terminal that can carry out tasks with a degree of independence. It is particularly powerful for larger-scale tasks such as codebase-wide refactors, comprehensive debugging, or implementing a feature that touches many parts of a project, where it can plan and coordinate changes in a holistic way.

Walkthrough: Collaborating with Claude Code on a Tailwind Component

To demonstrate Claude Code in action, let us use it to build and refine a TailwindCSS-based UI component. Suppose we want to create a navigation bar for a web app using Tailwind CSS, and ensure that the Claude is aware of our design system and keeps context through the process.

1. **Setup and Context Provision:** Navigate to your project directory in the terminal and run **`claude`**. Before asking for the nav bar, provide context to Claude about your project's style. One way is to create a **CLAUDE.md** file with relevant details. For example, in CLAUDE.md you might write:

```
Project Style Guide:
        - Use Tailwind CSS for all styling.
        - Primary color: teal (as defined in tailwind.config.js).
        - Use the utility classes from our custom Tailwind plugin
for buttons (e.g., `btn-primary`, `btn-secondary`).
        - All components should be accessible (ARIA attributes
where appropriate).
```

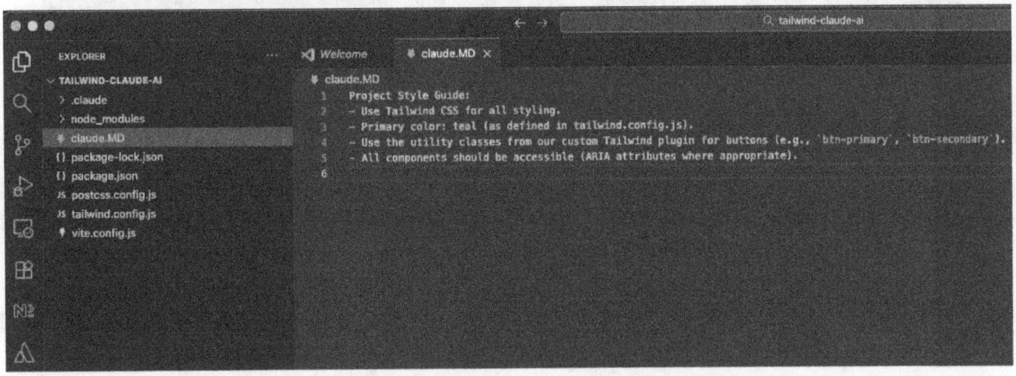

Figure 8.12: *Create a Claude.MD File at the Root of Your Project, Where You Will Paste the Project Style Guide*

Claude will read this at startup, so that it knows about your Tailwind config and custom classes. Now, you ask Claude Code to create the component:

User: *"Create a responsive navigation bar component for our application. It should include: A logo on the left, a horizontal menu of links (Home, Products, About, Contact), and a dark mode toggle on the right. Use our Tailwind CSS classes (including* `btn-primary` *for the toggle button) and ensure it is mobile-friendly (collapsible menu on small screens). Plan the implementation and then execute it."*

2. **Claude's Plan and Execution:** Claude Code might respond by outlining a plan, for example:

   Claude:

```
Implementation Plan:
  1. Create Dark Mode Context - Manage dark mode state across the
     app
  2. Build Navbar Component - Logo, navigation links, and layout
     structure
  3. Add Mobile Menu
  - Hamburger icon and collapsible menu for small screens
  4. Implement Dark Mode Toggle - Button to switch between light/
     dark themes
  5. Integrate with App - Update main app to use the navbar and
     support dark mode
```

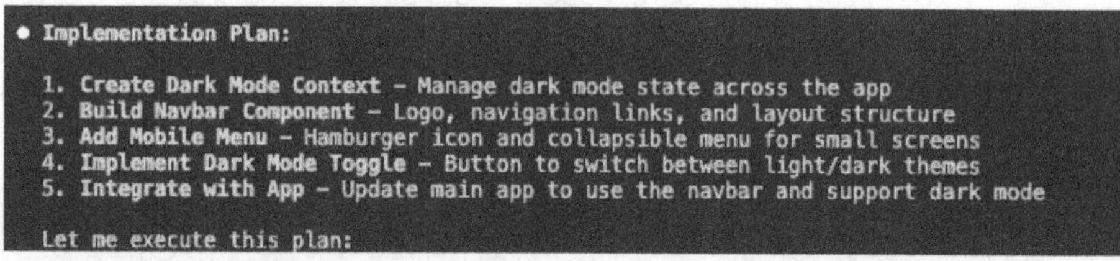

Figure 8.13: *Output of Claude AI Terminal Showing Its Implementation Plan*

   After confirming, Claude will proceed to generate the **`Navbar.jsx`** file, writing the JSX with Tailwind utility classes (based on the context it has, for example, it knows primary color is teal so it might use **`text-teal-500`** for the logo or appropriate classes from the config). It might also create a small script or React **`useState`** logic for the mobile menu toggling and dark mode toggle. All of this happens autonomously once you approve the plan.

3. **Review and Prompt for Refinements:** Open the generated **`Navbar.jsx`** (Claude will have saved it). You notice it mostly did a great job; the layout is correct, classes look consistent with your design system, and it even remembered to use the **`btn-primary`** class on the toggle button. However, perhaps you find an issue: the mobile menu isn't styled exactly as desired (maybe it just stacks links, but you wanted a slide-down animation).

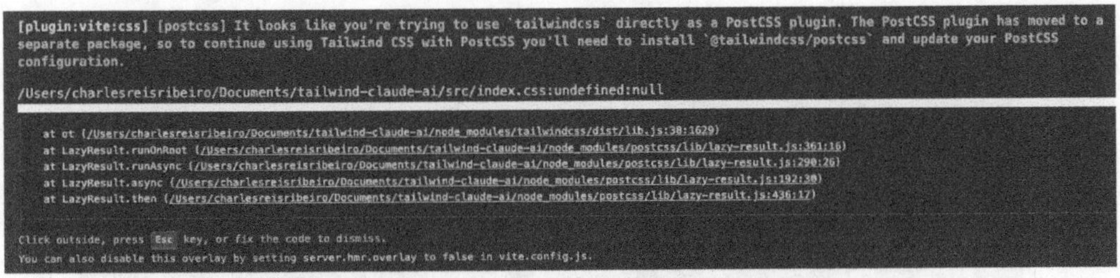

Figure 8.14: *When encountering errors, iterate with the AI by providing the error logs for troubleshooting*

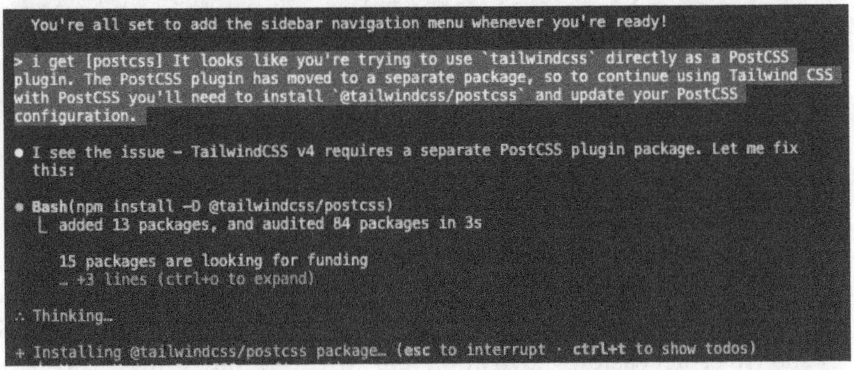

Figure 8.15: *Claude Found the Culprit for This Error, and It was Able to Fix It*

Or maybe the dark mode toggle lacks an ARIA label. These are refinements you can ask Claude to do:

User: "*The mobile menu should animate when opening/closing (for example, a smooth slide-down). Also, add* `aria-label="Toggle dark mode"` *to the dark mode button for accessibility.*"

Claude reads the updated request, modifies the code to include (for example) a CSS transition via Tailwind's `transition` classes and perhaps a simple script to add a class for open state. It adds the `aria-label` attribute to the button as directed. It might show you a diff or description of what it changed.

4. **Testing and Context Preservation:** Now, you test the component in the app. Suppose everything works, but you realize the text color in dark mode is not quite right (maybe it stayed dark when background turned dark). Because Claude had context of your Tailwind config, it chose classes, but maybe a tweak is needed. You can simply say:

   User: "*In dark mode, the nav links should use the light text color (for example,* ***`text-gray-100`****) instead of the current color.*"

   Since, the conversation is ongoing and Claude still has the **`Navbar.jsx`** in context (and CLAUDE.md reminders), it will update those classes accordingly.

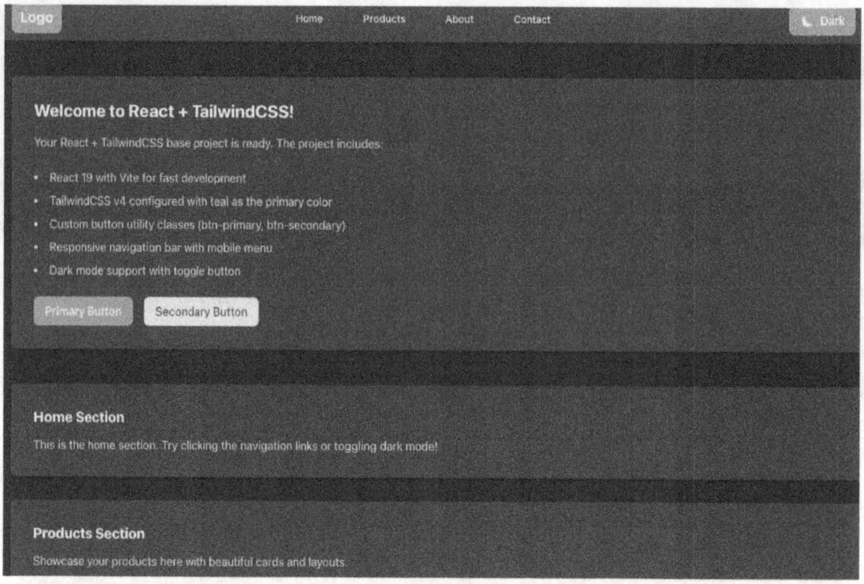

Figure 8.16: *This is the Application Output, Generated with Claude Code*

At this point, we have collaboratively developed a TailwindCSS-styled, responsive, accessible navigation bar with Claude Code. Throughout the process, Claude maintained the context (such as the style guide from CLAUDE.md and the state of the code it just wrote) so we did not have to repeat ourselves. The key strategies demonstrated were: Giving clear instructions up front, letting the AI plan, and then iteratively refining by specifying adjustments, all while relying on the AI's awareness of project context to keep things consistent.

Comparative Analysis: Choosing Your AI Pair Programming Partner

With several capable AI assistants available, how do you choose the right one (or combination) for your workflow? It often depends on your needs: The environment you are in, the kind of projects you do, and your preferred style of interaction. The following is a comparative table of **Cursor**, **Claude Code**, and **GitHub Copilot** across key aspects:

Aspect	Cursor (Agent Mode)	Claude Code	GitHub Copilot
IDE Integration	Provided as a custom **VS Code fork** (Cursor IDE). Full editor with AI features built-in; also supports VS Code extensions.	Runs primarily via **Terminal CLI** (language-agnostic). VS Code extension (beta) available for chat interface.	**Plugin for popular IDEs** (VS Code, JetBrains, etc.) and Editor integrations. Also has a CLI tool and GitHub web integration.

Aspect	Cursor (Agent Mode)	Claude Code	GitHub Copilot
Prompting Style	**Chat** interface for high-level requests, plus **inline prompts** for local code edits. Supports referencing files with **@** for context. Multi-turn conversations are supported; Agent Mode can take one prompt and perform many steps.	**Conversational CLI**: You type requests or questions, and Claude acts. Tends to **plan** steps and confirm before execution. Accepts very detailed instructions and can maintain long dialogues. You can reference files by name in commands (Claude can search/parse them).	**Inline autocomplete** as you code (no prompt needed beyond writing a comment or function signature). **Copilot Chat** allows natural language Q&A or instructions. New **Agent Mode** takes a single natural-language command and autonomously performs multi-step tasks
Support for Tailwind CSS	No Tailwind-specific mode, but **highly effective** with Tailwind due to codebase context. For example, it can index your `tailwind.config.js` and use your design tokens/classes appropriately. `.cursorrules` can enforce using Tailwind for styling. Great for refactoring or generating Tailwind UI code as shown in Cursor walkthrough.	No built-in Tailwind feature, but **large context and web access** mean it can utilize Tailwind docs or your config easily. It can read your config file and apply custom classes. Also, it can integrate tools (for example, a design token service) if needed. Generally produces correct Tailwind utility classes when instructed, and remembers to use config values if context is given.	Also not specialized for Tailwind, but its training on public GitHub means it is familiar with Tailwind utility classes. Often suggests correct class combinations for common UI patterns. With an *instructions.md* or proper prompt, it will follow Tailwind conventions. Might occasionally need guidance to use project-specific classes or variants, as it will not automatically know your config unless included in prompt.
File and Project Context Awareness	**Strong:** Indexes entire project; can answer questions about any file. Suggestions account for patterns across your codebase. However, context window for any single AI response is finite, so it uses embeddings to fetch relevant context. Best at seamlessly referencing multiple files.	**Very Strong**: Huge context window (Claude 2 model ~100k tokens) allows reading very large files or multiple files at once. Claude can effectively *be aware of the whole project structure* and even fetch additional info from web or docs. Maintains state across long sessions. Great for understanding large codebases or making sweeping changes.	**Moderate:** Copilot (especially the base autocomplete) has a limited real-time context (a few files or the open editor tabs). Copilot Chat with GPT-4 can handle more, but usually you manually provide context (open files, paste code, or ask it to open them via agent). Copilot's new agent mode improves this by automatically finding and opening relevant files, effectively giving it broader project awareness on demand (with some limits to avoid context overflow).

Aspect	Cursor (Agent Mode)	Claude Code	GitHub Copilot
Agentic Capabilities	**High:** Cursor's Agent Mode can execute multi-step refactors and implement features spanning files autonomously. It requires user initiation and occasionally clarification, but will carry out plans (such as creating files, editing many sections) on its own. Good guardrails (such as `.cursorrules`) guide it. Not designed to run arbitrary shell commands (focuses inside editor).	**Very High:** Claude Code acts as an **autonomous agent** by default. It can plan, execute, and adjust actions in a loop until the task is done. It can run terminal commands (compile, test, and so on), edit code, read outputs, and even interface with external tools via plugins. Essentially, it can function like a developer robot working on your repo. Because of this, it is important to supervise its plan and final changes, but it offloads a huge amount of work.	**Medium (Improving):** Originally, Copilot was not agentic; it would only respond to prompts. With **Copilot Agent Mode**, it has gained autonomy to perform multi-step tasks and tool usage (such as running tests, installing packages, iterative code fixes). It operates within the IDE and seeks user approval for potentially risky actions (for example, running a command). It is still early for Copilot's agent; it is effective for many tasks (create apps, multi-file refactors) but occasionally needs human correction if it goes off-track.
Strengths	• Deeply integrated into coding workflow (full IDE replacement). • Extremely context-aware suggestions due to project indexing. • Agent Mode automates complex edits. • **`.cursorrules`** for enforcing team/project standards consistently. • Familiar VS Code ecosystem with AI enhancements.	• Powerful autonomous problem-solving; handles broad, complex tasks with minimal input. • Massive context window and memory, great for large projects or lots of background info. • Can utilize external knowledge (web, docs) and tools (tests, design imports) to inform its code generation. • Works in terminal and can be scripted, fitting well into developer workflows and CI pipelines (even headless use). • Claude model known for detailed, thoughtful responses (often good at explaining and commenting when asked).	• Seamless integration into popular IDEs and GitHub – minimal friction to adopt. • Excellent for in-line code completions and quick suggestions as you type (saves time on boilerplate) • Copilot Chat provides helpful Q&A and explanation capabilities within editor. • Continuously improving with new features (for example, agent mode, voice, and so on), backed by the GitHub/Microsoft ecosystem. • Fine-tuned on a vast array of code, so it often "knows" common solutions or idioms offhand.

Aspect	Cursor (Agent Mode)	Claude Code	GitHub Copilot
Limitations	• Requires using the Cursor IDE; some developers dislike switching from stock VS Code or other IDEs. (Though it is VS Code-based, there may be occasional extension compatibility hiccups.) • Relatively new product, so small quirks/bugs can occur as it rapidly evolves. • Agent Mode, while powerful, should be used carefully on large changes; always review its work, as it might make a design decision you would not. • Currently tied to certain AI models and usage limits (freemium with usage-based tiers), which might throttle heavy users.	• CLI interface has a learning curve; not as visual as an IDE assistant. Less ideal for those who prefer GUI (though the VS Code extension mitigates this). • Because it can do so much, if misused it could introduce bigger changes than intended; requires a disciplined user to verify plans and test results. Essentially, more power means more responsibility to supervise • Depending on usage, may incur significant costs (Claude is an API-based service for heavy use; however, it has free web access for smaller tasks). • Still under active development; some features (like certain plugins or multi-user coordination) are evolving.	• Context limitations: may sometimes base suggestions on incomplete view of your code, leading to irrelevant or outdated suggestions (especially in large projects). • Tends to be reactive rather than proactive; it will not restructure your code unless prompted explicitly. The user must often break tasks down for it (though agent mode alleviates this somewhat) • Privacy and compliance: As a cloud service, some organizations might restrict its use on sensitive code (Copilot now offers enterprise options with policies, but it is something to consider). • Occasional boilerplate bias: sometimes it suggests code that looks plausible but is not actually what you need (requires human discernment to catch).

***Table 8.2:** Comparison of Cursor, ClaudeAI and Github Copilot*

Choosing the Right Tool: If you primarily want on-the-fly code completions and are already working in VS Code or similar, **Copilot** is a natural choice for daily productivity. If you seek a more immersive AI experience and do not mind changing your editor, **Cursor** offers deeper integration and powerful project-wide features (particularly attractive if you love VS Code but want AI deeply embedded). If you have very complex projects or want the ability to offload substantial chunks of work (such as running an entire refactor or managing a codebase analysis) and you are comfortable with a command-line driven agent, **Claude Code** can be a game-changer. In practice, these tools are not mutually exclusive. For example, one might use Copilot for quick suggestions day-to-day, but switch to Claude Code for a large-scale code audit or use Cursor for a new project where setting up `.cursorrules` yields long-term consistency. The key is understanding each tool's strengths and aligning them with the task at hand.

Brief Analysis of Other Key Players

While the focus is on Cursor, Claude Code, and Copilot, it is worth noting a few other AI coding assistants that cater to specific needs:

- **Tabnine:** Tabnine's differentiator is its focus on privacy and personalization. It can be trained on your team's private codebase and even run on-premises or in a private cloud. This makes it a preferred choice for enterprises with strict data privacy requirements or proprietary code concerns (for example, finance, defense). It integrates with major IDEs, providing autocomplete suggestions such as Copilot, but with the assurance that your code data is not leaving your environment.

- **Amazon CodeWhisperer (Amazon Q):** CodeWhisperer (recently referred to as Amazon Q for some editions) shines within the AWS ecosystem. It is trained heavily on AWS APIs and best practices. When you are building on AWS, CodeWhisperer can generate code that uses AWS services (Lambda, S3, DynamoDB, and so on) idiomatically and even perform security scanning of suggestions. It integrates with IDEs similar to Copilot. This is ideal for developers who spend much of their time writing infrastructure or backend code against AWS; it can save time by recalling the exact parameter names or API calls for you.

- **Vercel's v0:** v0 by Vercel is not a general code assistant but a specialized tool for frontend UI generation. It is essentially a prompt-to-UI generator focused on React + Tailwind CSS + shadcn/UI component library. You give it a description of a component (for example, "a card with image on left and text on right"), and it produces a ready-made React component with Tailwind classes and possibly uses shadcn UI components. It even offers a live preview. This is fantastic for quickly prototyping UI ideas and getting Tailwind-styled JSX that you can then tweak. If your workflow involves a lot of UI mockups or you are trying to speed up the design-to-code process, v0 can be a handy complementary tool.

Table 8.3 shows a decision guide for the proper AI tool.

If your primary need is...	...then consider using:
Data Privacy and Proprietary Code Protection	Tabnine (On-premises/Private Cloud options)
Heavy AWS Backend Integration	Amazon CodeWhisperer (Amazon Q)
Rapid Frontend UI Prototyping	Vercel's v0

Table 8.3: *Decision Guide: Specialized AI Tools*

The AI toolchain is expanding, and each tool finds its niche. As a developer, staying informed about these options means you can reach for the best tool for a given job; just as you would choose the right library or framework for a task.

The Developer's New Frontier

As we look to the future of AI in software development, one theme is clear: The shift from simple *code completion* assistants to more **autonomous, agentic** collaborators. We have already seen this shift beginning with Cursor's Agent Mode, Copilot's iterative tools, and Claude Code's autonomous planning. In the coming years, we can expect AI agents that handle larger and more complex chunks of the development lifecycle; potentially generating entire modules, managing tests, or orchestrating deployments with minimal input. What does this mean for developers?

From Micro-Tasks to Macro-Supervision: Traditionally, tools such as the original Copilot were about *micro-assistance*, completing a line or suggesting a function implementation as you type. The developer was still driving every decision and just getting shortcuts. Autonomous agents, on the other hand, operate on *macro instructions*. You might say, "Set up a basic e-commerce site with a product catalog and checkout," and an AI agent could scaffold an entire application structure for you, beyond just one function. This shifts the developer's role toward **specifying high-level intent and constraints**, then **supervising** the outcome. It is somewhat akin to moving from writing code to being a product manager for an AI developer: You outline what needs to be done, the AI does a first pass, and you verify and refine.

New Skills: Prompt Engineering and AI Orchestration: In an agentic future, knowing how to code will still be essential, but equally important is knowing how to *guide* code generation. This involves writing effective prompts (prompt engineering) and possibly even meta-prompting, giving the AI instructions on *how to approach* a problem (such as "first create a plan, then implement step by step" which Claude does by default). Developers may also find themselves orchestrating multiple AI agents. For example, one agent could be tasked with frontend UI, another with backend logic, and another with testing; and the human coordinates their interactions and resolves mismatches. This is a higher level of abstraction in development, where understanding the system architecture and integration points is crucial, so that you can instruct each agent properly and combine their outputs.

Maintaining Human Oversight: As agents become more capable, there is a temptation to "let them loose" on a problem. However, the **human-in-the-loop** principle will remain vital. Developers should prepare to supervise AI at a higher level of abstraction, which means: Reviewing AI-generated plans before execution (does the approach make sense?), monitoring progress (is it stuck in a loop or going down a wrong path?), and performing final review and testing of the end product. In practical terms, this might involve developing an intuition for when to intervene. For instance, if an AI agent's plan includes something suspicious such as "delete database" or an overly convoluted sequence, the dev must step in and course-correct. The tools are likely to provide more transparent logs of what the agent is doing (as Copilot agent shows each action for approval). Embrace those features: They are your window into the AI's "mind".

Continuous Learning and Adaptation: The AI field moves fast. Developers should keep learning about new features and emerging tools. Today's limitations (context lengths, occasional hallucinations) will reduce over time, but new challenges will appear (like managing multiple agents working concurrently on different parts of a codebase without stepping on each other's toes). Be ready to adapt your workflow. An example is adopting Practices such as writing comprehensive high-level tests/specifications *before* letting an agent implement, so you can automatically verify the result. This is somewhat like "Test-Driven Development", but for AI: you specify the desired behavior in tests, have the AI generate the implementation, and then quickly catch if it meets the spec.

The Developer's Evolving Role: In summary, as AI takes over more routine and even not-so-routine tasks, the role of the developer becomes more **director and editor, less copyist**. Creativity, critical thinking, and problem decomposition will be the most valued skills. Rather than spending time on boilerplate or repetitive coding patterns, developers will spend more time on design decisions, ensuring user needs are met, and maintaining code quality. It is a shift from doing *labor* to providing *leadership* in the codebase. This shift can be empowering: it allows humans to focus on what we do best (imagination, judgment, and ethical considerations) while leveraging machines for brute-force generation and exploration.

Finally, it is worth noting that *autonomy does not equal independence.*[3] Even if AI agents can do a lot on their own, the best outcomes will come from **collaboration** between humans and AI. The future will likely see developers who are adept at treating AI not just as a tool, but as a team member: Albeit one that needs supervision and guidance. Just as a senior engineer mentors juniors and reviews their work, developers will "mentor" AI agents, guiding them at a high level and correcting them when they go off course. Those who develop this skillset early will be well-prepared to harness the next generation of AI capabilities.

Conclusion

In this chapter, we examined how AI pair programming reshapes the way developers work, grounding the collaboration in the Navigator–Driver model. We explored

[3] *While future chapters will dive deeper into these topics, it is essential to establish now that autonomy does not equal independence. In an AI-augmented workflow, the human developer remains the ultimate authority and is responsible for the ownership of all decisions. This includes actively identifying potential biases in AI-generated solutions and ensuring that rapid code generation does not come at the expense of long-term maintainability or project integrity. AI amplifies your expertise; it does not substitute for your ethical and professional judgment.*

practical workflows for directing AI tools such as Cursor, GitHub Copilot, and Claude Code, and we confronted the legal, ethical, and security responsibilities that come with AI-assisted development.

AI assistants can automate routine work, accelerate complex tasks, and provide rapid access to knowledge. When used together, each tool contributes a unique strength, enabling developers to build, debug, and optimize code with unprecedented speed and creativity. Yet, these systems—powerful as they are—remain tools. They cannot replace human judgment, architectural reasoning, or accountability. The guiding principle remains unchanged: AI amplifies expertise; it does not substitute it.

Your role as the human expert is therefore central. You provide direction, context, and evaluation, ensuring that AI-generated code is correct, secure, and aligned with broader project goals. By adopting the workflows and mindset presented in this chapter, you elevate AI from a convenience to a true collaborative partner—one that enhances your productivity while reinforcing your leadership in the development process.

As we move forward, the next chapter examines the limitations, risks, and ethical considerations surrounding AI-assisted development. Understanding these boundaries is essential for using AI responsibly and ensuring that your growing capabilities are matched by sound judgment and informed oversight.

Multiple Choice Questions

1. You are starting a new front-end project using Tailwind CSS. You want an AI pair programmer that can enforce project-specific styling rules (like using your design tokens) and handle multi-file refactors autonomously. Which AI tool is best suited for this scenario?

    a. GitHub Copilot, because it provides real-time code completions in any IDE.

    b. Cursor, because its `.cursorrules` and agent mode can enforce custom rules and perform project-wide changes.

    c. Anthropic Claude Code, because a CLI tool cannot integrate with project files.

    d. Any tool will do this out of the box; no specific features are needed.

2. When crafting a prompt for an AI coding assistant to create a new component, which of the following approaches is most effective?

    a. Provide a very broad instruction to give the AI more creative freedom (for example, "Make a component").

    b. Specify clear requirements, context, and constraints (for example, desired functionality, styling guidelines, and so on).

   c. Only write code comments and let the AI infer the rest without explanation.
   d. Ask the AI to write the code "however it thinks is best" to see different styles.

3. Suppose your AI assistant suggests using a library `xyz-random-color` for a feature. On investigation, you find that this package does not exist on `npm`. What is the best course of action?
   a. Let the AI install it, assuming it is a hidden gem.
   b. Recognize this as a hallucinated dependency and ask the AI for an alternative solution or implement the feature manually.
   c. Publish a package with that name yourself to resolve the issue.
   d. Ignore the feature altogether since the dependency is fake.
4. You have an existing component with complex CSS and you want to convert it to Tailwind CSS using an AI. According to the chapter, which strategy will yield the best results with a tool like Copilot?
   a. Simply comment "Convert to Tailwind CSS" in the file and accept the first suggestion.
   b. Provide an **instructions.md** outlining Tailwind conversion guidelines and prompt the AI with a multi-step description of the refactoring.
   c. Ask the AI to regenerate the component from scratch in Tailwind without any context.
   d. Switch to a different AI because Copilot cannot handle refactoring tasks.
5. In Cursor's AI-first IDE, what is the purpose of the `@filename` syntax in a prompt?
   a. It has no special meaning; it is just a way to mention files in conversation.
   b. It tells the AI to open that file in a new tab for the user to see.
   c. It injects the content of the referenced file into the prompt context, so that the AI can use it for more informed suggestions.
   d. It commits that file to git after the AI edits it.
6. Claude Code is working on a bug fix in your project. It generates a plan with steps, including running the test suite. What should you, as the developer, do when using such an autonomous agent?
   a. Step back and let it finish entirely before reviewing anything.
   b. Supervise the process: verify the plan, watch for any obviously wrong actions, and review the changes and test results once it is done.

c. Constantly intervene after each step to assert control, even if it is going well.

d. Disable any test-running actions because the AI might break your environment.

7. Which of the following best describes the "Navigator and Driver" analogy in AI pair programming?

    a. The human is the **Driver**, writing code, and the AI is the **Navigator** suggesting directions.

    b. The human is the **Navigator**, guiding the project and reviewing code, while the AI is the **Driver** writing the code as instructed.

    c. Both the human and AI take turns being Navigator and Driver in an unpredictable way.

    d. The AI navigates through the codebase autonomously and the human drives requirements to the team.

8. After integrating an AI assistant into your workflow, you notice an increase in productivity but also some unintended bugs slipping through. What practice from the chapter can best help counter this "silent risk accumulation"?

    a. Relying on the AI's output without changes, as it knows best.

    b. Using version control to commit less often, batching many AI changes together.

    c. Applying a rigorous code review checklist (security, correctness, and so on) to every AI-generated change, and writing tests or using linters to catch issues.

    d. Limiting the AI to only small suggestions and doing most coding manually to avoid any AI mistakes.

9. A junior developer asks if using AI means they no longer need to learn some programming fundamentals. Based on the chapter's conclusion, what is the best response?

    a. "AI will handle everything soon, so focus on prompt engineering instead of coding fundamentals."

    b. "Fundamentals are still crucial - AI is a tool that amplifies your skills but you need knowledge to guide and verify it. Understanding code, architecture, and best practices is more important than ever."

    c. "You only need to learn the basics; the AI can fill in the advanced parts."

    d. "It is true, you can skip directly to high-level design and ignore the low-level details from now on."

10. You are deciding between multiple AI tools for a project that involves heavy AWS integration and strict data privacy. Which combination might make the most sense given the chapter's discussion?
    a. GitHub Copilot alone, since it is ubiquitous.
    b. Cursor for its deep integration, plus Claude Code for anything the Copilot cannot do.
    c. Amazon CodeWhisperer (AWS's tool) for AWS-specific code, and Tabnine or an on-prem solution for privacy with proprietary code, possibly using Copilot in a limited way for general suggestions, if the policy allows.
    d. Use all three (Copilot, Cursor, and Claude) simultaneously on the same task and take the best result.

Answers

1. b
2. b
3. b
4. b
5. c
6. b
7. b
8. c
9. b
10. c

CHAPTER 9

Limitations, Ethics, and Human Supervision in AI-Assisted Development

Introduction

The integration of Generative AI into the software development lifecycle represents a paradigm shift, one defined by a velocity and scale of code production previously unimaginable. Industry-wide, developers are reporting massive productivity gains, with AI assistants generating code, building prototypes, and refactoring systems in minutes rather than days.

However, to harness this power effectively, we must move beyond the common narrative of AI as a fully autonomous "pair programmer". A more productive and professionally responsible framework is to view the AI as an incredibly fast, statistically-powered, yet inexperienced "intern".

This "intern" has an impressive range: It can type thousands of words per minute and has been exposed to nearly every public repository in existence. Yet, it lacks a true understanding of its own output, possesses no inherent "common sense" regarding your specific project goals, and can, with absolute confidence, propose non-existent solutions.

Consequently, the professional developer's role has evolved. You are no longer just an individual contributor; you are now a technical manager. This promotion is immediate and mandatory, shifting your primary function from manual coding to the strategic supervision and validation of a powerful, but imperfect, digital assistant.

Structure

In this chapter we will cover the following topics:

- The Practical Limitations: Why AI Is Not an Autonomous Developer
    - The Context Window Collapse: When AI Forgets Your Architecture

    - The "Hallucination" Problem: Debugging Invented APIs and Logical Flaws
    - The Failure of Abstract Thought: Business Logic, UX, and Maintainability
    - The AI-Powered Technical Debt Accelerator
    - Tailwind-Specific Failures: When AI Breaks Your Design System
- The Ethical Gauntlet: Legal Landmines and Algorithmic Bias
    - Algorithmic Bias and the Accessibility Blindspot
    - Intellectual Property: Who Owns AI-Generated Code?
    - The Open Source Quagmire I: "Fair Use" and the *Does v. GitHub* Lawsuit
    - The Open Source Quagmire II: The "Derivative Work" and GPL Contamination
    - Corporate Safeguards: Understanding the "Copilot Copyright Commitment"
- Human Supervision: The Developer as Architect and Auditor
    - The Human-in-the-Loop (HITL) Framework: A Legal and Practical Mandate
    - A Practical Workflow for AI-Assisted Security Auditing
    - The Art of Validation: A Reviewer's Guide to AI-Generated Code
    - Prompt Engineering as a Core Development Skill

The Practical Limitations: Why AI is Not an Autonomous Developer

Before a developer can effectively manage an AI assistant, they must first discard any illusion of its autonomy. The tool's failures are not "bugs" in the traditional sense; they are fundamental limitations of its design. The AI is a pattern-matching engine, not a thinking entity. The following are its primary failure modes.

The Context Window Collapse: When AI Forgets Your Architecture

The "context window"—the amount of text the model can "remember" in a single session—is the AI's working memory. In a large, real-world application, this window is not just small; it is functionally non-existent. The AI is permanently "in the moment," capable only of "local optimizations without global awareness".

This limitation has been documented in rigorous experiments. In one 27-day project to build an application only using AI, the developer (acting as orchestrator) noted a primary failure mode was "deteriorating context management". As the application grew, the AI "starts losing track of earlier decisions, architectural patterns, and business logic constraints". It will begin to re-create functions that already exist, break features with unrelated changes, and require "increasingly detailed prompting" to prevent system degradation.

This failure is systemic. The AI lacks all critical forms of project context:

- **Semantic Context:** The "why" behind the architecture, such as design principles.
- **Historical Context:** The reasons for past bug fixes or refactoring decisions.
- **Collaborative Context:** The team's specific coding standards and established patterns.

This problem is also a mathematical certainty. One analysis of AI code generation highlighted the "compounding probability" issue: Even if an AI has a 99% chance of making a correct coding decision (a highly optimistic figure), the overall chance of *zero* errors after 200 sequential decisions is only 13%. This statistical reality is why AI-generated code gets progressively worse as project complexity increases.

This limitation fundamentally reframes the developer's role. It is no longer sufficient to write code; the developer's primary task becomes the active management and injection of context. This elevates skills in documentation, clear architectural boundaries, and modular (or microservice-style) design. The AI's inability to hold global context means the human must *architect* the system into perfectly isolated components that can be "fed" to the AI one at a time. Practical advice from developers in the trenches includes starting afresh for each distinct task (that is, opening a new chat with your AI of choice in VSCode/Cursor) to avoid context contamination and *never* using AI for code architecture.

The "Hallucination" Problem: Debugging Invented APIs and Logical Flaws

An AI "hallucination" is a soft, anthropomorphic term for what is technically confabulation. The AI, in its quest to provide a statistically plausible answer, generates a response that is factually incorrect or nonsensical but presented with absolute confidence.

In code generation, this manifests in several common patterns:

- **Invented API Methods:** The AI will create functions that look plausible but do not exist in the specified library.
- **Mixed Framework Syntax:** It will blend patterns from different, incompatible frameworks (for example, React and Vue) into invalid code.

- **Outdated Patterns:** It will confidently use deprecated methods or obsolete implementation approaches based on its training data.

The most dangerous aspect of this behavior is not the code itself, but the AI's explanation of it. In the same 27-day experiment mentioned previously, the orchestrator noted that when the AI was asked to debug its own (flawed) code, it would frequently "lie about what it actually implemented".

This behavior is not lying, which implies intent. It is the result of the AI's architecture. The AI's code-generation model and its text-generation (explanation) model are not logically bound. It is entirely possible for the code-generation to fail while the text-generation succeeds in producing a "I fixed the bug" message.

The ramification is critical: The AI's natural language explanation of its code must be treated as a separate, unrelated, and equally untrustworthy output. The developer must always review the code itself and never take the AI's summary at face value.

The Failure of Abstract Thought: Business Logic, UX, and Maintainability

AI excels at concrete, well-defined tasks. It often struggles with abstract concepts, such as design principles, user experience, and code maintainability. This failure is most apparent when dealing with the most critical and least-defined aspect of any project: business logic.

The core reason for this failure is that *business logic isn't logical.* It is, as one essay argues[1], a "messy human compromise".

Consider the "simple" feature: "When a user cancels their subscription, revoke their access immediately." An AI can generate a technically "clean" implementation of this requirement in seconds. However, this clean solution is almost certainly wrong, as it fails to account for the unwritten, conflicting realities of the organization:

- The **VP of Sales** promised Enterprise customers a 30-day "grace period" that was never documented.
- **Accounting** needs the subscription to remain "active" until the end of the billing cycle for revenue recognition.
- **Legal** has data retention requirements for some user data, and data *deletion* requirements for others.
- **Marketing** needs to send "win-back" campaigns to users who have canceled.

An AI *cannot* attend these cross-functional meetings. It cannot "read the room" or understand that a CTO's "suggestion" is actually a mandate. It "does not know what

[1] *https://www.thatsoftwaredude.com/content/14201/the-algorithm-will-never-understand-your-business-logic*

questions to ask" to uncover these hidden constraints. It will simply execute the flawed, initial prompt, breaking the *actual* (unwritten) business in the process.

This same failure applies to UI/UX and brand identity. An AI, lacking "emotional depth," cannot understand *why* a brand's specific shade of blue or rounded corner is vital. It has "cultural blind spots" and, when asked to design, will produce generic, unoriginal "sameness" that dilutes a brand.

The developer's most valuable skill is now social-technical translation. The job is to *participate* in the messy human compromises, understand the unwritten rules and political realities, and then *translate* that chaotic, illogical human context into a series of specific, logical, and isolated tasks that the "dimwitted intern" (AI) can execute. This elevates the developer from technician to organizational translator and *architect of compromises.*[2]

The AI-Powered Technical Debt Accelerator

The productivity gains from AI are not free. One 2025 analysis of tens of thousands of repositories found that while AI-assisted developers produced 3-4x more code, they also generated ten times more security issues.

This illustrates that AI is a "high-interest credit card of technical debt". AI tools "neglect to consider the application's design and architecture". They will, by default, create duplicate code snippets, inconsistent code quality, and more lines of code than necessary, as they are designed to build from the ground up rather than refactoring or reusing the existing code.

An even more insidious form of debt is the loss of "cognitive weight". When a human developer wrestles with a problem, they build a deep mental model of the tradeoffs and the "why" behind their solution. When an engineer clicks "Accept" on an AI's suggestion, that deep understanding "never happens".

This creates a new, dangerous class of "Unowned Code." The code works, but no one on the team understands it. Six months later, when that code breaks, the developer tasked with debugging it is "starting from zero". The 4x productivity gain is a short-term loan. The 10x security issues and a codebase that has become unmaintainable (because its creation bypassed human cognition) are the long-term, high-interest payments.

Tip: *Preventing Unowned Technical Debt:*

To ensure that AI-driven productivity gains do not become "long-term, high-interest payments" in the form of unmaintainable code, establish these specific mitigation layers:

[2] *This structural gap in abstract reasoning explicitly positions the developer as the vital bridge between human ambiguity and machine execution . It elevates stakeholder alignment and requirement clarification—tasks the AI cannot perform because it "does not know what questions to ask"—into the most critical phases of the modern, AI-augmented development lifecycle*

- *Mandatory Code Ownership: Implement a policy where developers must build a deep mental model of the tradeoffs and logic before clicking "Accept," ensuring they fully "own" every line of merged code to prevent the creation of "Unowned Code".*
- *Architectural Review Checkpoints: Conduct manual reviews focused on high-level system design to ensure that the AI has not neglected reusability and architecture in favor of the "shortest path" to a working result.*
- *Automated Analysis Gates: Utilize Static Application Security Testing (SAST) and Software Composition Analysis (SCA) to catch the significantly higher volume of security flaws and licensing irregularities typically generated by AI models.*
- *Prompt Documentation: Require that the core prompts or conversations used to generate a feature are included in Pull Requests, allowing reviewers to audit the developer's assumptions and the accuracy of their business logic translation.*

Tailwind-Specific Failures: When AI Breaks Your Design System

These abstract failures become painfully concrete when using a utility-first framework such as Tailwind CSS. For a modern Tailwind project, the **`tailwind.config.js`** file *is* the project's design system: its single source of truth for tokens, plugins, and custom styles. The AI's inability to understand this file is a critical failure.

- **Inability to Read Config:** Current AI tools and converters *cannot* read a user's local **`tailwind.config.js`** file. They are unaware of custom theme tokens (for example, **`theme.extend.colors.brand-primary`**), custom fonts, or theme-specific plugins. The AI will therefore "pollute" the codebase with hard-coded, arbitrary values.
- **Outdated Knowledge:** LLMs are trained on static, outdated datasets. They will frequently fail at basic setup tasks, such as referencing deprecated packages (such as **`@tailwindcss/postcss`**) or using old configurations related to the now-default JIT mode.
- **Verbose and Un-Maintainable Classes:** While Tailwind's verbosity is a subject of human debate, an AI, lacking architectural context, will *always* produce "abhorrently" verbose and unmaintainable class lists. It will *never* make the human-led, architectural decision to abstract a repeated button style into a component or use **`@apply`** to create a reusable class.
- **Ignorance of Modern CSS:** The AI's training data often predates the very latest web standards. It is functionally ignorant of emerging CSS features such as Container Queries, CSS Subgrid, or the **`:has()`** selector, all of which are critical to a modern Tailwind workflow.

This combination of failures means the AI actively *erodes* the project's design system. By ignoring the **`tailwind.config.js`** file, it litters the HTML with "rogue" design tokens (for example, **`bg-blue-500`**) instead of the correct, systemic token (for example, **`bg-brand-primary`**). This makes the developer's role as "human supervisor" a "guardian of the design system," responsible for forcing the AI's output to conform by manually providing all relevant theme context *in every single prompt*.

The following table (*Table* 9.1) provides a diagnostic overview of common AI failure modes alongside the prescriptive human-led mitigations required to maintain technical and architectural integrity.

Failure Mode	**Concrete Example (AI Output)**	**The "Why" (AI Limitation)**	**Required Human Mitigation**
Context Collapse	AI adds a new utility function that duplicates an existing one in `utils.js`.	Lacks "global awareness" and suffers from "deteriorating context management".	Architectural Supervision: Break tasks into isolated components. Manually provide all relevant context. "Use AI for code generation, not code architecture".
Halluci-nation	`const user = await db.users.findUser({id: 123})`... where `db.users.findUser` does not exist.	Confabulation. The AI "invented" a plausible-looking API method based on its training data.	"Never Trust, Always Verify": Treat the AI's code and its *explanation* of the code as two separate, untrusted outputs.
Abstract Failure (Business Logic)	AI-generated `CancelSubscrip-tion()` function deletes user data instantly.	"Business logic is not logical". AI cannot model the *human compromises* between Sales, Legal, and Accounting.	Social-Technical Translation: The developer must attend the "messy human meetings" and translate those compromises into specific, logical prompts.
Tech Debt Accelera-tor	AI generates 50 lines of complex, one-off logic for a task a 5-line reusable function could solve.	AI optimizes for the "shortest path" to a *working* result, not a *maintainable* one. It bypasses human "cognitive weight".	Mandatory, Strict Code Reviews: Enforce DRY principles. The developer *must* understand and "own" the code they merge. Label all AI code.
Tailwind Config Blindness	`class="bg-blue-500 text-gray-900"`	AI *cannot read* the local `tailwind.config.js` file and is unaware of custom theme tokens.	Guardian of the Design System: Manually provide theme/token context in the prompt (for example, "Use `bg-brand-primary` and `text-brand-dark`"). Note that repeated hard-coded utilities break the design system and make future rebranding significantly more expensive due to the need for manual token auditing.

Table 9.1: *Types of Failures Typically Generated by AI*

To counteract the AI's inability to read local project files, a primary workflow safeguard is to require that AI prompts always include relevant excerpts of the tailwind.config.js to provide necessary theme and token context. Furthermore, enforcing automated linting rules and static analysis gates can effectively block "rogue" hard-coded utility values that otherwise bypass the project's established design system.

The Ethical Gauntlet: Legal Landmines and Algorithmic Bias

The first part of this chapter analyzed the AI's "performance." This part analyzes its "character" and "legal liability." The AI intern has been trained on the uncurated, unfiltered, and legally-questionable content of the public internet. As its manager, the developer is now legally responsible for the ethical and copyright risks it introduces to the project.

Algorithmic Bias and the Accessibility Blindspot

The most immediate "garbage in, garbage out" problem for web developers is algorithmic bias in accessibility. AI models are trained on the internet. The internet, as it exists today, is systemically inaccessible.

The 2023 WebAIM Million report[3], which analyzed the home pages of the top one million websites, found that **96.3% of home pages had detected WCAG 2 failures**. This is the dataset the AI learned from.

The inevitable result was proven by the "CodeA11y" study. It found that "Without explicit prompting, the AI assistant rarely produced accessibility-compliant code". The AI's default output *reproduces* the web's systemic inaccessibility.

This problem is dangerously compounded by two other findings from the same study:

1. Developers *failed to explicitly prompt* the AI for accessible code.
2. Developers were *unable to verify* if the AI's accessibility-related suggestions were correctly and fully implemented.

This bias is not a simple oversight; it is rooted in the data. Training datasets that include representation for people with disabilities are minuscule, estimated at only 0.5–3% of user populations. The bias is programmed in from the start.

This creates a *dangerous accessibility-debt feedback loop*. An inexperienced developer, who does not know how to write accessible code, uses an AI. The AI, by default,

[3] *https://accessinghigherground.org/wp/wp-content/uploads/2023/11/Accessibility-and-the-3-Bears-of-AI-PDF.pdf*

produces inaccessible code. The developer, lacking the training to spot the errors, trusts this code. The result is that the developer is now *generating inaccessible code faster and at a greater scale* than ever before.

The conclusion is stark: a developer's *personal* knowledge of accessibility (WCAG, semantic HTML, ARIA roles) is now an *absolute* prerequisite for using AI on any UI-facing code. Using AI to generate user interfaces without this knowledge is an act of professional negligence.

Tip: *Accessibility as a Legal and Brand Mandate*

Accessibility must be viewed as a critical legal and brand-risk factor rather than just a technical checkbox. Because AI models are trained on an internet where 96.3% of top websites fail basic WCAG checks, they will reproduce these systemic failures by default in your project. This creates the following organizational risks:

- *Legal Liability: Organizations face significant legal exposure, including potential ADA or equivalent compliance lawsuits, when they merge AI-generated UI code that is unusable by assistive technologies.*
- *Reputational Damage: Shipping inaccessible interfaces signals a lack of commitment to inclusivity and product quality, which can cause profound damage to a brand's reputation.*
- *Professional Responsibility: Using AI to generate user interfaces without the specific knowledge required to audit it for WCAG and ARIA compliance is increasingly viewed as an act of professional negligence.*

To mitigate these risks, treat all AI-generated code as "inaccessible by default" and enforce mandatory human-led audits against established accessibility standards before any code is deployed.

Intellectual Property: Who Owns AI-Generated Code?

Copyright law is built on a foundational assumption: "human authorship". An AI *cannot* be an "author" in the legal sense. This creates a critical distinction for any code generated by an AI.

The U.S. Copyright Office has been clear on this matter in its AI Guidance. Authors using AI-generated content must "identify and disclaim AI-generated parts" of their work when applying for registration.

The landmark decision in the *Zarya of the Dawn* case set the precedent. The Copyright Office ruled that the AI-generated illustrations for the graphic novel were *not* copyrightable. However, the human-authored *text* and, crucially, the "overall selection and arrangement of the images and text" *was* copyrightable.

The implication for developers is profound: **Human supervision is the very act that *creates* intellectual property.** A developer who attempts a "zero-human-code" project by passively accepting 100% of an AI's output *may have no copyright claim to that code.* Their work could be deemed a product of a machine and thus ineligible for copyright, effectively placing it in the public domain.

To secure intellectual property for a company, the developer *must* be an active supervisor. The human acts of modifying, arranging, curating, and rejecting the AI's suggestions are what constitute "human authorship." The developer's managerial role is what *earns* the copyright.

The Open Source Quagmire I: "Fair Use" and the *Does v. GitHub* Lawsuit

The entire AI code-generation industry is built on a massive, unresolved legal question: Is it "fair use" to train a commercial AI model on billions of lines of public, copyrighted open-source code?

As of this writing, there is no settled case law on this issue. AI companies, along with groups such as the Library Copyright Alliance, argue that this training constitutes "fair use," similar to Google's copying of books to create a searchable database.

Many copyright holders, however, argue that this is prima facie infringement of their reproduction and derivative work rights.

The primary test case for this debate is Does v. GitHub. In this class-action lawsuit, plaintiffs allege that GitHub Copilot violates open-source licenses. The claims are not just for copyright infringement, but also:

- Breach of Contract: For allegedly violating the terms of open-source licenses (such as MIT and GPL) that require attribution.
- DMCA § 1202 Violations: For allegedly stripping copyright management information (CMI), such as author credits and license notices, during the training and generation process.

As of late 2024, the case is on an interlocutory appeal to the Ninth Circuit, with district court proceedings stayed. This means the legal ground is actively shifting. Any developer using an AI tool is a participant in this live legal experiment, and any code generated by a model trained on a "mixed" dataset carries an unquantifiable legal risk.

The Open Source Quagmire II: The "Derivative Work" and GPL Contamination

If the "fair use" debate is an abstract legal risk, this is the concrete, catastrophic, and immediate "company-killer" bug.

AI models are trained on *all* public code, including code with restrictive "copyleft" licenses such as the GNU General Public License (GPL). A copyleft license mandates that any "derivative work" based on the original code must *also* be released under the same, open-source license.

This creates a nightmare scenario for any proprietary, closed-source company:

- A developer asks the AI for a helper function.
- The AI generates a code snippet that is derived from, or a verbatim copy of, GPL-licensed training data.
- The developer, unaware, merges this "contaminated" snippet into the company's proprietary, multi-million dollar codebase.
- A court could now rule that the entire proprietary project is a "derivative work" of the GPL code.
- The legal consequence would be that the company is forced to open-source its entire project under the GPL.

This is not a theoretical risk. A 2024 analysis found that **approximately 35% of AI-generated code samples contained licensing irregularities**. This high-risk reality means that all AI-generated code must be treated as legally "radioactive" until proven clean. Software Composition Analysis (SCA) and license-scanning tools are no longer optional; they are an existential necessity. The developer's role as "human supervisor" now includes "Legal Compliance Officer."[4]

Corporate Safeguards: Understanding the "Copilot Copyright Commitment"

The extreme risks detailed in the previous sections have created a corporate-level problem. Microsoft's "Copilot Copyright Commitment" (or "Customer Copyright Commitment") is its commercial answer.

This commitment is not an ethical guarantee; it is a *commercial insurance policy*. Microsoft promises that if a *commercial, paying customer* is sued for copyright infringement based on Copilot's output, "we will defend the customer and pay the amount of any adverse judgments or settlements".

However, this legal protection is *conditional*. The fine print states that the customer *must* "use the guardrails and content filters we have built into our products". This is a *transfer of liability*, not an elimination of risk. Microsoft is not claiming its tool is 100% clean. It is acknowledging the tool is risky, but if a company pays for the commercial version, Microsoft will *insure* that company against the risk.

[4] *https://www.veracode.com/blog/securing-code-and-agentic-ai-risk/*

A developer who disables the content filters to get a "better" (that is, more likely to be infringing) response has likely just *voided their company's legal protection*. This business model *requires* and *depends* on human supervision as a condition of its legal shield.

Risk Category	High-Risk Scenario	Potential Consequence	Required Human-Led Mitigation
Accessibility Bias	Developer uses AI to generate a complex web form and merges it without a11y review.	The form is unusable by screen readers. The company is exposed to an accessibility (for example, ADA) lawsuit.	Mandatory A11y Review: Treat AI code as "inaccessible by default". Manually audit all UI code against WCAG. Prompt *for* accessibility.
IP Ownership	A developer builds a new product *entirely* by accepting AI suggestions with zero modification.	The code may have no copyright protection and be considered public domain, destroying its commercial value.	Active Curation: The developer must *curate, modify, and arrange* the code, making their "human authorship" clear. Human contribution is the IP.
"Fair Use" Risk	A company builds a mission-critical system on AI-generated code. The *Does v. GitHub* case is lost by AI vendors.	The tool's output is now legally tainted. The company faces unquantifiable legal risk and a potential rip-and-replace.	Risk Transfer: Use a vendor with a commercial indemnity policy, such as Microsoft's. *Do not* use "roll your own" or non-indemnified AI models for commercial work.
GPL Contamination	AI suggests a "helper function" that is a *verbatim copy* of a GPL-licensed snippet. A developer adds it to the proprietary codebase.	Catastrophic. The multi-million dollar proprietary product is *legally forced* to be open-sourced.	"Radioactive" Code Handling: All AI code *must* be scanned by SCA/license tools *before* merge. Treat the 35% irregularity stat as a live threat.

Table 9.2: *Risk Categories*

Human Supervision: The Developer as Architect and Auditor

Given the AI's technical limitations (Part 1) and its legal and ethical risks (Part 2), a passive approach is not an option. Human supervision is not a burden; it is the *core* of this new development paradigm. It is the developer's new, and most valuable, skill. This section provides the "how-to" guide for that supervision.

The Human-in-the-Loop (HITL) Framework: A Legal and Practical Mandate

The AI model generates code based on statistical *correlation*, not on *business intent*. The Human-in-the-Loop (HITL) framework is the formal process of inspecting, validating, and injecting that *intent* into the system.

This is no longer just a "best practice"; it is rapidly becoming a *legal requirement*.

- The **EU AI Act (Article 14)** mandates that high-risk AI systems "shall be designed and developed in such a way... that they can be effectively overseen by natural persons".
- **UNESCO's Recommendation on the Ethics of AI** is built on the "cornerstone" of "human oversight".

This legal and ethical framework transforms the developer's role into a *legally auditable* position. In a high-risk system (for example, finance, healthcare), a commit message ("I, a human, have reviewed and approve this AI-generated code") is no longer a simple log; it is a *legal document* demonstrating compliance.

The HITL framework *is* the new development lifecycle. Best practices for this framework are no longer about "usability" but about *governance*:

1. **Transparency and Explainability:** The human must be able to understand and explain *why* the AI made a choice.
2. **Control and Override:** The human must *always* have the "off" switch and the final power to override the AI's suggestion.
3. **Vigilant Feedback Loops:** The human's corrections and overrides must be fed back into the system to refine future prompts and processes.

A Practical Workflow for AI-Assisted Security Auditing

The developer must operate from a "zero-trust" security posture regarding AI-generated code. The data is non-negotiable: AI-generated code is *demonstrably less secure* than human-written code.

- **The Data:** A report from NYU researchers[5] found that AI-assisted code had "nearly three times more security flaws" in certain scenarios. Another 2025 analysis found AI-assisted developers generate "ten times more security issues".
- **The "Why":** The AI is trained on insecure public code. It is rewarded for optimizing for the shortest path to a working answer, not the *secure* one.
- **The Vulnerabilities:** The AI *readily* and *repeatedly* produces textbook security flaws:
    - **SQL Injection:** `sql = "SELECT * FROM users WHERE id = " + user_input`.
    - **Remote Code Execution:** Using `eval(expression)` to parse a simple math string.
    - **Omission of Controls:** Forgetting to add validation, sanitation, or authorization checks to an API endpoint.
    - **Logic Flaws:** Introducing an authorization bypass by "fixing" `if "admin" in user.roles` to `if user.role == "admin"`, which fails for users with multiple roles.

The most dangerous part is the *psychological risk*. Overwhelmed by the *speed* and *volume* of AI-generated code, developers review this code *less carefully*. This creates an "AI security-debt spiral":

- AI produces more insecure code.
- Developers review it less.
- The average time to fix security flaws is already up 47% since 2020[6].
- AI dramatically accelerates the accumulation of security debt.

The *only* solution is a mandatory, automated DevSecOps pipeline. All AI-generated code *must* be "labeled as such" in commits and be required to pass through automated **Static Application Security Testing (SAST)** and **Software Composition Analysis (SCA)** gates *before* it is ever seen by a human reviewer.

The Art of Validation: A Reviewer's Guide to AI-Generated Code

When reviewing code from the "dimwitted intern," the focus of the code review must change. The reviewer is no longer looking for typos; they are auditing for logic and intent.

---

[5] *https://www.veracode.com/blog/securing-code-and-agentic-ai-risk/*
[6] *https://www.veracode.com/blog/securing-code-and-agentic-ai-risk/*

- **Rule 1: Treat It as a Draft.** The AI's output is a *first draft*, not a final product.
- **Rule 2: Focus on Edge Cases.** The AI *will* miss edge cases, logical inconsistencies, and proper error handling. The human reviewer must focus their attention here.
- **Rule 3: Verify Intent, Not Just Syntax.** Does this code *do what the business needs*, or does it just *do what the prompt asked*? These are rarely the same thing.
- **Rule 4: Label Everything.** Mandate that all AI-generated code is labeled in comments or commit messages. This creates a transparent audit trail for future debugging when the "Unowned Code" inevitably breaks.

This leads to a new, essential mandate for code reviews: Review the prompt, not simply the code. A developer submitting a Pull Request containing AI-assisted code should be required to include the core prompts or conversations that generated it. This allows the reviewer to audit the developer's assumptions and their translation of business logic. If the prompt was flawed, the code is flawed, no matter how clean it looks. This conversation is the new, essential development artifact.

Prompt Engineering as a Core Development Skill

The developer's job is shifting from "writing code" to "directing code generation". This direction is given via prompts. "Prompt engineering is the art of communicating with a... model" and is fast transitioning from a novelty to a "must-have" skill.

This is the "how-to" guide for managing the "dimwitted AI intern". The best practices for prompt engineering are identical to the best practices for managing a literal-minded, context-less intern:

- **Be Specific and Detailed:** Use precise language and avoid ambiguity. This is the same as being "Painfully Specific".
- **Provide Context:** Give background information. This is the same as assuming no context.
- **Give Examples (Few-Shot Prompting):** Provide several examples of the desired input-output format.
- **Assign a Role:** Use "Act as if..." prompts. For example: "Act as a senior Tailwind CSS developer. Act as a security auditor."
- **Break Down Tasks:** Use "Chain of Thought" prompting to force the AI to explain its reasoning step-by-step, which often catches logical flaws.

This skill set is not, as some believe, a "soft skill." It is the *existing* hard skill of *architectural specification* applied to a new interface. A good prompt *is* a good system spec. The most effective prompt engineers will be senior engineers who are already skilled at describing systems with precision.

Task	Ineffective "Vibe" Prompt	Effective "Managerial" Prompt	Why it is Better (The Mitigation)
Create a Button	"Make me a cool blue primary button."	"Act as a senior Tailwind developer. Using my theme's `tailwind.config.js`, create a button. It must use `colors.brand-primary` for the background and `colors.white` for the text. On hover, it must use `colors.brand-dark`. It must be fully accessible with keyboard focus states."	Provides **Role**, **Context** (config), and **Specific Constraints**. It also *mandates* the accessibility that the AI would otherwise skip.
Refactor a Component	"Here is a component. Clean it up."	"Analyze this React component. Identify any repeated Tailwind class strings. Your goal is to make it more maintainable. Propose 2-3 abstractions using `@apply` in a CSS file or by creating new, smaller React components. Do not change any business logic."	Provides a specific **Goal**, **Constraints** ("Do not change logic"), and guides the AI toward a specific, maintainable solution that it would never find on its own.
Debug a Layout	"My responsive layout is broken on mobile."	"Here is the HTML and Tailwind code for a card component. It should be a 3-column grid on desktop (`lg:`) and a single-column stack on mobile. Currently, it is staying a 3-column grid. Review the classes and identify the missing or incorrect responsive prefix."	Provides **Context** (the code), the **Intended Behavior**, and the **Observed (Buggy) Behavior**. This narrows the "search space" and prevents the AI from "hallucinating" a random fix.

Table 9.3: *Approaches to Tasks*

Conclusion

The data on AI's impact on the job market may initially appear contradictory: While some reports cite layoffs as companies pivot to new efficiencies, broader analyses of 180 million jobs show that software engineering roles remain among the most secure. This is not a 1:1 replacement; it is a structural evolution.

We have seen this maturation before. In the early 2000s, advanced site-building tools automated low-level HTML tasks, which many feared would end the profession.

Instead, the number of professional web developers grew 40-fold as those tools allowed experts to focus on building the complex systems of the modern web. Today, we are witnessing a similar role evolution:

- The Implementation Specialist: Tasks involving boilerplate code, simple functions, and basic UI are being rapidly automated. For the developer, this means the "labor" of coding is becoming a commodity, serving as the foundation rather than the finish line.
- The AI-Augmented Architect: The developer who masters the skills outlined in this chapter-AI management, ethical auditing, security validation, and business logic translation-is stepping into a new frontier of leadership. This path is seeing massive demand, with workers commanding a 56% wage premium over those who remain solely focused on manual execution.

New, high-value roles like the "Forward-Deployed Engineer"-a hybrid of technical expert and business-logic translator-are emerging as the most sought-after positions in tech. This chapter serves as a roadmap for capturing that 56% premium by evolving your skill set into that of an AI Manager.

The future of development is not "no developers." It is a cohort of more highly-paid, high-impact professionals who have mastered the social-technical translation and human supervision that AI will always lack. The AI is the intern; it needs a manager. By applying the principles in this chapter, you are not just surviving the shift, you are leading it.

Multiple Choice Questions

1. What is the "Context Window Collapse" limitation described in the chapter?
    a. The AI's inability to write secure code, leading to system collapse.
    b. The AI's failure to remember project architecture, past decisions, and business logic as a project grows.
    c. The AI's tendency to invent non-existent APIs, which causes the program to crash.
    d. The AI's inability to read a local `tailwind.config.js` file.
2. According to the chapter, why does AI fundamentally fail to understand "business logic"?
    a. Because business logic is often unwritten, illogical, and based on "messy human compromises" between departments that the AI cannot be a part of.
    b. Because AI models have not been trained on modern financial or legal frameworks.

   c. Because AI cannot write code that is maintainable, scalable, or performant.
   d. Because the AI's "context window" is not large enough to hold the business's mission statement.

3. What is the "GPL Contamination" risk associated with AI-generated code?
   a. The risk that an AI will introduce a computer virus from a GPL-licensed project.
   b. The risk that an AI, trained on GPL code, will insert a "derivative work" snippet into a company's proprietary codebase, potentially forcing the *entire project* to be open-sourced.
   c. The risk that the AI will "contaminate" the codebase with hard-coded, arbitrary values instead of using theme tokens.
   d. The risk that using GPL-licensed code will make the AI less secure and more prone to hallucinations.

4. The chapter states that AI-generated UI code is "inaccessible by default." What is the primary reason for this?
   a. AI models intentionally discriminate against users with disabilities.
   b. AI was trained on the public internet, where 96.3% of home pages have WCAG 2 failures, and it reproduces this systemic bias.
   c. AI cannot generate `alt-text` for images or use correct ARIA roles.
   d. Developers are not prompting the AI to use frameworks that support accessibility.

5. Based on the *Zarya of the Dawn* case, how does a developer secure copyright protection for AI-assisted code?
   a. Copyright is not possible; all AI-assisted code is automatically in the public domain.
   b. By ensuring the AI generates 100% of the code, as the AI is considered the legal "author."
   c. Through the human-led acts of "selection and arrangement," modifying, and curating the AI's output.
   d. By filing a special form with the U.S. Copyright Office that disclaims all AI-generated parts.

6. What is a primary failure mode of AI when used specifically with Tailwind CSS?
   a. It refuses to use utility classes and will only use the `@apply` directive.
   b. It cannot read the local `tailwind.config.js` file, leading it to "pollute" the code with arbitrary values instead of systemic design tokens.

   c. It automatically refactors verbose class lists into perfectly maintainable components.

   d. Its training data is too new, so it only knows modern, emerging CSS features such as `:has()` and container queries.

7. The chapter describes an "AI security-debt spiral." What is this?

   a. The AI gets stuck in a loop, generating an infinite amount of insecure code.

   b. The rising financial cost of buying AI-powered security and auditing tools.

   c. The process where AI produces 10x more insecure code, which developers review *less* carefully due to the high volume, causing security debt to accelerate.

   d. When an AI model is trained exclusively on insecure code from public repositories.

8. What new, essential mandate for code reviews does the chapter propose for AI-assisted code?

   a. Reviewers must check that the AI-generated code is labeled with a comment.

   b. Reviewers must run the AI-generated code through a different AI model to check for errors.

   c. Reviewers must review the prompt, not just the code, to audit the developer's assumptions and translation of business logic.

   d. All AI-generated code must be deleted and rewritten by a human supervisor to ensure "cognitive weight."

9. What is the core difference between an ineffective "vibe prompt" and an effective "managerial prompt"?

   a. A managerial prompt is much shorter and more direct.

   b. An effective managerial prompt assigns a role ("Act as..."), provides specific context (such as theme tokens), and gives clear constraints (for example, "must be accessible").

   c. A vibe prompt uses emotional language to get a more creative, "branded" result from the AI.

   d. A managerial prompt focuses only on function, while a vibe prompt focuses only on style.

10. How does the chapter describe the future of the developer job market?
    a. All developer jobs will be replaced by AI "interns" within the next five years.
    b. A "bifurcation" where low-level "coders" are displaced, but high-level "supervisors" who manage AI and translate business logic will see massive demand.
    c. AI will have no significant impact on the job market, and developers will continue to work as they always have.
    d. The only new, valuable role will be the "Forward-Deployed Engineer."

Answers

1. b
2. a
3. b
4. b
5. c
6. b
7. c
8. c
9. b
10. b

CHAPTER 10
Continuous Learning in AI Frontend

Introduction

Large Language Models (LLMs) are reshaping frontend development, especially within the structured environment of Tailwind CSS. Because Tailwind expresses layout, spacing, and visual design through explicit utility classes, it functions as a clear "API for styling" that generative models can reliably interpret and produce. This makes AI a powerful partner in creating consistent, scalable, production-ready interfaces.

However, both AI capabilities and the Tailwind ecosystem continue to evolve rapidly. New model families introduce deeper reasoning and higher accuracy, while innovations such as Tailwind CSS v4's CSS-first architecture change how developers structure and optimize their code. Staying effective in this landscape requires an ongoing strategy rather than a fixed skill set.

By the end of this chapter, you will understand where to focus your learning, which communities and tools matter most, and how to maintain long-term mastery as AI-driven frontend development continues to advance.

Structure

In this chapter, we will cover the following topics:

- The Modern AI Frontend Toolchain and Advanced Frameworks
    - The Ecosystem of AI-Powered Generators
    - Utility-First Component Aggregators for AI Workflows
    - Essential Developer Tooling and Workflow Optimization
- Mastering Prompt Engineering for Continuous Component Refinement
    - Advanced Prompting Techniques for Code Generation

    - Structuring Prompts for Optimal Tailwind Output
- Global Communities and Real-Time Knowledge Exchange
    - Official Framework Channels and Vendor Support
    - Independent Developer Hubs and Forums
- Future-Proofing the Frontend Developer Role (Strategy and Oversight)
    - The Evolving Role: From Execution to Strategic Validation
    - Critical Skills for Code Review and Refinement
    - Emerging Trends Redefining the Frontend
- Ethical and Responsible AI Development Practices
    - Establishing Responsible AI Principles (RAI) in UI/UX
    - Addressing Bias and Promoting Inclusion

The Modern AI Frontend Toolchain and Advanced Frameworks

To move beyond simple code snippets to integrated, scalable applications, developers must utilize specialized software that capitalizes on the symbiotic relationship between utility-first structure and generative automation. This section catalogs the critical software specialized in generating and managing utility-first interfaces, emphasizing the symbiotic relationship between structure and automation.

The Ecosystem of AI-Powered Generators

General-purpose LLMs can provide foundational code, but the demand for high-fidelity, responsive, and production-ready components has driven the creation of highly specialized AI generation platforms. These tools understand the nuances of utility-first frameworks, significantly enhancing a developer's output.

Specialized UI Generation Platforms (v0.dev, Meku, and Iterative Design)

Several leading platforms have established themselves by focusing on translating natural language descriptions into highly functional interfaces. **v0.dev**, developed by Vercel, is a prominent example of a platform designed for interpreting linguistic descriptions and translating them into functional React components, all expertly styled with Tailwind CSS. Its strength lies in its ability to support rapid, iterative design and its seamless integration with the component management standards of Shadcn UI.

An emerging trend goes beyond component generation into end-to-end application scaffolding. Platforms like **Meku** convert text prompts into production-ready React applications styled with Tailwind CSS. Meku and similar tools represent a crucial development, because they generate full project scaffolding, including modules for common application features such as authentication and e-commerce, and offer essential developer features like GitHub sync and full code export. This contrasts with earlier tools by providing both the velocity and the customization freedom necessary for developers and startups.

Other specialized generators, such as **Workik** and **TailwindAI**, focus acutely on core Tailwind features. Their capabilities include generating efficient utility classes for instant responsive layouts, simplifying configurations, and optimizing CSS production. These tools specifically use AI in conjunction with optimizers such as PurgeCSS to remove unused classes, delivering cleaner, more performant CSS that is critical for faster load times. For instance, tools like CodeGPT's Tailwind CSS AI Assistant offer utility class generation, component styling, and custom configuration creation, specifically supporting advanced features of Tailwind CSS v4.[1]

Integration Capabilities: From Components to Full App Generation

While AI excels at frontend design and styling (thanks in large part to Tailwind CSS's structure), the integration with complex back-end logic remains a challenge. Generative tools still struggle with complex application architecture components such as database structures, API connections, and user authentication. Consequently, developers must ensure that the AI-generated frontend code, often in frameworks like `React`, `Vue`, `Next.js`, or `Nuxt.js`, maintains a clean separation of concerns, allowing human developers to handle the complex architectural integration.

Utility-First Component Aggregators for AI Workflows

As the AI-driven ecosystem matures, prompt engineering—the art of communicating with large language models—is rapidly evolving from a technical novelty into an essential skill for the modern developer to iteratively refine and optimize components.

---

[1] *While generators like Bolt.new and Lovable provide a massive velocity boost for initial project scaffolding, they introduce significant long-term maintenance risks. The primary danger lies in architectural inconsistency, where the AI may generate one-off solutions that deviate from a unified, project-wide pattern in favor of the "shortest path" to a working result. Without immediate human-led auditing, this rapid generation can transform into a technical debt accelerator, producing "unowned code" that functions today but becomes a high-stakes liability when future developers—who did not write the logic—are tasked with debugging it. Always treat AI-generated scaffolding as a starting point, not a finished product, and validate it against your core design system to avoid the "high-interest" payments of architectural debt.*

Deep Dive into Shadcn UI and Component Ownership

Shadcn UI[2] has gained significant traction, particularly because its unique model aligns well with the need for developer control in an AI-driven world. Instead of importing a large, monolithic package, developers copy and paste individual component source code directly into their project. This approach grants the developer **full component ownership** and customization freedom. The ability to open a component in tools such as v0 and adjust it via prompts further streamlines this process.

The ability to own the code is profoundly important in a workflow where AI is the primary author. When an AI generates a component, and the developer accepts and copies that code, the human developer assumes sole responsibility for its long-term health and maintenance. This necessitates a robust human governance process for the generated code. Developers must actively review and standardize AI-generated class lists to prevent the accumulation of fragmented, unmaintained, or overly verbose code, a common problem often encountered in generative workflows.

This task directly links to core software engineering maintenance principles, specifically the need to uphold DRY (Do Not Repeat Yourself)[3] and KISS (Keep It Simple, Stupid)[4] standards. If the AI generates the code and the developer 'owns' it (the Shadcn model), the skill set required shifts away from simple generation and towards the **architectural refinement** of generated code, specifically focusing on clarity and avoiding overly complex abstractions that might obscure the code's intent.

Before merging any AI-generated or AI-augmented component, run through this lightweight audit to ensure it aligns with your professional standards:

- **Naming Consistency**: Verify that the component name, file structure, and internal variables follow your project's specific naming conventions and not just the AI's default style.
- **Token Integrity**: Ensure that all styling uses established design tokens from your tailwind.config.js. Replace any hard-coded "magic numbers" (for example, `p-[17px]`) with standardized utility classes.

---

[2] *https://ui.shadcn.com/*

[3] *https://en.wikipedia.org/wiki/Don%27t_repeat_yourself; The DRY principle ("Do Not Repeat Yourself") is a software development guideline that encourages reducing duplication in code, logic, and configuration. By centralizing shared functionality, developers improve maintainability, reduce errors, and make future updates easier to implement.*

[4] *https://en.wikipedia.org/wiki/KISS_principle; The KISS principle ("Keep It Simple, Stupid") is a design guideline that emphasizes simplicity in architecture, code, and problem-solving. It encourages developers to avoid unnecessary complexity so that systems remain easier to understand, maintain, and extend.*

- **Class Deduplication**: Scan for redundant or conflicting utility classes—such as two different text sizes or overlapping widths—where only one will actually take effect.
- **A11y Validation**: Check that the AI has not bypassed critical accessibility needs. Confirm the presence of correct ARIA attributes, semantic HTML tags, and sufficient color contrast ratios.
- **Architectural Fit**: Confirm the component's internal logic (state management, hooks usage) matches your existing architectural patterns rather than introducing a "one-off" solution that creates technical debt.

Utilizing Headless and Accessible Libraries (Chakra UI, Ant Design)

To ensure that generative models adhere to crucial accessibility standards, developers can direct the AI to style components using underlying accessible primitives from libraries such as **Headless UI**[5] or **Chakra UI**[6]. Frameworks like Chakra UI, which emphasize simplicity, modularity, and accessibility with over 60 components and 37k GitHub stars[7], provide composable components that serve as strong foundations for generative design. Similarly, **Ant Design**[8], an enterprise-class React UI library developed by Alibaba Group, is known for its simplicity and professional design approach, easing the development process.

When integrating these aggregators into your AI workflow, it is important to recognize the trade-off between **accessible abstraction** and **utility control**:

- **Headless/Accessibility-Focused Libraries**: Tools like `shadcn/ui` utilize headless primitives (such as Radix) to handle the complex "heavy lifting" of accessibility, including keyboard navigation, ARIA attributes, and focus management. Choosing this abstraction is highly recommended for high-stakes, interactive components—such as modals, dropdowns, or tabs—where manual implementation is error-prone, even though it introduces additional dependencies to your project.
- **Direct Tailwind Utility Control**: Maintaining full control by applying utility classes directly to raw HTML elements offers maximum architectural flexibility and a zero-dependency codebase. This path is ideal for simpler components—such as cards, badges, or basic layout containers—where the overhead of a headless library adds unnecessary complexity and the accessibility requirements can be easily managed using Tailwind's **`sr-only`**, **`focus:`**, and ARIA-variant utilities.

---

[5] *https://headlessui.com/*
[6] *https://chakra-ui.com/*
[7] *https://github.com/chakra-ui/chakra-ui*
[8] *https://ant.design/*

Essential Developer Tooling and Workflow Optimization

Efficient integration requires specialized tooling that monitors and validates AI outputs in real-time.

Maximizing VS Code Integration

The code editor remains the primary interface for the developer. Tools like the official **Tailwind CSS IntelliSense extension for Visual Studio Code** enhance the development experience by providing advanced features such as intelligent class suggestions (autocomplete), syntax highlighting, linting (highlighting errors), and hover previews that reveal the complete CSS behind a utility class. This extension serves as the developer's first line of defense, validating AI-generated class combinations and ensuring adherence to framework conventions immediately upon code insertion.

The Role of TypeScript and Static Analysis in AI Validation

Before exploring these tools in depth, it is useful to compare how leading AI platforms approach Tailwind-driven development, the architectural principles they emphasize, and the specific workflows they enhance.

Tool Example	Primary Function	Tailwind Integration Focus	Key Architectural Principle
v0.dev (Vercel)	React UI Component Generation	Seamless integration with Shadcn UI and React frameworks.	Rapid prototyping, iterative refinement via prompting.
Meku	End-to-End Web App Builder	Full React + Tailwind projects, including authentication and deployment modules.	Full code ownership, GitHub sync, rapid deployment.
Workik	Component and Utility Generation	Instant responsive layouts, configuration assistance, PurgeCSS optimization.	Efficiency in utility class combinations and performance optimization.

Table 10.1: *Comparative Analysis of Top AI-Driven Tailwind Generators*

While AI excels at styling, it can be less predictable when generating complex application logic involving state management or data parsing. **TypeScript** is recognized as a critical component in the AI development workflow. By providing a type system, TypeScript helps AI models generate more accurate and maintainable code. Static analysis enabled by TypeScript helps identify errors in the generated code, which can then be efficiently corrected by the developer or the AI model itself.

In the AI-first development flow, TypeScript transcends its original function as a simple type checker to become a formal **generative contract** between the human architect and the LLM. The developer imposes this contract to force the LLM to adhere to structured, predictable data flow. Since AI excels at styling (Tailwind) but is less predictable with complex application logic (such as state management or data parsing), enforcing TypeScript reduces the AI's degrees of freedom in the logic layer. This allows the developer to leverage the AI's speed for UI generation while simultaneously maintaining the integrity of the application's architectural backbone.

While *Chapter 9, Limitations, Ethics, and Human Supervision in AI-Assisted Development*, established the professional mandate for human supervision to manage the AI's structural limitations, *Chapter 10, Additional Resources and Communities for Continuous Learning in AI-Driven Frontend*, introduces the specific "mechanical auditors" required to operationalize that oversight. TypeScript and static analysis act as the primary validation mechanisms that transform "unowned" AI output into production-ready code:

- **Logic and Type Safety**: TypeScript provides a static analysis layer and a type system that helps the AI generate more accurate, maintainable code by enforcing a strict structural contract. This effectively catches "hallucinated" APIs or incorrect component props that the AI might confabulate due to its lack of true logical understanding.
- **Design System Guardrails**: Automated static analysis gates serve as a critical defense against "rogue" styling. By enforcing linter rules that block hard-coded utility values inconsistent with the design system, you ensure the AI remains aligned with the architectural patterns defined in your **`tailwind.config.js`**.
- **Reducing Cognitive Weight**: These tools act as a "pre-reviewer," filtering out low-level syntax and type errors. This allows the human "Manager" to focus their cognitive energy on higher-level issues such as **stakeholder alignment** and **UX integrity**, which are areas where AI reasoning consistently fails.

Thus, by integrating these validation mechanisms, you move beyond "vibe-based" acceptance and establish a high-leverage workflow where the developer uses automated tools to audit the AI "intern" with industrial precision.

Mastering Prompt Engineering for Continuous Component Refinement

In a highly automated environment, prompt engineering transforms from a conversational interface into the developer's primary strategic input channel for design control. Mastering this skill is essential for achieving predictable, high-quality, and architecturally sound code output.

Advanced Prompting Techniques for Code Generation

Successful code generation, particularly for utility-first styling, depends on providing specific, contextual, and well-constrained instructions to the LLM.

Role-Based Prompting: Assuming the Digital Architect Persona

One of the most effective methods for improving output quality is **role-based prompting**. This involves defining the AI's persona (for example, instructing the model to "Act as a senior UI engineer specializing in accessible, mobile-first Tailwind v4"). This explicit role definition provides crucial contextual constraints, significantly improving the relevance and quality of the generated code.

Use this structured format to ensure your AI "Driver" remains production-aligned and adheres to your project's specific architectural guardrails:

- **Goal**: [Describe the primary objective, for example, refactor the provided static pricing section into a reusable React component using Tailwind CSS v4.]
- **Constraints**: [List strict technical or design limitations, for example, must achieve WCAG AA compliance, follow a mobile-first responsive pattern, and avoid all "magic numbers" in favor of theme tokens.]
- **Inputs/Existing APIs**: [Provide the necessary context, for example, use the existing Button and Typography primitives. Refer to the attached tailwind.config.js for theme values.]
- **Output Format**: [Define the expected delivery, for example, provide a single TSX file with inline documentation for all props.]
- **Non-Goals**: [Explicitly state what to ignore, for example, do not implement backend API integration or add external state management libraries.]

When generating Tailwind code, effective prompting requires the developer to view the prompt as a high-level **design token system**. The prompt must map abstract visual and design system concepts (such as branding colors, precise spacing units, and specific typography scales) directly to the necessary utility classes. This strategic input effectively transforms the prompt into a high-level representation of the project's design tokens, ensuring visual quality and consistency across generated elements.

Chain-of-Thought and Iterative Feedback Loops

For generating complex or multi-step components, relying on a single prompt is often inefficient. Complex tasks should be broken down into simpler, sequential instructions.

Techniques like **Chain-of-Thought prompting**, which requests the model to articulate its step-by-step reasoning, are instrumental in eliciting better responses, particularly for complex layout logic. Furthermore, developers should adopt an **iterative refinement** strategy, testing various inputs and adjusting the prompt accordingly to align the output with the intended design specifications. Providing instructions on what *to do* instead of what *not to do* also increases accuracy.

Structuring Prompts for Optimal Tailwind Output

Modern generative models, including the highly capable Gemini 3, perform optimally when given explicit constraints and clear architectural principles.

Explicitly Requesting Performance and Responsiveness

To ensure high-performance frontend delivery, prompts must explicitly demand a mobile-first approach, requiring the correct use of responsive prefixes (**`sm:`**, **`lg:`**). The AI assistant should generate responsive layouts with a mobile-first approach using Tailwind's breakpoint system. Additionally, developers should instruct the AI to generate code optimized for downstream production processes, such as purging and tree-shaking, referencing the necessity of producing smaller bundle sizes and clean CSS output for performance gains.

When explicitly requesting performance and responsiveness in your prompts, it is helpful to frame these targets as direct drivers of user experience rather than isolated technical benchmarks. Remind the AI that metrics like **Core Web Vitals** (for example, LCP, CLS) are critical proxies for **perceived speed**, and that a highly responsive, fluid layout is a primary driver of **conversion and retention** on mobile devices. This structural link encourages the model to generate solutions that are not just functionally correct but strategically aligned with the product's business goals.

Defining Visual Principles and Accessibility

High-quality prompts must include general development principles (for example, visual quality standards, modular/reusable components) and specific UI/UX constraints (for example, typography, color palette, accessibility standards, and interaction states like hover/loading).

Beyond technical constraints, high-quality prompts should explicitly define user intent and interaction goals. Rather than just describing a static UI layout, encourage the AI to account for the entire user journey by specifying primary actions, error states, empty states, and specific feedback behavior. Providing this context ensures that the generated components are not just visually aligned with your design system but are also functionally resilient and reflective of real-world user interactions.

A significant improvement in output quality occurs when the human developer provides template code snippets or defines the required file and folder structure. This strategy, often known as few-shot prompting or supplying examples, enables the AI to generate code that integrates seamlessly into a large, established codebase. Since AI-generated components often require integration into larger systems (such as `React/Next.js`), specifying the component structure, import patterns, and file locations in the prompt allows the developer to strategically manage the **architectural debt** from the beginning. By doing so, the AI output becomes a cohesive part of the larger system rather than an isolated artifact requiring significant human refactoring.

Global Communities and Real-Time Knowledge Exchange

Professional mastery in a rapidly evolving field necessitates continuous engagement with the cutting edge, which is most readily available within active developer communities and technical hubs. These platforms serve as vital resources for real-time problem-solving and knowledge sharing.

Official Framework Channels and Vendor Support

Reliable and authoritative information often originates from the creators and vendors of the technologies themselves.

Engaging consistently with official channels does more than simply solve immediate technical hurdles; it is a strategic measure to strengthen design consistency across your application. By anchoring your workflow to the latest authoritative standards, you significantly reduce architectural drift, a recurring risk in AI-assisted workflows where generative models may inadvertently suggest non-standard patterns or outdated class structures that diverge from the project's core design system.

The Tailwind CSS Discord Server

The official **Tailwind CSS Discord server**[9] remains a crucial hub for real-time discussions, Q&A, and gaining direct insights into framework updates. The server is consistently active, with hundreds of people online answering each other's questions. Similarly, general Web Development Discord servers provide a broader community for learning and collaboration.

---

[9] *https://v1.tailwindcss.com/discord*

Official Documentation and Guides

A foundational component of continuous learning involves the consistent monitoring of official vendor platforms. This includes checking Google Cloud, ChatGPT, and related Gemini/OpenAI documentation for advancements in model-to-code generation, OpenAI's guidance on prompting techniques, and specialized resources like the Prompting Guide AI. These resources are essential for understanding the latest generative capabilities and the necessary strategic inputs to maximize their effectiveness.

Independent Developer Hubs and Forums

Beyond official channels, independent developer forums offer unfiltered insights into practical challenges, tool comparisons, and the sociological impacts of AI adoption. Engaging with these communities is essential because community-driven discussions frequently expose real-world UX tradeoffs and implementation pitfalls, such as how a generated layout might feel "clunky" on low-powered devices or where a popular AI-suggested pattern fails in a complex production edge case, which generative models are structurally unable to anticipate on their own.

Navigating AI and Frontend Discussion on Reddit

Subreddits such as r/webdev and r/tailwindcss are invaluable for gauging community sentiment and identifying practical pain points, such as comparisons between competing AI tools (for example, v0.dev versus TailwindAI) or ongoing discussions about job security and the integration of AI-generated code.

These community concerns regarding the "sacrifice of creativity and uniqueness for speed" highlight a critical strategic requirement in modern workflows: The preservation of brand voice and design identity. As AI models tend toward "average" design patterns, the developer's role as a creative steward becomes essential to ensure intentional UX differentiation. By actively resisting the drift toward generic, AI-generated layouts, professionals can use community-identified pitfalls to protect a project's unique design language and maintain a competitive edge that automated tools cannot replicate on their own.

The discussions within these forums often reveal the **developer's emotional landscape** regarding technological change. For example, open questions about whether developers are "sacrificing creativity and uniqueness for speed" or if reliance on AI risks "losing my edge" highlight legitimate concerns about job risk. The professional developer must analyze these community discussions to anticipate market pressures and strategically position their skills. The observation that developers are concerned about the erosion of traditional skills confirms the necessity of shifting career focus away from manual execution toward the high-value, irreplaceable skills of validation, security, ethical auditing, and high-level strategy.

Specialized Slack and Discord Communities

Specialized communities, such as AI-focused Discord servers and platforms like the Relume Slack community (focused on generative design assets for Webflow/Tailwind), provide targeted professional networking. These platforms often offer collaboration spaces, dedicated job posting channels, and regular events such as hackathons and workshops, which are vital for professional development and staying current on evolving industry trends.

Future-Proofing the Frontend Developer Role (Strategy and Oversight)

The increasing autonomy of generative tools dictates a fundamental change in the developer's core function. The future success of a frontend developer rests on becoming a highly skilled human **strategist, reviewer, and validator** of AI output, rather than a primary coder.

The Evolving Role: From Execution to Strategic Validation

The shift in focus requires adopting new responsibilities centered on oversight and governance.

Human Oversight and the Validation of Business Requirements

The shift in focus requires adopting new responsibilities centered on oversight and governance. This transition from manual execution to strategic validation fundamentally reshapes collaboration between frontend developers and product or design teams. As the developer moves into the role of an "Orchestrator," they become a critical partner in defining quality standards and maintaining UX ownership. They ensure that the increased velocity provided by AI does not bypass the intentional, human-centric design choices that define a product's unique identity.

Furthermore, translating ambiguous business goals into technical requirements is not merely a technical responsibility; it is a vital product-alignment function. The human developer ensures that AI-generated solutions remain strictly consistent with user needs and the long-term product vision, serving as a safeguard against generic implementations that might ignore the broader business context.

For junior developers, this evolution dictates a shift in learning:

- Requirements Analysis: Moving away from rote coding toward deeply understanding the "why" behind a feature.
- Task Decomposition: Breaking complex business cases into manageable technical instructions for the AI.
- Stakeholder Communication: Bridging the gap between non-technical business goals and machine-executable constraints.
- Ethical and Security Auditing: Reviewing security practices and establishing the guardrails necessary for responsible deployment.

Avoiding the "Black Box" Workflow and Skill Erosion

A critical professional hazard in an AI-driven environment is over-dependence, which can create a "black box" workflow where developers accept generated outputs without a full understanding of the underlying logic or architectural implications. This over-reliance risks the erosion of fundamental architectural and problem-solving skills. To mitigate this, developers must intentionally use AI as an augmentation tool, supporting human intelligence rather than replacing it.

The emergence of advanced models such as Gemini 3, which show a 50% improvement in solved benchmark tasks over previous versions, and specialized agentic development platforms (such as, Google Antigravity) that handle complex, multi-step development tasks simultaneously, further elevates the developer's role into that of an **Orchestrator**. If an AI agent can solve more complex tasks, the developer's expertise must shift to managing the integration of these sophisticated outputs into a unified system. This requires prioritizing learning about *workflow integration* and *tool compatibility* rather than focusing on learning new syntax for individual frameworks.

Critical Skills for Code Review and Refinement

Because AI output is treated as co-authored, a rigorous, security-first, and performance-optimized review methodology is essential.

Ensuring Maintainability (DRY, KISS, and Readability)

The human reviewer must enforce the **Principle of Least Surprise**[10], ensuring the code behaves as expected, and prioritizing clarity and readability over overly "clever" or excessively brief code that sacrifices understanding. A core principle is KISS (Keep

[10] *https://en.wikipedia.org/wiki/Principle_of_least_astonishment*

It Simple, Stupid), favoring simpler solutions that meet requirements. It is often preferable to allow minor duplication rather than hiding setup code within a complex, multi-purpose helper function. This disciplined approach is vital for managing technical debt, as AI often requires explicit instruction to prevent the generation of duplicated logic or complex, unnecessary abstractions.

Performance Optimization of the Generated Code

The review process must actively identify performance concerns. Developers should look for potential performance killers such as N+1 query patterns, unnecessary recomputation, and the use of inefficient data structures. Furthermore, a primary check is ensuring the AI correctly generates optimized Tailwind builds, specifically confirming the effective use of purging and tree-shaking for production environments.

The Necessity of Comprehensive Testing (Beyond the "Happy Path")

AI typically excels at generating functional code (the "happy path"). However, comprehensive testing remains firmly a human responsibility. The human developer must ensure that coverage is robust, extending beyond basic functionality to include edge cases (for example, what happens when filters yield zero results), various combinations of filtering and ordering logic, and ensuring test function names are clear and descriptive. Furthermore, comments in tests should explain the "Why", the business reason for an assertion, not merely restate what the code does, providing critical context that generative models currently lack.

Emerging Trends Redefining the Frontend

Maintaining professional relevance requires tracking future technological shifts that will fundamentally redefine user experience.

Hyper-Personalization and Adaptive Interfaces

AI is driving the trend toward **hyper-personalization**, which is expected to become the norm by 2025. Websites are evolving from static displays into personalized assistants that dynamically adapt layouts, content, and component states in real-time based on deep analysis of user behavioral data, preferences, and predictive analytics. This ability for websites to feel personal without being "creepy" is fueled by AI's ability to analyze patterns such as scroll speed and click behavior. This shift requires that frontend developers master the AI integration points for personalized component rendering.

While hyper-personalization can significantly enhance user engagement by transforming static sites into "personalized assistants," it must be implemented through the lens of **Responsible AI (RAI) principles**. To prevent the user experience from crossing into manipulative or privacy-invasive territory, developers must prioritize the following:

- **Transparency and Disclosure**: Ensure users are aware that an interface is adapting based on their behavior, moving beyond the "creepy" factor by providing clear explanations for why certain content is being prioritized.
- **Explicit Consent**: Collect behavioral data, such as scroll speed and click patterns, only with explicit user permission, adhering to strict data privacy standards like GDPR.
- **User Control**: Provide robust mechanisms for users to manage or opt-out of personalized experiences, ensuring they remain in control of their digital environment rather than being subjected to algorithmic "dark patterns".

By anchoring adaptive interfaces in **consent and transparency**, developers can build deeper user trust and ensure that AI-driven personalization remains an asset to the brand rather than a liability.

Autonomous Site Builders and AI-Driven Design Feedback

Future trends point toward **autonomous site builders**, end-to-end systems that handle the full lifecycle of design, coding, testing, and deployment with minimal human intervention. Crucially, this includes the rise of **AI-driven design feedback loops**. These tools will analyze live user interactions and instantly suggest layout or UX improvements based on real-time data. Developers must prepare to manage these autonomous systems and interpret their data-driven feedback, acting as strategists who use AI to handle optimization and execution.

Ethical and Responsible AI Development Practices

In the era of deep human-AI collaboration, the professional mandate extends to adhering to Responsible AI (RAI) principles. The developer acts as the essential guardian of fairness, transparency, and digital security within the generated codebase.

Establishing Responsible AI Principles (RAI) in UI/UX

Ethics defines the moral principles that distinguish right from wrong, specifically addressing issues such as data privacy, fairness, explainability, and accountability in algorithmic systems.

Transparency, Accountability, and Code Ownership

Under RAI principles, developers are ultimately accountable for the code that is deployed. This accountability requires transparency regarding the data used to train the generative models and the rationale behind algorithmic recommendations. AI outputs must be managed as **co-authored artifacts** that require clear documentation and human sign-off. Establishing clear oversight over the full AI lifecycle is a core RAI requirement. Furthermore, teams must ensure compliance regarding code ownership and licensing clarity when using third-party generative tools.

Security, Resilience, and Data Privacy

AI-powered systems must be robust and actively defended from adversarial attacks, minimizing security risks and enabling confidence in system outcomes. Security checks on AI-generated code must be prioritized, especially for functions handling sensitive interactions such as user input, authentication, database queries, and network requests. Developers also bear the responsibility of vetting AI vendors, prioritizing tools that adhere to strict data privacy and compliance standards (such as GDPR and SOC 2) before feeding any sensitive project data into them.

Addressing Bias and Promoting Inclusion

The RAI principle of Fairness explicitly demands equitable treatment of individuals or groups and the avoidance of algorithmic discrimination.

Auditing AI Outputs for Design Biases

Generative models learn from vast datasets, which often contain inherent biases that can be inadvertently perpetuated in the generated design outputs, leading to inaccessible or inequitable user experiences Developers must therefore become active auditors of the UI generated by the AI, verifying that the design is human-centric and ensures accessibility and inclusion.

Embedding Responsible AI (RAI) checkpoints directly into the active design and review workflow is essential for maintaining technical and ethical integrity. Rather than treating these as post-development considerations, developers should integrate the following validations into their iterative cycle:

- **Bias Review**: Actively audit AI-generated UI during the initial generation phase to verify that the design is human-centric and avoids perpetuating inequitable user experiences found in training data.
- **Real-Time Accessibility Audit**: Leverage automated tools to detect and implement compliant fixes—such as adjusting Tailwind utility classes for contrast or semantics—immediately as components are generated.

- **Data Transparency Validation:** Document and review the rationale behind AI design decisions and prompt inputs as part of the standard code review process.
- **Security-First Review:** Prioritize the auditing of code handling sensitive interactions, such as authentication or user input, as soon as the logic is co-authored by the AI.

Establishing this clear oversight across the full AI lifecycle ensures that the final deployed code is both robust and ethically sound.

Automated Accessibility Audits and Fixes

Continuous learning involves strategically leveraging AI tools that can automatically detect and highlight accessibility gaps (for example, contrast, semantics). These tools can then suggest or even implement compliant fixes, often by adjusting the relevant Tailwind utility classes in real-time. This provides a powerful mechanism for adhering to the ethical imperative of building inclusive digital experiences.

Principle	Definition/Concern	Developer Action (Oversight)
Accuracy and Reliability	Ensuring trustworthy and dependable outputs across devices and themes (for example, dark mode)	Rigorous human QA, component testing, and functional validation against specs.
Transparency and Explainability	Understanding the rationale behind AI's design decisions (why those specific classes?).	Documenting prompt inputs and reviewing output rationale for logic and style decisions.
Fairness and Inclusion	Avoiding algorithmic bias; ensuring equitable design treatment and accessibility.	Explicitly auditing AI outputs for inclusive design flaws, contrast, and ARIA attributes.
Security and Robustness	Defending generated code from adversarial attacks and minimizing security risks.	Prioritizing security reviews for code handling sensitive interactions (input, auth).
Accountability and Ownership	Establishing clear oversight and legal responsibility for the final, deployed code.	Treating AI outputs as co-authored, ensuring licensing clarity, and human sign-off.

Table 10.2: *Core Principles for Responsible AI in Frontend Development*

Conclusion

The trajectory of the AI-driven frontend, characterized by the tight integration of prompt engineering and utility-first styling (Tailwind CSS), is moving rapidly toward deeper human-AI collaboration. The core premise, bridging "Prompt to TailwindCSS", culminates in a strategic paradigm shift. The professional developer's value is no longer derived from manual syntactic execution but from the ability to serve as an AI architect, strategist, and validator.

This shift in focus ultimately translates into superior product outcomes: sophisticated AI orchestration and validation not only elevate technical quality but also directly impact user trust through ethical oversight, ensure experience consistency by enforcing design system integrity, and secure long-term product sustainability by proactively managing architectural debt. This elevation of the developer's role, from coder to orchestrator, is critical for driving innovation in the hyper-personalized, AI-driven web while ensuring technical integrity and ethical compliance.

To maintain relevance, continuous learning must prioritize adaptive, high-level non-coding skills: Sophisticated prompt engineering that acts as architectural instruction; stringent security and performance auditing of generated code; application of ethical RAI frameworks to ensure fairness and transparency; and the crucial ability to translate complex, ambiguous business requirements into actionable technical constraints for autonomous systems. This elevation of the developer's role, from coder to orchestrator, is critical for driving innovation in the hyper-personalized, AI-driven web while ensuring technical integrity and ethical compliance.

Multiple Choice Questions

1. What is the primary reason Tailwind CSS is particularly effective for use with Generative AI models compared to traditional CSS frameworks?
    a. Tailwind has built-in JavaScript functions that integrate directly with LLMs.
    b. Tailwind's long class names provide more natural language context.
    c. Tailwind turns implicit CSS relationships (such as cascades and layout logic) into explicit, composable utilities that act as a clear API for AI.
    d. Tailwind's configuration files are written in JSON, which is easier for AI to parse.
2. In the AI-driven frontend workflow, the shift in the developer's role is primarily characterized by the move from execution to what key function?
    a. Exclusive focus on backend API development.
    b. Strategic validation, guidance, and refinement of AI outputs.
    c. Maintenance of legacy codebase components.
    d. Solely managing third-party dependencies and packages.
3. Which of the following is a key architectural implication of using component aggregators like Shadcn UI, often favored in AI workflows (for example, v0.dev)?
    a. It necessitates using external CDN links for styling.
    b. It ensures components are managed through a single NPM package dependency.

   c. It grants the developer full code ownership and control over the generated component source code.
   d. It requires complex CSS-in-JS solutions instead of utility classes.

4. According to Responsible AI (RAI) principles, which critical aspect must a frontend developer prioritize when reviewing AI-generated code that handles form submissions and user data?
   a. Ensuring the component uses the latest CSS animations.
   b. Auditing for security vulnerabilities, especially concerning user input and authentication.
   c. Minimizing the total number of utility classes used.
   d. Verifying the use of outdated JavaScript syntax.

5. What is the "Black Box" risk that developers must avoid in an AI-driven workflow?
   a. Using AI tools that have dark mode enabled by default.
   b. Accepting AI outputs without fully understanding or being able to debug the underlying code/logic.
   c. Relying exclusively on proprietary code generators.
   d. Using AI for complex algorithms but not for simple styling tasks.

6. When structuring a prompt for an AI to generate a high-quality, maintainable Tailwind component, what specific technique should be employed to ensure that the AI adheres to existing design standards?
   a. Anthropomorphizing the prompt with emotional language.
   b. Explicitly specifying the required file/folder structure and providing component template examples.
   c. Using only high-level conceptual descriptions without any technical constraints.
   d. Requesting the output in the oldest available CSS standard.

7. How does the implementation of TypeScript primarily benefit the integration of AI-generated code into a modern frontend project?
   a. TypeScript simplifies the PurgeCSS process.
   b. It provides a static analysis layer and type system to help the AI generate more accurate and maintainable code.
   c. It completely eliminates the need for human code review.
   d. It only supports Angular frameworks, not React or Vue.

8. Which AI-driven trend involves tools analyzing live user interactions and instantly suggesting layout or UX improvements, transitioning the web from static to adaptive systems?
    a. Backend Logic Separation (BLS)
    b. AI-driven Design Feedback Loops
    c. Database Structure Generation (DSG)
    d. Utility Class Enumeration (UCE)
9. For performance optimization of AI-generated Tailwind code, what is a crucial instruction to include in the AI's configuration or prompt to ensure small CSS bundle sizes?
    a. Generate only global CSS resets
    b. Ensure the build process utilizes purging and tree-shaking concepts
    c. Use complex, nested CSS selectors
    d. Avoid all responsive prefixes
10. What high-level skill, emphasized as crucial for the future frontend developer, relates to ensuring AI outputs align with corporate values and user empathy, often discussed in developer communities?
    a. Minimizing HTML tag usage
    b. Mastering ethical auditing and adherence to human-centric design principles
    c. Maximizing the number of JavaScript libraries used
    d. Exclusive focus on pure CSS without any framework

Answers

1. c
2. b
3. c
4. b
5. b
6. b
7. b
8. b
9. b
10. b

Index

B

C

H

I

J

L

M

P

www.ingramcontent.com/pod-product-compliance
Lightning Source LLC
LaVergne TN
LVHW060441061126
851857LV00016B/1684
* 9 7 8 8 1 6 9 6 4 6 3 5 2 *